Food and Beverage Management

For the hospitality, tourism and event industries

Fifth edition

John Cousins, David Foskett and Amy Hollier

The Food and Beverage Training Company, London

David Foskett Associates, London

Service Sector Management, Sheffield Hallam University

College of Food, University College Birmingham

(G) **Goodfellow Publishers Ltd**

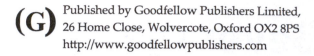 Published by Goodfellow Publishers Limited,
26 Home Close, Wolvercote, Oxford OX2 8PS
http://www.goodfellowpublishers.com

British Library Cataloguing in Publication Data: a catalogue record for this
title is available from the British Library.

Library of Congress Catalog Card Number: on file.

ISBN: 978-1-911635-10-9

 Design and typesetting by P.K. McBride, www.macbride.org.uk

Cover design by Cylinder

Cover images reproduced by kind permission of Gleneagles

Printed and bound in Great Britain by Marston Book Services Ltd, Oxfordshire

Contents

Preface

Food and restaurant styles are continuing to change to meet the challenges of the demands being made by increasingly diversified, knowledgeable and value conscious customers. Underlying trends include an increasing interest in common causes such as environmental concerns, humanitarianism and animal welfare, requirements for enhanced business ethics, and changes in dietary demands.

In addition, there continue to be staggering developments in food technology, kitchen and production methods, the application of operations management techniques, greater application of information technology, and a greater understanding of the use of architectural and interior design, have created new possibilities and alternatives.

Expansion of the industry has generally meant greater choice. This, together with potential skill shortages and drives for efficiency, has seen a streamlining of food and beverage operations. Increasing competition has also meant the quality of the service and the perceived value of the experience by customers are now the main differentiators between those operations that are endeavouring to attract similar customers.

It is against this background that this book has been revised.

Content

The content of this book reflects current industrial practices. It provides information and viewpoints on a variety of aspects of food and beverage management and considers various approaches, which students and food and beverage practitioners will find useful. The book will also be of value to those in the hospitality, tourism and events industries who are responsible for purchasing food and beverage services.

Aims

The principal aims of the book are to:

- provide supporting information for those involved, or likely to be involved, at a variety of levels, in food and beverage management;
- meet the needs of students and practitioners who want to acquire underpinning knowledge and skills in order for them to achieve competence in the industry;
- meet the needs of students studying for a range of qualifications, including City and Guilds, BTEC, Institute of Hospitality and foundation and undergraduate degrees, higher apprenticeship and post-graduate programs;

- provide support for in-company training programmes, and
- provide a foundation on which to build further knowledge and skills.

The book covers aspects of the management of food and beverage (or food service) operations that are applicable to a wide variety of industrial sectors. We have assumed that those using this text will have already acquired knowledge and skills in food and beverage operations.

Structure

The structure of the book has continued to be based on an adaptation of the food service cycle. Thus, the reader is led from consideration of food and beverage operations in Chapter 1, to concentrating on concept development in Chapters 2 and product development in Chapter 3. Chapter 4 covers operational areas, equipment and staffing considerations before moving on food production, in Chapter 5; beverage provision, in Chapter 6; and food and beverage service in Chapter 7. Chapter 8 considers events management in more detail and the book culminates with performance appraisal in Chapter 9 and strategic decision making in Chapter 10.

Using the book

The book can be approached in two main ways: either by working through the various chapters in the order they are presented, or by selecting what parts of the book are relevant to a particular learning programme or job. The structure of the book is outlined in Figure 1.2, which is on page 4. The structure identifies the relationship between the chapters of the book and it can also be used to identify what parts of the book might be relevant at the time

Whatever approach is adopted it is recommended that all of Chapter 1 should be covered first, as this chapter essentially lays the foundations for the rest of the text. It also places the consideration of food and beverage (or food service) operations and management within context.

Learning support

Learning is supported through the provision of an aim and identification of objectives for each of the chapters. These objectives indicate the learning outcomes that may be achieved. These outcomes can be mapped against the learning outcome requirements of different education programmes, or in-company training courses. Also included within the text are examples of a range of learning activities.

Three appendices are also provided, which detail particular approaches: Appendix A contains a listing and explanation of performance measures - also referred to as key performance measures (KPIs); Appendix B provides an example operational calculations exercise, and Appendix C sets out an example exercise on trading results comparison and evaluation.

Teaching and learning are also supported through the provision of PowerPoint presentations, which are available from the publisher's website at: http://www.goodfellowpublishers.com.

Focus

The main focus of the material is directly relevant to the management of food and beverage operations. Business management areas such as marketing, personnel and finance are already supported by a wide range of well-established resources. Although some applications of these are covered within the book, references are given to other information sources and further reading.

Overall

Our view remains that successful food service operations are those that have a clear understanding of their customers' needs, which they continually seek to meet.

John Cousins, David Foskett, David Graham and Amy Hollier
May 2019

Acknowledgements

We would like to express our grateful thanks to all the individual and organisations and who gave us assistance and support in developing this text, and especially those who have provided feedback on the previous editions.

In particular we would like to thank:

Academy of Food and Wine Service, UK; Foodservice Consultants Society International, UK&I; Croner's Catering, Croner Publications, London; Andrew Durkan, independent food and wine consultant; Food Service and Executive Management Teams, University College Birmingham; Cailein Gillespie, formally lecturer in Management at Strathclyde University, Glasgow; Robert Hayward, Senior Lecturer, Service Sector Management, Sheffield Hallam University; Hotel F&B magazine, H2O Publishing; Institute of Hospitality; IFS Publications, Bedford; Royal Academy of Culinary Arts; and Suzanne Weekes, Director, Hospitality Accreditation Training and Consultancy Service.

A special thank you also goes to Andrew Pennington who had contributed to the third edition.

1 Food and beverage operations and management

Aim

To introduce the concept of food and beverage operations and management and to provide an underpinning to the rest of the book.

Objectives

This chapter is intended to support you in:

- Identifying the food service cycle as a tool for the systematic examination of food service operations

- Establishing the relationship between the food service cycle and the content and structure of this book

- Identifying and applying service operations management principles to food service operations

- Exploring the nature of the food service product

- Categorising the industry sectors

- Identifying types of cuisine and restaurant styles

- Identifying the nature of customer demand

- Exploring the key influences on food service organisations

- Identifying the legal framework in which the food service industry operates.

1.1   Food and beverage operations

Food and beverage (or food service) operations are concerned with the provision of food and a variety of beverages within business. The international food service industry provides millions of meals a day in a wide variety of types of food service operation.

For managers in food and beverage operations, skills in marketing, merchandising, staff management, team development, training, customer relations, financial management and operational management are necessary for the management of both the service sequence (delivery) and the customer process (experience), and ultimately for the survival of the business.

The various elements that make up a food and beverage operation can be summarised into the eight stages of the Food Service Cycle. The eight stages follow a logical sequence from determining the market needs that the operation is intended to meet, through to checking whether this is actually being achieved, as illustrated in Figure 1.1. Food service operations are therefore concerned with:

1 **Consumer and the market:** the existing and future consumer needs and the potential market being served by the operation.

2 **Policy and objectives:** guiding the choice of the operational methods that are used.

3 **Customer service specification:** decisions on the range and type of menu and beverage lists to be provided, as well as other services, and the service levels to be offered and the prices to be charged.

4 **Facilities:** the planning and design, and operational capability of the facilities, plant and equipment to support the customer service specification.

5 **Purchasing:** developing purchasing, storage and stock control methods to meet the needs of the food production, beverage provision and other services being provided.

6 **Production and service:** using efficient food production and food and beverage service methods to support the requirements of the customer service specification.

7 **Control of costs and revenue:** maintaining robust systems for the accounting of revenue and the monitoring of costs of materials, labour and overheads.

8 **Monitoring of customer satisfaction:** regular checking on the extent to which the operation is meeting customer needs and achieving customer satisfaction.

The food service cycle is not just a statement of what food and beverage operations are concerned with. It also provides a comprehensive framework for the planning of a new food and beverage operation, as well as the appraisal of existing ones.

Figure 1.1: The Food Service Cycle

Source: developed from Cracknel and Kaufmann, 2002.

Using the same eight stage template means that information about a single or multiple operations can be organised in the same way. This helps when comparing the similarities and differences between the operations. Not all of the information may be able to be obtained but the template will help to identify what information is needed, what has been found out and, importantly, what information is not known about the operation.

Although the eight stages are presented as a sequence, they are also interdependent. The causes of difficulties in one stage are often one or two stages before that stage, rather than being within that stage itself. For example, difficulties with food and beverage service can often be traced back to equipment shortages, stock outs, incorrect pricing information etc. Similarly difficulties identified in one of the stages will also have knock-on effects on all the stages that follow. For example, difficulties with purchasing will then have effects on production and service, and control.

Identifying and understand the various interrelationships between the eight stages of the Food Service Cycle is important. It helps to ensure that decisions about operations will only be considered after looking at the effect any decisions might have throughout all the stages of the Food Service Cycle.

Food and beverage definitions

For the purposes of this book these definitions are used:

- *Food* – includes a wide range of styles and cuisine types. These can be classified by country, e.g. traditional British or Italian; by type of cuisine, e.g. oriental; or a particular speciality such as fish, vegetarian or health food.

- *Beverages* – includes all alcoholic and non-alcoholic drinks. Alcoholic beverages include wines and all other types of alcoholic drink such as cocktails, beers and cider, spirits and liqueurs. Non-alcoholic beverages include mineral waters, juices, squashes and aerated waters, as well as tea, coffee, chocolate, milk and milk drinks and also proprietary drinks such as Bovril.

Activity:

- Using the eight stages of the food service cycle as a framework, visit and collect information about three different types of food and beverage operations.

- Once you have collected the information, identify the key differences between the operations under each of the eight headings of the food service cycle.

The structure of the book

The Food Service Cycle, and the systematic approach it supports, is the basis of the structure of this book. This is indicated by the presentation of the structure of the book in Figure 1.2, which has been developed from an application of the food service cycle.

Figure 1.2: The structure of the book

Although presented in a form which is predominately linear, the actual management of food and beverage operations is organic. The structure of the book therefore also attempts to indicate the nature of the interrelationship that exists between the various components. Thus all the issues raised in Chapter 1 provide an underpinning to the rest of the chapters. Any consideration of a food and beverage operation must be carried out taking account of the nature of demand being met, the key influences on the food service industry and the legal environment. Equally any review of the performance of the operation, as discussed in Chapter 9, must also take account of all the discussions in the preceding chapters. Additionally any strategic decisions, as discussed on Chapter 10, are as dependent on the outcome of appraising the performance of the operation as they are on appraising the trends in the business environment.

Food and beverage management then, is the management of all the eight stages of the food service cycle. It is also systematic and organic; quantitative and qualitative; academic and pragmatic, and also both serious and fun. This is its fascination.

1.2   Service operations management

The underlying thinking behind much of this text relies on the application of a systems approach to the management of food and beverage operations. The systems approach recognises that operations are made up of systems that have inputs, processes and outputs, all of which need to be managed (Johnston *et al.* 2012). There are, however, two dimensions to a systems approach:

■ The first dimension of the systems approach is concerned with being systematic in the design, planning and control of a food and beverage operation.

■ The second dimension of the systems approach is concerned with the management of the operating systems within a food and beverage operation.

A system, or operations management approach, varies from the more traditional approaches to food service management. These differences are summarised and contrasted by the comparisons presented in Table 1.1.

Table 1.1: Comparison of traditional and system approaches

Traditional approach	Systems approach
Based on assumptions of linearity in the marketplace	Sensitive to changes in business conditions
Depends on the experience of key people	Depends on staff experience and good data
Information not readily available	Information available as needed
Intuitive	Quantitative
Reactive in nature	Proactive in nature
Service driven	Cost and service driven
Vulnerable to turnover of key people	Less vulnerable to turnover of key people
Weak in accountability	Strong in accountability

Source: Developed from Records and Glennie, 1991.

The benefits of adopting the systems, or operations management, approach have also been reinforced and further supported by various writers (see, for example, Johnston *et al.* 2012, Parker, 2018, Mele *et al.* 2010, Jones *et al.* 2003 and Johns and Jones, 2000).

Traditionally a food and beverage operation, and therefore food and beverage management, were seen as the management of the whole operation. With the application of systems thinking, three distinct operating systems can be identified within a single food and beverage operation: a system for food production, one for beverage provision, and one for food and beverage service. In this traditional view, food and beverage service was primarily seen as a delivery system. With this approach the customer was largely seen as a passive recipient of the service.

However the increasingly diverse range of food service operations has also led to developments in approaches to the customer. The customer is now seen as being central to the process and also as an active participant within it. Consequently understanding the customers' involvement, and identifying the experience they are likely to have, and should expect, have become critical to the design of successful food service operations.

One of the key outcomes of these changes was recognising that food and beverage service actually consists of two separate systems, albeit operating at the same time (Cousins, 1988). These are the **service sequence** (as a delivery system) and the **customer process** (the management of the customer experience**)**.

The four systems operating within a food service operation are:

1 The system for **food production**
2 The system for **beverage provision**
3 The system for delivery: the **service sequence**
4 The system for customer experience management: the **customer process.**

These four systems are tangible systems whose properties are known and can be defined. Figure 1.3 presents a simple model of a food service operation.

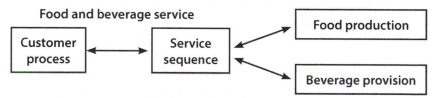

Food and beverage service

Figure 1.3: Simple model of a food service operation

The customer receiving the food and beverage product is required to undertake or observe certain requirements: this is the **customer process**.

The **service sequence** is essentially the bridge between the **food production, beverage provision** and the **customer process** (or customer experience). The **service sequence** consists of a number of stages from taking customer bookings through to clearing following service.

Bringing these aspects together, it is possible to summarise the relationship between the various systems with a food service operation, as shown in Figure 1.4. This model identifies the key stages of a food service operation: for the customer, for the food and beverage service staff and for those involved in food production and beverage provision. It also reinforces the existence of the two sub-systems within food and beverage service that have to be managed at the same time. (Food production is explored in more detail in Chapter 5, beverage provision in Chapter 6 and the systems of food and beverage service in Chapter 7.)

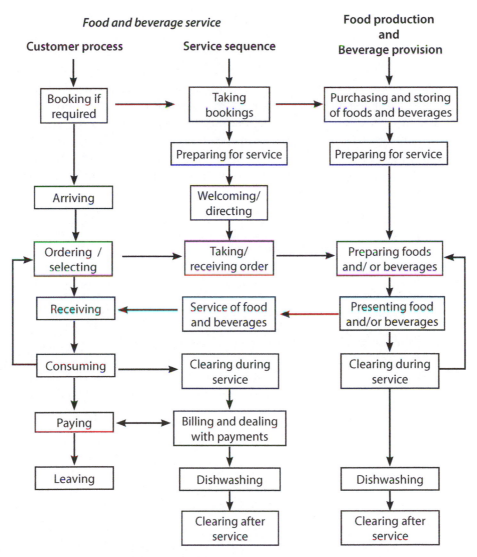

Figure 1.4: Outline of the relationship between the different operating systems within a food service operation

Source: Cousins *et al.* 2014, developed from Cousins, 1988

For a food service operation, **food production** and **beverage provision** are considered as two 'hard' systems, which are expected to behave predictably. The **customer process** is considered to be a 'soft' system because it involves emotional reactions, personal values and attitudes and shifting expectations, which are personal rather than technical in construction. However the **service sequence** contains characteristics of both 'hard' and 'soft' systems. It is 'hard' in the technical and procedural aspects of service and 'soft' because there are aspects of it that are to do with interactions between staff and customers and between staff and staff in the same or from other departments.

Food and beverage management therefore is concerned with the management of an operation, which is constructed from four core operating systems that are interlinked; and each of these four systems is made up from a variety of sub-systems. Thinking in this way can be useful. Figure 1.5 summarises the overlapping relationship between the Service Operation and the Service Product. For food and beverage managers, understanding the characteristics of systems, and the ways in which they behave, helps in the control of resources (**inputs**), the maintenance of efficient and effective processes (**service sequence** and **customer process**), and assuring the achievement of the required system outputs (**outcomes**). The central links between the operation and the customers are the **service sequence** (delivery) and the **customer process** (or experience).

Food and Beverage Operation

Figure 1.5: Managing service and service operations
Source: Developed from Johnston *et al.* 2012

Johnston *et al.* (2012) confirm that service operations consist of a combination of outcomes delivered to and received by customers. They also discuss the nature of service operations management and the potential conflict between the demands of the short-term management of the day-to-day operations against the longer-term needs of developing an operations strategy. Additionally they identify the constant need for operations managers to improve processes and to motivate people in order to carry out the operations more effectively, so as to achieve greater quality of service and productivity. (See also Slack *et al.,* 2016)

1.3   The hospitality industry and its products

The hospitality industry is usually identified by its output of products that satisfy the demand for food, drink and accommodation away from home. The hospitality industry is often split into the accommodation and food service industries and it is the latter that this book focusses on.

The word 'hospitality' encompasses all aspects of the hotel and catering (or food service) industry. It is a relatively modern word, originally meaning the friendly and generous treatment of guests and strangers (O'Gorman, 2010). Pizam and Shani (2009) highlighted the distinction between hospitality and hospitableness, arguing that the latter refers to authentic kindness and generosity while the former refers to the creation of experiences; which is what people working in hospitality do.

Over the years there has been much discussion about possible differences between products as being divided into goods and services. The approach of this book is to follow the lead of many in talking only about service products.

All products, that are produced and sold, have production and delivery elements, although these may be separated by distance, time or both, as in the production of cars, which is separated from the selling of cars in showrooms. All products then have some form of tangible (or physical) element and all products have some intangible (or non-physical) element. In the hospitality industry these two are operating side by side at the same time and place; there is an inseparability of production and delivery.

■   The Experience Economy

Hemmington (2007) amongst others, identified that customers do not buy service delivery, they buy experiences; they do not buy service quality, they buy memories; they do not buy food and drink, they buy meal experiences. The service product is now no longer being managed solely by the traditions of the service economy. The service product has to offer unique and memorable experiences as part of the delivery interaction, termed by Pine and Gilmour (1999) as the 'experience economy'.

The concept of the 'experience economy' is the new delivery mind-set required by staff and management within the food service offer. The 'experience' and 'service' is nothing new – it is perhaps the articulation of the concept into a theoretical construct that has captured the imagination and engaged the service industries into developing offers, which deliver uniqueness. It is through this 'Americanisation' which can perhaps best be illustrated through the 'Disneyfication' of guest encounters. Requiring highly skilled 'actors' who can dynamically personalise each service event, according to the needs, the responses and the behaviour traits of the guest. Guests must be drawn into an offering that they feel a sensation for, while the delivery must be authentic in nature (Fineman, 2000). It is through this Disneyfication that the food and drink service industry identifies the environment (stage) and the stakeholders (actors and guest) in a new terminology of delivery thought; the roles have not changed, just the manner in which we perceive and discuss the engagement. Table 1.2 compares some roles.

Table 1.2: Example comparison of roles.
Source: Developed from Pine and Gilmour (1999)

Theatrical	Operational type	Operational type
Stage	Restaurant	Coffee Shop
Actors	Waiting Staff	Barista
Guest	Customer	Customer

It is not necessarily the renaming of the building blocks of delivery, but a reshaping of the manner in which these blocks are framed by management and the engagement of the staff, which have been the key delivery shifts.

Corporate phrases can be used in management to generate a culture in service that embodies this, for example, in an American style burger outlet, the buzz expression of food service is perhaps about "rocking your restaurant".

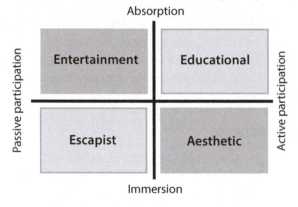

Figure 1.6: The four realms of the experience economy.
Source: Adapted from Pine and Gilmour (1999)

The experience economy has been articulated to exists in four realms: entertainment, education, escapist and aesthetic, which can be used to explain the manner in which the food and beverage product can be explored. The manner in which the customer engages with these is absorption, active participation, immersion and passive participation, as illustrated in Figure 1.6. Table 1.3 gives examples of the four realms in the food and beverage offer.

Table 1.3: Examples of the four realms in the food and beverage offer

Realms of experience	Elucidation example	Operational example
Entertainment	A key element is the engagement of all the senses	Hard Rock Café, www.hardrock.com/ or Rainforest Café, www.rainforestcafe.com/
Educational	Food and wine paring menu with a gastronomic tour	Castello di Amorosa, Napa Valley, USA www.castellodiamorosa.com/Visit-Us/ Wine-and-Food-Pairing
Aesthetic	Dinning in a restaurant of high environment visibility	Sketch restaurant, London http://sketch.london/
Escapist	Engaging in a food service offer which is not perhaps the guests' norm	Orient Express train www.orient-express.com/en

These examples reiterate the work of Goffman (1967) who proposes that the service worker is required to give a 'theatrical' performance while offering an effective experience is the requirement in contemporary food service (Lugosi, 2008).

This has been referred to elsewhere as the 'aesthetic economy' (Warhurst *et al.*, 2000; Postrel, 2003) the 'entertainment economy' (Wolf, 1999), the 'attention economy' (Davenport and Beck, 2002) and the 'dream society' (Jenson, 1999). Within the hospitality industry, and the food service industry in particular, the notion of the product delivery is one which requires hospitality to be delivered with hospitableness as the fundamental of the offer (Lashley and Morrison, 2000) while delivering authenticity (Fineman, 2000) to the customer.

Hemmington (2007) demonstrated that exploring and defining hospitality as experience created five different perspectives which all had implications for hospitality in commercial contexts. These five dimensions can be summarised as:

- **Host/guest relationship** – taking responsibility for the guest experience
- **Generosity** – allowing the hospitality relationship to develop without constant reminders to the customer of the economic nature of the relationship; for example, by reducing the number of extras the customer must pay for.
- **Theatre and performance** – providing experiences that are personal, memorable and add value to customers' lives.
- **Creating lots of little surprises** – recognising that the hospitality experience takes place over time and should be revealed at difference points throughout that time. For example, restaurants offering canapés or amuse bouche before the meal; revealing and presenting courses one by one and ending with items such as chocolates or mints or petit fours.
- **Safety and security** – recognising that customers are often in an unfamiliar environment and need hospitality operations to provide a feeling of sanctuary; with customers being aware of the genuine concern for their safety and security.

■ Dimensions of hospitality industry

Kotler *et al.* (2016) propose that there are particular dimensions of the hospitality industry's products that should be taken into account, as they make the service conceptual in nature and difficult to manage. These are:

- **Intangibility** – referring to the nature of the service element of the product. The accommodation and the food and beverages can be described and defined but the service element is potentially variable both in the process itself and in the way it is carried out.

- **Perishability** – the inability to sell tomorrow the rooms or restaurant seats which were not occupied today.

- **Inseparability** – Services cannot be separated from their providers.

- **Variability** – the potential for highly variable procedural execution and level of conviviality.

In addition other dimensions that affect the provision of the food and beverage product include:

- **Simultaneous production and consumption** – the product (from the customer's perspective) is not created until the customer requests it.

- **Ease of duplication** – the core of the product (the food and beverages) is the most easily duplicated. The procedural aspects of service are less so, and the convivial aspects (the way the procedures are carried out by staff) the least easy to duplicate.

- **Demand variation** – demand for the hospitality product varies dramatically throughout the day, week, month, or the year and over a period of years. Sustaining consistency of the product within these fluctuations is a major challenge for the hospitality operator.

- **Difficulty of comparison** – the intangible elements of the service product make direct comparison of the service product difficult. Customers tend to use three comparators when purchasing. These are:

  1 Search qualities – attributes that can be identified before purchase.

  2 Experienced qualities – attributes that can be identified only after consumption.

  3 Credence qualities – attributes that customers may find impossible to evaluate because of a lack of experience, knowledge or evaluative skills.

  Hospitality-related purchase decisions tend to derive from experience and credence decisions. Consequently customers tend to rely more on personal sources of information than they might for other products. This may explain the phenomenal demand for published reviews and guidebooks and the extensive use of social media.

■ The sectors of the food service industry

There are many types of eating out premises, but differing premises do not necessarily indicate the nature of the demand being met. For instance, a cafeteria may be found in industrial catering, motorway service stations, hospitals and retail operations. For marketing purposes, sectors are better identified based upon the nature of customer demand being met and not on the type of operation. The list of the sectors given in Table 1.4 is based upon identifying the purpose of the sector, i.e. the nature of demand being met by the food service operations. This method of classification of sectors by purpose provides for either the small company to identify its immediate competitors, or for the larger company – which may be operating in a number of markets – to identify immediate competitors within a specific sector. It also provides for the identification of other sectors where competition might exist for the sector under consideration, i.e. alternatives (hotels, popular catering, or fast food) may attract the same customers at different times.

Table 1.4: Sectors of the food service industry (including UK and international terminology comparison)

Industry sector: UK terminology	Purpose of the food service operation	Industry sector: international terminology
Hotels and other tourist accommodation	Provision of food and drink together with accommodation services	**Hotel, motel and other tourist accommodation**: often referred to as the *Lodging industry*
Restaurants including conventional and specialist operations	Provision of food and drink generally at high price with high levels of service	
Casual dining/ Popular catering including cafes, pizza, grills, specialist coffee shops, roadside restaurants and steak houses	Provision of food and drink generally at low/medium price with limited levels of service	**Separate eating and drinking places** Categories usually defined by reference to three criteria: Level of service, e.g. quick service to full service or fine dining
Fast food including McDonalds and Burger King	Provision of food and drink in highly specialised environment characterised by high investment, high labour costs and vast customer throughput	Extent of menu, e.g. limited to full Price range, e.g. low to high
Takeaway including KFC, snacks, fish and chips, sandwich bars, kiosks and street market stalls	Provision of food and drink quickly	
Retail stores	Provision of food and drink as adjunct to retail provision	**Retail market**

Events including banqueting/conferencing/exhibitions	Provision of large-scale food and drink alongside services such as conferencing	**Leisure and special event market**
Leisure attractions such as theme parks, galleries, theatres, airline terminals	Provision of food and drink to people engaged in another pursuit	
Motorway service stations	Provision of food and drink together with petrol and other retail services often in isolated locations	**Highway (interstate)**
Industrial catering either in-house operations or through contractors	Provision of food and drink to people at work	**Business and industry markets**
Welfare catering	Provision of food and drink to people in colleges, universities, the forces and through established social need	**Social caterer** **student**, **healthcare**, **institutional** and **military**
Licensed trade including public houses, wine bars, licensed clubs and members' clubs	Provision of food and drink in an environment dominated by licensing requirements	**Separate drinking places** but also some units included in separate eating and drinking places above
Transport catering including railways, airlines and marine	Provision of food and drink to people on the move	**Transportation market**
Event catering (or off premises catering)	Provision of food and drink away from home base and suppliers usually associated with a major event	**Catering market**

Source: developed from Cousins *et al.* 2014

Note on definitions: The word 'catering' is often used to refer to all food and beverage operations. There is also the more internationally understood one word term 'foodservice' which is often used to mean the same. However, the term 'foodservice' in the UK has now become more associated with cost sector and contract catering. More recently food and beverage operations are being referred to by the two word term 'food service'. This book follows this trend and refers to 'food service' operations, and the catering industry as the 'food service' industry.

Activity:

- Consider what operations there are in the locality.

- List up to 10 and identify which sector of the food service industry they belong to.

In order consider the sectors in more detail, each sector may be further analysed by reference to a set of variables that exist in the different sectors as indicated in Table 1.5. These variables represent elements that vary in particular sectors and thus provide a basis for examining the operation of different types of food service operation within specific sectors. They enable a comprehensive picture of industrial sectors to be compiled, and also provide the basis for the comparison of the different sectors.

Table 1.5: Variables in food service sectors

Historical background	Interpretation of demand/catering concept
Reasons for customer demand	Technological development
Size of sector:	Influences
In terms of outlets	State of sector development
In terms of turnover	Primary/secondary activity
Policies:	Types of outlets
Financial	Profit orientation/cost provision
Marketing	Public/priva te ownership
Catering	

There are many different industry sectors such as hotels, independent and chain restaurants, popular catering, pubs and wine bars, fast food, leisure attractions and banqueting where the hospitality provision and therefore the food and beverage provision is part of the main business. There are also sectors where food and beverages are provided as part of another business. These include transport catering, welfare, clubs, education, industrial feeding and the armed forces.

Some sectors are providing food and beverages for profit, whereas others are working within the constraints of a given budget, often called *cost provision* or *cost sector*, for example welfare and industrial. In addition, some sectors provide services to the general public whereas others provide them for restricted groups of people.

A summary of the sectors of the food service industry is given in Table 1.6, with the sectors categorised according to whether they are profit orientated or cost sector, and also according to whether the market is general or restricted.

Table 1.6: Summary of sectors in the food service industry

Profit orientated		Cost provision
Restricted market	**General market**	**Restricted market**
Transport catering	Hotels/restaurants	Institutional catering
Clubs	Popular catering	Schools
Industrial (contract)	Fast food/takeaway	Universities and colleges
Private welfare	Retail stores	Hospitals
	Events/conferences/exhibitions	Armed forces
	Leisure attractions	Prisons
	Motorway service stations	Industrial (in-house)
	Pubs and wine bars	
	Event catering (off-premises catering)	

Within the cost provision sector the food service provision can be either carried out by in-house caterers or contracted out to a third party, often a commercial contract catering business. Leaders in the global contract catering industry are Aramark, Sodexho and Compass who have seen significant growth as food and service delivery providers.

Within the profit orientated sector, there are also examples where the food and beverage provision has been contracted out to a third party, or is being provided though a franchise/concession operation.

Activity:

- Review the corporate websites for Aramark, Sodexho and Compass.
    www.aramark.com
    www.sodexo.com
    www.compass-group.com

- Identify where the corporate head office is and the company history and country of origin.

- What sectors do they operate in?

- What is their international reach?

- How diverse are the food service and service operations?

Cuisine and restaurant styles

Over the past 20 years a number of terms have been adopted to signify differing types of food and establishment styles. Examples of these are given in Table 1.7.

Table 1.7: Examples of cuisine and restaurant styles

Cuisine or restaurant style	Description
Bistro	Often a smaller establishment, with check tablecloths, bentwood chairs, cluttered decor and friendly informal staff. Tends to offer honest, and robust cooking styles.
Brasserie	Generally, a largish, styled room, with a long bar, normally serving a range of meals. Often it is possible just to have a drink, coffee or just a snack. Service by waiters, often in traditional style of long aprons and black waistcoats.
Cafeteria	Primarily self-service with customer choosing selection from a counter or counters in varying designs and layouts. Originally developed for the industrial feeding market but now seen in a variety of commercial sectors.
Casual dining	Term often associated with a range of medium-priced, usually table service operations, serving a range of meals, from beverages and snacks though to main meals. Sometimes referred to as popular catering.
Fine Dining	Classical style of cooking evolved through many centuries. Greater depth of flavour. Style does not necessarily mean the most expensive ingredients. Classical presentation of food with full table service. Good quality table ware is generally an important feature in the dining experience.

Coffee shop	Similar to brasserie-style operations, often themed. May be open all day and serve all meal types from breakfast through to supper.
Country house hotel cooking	Varies from establishment to establishment but food is often modern British style with some influence from classic or even farmhouse style. Often the home of high-end destination restaurants.
Farmhouse cooking	Simply cooked with generous portions of basic, home-produced fare using good, local ingredients.
First class restaurants	Tend to be formal fine dining restaurants with classical preparation and presentation of food and offering a high level of table service. Often associated with classical/haute cuisine.
Fusion/eclectic cuisine	Based on an inter-mix of cuisine cultures, for example a fusion of, particularly, western and eastern styles. Also described as eclectic cuisine. Can often be based on mixing a variety of apparently random ingredients. Most successful when the approach is based on the principles from one main traditional cuisine.
Health food & vegetarian restaurants	Increasing specialisation of operations into vegetarianism and/or health foods (though vegetarian food is not necessarily 'healthy'), to meet lifestyle needs as well as dietary requirements.
International destination restaurant	Often Michelin-starred fine dining restaurants, offering a distinctive personality, cuisine, ambiance, beverages and service. Usually table service at various levels but mostly personal and highly attentive. Generally considered as the home of gastronomy. Expensive but also value-laden.
International cuisine	Indian, Oriental, Asian, Spanish, Greek, Italian, English, French, Creole and Cajun are just some of the many types of cuisine available, with establishments tending to reflect specific national or ethnic origins. Many of the standard dishes are now appearing within a range of other menu types.
Molecular gastronomy	Term sometimes used to describe the greater combination of food with science using many of the technical advances in equipment and ingredients, in order to reflect the combination of the social, artistic and technical aspects of food and beverages
New wave brasserie (gastrodome)	Slick modern interior design coupled with similar approaches to contemporary cuisine and service. Busy and bustling, and often large and multi-leveled.
New/modern British/French	Cuisine drawn from the classical style but with new style saucing and the better aspects of nouvelle presentation. Plated in the kitchen, allowing the chef the final responsibility for presentation.
Pop-ups	Restaurant operations that appear for a day or for several months. Can be established restaurant operations in a different location or new talent showing off their skills without long-term financial risks. Cuisines vary. Heavily reliant on social media for success.
Popular catering	Often now referred to as casual dining. Variety of styles of operation with all-day (grazing) menus. Mostly plated table service.
Public houses Gastro pubs	Licensed environment primarily for drinking alcoholic beverages. May be simply a serving bar with standing room for customers or may have more plush surroundings incorporating the offer of a variety of foods. Can range from simple plated dishes to establishments offering full restaurant service (sometimes called gastropubs).
Restaurant	Term used to cover a wide variety of operations. Price, level and type of service, decor, styles, cuisines and degree of choice varies enormously across the types of operation. Service ranges from full table to assisted service such as in carvery-style operations.
Street food	Specialising in a variety of local and international food offerings, often cooked at the market stall. Found in night-time markets, night bazaars, or souvenir and food markets, and also markets with a number of other similar titles, including Christmas markets.

Takeaways and fast food outlets	Providing 'grab and go' service (some have seating areas). Includes kiosks, takeaways and quick service outlets, sandwich shops, branded coffee outlets and modern-day burger, chicken and fish concepts, as well as providing a variety of international foods. Often also called quick service restaurants.
Themed restaurant	Often international in orientation, for example, Icelandic hot rock with food prepared and cooked at the table, 'Beni-hana' oriental theme, again with food prepared and cooked at table. Also includes themes such as jungle, rainforest, or music/opera where waiting staff will perform as well as serve.
Wine bars	Often offering a mixture of bar and brasserie-style operation, commonly wine themed, serving a variety of foods.

Source: based on Cousins and Weekes (2018).

■ The nature of demand

There are many different kinds of food and beverage (or food service) operations that are designed to meet a wide range of types of demand. However the type of operation does not necessarily indicate the type of customer demand being met. It is the needs that people have at the time, rather than the type of people they are, that these different operations are designed for. For example, the same person may be a business customer during the week, but a member of a family at the weekend; he or she may want a quick lunch on one occasion, a snack while travelling on another or a meal for the family at another time. Additionally the same person may be booking a wedding or organising some other special occasion. Clearly there are numerous reasons for eating out, other examples being: to do something different, to try different foods, or for sheer convenience because of already being away from the home, out shopping, at the cinema, a conference or an exhibition.

The reasons for eating out vary and with this, the types of operation that may be appropriate at the time. Differing establishments offer different service, in both the extent of the menu and the price as well as varying service levels. Also the choice offered may be restricted or wide. Basically there are three types of markets in which operations may be meeting demand. These are:

1 **Captive markets** – where the customer has no choice, e.g. hospital patients or people in prison.

2 **Non-captive markets** – those people who have a free choice of establishments.

3 **Semi-captive markets** – where there is some restriction, e.g. people travelling by air who have a choice of airline but once the choice is made, are restricted to the food and drink on offer. This category also applies, for instance, to railways, some inclusive-term holidays and people travelling on motorways.

Identifying what business a food service operation is in then is not simply about what sector it is in or what type of operation: it is also about identifying the range of types of demand that are being met by the operation. This will then help with identifying the direct or indirect competition that might exist.

The nature of the food service product

To every product (and the food service product is no exception) there are two dimensions: features and benefits. Features are the physical characteristics of the product but marketers tend to stress benefits, because of the realisation that products are bought for the satisfaction they provide.

The food service industry's products may be defined as the set of satisfactions or dissatisfactions which a customer receives from a food service experience. The satisfaction may be physiological, economic, social or psychological or convenience as follows:

- **Physiological needs:** to satisfy hunger and thirst, or the need for special foods.
- **Economic needs:** staying within a certain budget, wanting good value, a convenient location or fast service.
- **Social needs:** being out with friends, business colleagues or attending special functions such as weddings.
- **Psychological needs:** responding to advertising, wanting to try something new, fulfilling life-style needs or satisfying or fulfilling the need for self-esteem.
- **Convenience needs:** it may not be possible to return home or there may be the desire for someone else to prepare, serve and wash up.

Potential dissatisfaction falls into two categories:

- **Controllable by the establishment:** e.g. scruffy, unhelpful staff and cramped conditions.
- **Uncontrollable:** e.g. behaviour of other customers, the weather, and transport problems.

Customers may want to satisfy some or all of the needs identified above. The reasons behind wanting, or having, to eat out, rather than the food and drink themselves, often play a more important part in determining the resulting satisfaction or dissatisfaction with the experience. It is quite possible that the motivation to eat out is not to satisfy basic physiological needs at all.

Product augmentation

Sometimes the product delivered to the customer is different from that received by the customer. In other words, the reason for the customer buying the product may determine the satisfaction, rather than specifically the product itself (e.g. out with friends). Distinctions are often drawn between the core, tangible and augmented concepts of the product, for example:

- The **core** of the product is the food and drink provision itself.
- The **tangible elements** of the product are the methods of delivery (silver service restaurant or vending machine) or portions of a certain size.
- **Augmentation** of the product takes into account the complete package.

Differing sectors of the food service industry are essentially meeting similar customer demands, i.e. offering the same core product. However, this can be modified and enhanced in cost-effective ways to make the product more attractive. Competition within specific sectors largely takes place at the augmented level. In the food service industry this augmentation might include:

■ Speed of service

■ Ordering/booking convenience

■ Reliability

■ Provision of special foods

■ Cooking to order

■ Home deliveries

■ Availability of non-menu items

■ Entertainment

■ Privacy/discretion

■ Acceptance of credit cards, or

■ Availability of account facilities.

These various elements are often drawn together with the core and tangible elements under the heading the 'meal experience' concept (Cousins *et al.*, 2014).

■ The meal experience

If people have decided to eat out then it follows that there has been a conscious choice to do this in preference to some other course of action. In other words, the food service operator has attracted the customer to buy his/her product as against some other product, for example theatre, cinema or simply staying at home. The reasons for eating out may be summarised under seven headings:

1 **Convenience**, for example being unable to return home, as in the case of shoppers or people at work or involved in some leisure activity.

2 **Variety**, for example trying new experiences or as a break from home cooking.

3 **Labour**, for example getting someone else to prepare, serve food and wash up or simply the physical impossibilities of staging special events at home.

4 **Status**, for example business lunches or people eating out because others of their socio-economic group do so.

5 **Culture/tradition**, for example special events or simply because it is a way of getting to know people.

6 **Impulse**, for example simply spur-of-the-moment buying.

7 **No choice**, for example those in welfare, hospitals or other forms of semi or captive markets.

People are, however, a collection of different types, as any demographic breakdown would show. While it is true that some types of food service operation might attract certain types of customers this is by no means true all the time; for example, McDonald's is marketed to the whole population and attracts customers depending on their needs at the time.

However, even a global fast food provider such as McDonald`s has had to customise elements of its product to take into account cultural differences and overcome product fatigue. Within the highly competitive experience economy, mass customisation of its product and the introduction of new product lines for international food service corporations has been an important element in ensuring continued success.

Activity:

- Visit to your local fast food offer and identify the level of customisation of the food offer.

- Identify to what extent they are willing to offer you the product outside of the stated menu.

- Review how the outlet may have diversified the range of products over the years.

- What level of cultural adaptability is occurring?

- Compare the food fast food offer to the same brand that you might have visited abroad and identify the similarity or differences between them.

- Visit the website of a global fast food corporation and investigate if cultural and menu diversity can be identified.

The decision to eat out may be split into two parts: first, the decision to do so for the reasons given above and then the decision as to what type of experience is to be undertaken. It is generally agreed that there are a number of factors influencing this latter decision. These factors extend the core, tangible and augmented distinctions drawn earlier. The factors that affect the meal experience may be summarised as follows:

- **Food and drink on offer** – the range of foods, choice, availability, flexibility for special orders and the quality of the food and drink.

- **Level of service** – Depending on the needs people have at the time, the level of service sought should be appropriate to these needs. For example, a romantic night out may call for a quiet table in a top-end restaurant, whereas a group of young friends might be seeking more informal service. This factor also takes into account services such as booking and account facilities, acceptance of credit cards and also the reliability of the operation's product.

- **Level of cleanliness and hygiene** – this relates to the premises, equipment and staff. Over the last few years this has increased in importance in the customers' minds. The recent media focus on food production and the risks involved in buying food have heightened awareness of health and hygiene aspects.

- **Perceived value for money and price** – customers have perceptions of the amount they are prepared to spend and relate these to differing types of establishments and operations. However, many people will spend more if the value gained is perceived as greater than could be obtained by spending slightly less. (Also see the notes on price, cost, worth and value in Chapter 2, page 39)

- **Atmosphere of the establishment** – this is difficult to quantify, as it is an intangible concept. However, it is composed of a number of tangible factors such as: design, decor, lighting, heating, furnishings, acoustics and noise levels, the other customers, the staff and the attitude of the staff. It is these tangibles which the food service organisation has control over and which, once bundled together, will create atmosphere).

Identifying the meal experience factors is important because it considers the product from the point of view of the customer. All too often food service operators can get caught up in the provision of food and drink, design, decor, equipment, etc. but ignore the actual experience. Untrained and poorly managed service members of staff are a good example of this problem. Operations can tend to concentrate on the core product and forget the complete package. A better understanding of the customer's viewpoint or the nature of customer demand leads to a better product being developed to meet it. (The meal experience factors are explored in more detail in Chapter 3 pages 53 to 64.)

1.4   Key influences on the food service industry

The role of the food and beverage manager is varied and complex. Managers have responsibility for the operation, as well as dealing with staff, reviewing financial performance, monitoring quality standards, overcoming obstacles and fine tuning the operation, whilst also considering changes in approaches to service delivery. In addition the manager has to monitor and respond to changes in the industry.

The key influences affecting the hospitality industry can be summarised using the PESTLE model, which is widely used by businesses to classify potential influences on the future of the business. PEST, STEP, PETS, PESTEL and STEEPL are all variations of the acronym that might be used to classify relevant factors that will impact on the food service industry. The influences they stand for are:

P Political
E Economic
S Socio/cultural
T Technological
L Legal
E Ecological.

The value of whichever version of the acronym is chosen is that it offers a simple mechanism for grouping related factors, although this might hide the interrelationships between them.

Applying the PESTLE framework leads to the identification of possible influences and the interrelated trends within the food service industry, such as:

- **Political** influences might include issues such as the availability of grants and subsidies, and the intervention of the Competition and Market Authority. For example, in the public house industry, UK government legalisation in the 1980s broke the monopoly on the ownership by national brewers, limiting each to a maximum of 2,000 pubs, and by doing so created increased competition and the diversity of food and beverage public house offers.

- **Economic** influences might include exchange rates (as they affect tourism), inflation and taxation. Tax as a percentage of direct sales within most European countries has been increased following the global recession. The dilemma for food service business is to decide whether to add the additional tax onto the food and beverages they sell, or absorb the increase tax and reduce profits, or find other cost savings to compensate.

- **Social** issues might concern changing market needs, demographic changes and changing patterns of employment. For example, the increase in casualization of society has created a greater acceptance of less formal modes and innovation in restaurant offers. One such societal change has influenced the development of the hipster restaurant and the branding of the individual worker as an aesthetic labourer for such operations.

- **Technological** issues might concern the operating systems of a business, channels of distribution (how a business communicates with its customers) and data and information gathering. Electronic Point of Sale (EPOS) systems are becoming key features of branded food service operators enabling greater detail in management information. The automated ordering from the kitchen, although arguably speeding up the table to customer food delivery, has the potential to disengage the food service worker from the kitchen staff and increased levels of misunderstanding. This is not a new phenomenon. Whyte (1947) in his seminal paper identified this as a restaurant issue in the USA in the 1940s when researching the coordinating of restaurant activity.

- **Legal** issues might mean changes in legislation, e.g. hygiene and food safety, opening hours, employment contracts and responsibilities, trade descriptions, licensing, etc. For example the, European Directive (Consumers Regulation EU No. 1169/2011) required that all non-packaged or pre-packed for direct sale must contain information so that individuals with food allergies can identify the ingredients to make informed choices. Another example is the General Data Protection Regulation (2018) which altered how businesses handle the information of their customers and aimed to harmonise data privacy laws across Europe.

- Ecological might mean the increasing requirements for energy conservation or the acceptability (or otherwise) of genetically modified foods. A related issue being the acceptance of certain foods on the menu and the corporate social responsibility (CSR) of the food service organisations in the service of foie gras, caviar and veal – food items which arguable have morale dilemmas in the production process and which, as a consequence, have been removed from the menu by some food service organisations. The use of materials with low levels of recyclability and high levels of waste pollutants is a factor in food business selection. Recent examples being the replacement of plastic cups and stirrers with biodegradable materials to reduce waste which contribute to the number of plastic microparticles being found in the sea and as a result in the human food chain through seafood consumption. An example of approaches to reducing plastic waste is at: https://disneyparks.disney.go.com/blog/2018/07/disney-expands-environmental-commitment-by-reducing-plastic-waste/

It may be very difficult to detect the impact of many of the PESTLE factors directly on the food service industry. There is also a danger of sterility in using a formal approach to PESTLE analysis. At worst, it can become a ritual listing of all possible influences. This has three possible dangers:

1 Data overload.

2 Failure to try to assess the potential impact of an environmental change, however unlikely it may initially seem.

3 Failure to recognise the combined impact of a number of influences.

So, looking outwards means also having to look inwards at the organisation to answer question such as:

■ Why are we, or how can we be successful?

■ Is it because there is a growing market out there?

■ Is it going to keep growing?

■ Will customers still buy our products?

■ Is it because our products are affordable?

■ If so, what are the major influences on our costs?

■ What changes of policy or price are we vulnerable to?

■ How can the product life cycle be extended?

■ Interactions between PESTLE elements

It can be an instructive and creative exercise to look out for interactions between the PESTLE elements. This is well illustrated by the advancement of the environmental factor: the ecological movement. Technology has produced damaging effects on the environment. These have led to social concerns, which have manifested themselves in political action and legislation. This has in turn spurred companies on to seek out technological developments to address the issue and also to gain competitive advantage. Thus food service operations have to respond to, for instance, consumer mistrust of genetically modified foods, with some firms making specific marketing claims based on not using such foods.

1

Additionally, one of the most important issues of the moment is sustainability. Sustainability refers to the ability to continue over time. This is not just about the environment (often also referred to as green issues). Food service operations need to be economically sustainable. Investment needs to continue in order to meet growing customer demands and increased national and international competition. Dealing with sustainability has now become a complicated combination of economic, social and environmental factors that present any business with having to make difficult decisions on trade-offs, in order to be able to prosper in the longer term.

Identifying changes in the PESTLE elements

In these turbulent times, it is important to keep a close watch on influences that may be unlikely to occur, but if they did, could have a major impact on the organisation. Many organisations are, or should be, aware of the main external influences that affect them at present. These could include factors that are fairly easy to identify and to monitor, such as the weather, government legislation, changes in the local business environment, changes in fashion, and developments in technology in directly related areas. Examples of these could be:

- The closure of a local manufacturing plant, which is a major source of local employment, directly affecting both business and leisure based demand for hotel and catering services and leading to a decline in the area generally
- The opening of a major tourist attraction which creates opportunities for local food service operations and may also encourage new businesses into the area and therefore increased competition, or
- The introduction of parking restrictions around a restaurant which might seriously reduce direct access and therefore business.

Other areas are less easy to grasp. These can include:

- Developments that are so new or unknown that most people have not realised they may be important and virtually nobody has any knowledge of the impact they might have, or
- Developments that seem extremely unlikely but may have a massive impact on a food service business if they do occur.
- The impact of the United Kingdom's future relationship with the European Union and the rest of the world.

There is no simple way of recognising and selecting developments. It can however be useful to try to identify reasons for the current success of an operation and the factors that might have affected them. It is also worth considering what developments might give a food service organisation the opportunity to build on its strengths.

The most difficult of all to pull together are those influences which, if taken separately, seem insignificant, but taken together can constitute a significant influence. It might not be recognisable by any one person or department because of the complex interlinking across many aspects of the organisation. Once again, this illustrates the need for cross-functional/cross-departmental creative forums to examine the interlinking of potential influences. This requires much more than a sterile listing of influences or naming of parts.

Most books on strategic management provide coverage of the analysis of the macro-environment. Kotler *et al.* (2016) discuss it as one component of a marketing audit and Johnson *et al.* (2017) link together the macro-environment with industry analysis. The key model for examining the industry analysis, or the micro-business environment, is Porter's Five Forces (Porter, 2004). This is examined in Chapter 10, page 309.

Activity:

■ Using the PESTLE framework, identify for each element a changed or changing factor and its associated impact on the food service organisation.

■ ## Sources of further information

Information about the industry can be obtained from a variety of sources. These include:

■ Trade magazines (and their associated websites) such as:
  □ *The Caterer* (www.thecaterer-magazine.co.uk)
  □ *Restaurant Magazine* (www.bighospitality.co.uk/Info/Restaurant)
  □ *Imbibe magazine* (imbibemagazine.com)
  □ *Cost sector catering* (www.costsectorcatering.co.uk)
  □ *Hotel F&B magazine* (www.hotelfandb.co.uk)

■ Various news media

■ Textbooks, journals, and on-line data bases

■ Government websites

■ Business link (www.businesslink.org.uk)

■ People 1st (www.people1st.co.uk)

■ Professional trade reports, such as those from Keynote (www.keynote.co.uk) and Mintel at (www.mintel.com).

■ Trade bodes such as UK Hospitality, formerly the British Hospitality Association (www.ukhospitality.org.uk) or the Catering Equipment Suppliers Association (CESA) (www.cesa.org.uk).

■ Professional bodies such as the Craft Guild of Chefs (craftguildofchefs.org), Institute of Hospitality (www.instituteofhospitality.org), Academy of Food and Wine Service (www.afws.co.uk) and the Royal Academy of Culinary Arts (www.royalacademyofculinaryarts.org.uk).

1.5   The legal framework

Part of considering the business environment is about considering the legal framework in which the food service organisation has to operate. For food service operations there are aspects that are the subject of legal regulation. Summaries of the key responsibilities of the food service operator are given below. However these are highly summarised guidelines and many of the issues highlighted are affected by the particular circumstances and legislation at the time.

■   Health, safety and security

There is a common law duty to care for all staff and lawful visitors. In addition establishments must not:

- Sell (or keep for sale) food and beverages that are unfit for human consumption,
- Cause food or beverages to be dangerous to health,
- Sell food or beverages that are not what the customer is entitled to expect, in terms of content or quality,
- Describe or present food in a way that is false or misleading, or
- Fail to comply with all local and national regulations in the operation of the business.

It is important for a food service operator to be able to demonstrate that steps have been taken to ensure good food hygiene (this is called *due diligence*).

An operator's responsibilities include ensuring that:

- Service standards comply with health, safety, environmental and food hygiene regulations
- There are adequate arrangements in place to ensure the safety, security and well-being of staff and customers
- Periodic risk assessments are carried out and recorded
- Emergency exits are clearly marked and regular fire drills are carried out
- Staff have been trained in fire procedures and how to use fire-fighting equipment
- Staff are aware of evacuation procedures in the event of fires or security risks such as bomb threats
- Health and safety notices are displayed in working areas
- Staff and customers are trained, as appropriate, on correct usage of equipment and facilities
- Food handlers have all been trained in safe and hygienic working practices, and
- Security policies and procedures are known and followed by all management and staff.

Further consideration of health and safety is given in Section 4.3. Health, safety and security issues related to staffing are identified in Section 4.6.

■ The licensing framework

The sale of alcoholic liquor is subject to liquor licensing requirements, which have four key objectives:

1 The prevention of crime and disorder.
2 Public safety.
3 The prevention of public nuisance.
4 The protection of children from harm.

There are usually requirements for:

- The display of a summary of the licence, including the days and times of opening, name of the registered holder, licence number and valid date.
- Drinks price lists to be displayed.
- Restrictions on under-aged persons being served alcohol and or being employed to serve alcohol.
- Requirements for an authorised person to be on site at all times.

Restrictions and penalties for infringement are applied, not only to the licensee or their staff, but also to the customer. In all cases of doubt as to legal issues and concerns, a licensing solicitor should be approached.

Other types of licences may include, for example, licences for music (live or pre-recorded), dancing, gambling, theatrical performance and television display. In all cases the supervisor and the staff should be aware of the provisions and limitations of the licences to ensure compliance. (For more detailed information on the local licensing arrangements refer to the various national and local government websites.)

■ Selling goods by weights and measures

All sales of goods by weight or measure should be in accordance with the legislative requirements. This usually requires the following:

- Display of the prices and the measures used for all spirits, wines, ales and any other alcohol served, and
- Ensuring that the food and beverage items for sale are of the quantity and quality demanded by the customer and can include, for example, spirits that have been inadvertently (or deliberately) watered down. This can occur through the use of speed pourers, which effectively leave bottles open for long periods of time, leading to evaporation of the alcohol. Equally, if the pourers are washed and then replaced in the bottles when they are wet, the water can become introduced to the spirit and cause a reduction in the percentage of alcohol by volume (abv).

■ Contracts

A contract is made when one party agrees to the terms of an offer made by another party. In food and beverage service there are essentially two types of customer: those who pre-book and those who do not (often called *chance* or *casual* customers). All food service operations should be clear on how they will deal with these different types of customers including:

■ Circumstances where the restaurant may seek compensation from the customer if they do not turn up or pay for their meals or services, and

■ Taking care when making contracts with minors (persons under 18).

■ Selling goods by description

It is good practice for the food service operation to ensure:

■ All food, beverages and services provided are fit for purpose and of satisfactory quality in relation to price and description.

■ Food, beverages and other services are accurately described in terms of size, quality, composition, production, quantity and standard.

■ All statements of price, whether in an advertisement, brochure, leaflet or on the Web, or given by letter or orally in person or over the telephone are clear and accurate.

■ Food, beverages and other services correspond to their description in brochures or other promotional material.

■ Times, dates, locations and nature of service promised are adhered to.

■ Customer billing is fair, transparent and reflects the prices quoted either orally or in writing.

Care must therefore be taken when:

■ Wording menus and wine lists

■ Describing menu and beverage items to customers

■ Stating if prices include local and/or government taxes

■ Describing conditions such as cover charges, service charges or extras

■ Describing the service provision.

■ Avoiding discrimination

The food service operator should be aware of, and work to ensure, that the operation and its staff do not discriminate on grounds of ethnic origin, race, creed, sex or disability. There are potentially three ways in which discrimination can occur.

■ *Direct discrimination:* for example, refusing service to customers of particular ethnic origin, race, creed, gender, sexual orientation or disability.

■ *Indirect discrimination:* for example, denying consumer services by imposing unjustifiable conditions or requirements that have ethnic origin, race, creed, gender, sexual orientation or disability implications.

- *Discrimination through victimisation*: for example, by (a) refusal of provision, that is refusal of admission on the basis of ethnic origin, race, creed, gender, sexual orientation or disability; or (b) omission of provision, that is providing services to ethnic customers that are markedly inferior to those available to the public in general or which may only be available at a price premium.

It is the manager's responsibility to ensure that no such discrimination occurs. This can create challenge where employees can be referred to as style labourers or aesthetic labourers. These are employees who have to `look good and sound right` (Warhurst *et al*. 2000). There is also a similar issue for some themed food service operators where a particular `look` of staff is required in order to deliver authenticity into the business.

Providing services

Generally a food and beverage operator is under no specific requirement to serve anyone. However, it is important that the managers and staff are aware of:

- Circumstances where there may be a mandatory requirement to provide services, and
- Valid reasons for refusal.

Customer property and customer debt

Good practice usually means that the operator needs to ensure:

- Proper care is taken of customer's property so as to minimise potential loss or damage. Notices warning customers of 'no responsibility' may help in defence but do not guarantee exemption from liability for the food and beverage operator, and
- Clear guidance is given on the procedures to follow if the customer is unable or unwilling to pay.

Data protection

Customers generally have a right to expect that data about them is kept secure and is only used for the published business purposes. The operator is generally required to ensure that:

- Information on customers is kept up to date, fairly, lawfully and securely
- Customer information is not passed on to third parties without prior consent from the customer, and
- Members of staff are aware of the importance of the protection of customer information and the procedures to follow to ensure it is held securely.

For further information on legal considerations see the various local and national government websites.

1.6 References and additional reading

Academy of Food and Wine Service at www.afws.co.uk (accessed Jan. 2019).

Catering Equipment Suppliers Association (CESA) at www.cesa.org.uk (accessed Jan. 2019).

Cost sector catering at www.costsectorcatering.co.uk (accessed Jan. 2019).

Cousins, J. (1988) Curriculum development in operational management teaching in catering education, in R. Johnson (ed.), *The Management of Service Operations*, Bedford: IFS Publications, pp. 437–459.

Cousins, J. and Weekes, S. (2018) *Food and Beverage Service for the Level 2 Technical Certificate*, London: Hodder Education.

Cousins, J., Lillicrap D. and Weekes, S. (2014) *Food and Beverage Service*, 9th edn, London: Hodder Education.

Cracknel, H.L. and Kaufmann, R.J. (2002) *Practical Professional Catering Management*, 2nd edn, Andover: Thomson Learning Vocational.

Craft Guild of Chefs at www.craftguildofchefs.org (accessed Jan.2019).

Davenport, T. and Beck, J. (2002) *The Attention Economy: Understanding the New Currency of Business*, Boston: Harvard Business School.

Disney (2018) Disney Expands Environmental Commitment By Reducing Plastic Waste at https://disneyparks.disney.go.com/blog/2018/07/disney-expands-environmental-commitment-by-reducing-plastic-waste/ (accessed Jan. 2019).

Fineman, S. (2000) Emotion in organisations, in: Fineman, S (ed.). *Emotional Labour and Authenticity; Views from Service Agents*, California: Sage Publications, 184-203.

Goffman, E. (1967) *Interaction Ritual: Essays in Face to Face Behaviour*. Chicago, Aldine Publishing Company.

Hemmington, N. (2002) From service to experience: understanding and defining the hospitality business, *Service Industries Journal*, **27**(6).

Hotel F&B at www.hotelfandb.co.uk (accessed Jan.2019).

Imbibe at www.imbibemagazine.com (accessed Jan. 2019).

Institute of Hospitality at www.instituteofhospitality.org (accessed Jan. 2019).

Jenson, R. (1999) *The Dream Society: How the coming shift from information to imagination will transform your business*, New York: McGraw-Hill.

Johns, N. and Jones, P. (2000) Systems and management: understanding the real world, *Hospitality Review,* January, 47–52.

Johnson, G., Whittington R., Scholes, K., Angwin, D. and Regnér, P. (2017) *Exploring Strategy Text and Cases*, 11th edition, Harlow: Pearson

Johnson, J., Scholes, K. and Whittington, R. (2008) *Exploring Corporate Strategy*, 8th edn, Harlow: Financial Times/ Prentice Hall.

Johnston, R., Clark, G. and Shulver, M. (2012) *Service Operations Management: Improving Service Delivery*, 4th edition, Harlow: Pearson.

Jones, P., Ball, S., Kirk, D. and Lockwood, A. (2003) *Hospitality Operations: a Systems Approach*, London: Continuum.

Keynote at www.keynote.co.uk (Accessed Jan. 2019).

Kotler, P., Bowen, J., Makens, J. and Balogau, S. (2013) *Marketing for Hospitality and Tourism*, Harlow: Pearson Education.

Kotler, P., Keller, K., Brady, M. Goodman, M. and Hansen, T. (2016) *Marketing Management*, 3rd edition, Harlow: Pearson Education.

Lashley, C. and Morrison, A. (2000) *In Search of Hospitality, Theoretical Perspectives and Debates*, Oxford: Butterworth Heinemann.

Lugosi, P. (2008) Hospitality spaces, hospitable moments: consumer encounters and affective experiences in commercial settings, *Journal of Food Service*, **19** (2), 139-149.

Mele, C., Pels, J. and Polese, F. (2010) A brief review of systems theories and their managerial applications, *Service Science*, **2** (1/2), 126-135.

Mintel at www.mintel.com (Accessed Jan. 2019).

O'Gorman, K. (2010) *The Origins of Hospitality and Tourism*, Oxford: Goodfellow Publishers.

Parker, D. (2018) *Service Operations Management: The Total Experience*, 8th edition, Cheltenham: Edward Elgar Publishing Ltd.

Pine, J. B. and Gilmore, J. H. (1999) *The Experience Economy: Work is theatre and every business a stage*, Harvard: Harvard Business School Press.

Pizam, A. and Shani, A. (2009) The nature of the hospitality industry: present and future managers' perspectives, *Anatolia: An International Journal of Tourism and Hospitality Research*, **20**(1), 134-50.

Pizam, A. and Tasci, A. (2019), 'Experiencescape: expanding the concept of servicescape with a multi-stakeholder and multi-disciplinary approach', *International Journal of Hospitality Management*, **76**, 25-37.

Porter, M. (2004) *Competitive Advantage*, New York: Free Press.

Postrel, V. (2003) *The Substance of Style*. New York: Harper Collins.

Qualman, E. (2011) *Socialnomics: How Social Media Transforms the Way we Live and Do Business*, New Jersey: Wiley and Sons.

Records, H. and Glennie, M. (1991) Service management and quality assurance, *Cornell HRA Quarterly*, **32**(1), 26–35.

Restaurant Magazine at www.bighospitality.co.uk/Info/Restaurant (accessed Jan. 2019).

Royal Academy of Culinary Arts at www.royalacademyofculinaryarts.org.uk (accessed Jan. 2019).

Slack, N., Brandon-Jones, A. and Johnston, R. (2016) *Operations Management*, 8th edn, Harlow: Pearson Education.

The Caterer at www.thecaterer-magazine.co.uk (accessed Jan. 2019).

UK Hospitality at www.ukhospitality.org.uk (accessed Jan. 2019).

Warhurst, C., Nickson, D., Witz, A. and Cullen, A. M. (2000) Aesthetic labour in interactive service work: Some case study evidence from the 'new' Glasgow. *Service Industries Journal*, **20**(3),1-18.

Whyte, W. F. (1947) The social structure of the restaurant, *American Journal of Sociology*, **54** (4), 302-310.

Wolf, M. J. (1999) *The Entertainment Economy - How mega media forces are transforming our lives*, New York: Times Books.

2 Concept development

Aim

To explore the nature of demand for food and beverage products through the application of a systematic approach to the development of the consumer–product relationship.

Objectives

This chapter is intended to support you in:

- Adopting a systematic approach to the development of a consumer product relationship

- Further identifying and appraising key issues associated with the nature of demand for food and beverage products

- Exploring the importance of market segmentation

- Developing the process of idea evaluation and understanding its relationship with concept development

- Setting organisational goals and objectives.

2.1   Developing a consumer–product relationship

In Chapter 1 we introduced issues regarding the nature of products, sectors of the industry, the nature of demand and the nature of the food service product. This chapter extends this material and proposes that a systematic approach needs to be adopted, in order to be effective in identifying the key issues, which shape the nature of demand for food and beverage products and create the consumer–product relationship.

Literature concerning consumers and markets is readily available, and much of it applies specifically to food and beverage operations. The literature explores the nature of demand for products from different viewpoints. These viewpoints include marketing, psychology, anthropology, economics, sociology, geography and social psychology.

■   Considering the consumer

Consumers of food and beverage products are increasingly sophisticated, complex and dynamic. Psychology, sociology, social psychology, geography and anthropology all identify the behaviour of individuals and groups in an attempt to understand the human condition, and relate to the consumer through the examination of human needs, wants, demands, goals and values. Economics focuses on the examination of the human condition as it relates to the commercial and business world through the examination of the allocation of scarce resources and the link between supply and demand. Marketing focuses on the human condition as it relates to products, i.e. the study of the consumer. Kotler *et al.* (2016) explain that marketing is managing markets to attract profitable customer relationships through identifying their needs and designing good product offerings. The consumer is the actual link. Without the consumer there is no link between the human needs and food and beverage products. A product is simply a consumer's satisfied need.

People who do not consume are not consumers. However obvious or trite this statement might appear it does eliminate the possible confusion between a consumer and a non-consumer. For example, families who eat four times a year in a motorway service area are consumers of the motorway service area food and beverage product, even if they rarely consume this product. They are potential consumers of many existing and future food and beverage products but at present are consumers of only one product from a vast range available, but are not consumers of the rest. They may have an unsatisfied food and beverage need, but a product is unavailable to them as yet which may satisfy this need.

When consumers are discussed they are often addressed as large groups comprising millions of people, which they are when all added together. But when consumers are examined in detail they are certainly not homogeneous; they consume, or choose not to consume, millions of products in a very dynamic and rapidly changing way. They are individuals who group together to form a market for a particular product. This market grouping may range from 300 people, as in a small rural exclusive restaurant, up to and beyond 300 million people for world-branded products like McDonald's. It is also true that the same consumers will group together at different time depending on the needs they have at the time. The question for food and beverage managers is: Who do we want our consumers to be?

Managers may say that their consumers are the same as the consumers they want them to be, i.e. 'We have achieved our objective of creating a consumer that fits our product.' However, even if such a desirable state exists, the nature of the consumer is continually changing and as such management need to understand their consumers and how changes are taking place, which affect consumers' choices. It is a clear argument for the establishment of a customer-oriented business. The first key issue in the framework is therefore centred on consumers.

Considering the product

The key issues concerning the nature of demand for food and beverage products are identified using a well validated, if somewhat oversimplified list of questions:

- Who are the consumers of the food and beverage product?
- What food and beverage product do they want?
- Why do they want a food and beverage product?
- When do they want a food and beverage product?
- Where do they want a food and beverage product?
- How do they obtain a food and beverage product?

These questions can be explored individually, but only one is key: What products do consumers want? Who, why, where, when and how are all part of the product and are inherent in answering the question as to the nature of the products consumers actually want. The second key issue in the framework is therefore centred on the product.

Activity:

Think of one example of a recent innovative food and beverage concept and analyse the following:

- Unique selling point of the concept.
- Target market for the concept.
- What impact has it had on the wider industry?

■ Being systematic in developing the consumer–product relationship

The two key issues, the **consumer** and the **product**, can each be examined by expanded them to identify their component parts. This expansion is illustrated in Figure 2.1. The component parts of the two frameworks represent the tasks required in order to develop a product–consumer relationship.

Figure 2.1: Consumer and product frameworks

The various component parts of the consumer and the product, as illustrated in Figure 2.1, may be merged together to form a single development framework, (Figure 2.2). This single framework then provides the basis for a systematic approach to the development of a consumer–product relationship. Although this framework can give the impression that it is a list of tasks, which are performed chronologically, in practice many of these tasks will be performed simultaneously. Additionally this is not a one-off process. It is a dynamic and organic process in which any food and beverage operation is continuously engaged.

Figure 2.2: Integrated consumer–product relationship development framework

The initial stages of the development process, through to setting goals and objectives, are covered in this chapter. The product development, quality management, sales promotion and completing the product-consumer relationship are covered in Chapter 3.

2.2   Market research

Researching into the food and beverage market can be performed at various levels. Large food and beverage businesses may invest considerable resources in acquiring market information. Marketing departments will use consumer panels, questionnaires, interviews, mystery customers, sales analyses, data capture from social media sources, market information from specialist publications, specifically commissioned market information and other generally available data. Small food and beverage businesses do not usually have a marketing department and in these instances the unit manager or owner-operator will perform the market research function. The sheer volume of information now available on the internet assists small businesses to conduct secondary research into the business environment. This leads to the identification of current trends and also of the competitors who are facilitating them.

■ The nature of needs

From Chapter 1 we identified that food and beverage needs arise as a consequence of the desire to satisfy a range of needs. Kotler *et al.* (2013) point out that these needs are inherent in human biology and the human condition and as such are not created by society or by marketers. This concept is reinforced by O'Gorman (2010) who demonstrates that hospitality is fundamental to human existence.

Food and beverage needs are basic needs for satisfaction but they do not arise independently. They are associated with other needs such as those for shelter, safety, belonging and esteem. Food and beverage wants are desires for satisfiers of this complex set of needs. Younger children, for example, may want to go to McDonald's to satisfy their need for belonging to their peer group, to satisfy their need for esteem within their peer group and to satisfy their need for food and drink. Wanting to satisfy their belonging and esteem needs may often outweigh their food and drink needs. A food and beverage product may therefore be satisfying needs not initially stimulated by hunger and thirst.

■ The nature of demand

We saw from Chapter 1 that it is important to recognise that it is the needs people have at the time, rather than the type of people they are, that different operations are designed for.

Food and beverage demands are wants for specific food and beverage products, but the level of demand is also affected by the capability of the consumer to buy them and to meet the other costs which may be involved. Food and beverage operators should try then to influence demand by making their product desirable, valuable, available and affordable. In essence this is following the four Ps of the marketing mix: Product, Price, Promotion, Place (location and availability). In service marketing the four Ps is often extended to include: Process, People and Physical evidence (see, for instance, Armstrong *et al.* 2015 and Kotler *et al.* 2016).

Consumers then have a variety of goals when they decide to choose a food and beverage product. These goals can include esteem, belonging, status, attention, entertainment, privilege, relaxation, intimacy, romance, convenience, physiological and psychological comfort, and satisfying hunger and thirst. Again sometimes satisfying hunger and thirst are not always goals needing to be achieved.

The collection of goals an individual has when choosing a food and beverage product may be referred to as the goal set. Each food and beverage product has the capacity to satisfy a different goal set. Accordingly, a consumer may perceive a takeaway as providing greater convenience and as being less expensive than an up-market à la carte restaurant, but the restaurant may be perceived as providing greater attention (level of service) and a higher level of esteem and status. The consumer will make a choice as to which is the most satisfying product for their particular goal set at the time. If a consumer's goal set is prioritised as food, convenience and variety, different food and beverage products may satisfy them in different ways. A consumer with this goal set may satisfy these goals with a fish and chip shop product, whereas another consumer may satisfy the same goal set with a public house meal product. This has important implications, as the direct competitors for a food service operation are not only those operations that are similar, but also those that the consumer may choose simply as an alternative. This can be for instance where the consumer is making a choice primarily motivated by the desire to save money or reduce travel time.

Individual consumers then will have different priorities depending on their needs at the time. An individual may prioritise convenience when purchasing coffee and croissants on the way to work in the morning, and prioritise low price at lunchtime when purchasing a meal in the workplace restaurant and high levels of service and entertainment when purchasing a celebration meal in the evening. These priorities will also change during an individual's life cycle as his/her needs, wants and demands also change in relation to their circumstances. Individuals may desire a nightclub product in their youth, a fast food restaurant when they have young children and a reduced price product for a pensioner in their old age. Additionally, consumers may give differing importance to the same product or parts of a product. One individual may value silver service because it is perceived as increasing the status of the occasion, while others may not value silver service because it makes them feel uncomfortable in an unusual situation.

2

Activity:

Using a food or beverage product/concept of your choice:

■ Answer the six key questions for consumer identification:

1   Who is involved in buying and consuming?

2   What are their choice criteria?

3   When do they buy/use the product?

4   Why do they buy/use the product?

5   Where do they buy the product?

6   How do they use the product?

■ Price, cost, value and worth

Although values are attached to various products because of the perception of the needs they can satisfy, the ability to realise those goals is dependent on the ability to pay. But payment is not just about having the required amount of money. Choices are also made by considering the relationship between price, cost, worth and value:

- **Price** is the amount of money required to purchase the product.
- **Cost** includes, as well as price, the cost of not going somewhere else, the cost of transport and time, the cost of potential embarrassment, the cost of having to look and behave in a required manner and the cost in terms of effort at work to earn the money to pay the required price.
- **Worth** is a perception of the desirability of a particular product over another in order to satisfy a set of established goals.
- **Value** is not only the personal estimate of a product's capacity to provide the benefits which satisfy a set of goals, it is also a perception of the balance between worth and cost.

Good value for a food and beverage operation is where the **worth** is perceived as greater than the **costs**, and **poor value** is where the **costs** are perceived as greater than the **worth.**

2.3   Market segmentation

Researching the market will facilitate the identification of consumers' needs, wants, demands, goals and values as they relate to food and beverage products. Having identified these it is possible to group them using a mix of criteria. These groupings are termed *market segments*.

There are many different ways to segment a market. Food and beverage operators will try different segmentation variables in the attempt to identify the needs, wants and demands of possible market groupings. These variables are most usually grouped using the following four sets of criteria:

1 Geographic segmentation

2 Demographic segmentation

3 Psychographic segmentation

4 Behavioural segmentation.

Geographic segmentation

This involves dividing the market into geographical areas such as nations, regions, cities, districts and neighbourhoods. Food and beverage products such as J. D. Wetherspoon and Harvester target regions of the UK's food and beverage market. T.G.I. Friday restaurants target international cities. Starbucks and Costa coffee shops have a global approach targeting major cities worldwide. Up-market restaurants may target a district, and a fish and chip shop may only target a neighbourhood.

A food and beverage product may operate in areas with different geographical needs, satisfying these different needs by making alterations to their product mix. Menu items can vary between the restaurants in different parts of the world. Well-known fast food restaurants operate discriminatory pricing by applying a different price to the same product in relation to location, e.g. higher prices at airports than on high streets, and different prices in relation to different countries. The reason this is done is because the needs, wants and demands vary by geographical location, and the product/marketing mix will be altered in an attempt to exploit and/or accommodate the differences.

Demographic segmentation

This will involve dividing the market into groups using such variables as age, gender, stage in the family life cycle, income, occupation, education, religion, race and nationality. A public house may segment their markets into, for instance, single, 25–35-year-old men with average incomes, whose education finished at 16, and who are employed in manual skilled and semi skilled professions. Another public house however may segment its market in a similar way but substitute married couples with two small children for the 25–35-year-old single males. The first public house could be located in a city centre, and the second in a seaside holiday resort. The needs, wants and demands of these two segments are very different and this will have implications for the nature of the food and beverage product being required and offered.

2

■ Psychographic segmentation

This is a stage further on from demographic grouping and identifies the social class, life style and personality characteristics of a consumer. Social class exists in all areas of our society with various individuals forming into sets whose patterns of behaviour and attitude vary widely. Food and beverage consumers may be segmented as to their social class with products designed specifically to satisfy their demands.

Different social groupings exhibit preferences for particular food and beverage products. Some social groupings will prefer seclusion and formality when consuming a food and beverage product while another group may prefer informal and crowded atmospheres. Life-style segmentation can be seen in the development of food and beverage products such as T.G.I. Friday and Wagamama, appealing to consumers who see themselves as young, fashionable, informal and adventurous. Personality segmentation is used to develop beverage products such as beers, appealing to consumers who see themselves as sharp and quick-witted (Foster's lager), or discerning traditionalists (real ale).

■ Behavioural segmentation

This divides the market into groups depending on the way in which customers use the product. The food and beverage product may be used as a place to meet others, or as a place of anonymity. The behaviour exhibited will relate to consumer needs which the product must try and satisfy, i.e. lots of open areas in the former, and booths in the latter.

Behavioural segmentation also includes identifying the position of consumers in the hierarchy of usage, from having never used the product through regular users to ex-users. Consumers who have never used the product before may need to be made psychologically comfortable by a genuinely friendly welcome and an informative introduction to the food and beverage product. Some steakhouse chains ask customers if it is their first visit to the brand as standard practice, with different procedures for either of the two, yes and no, responses.

First-time buyers

Attracting first-time buyers necessitates the identification of how first-time buyers behave. How often the product is consumed is another behavioural variable. A consumer may use a bar every day, a takeaway once a week, a pizza restaurant once a month or go to a dinner dance twice a year. Identifying the usage rate enables the identification of the needs, wants and demands of that segment, and will contribute to product design. Consumers may perceive a dinner dance as a special occasion and they must therefore be made to feel special with personalised attention from senior staff. A bar may be perceived as a place to rest and unwind after work and may therefore be designed to be peaceful and comfortable.

Loyalty

Loyalty is also a behavioural variable that applies to food and beverage products. This is the ratio between the consumption of a range of products. If a customer only eats in one restaurant he/she is 100 per cent loyal to that restaurant. If a customer eats in a mix of six restaurants, he/she may be 50 per cent loyal to one, and 10 per cent loyal to the rest. The consumer's needs, wants and demands may be different at different loyalty levels. Consumer loyalty is regularly courted by food and beverage businesses, offering generous discounts and special offers in return for the consumer's repeat business.

■ Identifying changes in variables is a continuous process

Using segmentation variables allow for a more objective view of food and beverage consumers, and adopting this approach assists in the identification of consumers with similar needs, wants and demands. However new groups are continually forming and older ones becoming no longer relevant, therefore the need to make the identification is also continual. Although market segmentation is a useful generic grouping to use for marketers, there is also a growing demand for bespoke products and uniqueness. Consumers increasingly want what others may not have. Many companies, alongside their usual range of products, now also offer a bespoke or tailored service to meet the needs of the most discerning individuals.

Apart from the traditional methods of segmentation, as discussed above, there are other approaches that achieve the same goal just in a different way. One method is detailed in Figure 2.3. This looks at the combination of the consumer's time availability and the budget (cash) and then identifies the possible dining experience that might be sought.

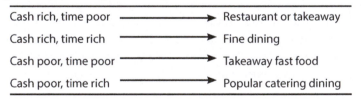

Figure 2.3: Cash/time model

Another approach used by large companies is that of typologies, which may include groups of consumers who are categorised and named and targeted as follows:

- Empty nest career ladies
- Comfortable retired couples
- Stretched single mums
- Career focused females/males, or
- Competitive male urbanites.

The ACORN classification is a UK-based system that uses geo-demographic segmentation to organise neighbourhoods into different consumer types and categories. Examples include: wealthy executives, affluent greys, flourishing families, aspiring singles, prudent pensioners and burdened singles. (Further information on the ACORN classification can be obtained from www.caci.co.uk/acorn-classification.aspx).

A further approach is based on characteristics of generations. The most identified recent groupings are:

- **Baby Boomers** – the result of increased birth rates in post-war years. Birth years are typically between the early to mid-1940s, to 1964. They grew up in a time of prosperity and enjoyed greater affluence and higher levels of income than their parents, and became the most active, and the most physically fit generation. They had a genuine belief that things would improve.

- **Generation X** – the generation after that of the Baby Boomers. Typical birth years are 1960s to late 1970s. Often originally perceived to be disaffected and directionless, in midlife they are mostly perceived as happy, active, achieving work-life balance and possessing entrepreneurial skills.

- **Millennials** – also known as *Generation Y*, millennials are the demographic cohort following Generation X. They refer to those who achieve adulthood in the 21st Century. Typical birth years are from 1980s to mid-1990s to early 2000s. Generally, most associated with increased and confident use of communications, media and digital technologies.

- **Generation Z** – demographic cohort following Millennials. Typically identified with birth years from mid-1990s to mid-2000s. Most of Generation Z are likely to be independent and entrepreneurial, and very comfortable with technology and social media, with high expectations that everyone else should be.

- **Snowflakes** – mostly young adults of the 2010s but can be used as a term for anyone with a highly exaggerated sense of being special and entitled. They are also the most easily outraged, and the most vocal about it.

Despite the differences in these groups, an underlying trend is an increasing unity in common causes such as environmental concerns, humanitarianism and animal welfare.

Groupings or market segments must be the focus of the food and beverage operators' business. Choosing which groupings and segments the product will be targeted at will then depend on the financial, technological, material and human resources available. Once a target segment has, or segments have, been decided this will drive how the company will create its product, price, promotion and distribution to fit the consumers. Food and beverage management is then concerned with the manipulation of these various resources to achieve customer satisfaction, organisational efficiency and effectiveness, and ultimately profitability.

2.4　Idea evaluation

How market segments are chosen, shaped, reached, targeted and satisfied by the operation, begins by generating ideas. Ideas can be generated using a variety of techniques and sources. In such a dynamic industry innovation can be crucial. It is imperative that a business captures a first-mover advantage with the implementation of new concepts and ideas.

Ideas can come from examining how existing food and beverage products are meeting the demands of various segments. Researching how well one's own and the competition's products satisfy customers' demands may stimulate ideas and identify key factors for success. Other methods of generating ideas include management and staff brainstorming sessions, and asking customers, with the focus for these approaches always being clearly on establishing customers' needs, wants and demands (Smith, 2015).

The generation of many ideas, which will then need to be considered, enables a more objective appraisal to be made. It is a sad situation that many new food and beverage operations fail because only one idea has been generated and no alternatives have been considered. Idea generation should be sought from all the stakeholders of the operation in an open and supportive atmosphere. If one idea is criticised, other ideas may not be forthcoming for fear of ridicule. Food and beverage operators can also benefit by formalising the idea generation process and by giving their employees information about segmentation variables. This would lead to a continuous flow of good new ideas to meet customer needs.

A flow of product ideas focused on consumers' needs, wants and demands should be screened. Screening out ideas and progressing the remainder into the next stage of concept development can be achieved by setting up processes through which the idea must successfully pass. Screening processes will be drawn up by the stakeholder(s) and applied accordingly. An example idea-screening process is as follows:

- Does the idea meet consumers' needs?
- Is the group of consumers with these needs large enough to make the idea worthwhile?
- Does the food and beverage operator or potential operator have the necessary resources available to deliver the idea?
- Will the idea generate customer satisfaction?
- Will the idea generate a benefit to the operation, economically, managerially and socially?
- Is the idea different from the competition?

This idea-screening process asks questions which may be very difficult, and sometimes impossible, to answer, but trying to answer them will give indications of what will be needed to make the idea worth investing in further. This approach to idea screening should reduce the amount of ideas considerably, but is by no means a foolproof system. Good ideas may still be discarded and poor ones adopted no matter how sophisticated the screening processes are.

These approaches to market research, market segmentation and idea generation and screening apply to all situations where new products are being developed. A restaurant concept, such as Nando's, will have gone through this development process, as will a change in the opening times, service methods and decor of an existing food and beverage product. All ideas need to be screened according to the stakeholders' objectives and resources. Screening processes should be individually tailored to suit the objectives of the business. It is also necessary to review the screening process periodically as business objectives may change. If a successful food and beverage operation decides to expand and open other operations, the idea-screening process may need to be changed to accommodate geographical location, product branding, continuity and consistency issues.

2.5   Completing the concept development

It is helpful to consider the generated ideas, which pass a screening process, in terms of how they might be conceptualised as products or parts of products. For example an idea to introduce a self-service buffet operation could be conceptualised as:

- An informal continental-style all-day restaurant
- A family meal occasion to satisfy all appetites, or
- An inexpensive, value for money, eat as much as you like concept.

Turning the ideas into concepts allows for the identification and consideration of the potential market as well as the potential competition if the concept was converted into a product.

Evaluating the competition, using for example, a relative strengths and weaknesses analysis, will help position the new product. The position of the product is related to key consumer needs variables. These variables will be directly related to a particular market segment and should be clearly focused on customers' needs. Product positioning draws a map of the food and beverage market and places the various products in relation to each other. For example, if speed of service and convenience are identified as key consumer needs for a particular target market, then the perceptions of various products might be related against each other as shown in Figure 2.4.

Figure 2.4: Perceptions of various products for a particular target market

Other variables, which may also be used to position a concept/product, include: price, quality, speed, dependability (and availability) and flexibility (capacity and volume). To be successful, food service operations need to plan the products to match the competitive factors against the proposed performance objectives. Table 2.1 gives examples of these variables factors and the corresponding performance that the business needs to concentrate on.

Table 2.1: Different competitive factors imply different performance requirements

Variable factors	Performance requirements
If the customer values these:	Then the operation will need to excel at these:
■ Low price	■ Price
■ High quality	■ Quality
■ Fast delivery	■ Speed
■ Reliable delivery	■ Dependability (and availability)
■ Wide range of products/services	■ Flexibility (choice and availability)
■ The ability to change the timing or quantity of products	■ Flexibility (capacity and volume)

Source: developed from Slack *et al.* 2013

■   Concept testing

Once the idea has been converted into a concept it should be tested in the identified market segment by asking consumers and potential consumer's questions about the concept. These questions might include:

■ How they view the concept in relation to the competition?

■ If they would purchase the product and how frequently, time of day, what price might they be prepared to pay?

- What they see as the benefits of the product?
- What improvements to the product could be made?

Asking these sorts of question can help to position the new concept more accurately.

Testing new product concepts is essential. Even if performed badly it is probably better than not testing at all. Large operations will test their new concepts thoroughly using consumer panels and sometimes actually create the real product in selected areas to test consumer reaction. Smaller operations with fewer resources to test the concept can still be thorough by talking, and most importantly, listening, to existing customers and likely competitors' customers. Well-structured interviews relating to a product's benefits and image will produce valuable data to inform the development of the new concept. Well-tested food and beverage concepts have a reduced risk of failure.

Activity:

- Identify four local establishments and determine the range of potential markets they will be attractive too.

2.6   Setting goals and objectives

As well as generating ideas for concept development, the organisation also needs to consider its potential goals and objectives. Developing an understanding of the business environment leads to greater confidence in determining appropriate goals and objectives for a food service organisation. This is important as the setting of goals and objectives will play a crucial role in the determination of the direction of a particular food service organisation and its likely success.

Goals, or aims, are the broad intentions of an organisation. Objectives are the measurable outcomes, which will indicate the progress being made by an organisation towards meeting its specific goals. Having goals and objectives is important: as the old adage says: if you have no idea of where you are going then you won't know if you are ever going to get there.

The orientation of organisational objectives can be classified under three broad headings as:

- Economic
- Managerial
- Social responsibility.

■ Economic objectives

Economic objectives assume that the sole purpose of an organisation is to maximise profit for its owners. This approach tends to be predominant where the food service operation is owner-managed and provides a single product, or a limited range of products, under near perfect market conditions. It is also likely to operate most successfully under the assumption of a unitary perspective; that is, where everyone within the organisation shares the same objectives.

There are however some problems when objectives are based purely on the economic theory of the firm. It can be difficult to define exactly what is meant by profit maximisation. Does it mean profit, for instance, in absolute terms or profit expressed as return on capital employed, return on equity or profit margin (that is profit as a percentage of sales) or some other measure of profit? The other dimension which needs to be determined is the time-scale over which this to be achieved; short-term profits, one, two, three years, or a much longer period?

Creating economic objectives also relies on the assumption that the achievement of profitability can actually be measured in a meaningful and consistent way. It also assumes that customers make their purchasing choices solely on economic grounds.

Moreover, it is easy to argue that such an approach ignores the reality of organisational life in today's complex organisations. Clearly, many organisations have non-economic goals, especially but not exclusively those in the public and charitable sectors. There are also likely to be circumstances under which the interests and objectives of the organisation's owners and its managers may be in conflict.

■ Managerial objectives

The maximisation of profit for the owners of a food service organisation may not always be perceived to be the desirable objectives for the managers. For example, food and beverage managers may seek to:

- Maximise revenue through a high market share, thereby increasing their own prestige in their industry
- Increase the assets of the organisation (for example, by acquisition), thereby increasing their own power and personal reward
- Empire-build inside the organisation, again increasing their own status, salary and associated perks, or
- Increase the technical sophistication and complexity of the organisation (for example, in products and processes) thereby achieving growth, increasing managerial independence and providing fresh challenges.

The existence of these types of managerial objectives can be very prevalent, especially in the private sector. On the other hand it can also be argued that the best interests of a firm are actually served by its managers. They may be more interested, for instance, in the long-term success of the organisation than its owners, whose interest may be transitory as they can sell the business or their shares in it.

The complexities of organisational life mean that managers are often faced with conflicting objectives. These may arise from their personal objectives, those of the owners, customers, suppliers, different groups of employees, the government, and other interested stakeholders. Under such conditions they may seek a compromise that satisfies every party to some extent. Such behaviour is termed 'satisficing'.

Social responsibility objectives

Such objectives stress the ethical aspects of a food service organisation's objectives. These can include objectives related to:

- Safety of products
- Working conditions for staff
- Working conditions for suppliers
- Honesty, for example, not offering or accepting bribes or other inducements
- Equal opportunities
- Ethical business practices
- Fairtrade
- Energy saving
- Sustainable and responsible sourcing
- Sustainability of the business, and
- Concern over pollution and other environmental concerns.

For many organisations, a code of business and social ethics is seen as good for business. It is also important, as increasingly businesses will only seek to trade with other businesses that have clear social responsibility policies. Additionally for many public, charitable and voluntary sector organisations, the entire *raison d'être* is allied to particular social and/or ethical objectives. However the issues raised under the preceding section on managerial objectives often also apply in the cost provision sectors.

Most businesses now recognise the need for robust Corporate Social Responsibility (CSR) strategies. Starbucks, for example, are well known for their CSR strategies which cover each element of their business from sourcing fair trade coffee through to environmental and community work.

It is however sometimes worth speculating as to whether social and ethical concerns among a profit seeking organisation's managers and owners derive from genuinely held beliefs, or whether they merely exist to satisfy the concerns of external stakeholders such as pressure groups, governments or society at large.

Activity:

Think about the impact a food and beverage establishment could have on wider society and the environment. Other than the example above (Starbucks), identify one business that demonstrates excellent corporate social responsibility and evaluate the following:

- Should the business invest time and labour into improving corporate social responsibility initiatives?

- Why is it so important?

- Which stakeholders of the business are affected by positive corporate social responsibility strategies?

For more information on sustainability issues see, for example, Hawkins and Bohdanowicz (2011). For information on business ethics see, for example, Hartman *et al.* (2017) or Crane and Matten (2015).

Summarising the need to set objectives

Generally, objectives for an enterprise tend to be a mixture of economic, management and social responsibility factors. In all cases, though:

- The goals of a food service organisation are bound to affect the strategic options that it will consider appropriate and the particular objectives that will be set.

- Organisational objectives have an implicit impact on planning when strategic choices are being considered.

- Setting objectives for a food service organisation provides a basis for making choices about the policies and plans to be adopted in order to achieve the goals of the organisation.

- Having agreed objectives, which are also made explicit, means that there is something to measure the performance of the organisation against.

- The agreed objectives may also be the criteria that are used when making future strategic choices and determining the resulting policies and plans.

2.7   References and additional reading

ACORN Classification at www.caci.co.uk/blog/acorn-explained (accessed January 2019).

Armstrong, G., Kotler, P., Harker, M. and Brennan, R. (2015) *Marketing: an Introduction*, Harlow: Pearson.

Bitner, M.J. (1992), Servicescapes: The impact of physical surroundings on customers and employees, *Journal of Marketing*, **56**, 57-71.

Crane, A. and Matten, D. (2015) *Business Ethics: Managing Corporate Citizenship and Sustainability in the Age of Globalization*, 4th edn, Oxford: Oxford University Press.

Hartman, L., Des Jardins, J. and MacDonald, C. (2017) *Business Ethics: Decision-making for Personal Integrity and Social Responsibility*, 4th edn, Boston, MA: McGraw-Hill International.

Hawkins, R. and Bohdanowicz, P. (2011) *Responsible Hospitality, Theory and Practice*, Oxford: Goodfellow Publishers.

Keynote at www.keynote.co.uk (Accessed January 2019).

Kotler, P., Bowen, J., Makens, J. and Balogau, S. (2013) *Marketing for Hospitality and Tourism*, Harlow: Pearson Education.

Kotler, P., Keller, K., Brady, M. Goodman, M. and Hansen, T. (2016) *Marketing Management*, 3rd edition, Harlow: Pearson Education.

Line, N., Hanks, L. and Kim, W.G. (2018), An expanded servicescape framework as the driver of place attachment and word of mouth, *Journal of Hospitality & Tourism Research*, **42**(3), 476-499.

Mintel at www.mintel.com (Accessed January 2019).

Slack, N., Brandon-Jones, A. and Johnston, R. (2016) *Operations Management*, 7th edn, Harlow: Pearson.

Smith, D. (2015) *Exploring Innovation*, 3rd edn, Maidenhead: McGraw-Hill Education.

The Caterer at www.thecaterer.com (Accessed January 2019).

3 Product development

Aim

To detail the process of developing the food and beverage product to meet the needs of its target consumer.

Objectives

This chapter is intended to support you in:

- Identifying key stages of product development

- Developing detailed knowledge of the meal experience factors

- Explore pricing methods

- Identifying and applying various approaches to the development of a consumer–product relationship

- Gaining an insight into service quality and quality management issues

- Setting standards for food and beverage operations

- Developing an integrated approach to service quality management

- Determining promotional channels

- Estimating profitability

- Developing approaches to sales promotion

- Developing the consumer–product relationship as a dynamic process.

3.1 The food and beverage product

In Chapter 2, the first stages of developing the consumer-product relationship were considered. These were market research, identifying potential markets, idea evaluation, concept development and setting goals and objectives.In order to progress from the concept development phase, the next requirement in developing a consumer–product relationship is to consider the nature of a food and beverage product. Within this phase, questions need to be addressed, and decisions made, in order to turn a consumer focus (the abstract concept that consumers purchase) into an operational focus.

Customers may view a food and beverage product as a quick snack, a night out, a celebration, an indulgent extravagance or an absolute necessity. The nature of the occasion and the expectations from the meal experience is varied. What is one customer's *dining out* is another's *eating out*. The concepts are what customers purchase, but the food and beverage product, as an amalgamation of the tangible and intangible elements, is what operators construct and provide in order to satisfy the customer requirements.

The marketing focus towards food and beverage service delivery tends to identify the product as: a central consumer concept known as the core concept; a surrounding layer of tangible features, and an outer layer of augmentation (see Section 1.3, p. 19 on product augmentation). Placing this framework on a food and beverage product might show that the core product is, for example, a wedding celebration, the tangible product is a full wedding banquet, and the augmented product includes the opportunity to pay by instalments. It is helpful to apply this type of product framework to the development of concepts. This is where frameworks such as the *meal experience* can be useful.

■ The meal experience

The concept of the *meal experience* was first put forward in the 1960s (Campbell-Smith, 1967). Others have developed the concept further with slightly different approaches. See for example, Jones (1988 and 1994), Wood (2000 and 2013) or the *Five Aspect Meal Model (FAMM model)* put forward by Gustafsson *et al.* (2006), orientated as "room, meeting, products, management control systems and making the meal an entirety (expressing an atmosphere)".

The *meal experience* concept was introduced in Chapter 1 as comprising the five factors: food and drink on offer; level of service; cleanliness and hygiene; value for money / price; and atmosphere (Cousins *at al.*, 2014b). These meal experience factors influence both the customers' choice of a food and beverage operation, and the potential enjoyment of a meal. Although the five factors can be identified for all operations, the relative importance of them, to the customer, is not the same for all occasions or all operations. Investigating the relative weighting given to the meal experience factors by the customer, can help guide the design of a new food and beverage operation, or the review of an existing one.

With five factors of the *meal experience* to consider, the inevitable question arises as to which one should be addressed first. Most food and beverage operators immediately explore the food and beverages, with the construction of a menu and beverage list being given the highest priority. However, it might be more appropriate to explore the price first, or the style and level of service that will be provided, the level of cleanliness and hygiene or the atmosphere and ambience to be created. The intended core, tangible and augmented concepts of the product, considered in the form of benefits to the consumer, will guide an operator when ranking the *meal experience* factors in order of priority to the consumer. Table 3.1 gives examples of how differing core concepts might change the order of importance, to the customer, of the *meal experience* factors.

Table 3.1: Possible meal experience factor ranking for different meal experiences

Core concept	Possible factor ranking
Night out	1. Atmosphere 2. Food and drink 3. Service 4. Price 5. Cleanliness and hygiene
Gourmet event	1. Food and drink 2. Service 3. Atmosphere 4. Cleanliness and hygiene 5. Price
Cheap meal	1. Price 2. Food and drink 3. Cleanliness and hygiene 4. Service 5. Atmosphere
State banquet	1. Service 2. Atmosphere 3. Food and drink 4. Cleanliness and hygiene 5. Price

When setting out to design a tangible product it is therefore appropriate to consider the core concept in order to establish the weighting of the meal experience factors and the priority given to them by the customer so that the operation can develop the product from this perspective.

Identifying the relative importance of the meal experience factors for differing type of operation is valuable because it considers the operation from the point of view of the customer. This approach also identifies that limitations in the operation in one part of the meal experience will create stronger expectations in the customers' minds for the other parts. For example a limited menu operation will find that customers are more concerned with value for money and the speed of service than they would be in an operation where the menu offered greater choice.

In all cases then, although the meal experience factors can be identified in all operations, the intended product will determine the emphasis or limitations placed on them. This in turn will affect the potential customer's expectations and this should determine the priorities for operational development of the product.

Activity:

■ Identify two different eating out experiences.

■ Place in order of importance the five meal experience factors.

■ Explain the reasons for your choices.

Exploring the meal experience further

There is a greater understanding of how the meal experience can affect customer enjoyment and sales. Across a range of service industries this concept is often referred to as the 'servicescape'. Although originally the concept of servicescape (Bitner, 1992) was solely concerned with the physical aspects of the service environment and how these affected the interaction of customers, it has now been broadened to include social interactions (Line *et al.*, 2018). In addition, Pizam and Tasci (2019) proposed the construct of the 'experiencescape', a holistic conceptualization consisting of social, cultural, sensory, functional and natural components that are all present in the dining experience and work together to create the overall meal experience.

The meal experience approach takes account of the physical aspects of the service environment within the broader context of the five elements of the meal experience. In addition, 'atmosphere' takes account of staff/customer and customer/customer interaction. In order to continue to explore product development more fully it can be useful to consider each of the five factors separately. They are:

■ Food and drink

■ Level of service

■ Cleanliness and hygiene

■ Price and value for money

■ Atmosphere.

Food and drink

The food and drink itself, usually in the form of a menu and beverage lists, must clearly focus on the needs and demands of the consumer. Operators need to focus on what food and beverages the different market segments require. The permutations of range, tastes, textures and presentations of food and beverages are almost endless. This facilitates the opportunity to be creative in its delivery as a means of generating product differentiation. However, the menu and beverage offerings are a list from which customers construct a package to suit their own needs, and therefore the range of food and beverages offered should be considered in this light. There may be vegetarians, dieters, customers who are hungry (and ones who are not), ones who like seafood and those who do not, ones who like steaks and not much else; all are potentially part of any intended market segment. However, if there are a very wide variety of demands in the intended market segment, it may be appropriate to consider further market segmentation. Trying to satisfy everyone can lead to satisfying no one.

The type of food and beverages that are offered is often used to identify operations. Food can include a wide range of styles and cuisine types. These can be by country, e.g. traditional British, Italian or Thai, by type of cuisine, e.g. eclectic cuisine, modern British, oriental, Mediterranean, Asia Pacific or aiming for a particular speciality such as fish, vegetarian or health food. These operations can all be identified by their cuisine. Other operations can be identified principally by the beverage provisions, e.g. pubs, wine bars and clubs. The food and beverage offering plays a considerable part in influencing the customers' perceptions and expectations of the product and consideration of the market's needs, wants and demands in terms of the food and beverages is important. Ideas can be generated and tested on consumer panels to identify these demands more specifically rather than relying on instinct and a propensity to deliver what the operator knows how to deliver, as opposed to what the customer actually wants.

Level of service

Service delivery is a part of the product and may be considered the human (usually) interface between the product and the consumer. The exception is vending and automated operations where the machine and technology form the interface. Food and beverage operators usually identify different service methods, such as silver service, buffet service, cafeteria service and so on, from which can be selected the most appropriate method to meet the demands of their customers: quick service when the customer is in a hurry; slower service for an intimate dinner; and stylish service for customers who want to be entertained, are examples of service methods meeting demand. However, service also involves a personal interaction between customers and service personnel. The quality and authenticity of this interaction can deliver benefits to the customer, such as feeling valued. It should therefore be designed into the product offer rather than just hoping that these benefits will be delivered. This is at all stages where interactions occur; each of the service-to-customer touch points and offers a unique encounter along the full meal journey. The journey being from the moment the customer engages with the restaurant business, to the moment that they depart; a journey which comprises many touch points, with each of these being positive encounters ensuing that the augmentation of the many contributes to an overall positive meal experience.

In food and beverage service, the two key service aspects are:

- **Efficiency:** how timely, consistent and organised the service is (procedural).
- **Conviviality:** the way the service is carried out, and the friendliness and attitude of the staff.

These two factors can be used to construct a matrix into which service styles can be placed. This is illustrated in Figure 3.1. Depending on the combination of the two service dimensions, *efficiency* and *conviviality,* the matrix identifies the four possible extremes of potential service styles, and how customers may view them. Without regular monitoring, any food and beverage operation can easily move towards any one of these four extremes.

	Conviviality	
	High	Low
High	Competent and responsive but can be intrusive	Customers are things to be processed
Low	Staff personality more important than competence	No idea what they are doing and don't care

Efficiency

Figure 3.1: Service dimensions matrix

Source: developed from Martin, 1986

The two key service dimensions of *efficiency* and *conviviality* are interdependent. If the procedural aspect of the service is poorly designed and delivered, resulting in overworked and poorly motivated staff, it is likely that the conviviality aspect will also deteriorate. Equally, if the convivial aspect is given too much prominence then the level of service efficiently will drop. To reduce the potential for problems, a food and beverage operator can seek to balance the level of the service efficiency with the level of service conviviality. This is achieved through ensuring that both of the two key service dimensions are always considered together, when designing or reviewing the service being offered.

The level of service can also be affected by the standards being achieved. However the level of service should not be confused with standards of service. Low levels of service, such as in a fast food operation, are often achieved with very high standards, which are also consistent over time. On the other hand an operation offering a high level of service, such as in fine dining, can be poorly regulated and standards can be low and variable.

The level of service provided can also be augmented and this can have a considerable influence on the success of a food service operation. Being able to reserve a table, pay by various credit cards, vary portion size, access health information and availability of highchairs, for example, will be factors that will influence consumer choice. There may be factors which particular market segments value highly and should be researched, and if thought worthwhile, introduced. It is also necessary for staff to be able to customise the offer for individual authentic service to be achieved, whilst maintaining the standards of the food service operation.

Cleanliness and hygiene

Cleanliness and hygiene issues are relevant to the premises, equipment and staff. In recent years the significance of this factor has increased substantially and has been reinforced with an increasing level of legislation. The media focus on food, staff and premises hygiene and the risks involved have heightened awareness of health and hygiene aspects. Customers are now far more aware of, and prepared to complain about, issues of cleanliness and hygiene, and to report them to regulatory bodies. Overall operations should be concerned about assuring the proper levels of cleanliness and hygiene through the systematic design of process and procedures of the operation, which are developed as a normal part of the working practices, rather than undertaking hygiene processes to avoid being caught out.

As well as ensuring that food and beverage product is prepared in hygienic conditions, and that customers are provided with a clean environment in which to consume the product, there is also the need to reinforce the perception of the foods service operation as being clean and hygienic. Tidy and clean premises, smart uniforms and well-groomed staff, for instance, can all have a positive effect on this perception. Negative impressions can be created by, for instance: scruffy staff; fiddling with hair; holding equipment badly (e.g. holding cups and glassware by the rim rather than the handle or the base), poor standards of personal hygiene amongst staff; poorly presented food items, food not being served at the right temperatures, stained menus and dirty toilets.

Price and value for money

Price is the element of the meal experience that relates to value, and is also directly related to profitability. However, price is also very flexible and can be changed relatively easily. This can be, for example, through product bundling such as offering early bird deals, or Buy One, Get One Free (BOGOF) promotions. This can change the customers' value perceptions and may change profitability. (Chapter 9, on operations appraisal, covers profitability in more detail.)

In Chapter 2, we also saw that good value is where the worth is perceived as greater than the cost. Therefore a successful operator must add value for the consumer into the product. Prices should also be set in relation to the quality and value perception that operators want consumers to have. A high-priced product might be perceived as either good value or a rip-off, and a low-priced product as poor quality or good value, indicating that it is more than just the absolute price which determines value, but rather the cash price together with the other costs relative to worth (see page 39).

When developing, changing or supporting a product concept, it is good practice to establish a price range within which the consumer will be prepared to pay. Another price range can be established within which the operator is prepared to offer the product. The overlap is the range available to the operator. Setting prices within ranges which the consumers will pay, should be accomplished with reference to the particular market segment and the core concept.

Market research can determine a range within which families travelling on motorways are prepared to stop and pay for food and drink, and will also be able to determine a price range for a particular menu item. This can be achieved through setting up consumer panels and asking them about price and product. The information to be gained from researching customers' attitudes and behaviour towards price will reveal that lowest price is far from always the main consideration, as Table 3.1 indicated.

Pricing methods

Pricing methods used by operators vary in their appropriateness and sophistication. The various pricing methods include the following:

- **Cost plus:** This is the most common method. The ingredient cost is established – not always very accurately – and the required profit (referred to as gross profit) is added. The result is a selling price that gives the operator the required profit for that dish once sold. This method is attractive because of its simplicity. However it ignores price sensitivity and demand (price is a determinant of demand) and that value for money must be factored into the pricing decision. It also makes the assumption that the required profit can be established by making it a standard percentage of the selling price (often between 60 and 75 per cent). But this approach fails to account for different restaurant types and different menu categories. It also does not take into account that each dish/ beverage is only part of a collection of items purchased to produce the meal experience. Where the cost plus method is applied, differentiated percentages are used so that low-cost starter items earn proportionately more gross profit than higher-cost main course items. This also fits in with the price ranges that customers expect to pay

- **Prime costing methods:** These methods attempt to factor-in the labour cost of a dish, and *actual* cost pricing attempts to include fixed and variable costs as well as labour. These additional costs are also established as a percentage of the final selling price (e.g. labour at 25% and variable costs at 10%). These methods are flawed in the same way as *cost plus*: labour is a factor related to the time needed to prepare a dish, not to the value of the ingredients used to prepare it; no account is taken of volume of business or item popularity in assessing the labour content of a dish, therefore not taking into account economies and diseconomies of scale; and allocating fixed and variable costs to each menu item should at least be related to the volume of each dish sold rather than a fixed percentage figure to be used for each menu item.

- **Backward pricing:** This method attempts to match costs to a price previously established for a desired potential market. This market-driven approach – which is not really backwards – is a good starting point in new product development but it is still difficult to establish the necessary gross profit, ingredient and labour costs, and care must be taken to avoid the problems of using percentages. However identifying what the customer is prepared to pay for a particular product and investigating whether the operation can provide the product, profitability, at that price may avoid an operation being created that was never going to be profitable anyway.

- **Profit-per-customer pricing:** This establishes the total profit required and allocates this to a forecast demand resulting in an average profit per customer. This 'profit' is then added to the material and/or other costs to produce a selling price for each dish. Again this may be used to produce a break-even analysis (see page 77), but caution should be exercised because profit is a factor of demand, which is a factor of price, which is a factor of demand, and so on. However, as with *backwards pricing* above, relating the required profitability of an operation to a given level of demand and within a price range that the customer is likely to pay can be used in determining if the operation can in fact ever be successful.

- **Elasticity pricing:** This asks how sensitive a market is to price changes. In order to determine menu prices the operator will try to determine the effect a price change may have on demand. It should be remembered that it is possible to increase demand and profitability through price decreases. However, it is very difficult to predict market responses to price changes, but considering elasticity may inform the pricing decisions.

- **Competition pricing:** This is copying the competitors' price. However, there is no guarantee that the cost structure of any competitor offering a similar product will be similar, so a particular market price may produce higher or lower profits. Copying the competition may also take the form of special offers, premium promotions, special meals, free wine and the provision of children's toys, all or which are short-term tactics, which can potentially lead to increasing costs and fierce price-based competition. (Sales promotion is discussed in more detail in Section 3.4.)

Other pricing methods include: marginal analysis; break-even analysis; cost margin analysis; individual menu item profit and loss, and frequency distribution pricing (see, for example, Bowie *et al.*, 2016 and Kotler *et al.*, 2016). There is no easy answer to making the right choice. Whichever methods are used, an operator should always have a clear pricing policy or objective in mind. Some of these pricing objectives might include:

- **Sales volume maximisation**, where the pricing objective is to achieve the highest sales possible.

- **Market share gain**, where the objective is to increase your number of customers relative to the total possible market and the competition.

- **Profit maximisation**, where the pricing objective is to achieve the highest profit possible.

- **Market penetration**, where the pricing objective is to move from a position of a zero or low market share to a significant market share.

Once a clear pricing objective is established, the pricing methods most suitable to that particular objective can be drawn from the various methods available, often being a combination of a range of pricing methods. (The nature of and the relationships between revenue, costs and profits are explored in more detail in Chapter 9, Appraising performance.)

Atmosphere

Atmosphere is an intangible element of the meal experience. It is created through the combination of a number of tangible factors such as: design, decor, lighting, heating, furnishings, acoustics and noise levels, the other customers, the staff and the attitude of the staff. It is the manipulation of these tangible factors which create atmosphere or restaurant mood. There are happy atmospheres and also gloomy, stressful, joyful, cheerful, angry, bustling, sedate, calming, invigorating, indulgent, peaceful, comfortable, uncomfortable, boring and inviting atmospheres. All of these different types of atmospheres can be created, and examples abound. The bright, young, clean atmosphere of McDonalds; the lively, musical atmosphere of a Hard Rock Cafe, the farmhouse atmosphere of Harvester, the luxurious atmosphere of the restaurant at the Ritz, London, the cosy and informal atmosphere of a local French bistro, are all created.

Atmosphere creation and maintenance needs to be managed as it can be as easily destroyed, as it can be created. Atmosphere is sensed through sight, sound, touch, taste and smell. Food and beverage operators' use:

- The sense of sight through the presentation of food and beverage products, furniture and textures, equipment, lighting, colours, employees, shapes, spaces and their own customers.

- The sense of sound can be controlled through acoustics, the use of materials and shapes, which alter sound, and the use of music, televisions, and operational sounds including speech.

- The sense of touch will be incorporated though, for instance, the quality of the air and the fabrics and equipment with which customers come into contact, the texture of the foods and the touching of other people.

- The sense of taste has great volumes of documentation dedicated to it through recipe and wine books and the variations are almost infinite.

- The sense of smell is used by many food and beverage operators to attract customers through coffee, bread, roast meat, etc. and any other aromas which may be associated with the core consumer concept.

Atmosphere is also created through the attitude of the staff. A pleasing environment soon becomes an unbearable one if members of staff are unhelpful, lacking in competence, unresponsive and rude. Conversely a potentially poor environment can be enhanced through genuine interest in customer needs, competence and good interpersonal skills.

Other customers have an impact on atmosphere. There is a range of customer related factors that operations need to consider which can affect the atmosphere. The proximity of other customers through the spacing of table in a restaurant for instance will affect the feeling of privacy or otherwise.

Additionally operations need to make decisions about policies, for example, for:

- Customer dress requirements
- Mobile phone usage
- Maximum group size
- Accepting children
- Alcohol over-consumption
- Minimum levels of acceptable customer behaviour, and
- Mix of customers (e.g. a bar showing a football match).

Having policies for these types of factors also means they have to be reinforced. There is no point having policies if they are not going to be enforced. Procedures for dealing with enforcement need to be developed so that the consistency in the application of the policies is maintained, and the potential for customer relations problems is minimised. (Also see the discussion in Section 7.4, p 197, on customer relations.)

There are always structural and cost constraints to atmosphere creation, but operators should invest in atmosphere to their best ability. If the right atmosphere is not created at the start, in the hope that business success will finance further atmosphere development, success might not come at all. It might be better to consider targeting a different market for which atmosphere creation is less expensive, and then moving on to the original target market when the atmosphere-creation funds are available.

Specialist designers are available to construct an atmosphere through the tangible elements for a food and beverage operation, with some large businesses employing their own design teams. Early designs concepts, (or redesign concepts) can be tested by showing them to consumer panels and recording the reaction, followed by initial low product or operational trial risks being undertaken. At whatever level a food and beverage operation is resourced, investing in a part of the product, which so heavily influences the customers' perception of the product, should be a priority.

Activity:

Using the Five Meal Experience Factors as a template:

- Compare and contrast the potential meal experience in two different food service operations.

- Place the five factors in order of importance for the customer and contrast this with the actual achievement of the operation.

3.2   Quality in the management of food and beverage operations

The term 'quality' is currently used in a variety of ways to mean a variety of things. To support the approach of this book, the term 'quality' relies primarily on the approach of the British Standard Quality Award BS EN ISO 9001, on an assessment: 'in the fitness for purpose and safe in use sense: is the service provided or product designed and constructed to satisfy the customer's needs'. Quality and service standards are often scripted and written down through operations manuals and service agreement handbooks; they set the benchmark which the organisation is required to meet and against which operational performance is measured.

■ British Standard EN ISO 9001

BS EN ISO 9001 identifies the systems, procedures and criteria that ensure that a product or service meets a customer's requirements. The key elements in quality management for most organisations in the hospitality industry include:

- Management responsibility: policy, objectives, and identification of key personnel.
- Quality system procedures: all functions must be covered.
- Auditing the system: it must be audited internally.
- Quality in marketing: honest promotional activities.
- Material control and traceability: supplies must be traceable.
- Nonconformity: ensuring that faulty products/service do not reach the customer.
- Corrective action: identifying reasons for faults, the measures taken to correct them and records to be kept.
- After-sales service: procedures for monitoring quality of after-sales service.
- Documentation and records: records of checks and inspections, action taken, audit reports.
- Personnel and training: identification of needs, provision and verification of training.
- Product safety and liability: procedures for handling, storing and processing materials, e.g. foods.

BS EN ISO 9001 offers a range of standards for industry sectors, and these are regularly updated. Although the food service industry is not specialty listed as a sector, the standard can be important to foods service operations for three reasons. First, when purchasing goods and services BS EN ISO 9001 indicates that a supplier operates a quality system of a high standard. Second, food service operators, particularly within the cost catering sector, may find that they will not be considered as potential tenderers if they have not achieved BS EN ISO 9001. Third BS EN ISO 9001 may provide useful evidence that *due diligence* had been exercised, for example, in the event of a food service operation being prosecuted under food safety legislation.

It is the front-line members of staff that offer this service: hence their training and development are crucial to the successful running of an operation. Total quality management offers a framework by which members of staff are given the scope to treat customers as individuals, and thereby offer superior service. In an increasingly competitive marketplace, the level of service provided and its quality become ever more important as key differentiators for operations attempting to attract customers in the same markets.

However, the costs involved in becoming BS EN ISO 9001 certified can be high and therefore, the introduction needs to be carefully cost benefit assessed, before implementation takes place. On the other hand, the reviews from many of the organisations moving towards and completing BS EN ISO 9001 have suggested that it full fills the requirements for their organisation. The complete documents on BS EN ISO 9001 and revisions of the standards are available from the British Standards Institution (BSI), at www.bsigroup.com.

■ European Foundation for Quality Management Excellence Model

The various approaches to quality management all support the systems approaches, and are intended to achieve total quality management within an organisation. This is summarised by the European Foundation for Quality Management Excellence Model, shown graphically in Figure. 3.2.

Figure 3.2: European Foundation for Quality Management Excellence Model

Source: adapted from EFQM, 2013

The EFQM Excellence Model is a non-prescriptive framework, which recognises that there are many approaches to achieving sustainable excellence in all aspects of performance and can be applied to any organisation regardless of size, sector or maturity. The model is based on nine criteria. Essentially the model tells us that **Results** for **People** (employees), **Customers** and **Society** are achieved through **Leadership** driving **Policy and strategy**, **People management**, **Partnership and resources** and **Processes**, leading ultimately to **business** (key performance) **results**.

Each of the nine elements, shown in the model as interlinked boxes, is a criterion that can be used to appraise an organisation's progress towards total quality management. The four **results** criteria (people, customer, society, business) are concerned with what the organisation has achieved and is achieving. The five criteria for **enablers** are concerned with how results are being achieved.

The arrows shown in Figure 3.2 are intended to emphasise the dynamic nature of the model. They indicate that **Learning, Creativity and Innovation** help to improve the **Enablers** and that this in turn leads to improved **Results.** The overall objective of a comprehensive self-appraisal and self-improvement programme is to regularly review each of these nine criteria and, thereafter, to adopt relevant improvement strategies. (Further information on quality matters can be obtained from European Foundation for Quality Management at www.efqm.org).

The formal quality `standards` discussed above (ISO 9001 and EFQM) are not necessarily relevant for some food service providers and in such instances restauranteur operators will develop their own systems, processes and measures of quality in line with the organisational goals and mission. The principles of which are discussed in the following section of this chapter.

Technical and service standards

Within food service operations, service standards may be identified under two headings:

- **Technical standards** refer to the items on offer such as: the portion size or measure, the cooking method, the degree of cooking, the method of presentation, the layup (cover), accompaniments, the cleanliness of items. These are highly tangible.

- **Service standards** refer to two aspects: first, the procedures for service and second, the way in which these procedures are carried out. Procedures include meeting and greeting, order taking, seeking customer comment, and dealing with complaints, payment and customers with additional needs. The methods in which the service is carried out includes, for example, paying attention to the attitude of staff attentiveness, tone of voice and body language. These processes are more subjective and open to interpretation by the staff and perceived level of delivery by the customer.

Accepting that any standard must be achievable and measurable, then this is quite possible with technical standards and with some aspects of service standards. However, it becomes increasingly difficult to set actual measureable standards for the way that the service should be carried out.

Below are a number of possible aims for the 'service' to achieve, but is it arguable whether all of these are in fact measurable standards or simply intentions:

- The supervisor should be visible in the room.
- The supervisor will visit all tables at least once during the customers' meal.
- The server will check back with the table after delivering each course.
- Service employees should have positive attitudes.
- Servers should be noticeably comfortable in their respective roles.
- Co-operation between staff should be noticeable.
- Customers should be addressed by name.
- All customers should be addressed by name at least once during the meal.
- Customers' needs will be met.
- Ninety per cent of customer requests will be met.
- Menu items can be substituted or combined.

The other difficulty is that these intentions may not suit all customers all the time. Therefore the service staff in endeavouring to meet these intentions may not be providing good service when considered from the customer perspective.

An alternative to this approach is first to recognise that the product is the totality of what the customer receives. The customer makes no real distinction between the physical tangible aspects of the product and the intangible aspects of service. It is often therefore more useful to view the product as a whole and to set standards only where it is actually possible. Standards of service are also discussed in Chapter 4, page 126.

■ Customer service and resource productivity

On the one hand, a food service operation is designed to provide customer service and on the other the achievement of profit is largely determined by the efficiency of the use of resources. Customer service can be defined as being a combination of five characteristics. These are:

- **Service level**: the intensity of or limitations in, the individual personal attention given to customers.
- **Availability of service**: e.g. the opening times, variations in the menus and drinks lists on offer.
- **Level of standards**: e.g. food quality, decor, equipment, staff professionalism.
- **Reliability of the service**: the extent to which the product is intended to be consistent in practice.

- **Flexibility of the service:** the provision of alternatives, variations in the standard product on offer.

The resources used in food service operations are:

- **Materials**: commodities and equipment
- **Labour**: staffing
- **Facilities**: basically the premises and the volume of business which the premises are able to support.

The customer service characteristics and the resources can be summarised as a model, shown in Figure 3.3. The management of the operation must therefore take account of the effect that the level of business has on the ability of the operation to maintain the service while at the same time ensuring a high productivity in all the resources being used. (This is discussed further in Chapter 7, page 207.)

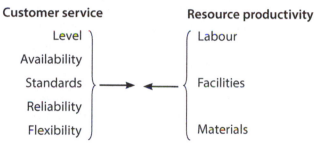

Figure 3.3: Customer service versus resource productivity

An integrated approach to quality management and service standards

Total Quality Management has had a controversial existence. The concept has on the one hand been praised by those who have successfully interwoven the TQM concepts into their organisational culture and, on the other hand it has been criticised by those organisations that have had problems with it.

There can be a tendency for quality management to be applied as a highly structured approach, which becomes internalised in the organisation, and as such is often supported by a weighty bureaucracy. Orientation to quality customer service is seen as a strategic dominant competitive tool, but, any strategy taking on board service quality must also consider the human element both within and external to the organisation. The customer can be too easily lost sight of in the highly regulated system of operating a business. In many ways the aim of management has been to reduce the aggregate cost of quality and so the cost of failure is likely to be reduced. Also businesses have often spent more money on prevention strategies, whereas the more prudent strategy is one of getting the job done correctly the first time through a quality assurance approach.

One further dimension is that most of the quality assessment processes do not include some external measure of the customers' satisfaction with a particular operation. They are primarily concerned with evidence of systematic processes, which are employed within an operation, which can demonstrate that there is a link between customer demand and the services and products on offer.

For hospitality industry, under the aegis of the Institute of Hospitality, an accreditation programme has been developed which is based on quality management assessment systems that do take into account a measure of the reality of customer service. This is the programme Hospitality Assured – more information on this can be obtained at www.hospitalityassured.com

The question of balance

The question then is: how can highly structured and systematised approaches to quality really allow service personnel to contribute from the heart in an authentic manner, which is the very essence of genuine good service? Product quality (in terms of technical standards) and service quality (in terms of service standards) are by their very nature different, and each service encounter should be unique within the organisational delivery framework. Technical standards can be identified, measured and compared. Service quality though is highly varied with elements which may be measured and others which are highly subjective. It is the degree of empowerment that staff have which creates the uniqueness of the service encounter as elements of a multi-dimensional layered activity.

However, it is possible to create an expectation that helps the customer to both perceive consistency and to recognise the variable factors that make that service what it is. There is a need then to develop a service culture which views quality as a natural part of what everyone is doing. Establishing standards, having operational manuals and regular auditing are appropriate as part of the process but it can only ever work if everyone in the organisation is focussed on real quality as viewed by the customer. There needs to be cohesion in moving toward ensuring emotional added value for the customer – in other words, doing the things your customers appreciate, but genuinely so. (Setting standards of performance is further discussed in Chapter 4, page 126.)

The nature of service

Overall, the extent to which customers appreciate a food service enterprise and its people is a function of the emotional value that has been added to the relationship, the product and the core design. When no emotional value exists in this relationship, there is in essence, no relationship. A food service organisation cannot blame customers from moving on to another business, when that other business recognises the importance of, and can support, rich, rewarding, physical and emotional relationships with its clientele, and through employing staff who demonstrate the right *attitude* and the correct *appearance* (Grandey and Gabriel, 2015; Warhurst, 2015).

A key element of the service product delivery is that the provider portrays a customer-friendly image, even though doing so may be contradictory to how the server is actually feeling, This concept has been termed as *emotional labour* (Hochschild, 1983; 2003). Front line workers, such as food service staff, are required to display certain types of positive emotions, such as friendliness, warmth, politeness, confidence, enthusiasm or cheerfulness, whilst interacting with the customer (Soares, 2003). This process also requires staff to change or control their own emotions when interacting with the customer, in exchange for a monetary reward (Grandey, Diefendorff and Rupp, 2013).

Providing service is not just about doing the job. It is also about doing it with the right attitude, the right degree of sincerity and the right amount of concern for the customers (Guerrier and Adib, 2001). The reasons why these factors underline how service is displayed are twofold:

1 Employees who participate in customer contact are the interface between the customer and the organisation and therefore represent the face of the business. Negative interactions from the employee will leave a poor impression of the business.

2 The unique attributes concerning the nature of the food and beverage service engagement, make it necessary for the business to establish policies and have rules and procedures to govern the standardisation of their product and service.

(Wong and Mei, 1999; Diefendorff, Croyle and Gosserand, 2005).

While emotional labour is concerned with the inner feelings and the display rules of the service worker, aesthetic labour is the concept that every front line service job requires the individual member of staff to *"look good and sound right"* (Warhurst and Nickson, 2001, p1; Karlsson, 2011, p51) and fit with the organisational values and image. In essence, the worker who is employed in a customer-facing role is required to embody the customer's pre-conception of the worker type and be able to engage with the customer in a manner that they would expect him or her to (Warhurst *et al.*, 2000; Pettinger, 2004). The employee is required to be well groomed, wear a uniform and communicate in a manner that the customer is able to relate to and hence enter into a dialogue with at an identifiable level (Warhurst and Nickson, 2005). The service worker is employed by the organisation for the way that they sound and the manner in which they effectively communicate along with their physical attributes (Harvey, Vachhani and Williams, 2014).

The level to which customers can appreciate a food service business and its people clearly has a critical impact on the success of the business. Consequently the benefits of true service quality, delivered with authenticity are most likely to come from giving service staff more freedom (empowerment) so that they can be themselves to do what they feel is in the best interests of their customers within a loose strategic framework. This empowerment of the worker enables flexibility in the customer interaction while adhering to the core values of the food service operation.

Towards an integrated approach

Taking account of the various thoughts about on quality management, the place of standards within it and also ensuring that there is scope for developing a relationship between the organisation and the customer, then it is possible to bring these various ideas together and to develop an integrated approach to service quality management. It is also very necessary as the food and beverage manager is having to manage the relationship between the four food and beverage systems: **food production**, **beverage provision** and between the **service sequence** (or service delivery system) and the **customer process** (for the relationship between these four systems see Figure 1.4, page 7).

Figure 3.4: Integrated Service Quality Management Model

The first stage of the integrated approach to service quality management is to draw up a customer service specification, using the five meal experience factors (identified on page 55 and the five customer service factors identified in Figure 3.3. The importance here is to define technical and procedural standards where they can be defined (and achieved, measured and compared) and also to describe what the customer experience should be like from their perspective. The next step is first to check that this customer service specification can be achieved and supported over time by the physical capabilities of the operation. Following this it is important to check that the customer service specification can actually be delivered through the service system (including being supported by the service staff). This can be seen as an **integrated service quality management model**. It is a six-stage process and can be summarised as shown in Figure 3.4.

This integrated approach to quality management ties in with the systems approach to operations and also follows from the philosophy of the various approaches to quality management.

3.3 Creating the consumer–product relationship

Once products to satisfy particular market segments have been designed it is necessary to undertake the steps to complete the product–consumer relationship. This final element in the process may be viewed as a four-stage sequence.

1 Determining promotional channels

2 Estimating profitability

3 Planning product launch

4 Offering product and appraising performance.

Determining promotional channels

Determining promotional channels is important because it will identify how consumers will be reached and attracted to the product. Food and beverage operators should identify and monitor consumers in order to be informed as to which promotional channels are best for their product.

When choosing promotional channels the target market segment variables are considered in relation to the product message and the medium through which it may be delivered. The message to be delivered should relate to the consumer's needs, wants and demands, and be delivered through a medium used by the target consumers, reflecting their life styles and self-images. Table 3.2 identifies possible messages and media for different food and beverage products.

Table 3.2: Possible message and media for food and beverage products

Product	Possible message	Media
Branded pizza restaurant	Meet friends and have fun	Television, local radio and press, mailshots
New Year's Eve dinner dance	Celebrate in style and spoil yourself	Local radio and press, in-house literature, direct suggestive selling to existing customer base, social media
Local bistro	A touch of Continental style	Word of mouth, social media
Public house	Traditional British hospitality	Word of mouth, local press, food guides, social media

Choosing the message and the medium is a critical element in promoting the product. Large businesses will often invest high levels of spend promoting their product through national television, radio, press and billboards. Small operations may only spend hundreds of pounds but the criterion is the same, is it effective? Regular reviewing of promotional activity and spending and how it relates to increased sales and profits, will enable effective evaluation of the process to take place. Consumers' responses to promotional activities should be researched.

On-line presence

Websites are a common way to communicate the product to a wide audience. Nowadays the organisation's website is one of the first stops for consumers when deciding on a product. Therefore operators need to ensure that their websites are easy to use, intuitive, presentable, communicative, current, and an honest reflection of what is offered. Furthermore, the website is now a platform to receive reservations directly through built-in online booking systems, to provide virtual menus and to stay in contact with customers through blogs and comments. Third-party booking sites (restaurant marketing portals) provide the opportunity to source bookings and to promote and monitor customer experiences. See for example www.Opentable.com.

Web 2.0 applications

In addition, when considering marketing activity, the use of Web 2.0 applications within hospitality organisations is becoming the norm. Web 2.0 refers to websites that allow users to interact and collaborate using social media, with a mixture of professional and user-generated content. These include, for example, Trip Advisor, Facebook and Twitter. These tools include applications that may include blogs, social networks, metaverse, podcast, wiki, tags and RSS enabling direct conversations with customers. The use of social media has become a significant influence in the selection of restaurants with many customers using this as a point of reference in restaurant selection. It has become a tool which if ignored can cause the business significant damage and as a result food service companies identifying effective approaches to it use.

Table 3.3 details some Web 2.0 examples of different applications being used and their uses within hospitality and food and beverage operations.

Table 3.3: Examples of Web 2.0 applications and their potential uses within the hospitality industry

Examples	Potential uses
Tripadvisor, Opentable	Consumers regularly post comments and ratings of their experiences of hotels and restaurants on specialised websites. These opinions are for the most part neutral and unbiased and can have a powerful impact on consumer decision and overall image. In an age of new media tools, consumers are more inclined to trust the recommendation of friends, relatives, or even strangers who have had a similar experience rather than generic marketing messages.
Facebook and Twitter	Operators can now use such social network sites as part of their customer relations management (CRM) system in order to have a better understanding of their customers and as a way to keep in contact. It is also a vast platform for advertising. Qualman (2012) notes that if Facebook were a country it would be the fourth largest in the world.
You Tube	Media such as You Tube is becoming very powerful because it is convenient for customers to upload videos with recommendation and critiques of visits to restaurants and other hospitality organisations. Organisations can also upload videos of their own to promote and showcase their operations.
Websites	Some operations are now encouraging complete interactivity with their customers allowing them to upload comments and videos of their experiences.
Podcasts	Chains, such as Jumeirah, now provides podcasts on its website informing potential customers of their facilities and what is taking place within their hotel.
Industry blogs	Operators should monitor and participate in industry blogs. There are various tools and resources available to inform operators when comments have been made about their business and brands.
Own blog	The operation's own blog being accessible through own website. This can be time consuming with some operators preferring to post short latest news items instead.
Custom apps	Many large restaurant chains now provide smart phones and tablets (mainly iPad) apps to inform customers of product updates, events and promotions.
Voucher sites	Some restaurants now use commercial voucher sites to inform consumers of discounted promotions.

Social media

Social media has become the new word of mouth about a good or bad dining experience. This is often termed 'word of mouse' or 'e-word of mouth' (eWOM) (Mooney, 2016 and Buzz Talk Blog, 2012) ,where customers participate in online reviews to understand what is new and what is out of fashion, engaging with it as they would do with face-to-face customers.

With the mass proliferation of social media, it is not just about the advertisements, as space and place through 'liking' the food service operator, but it is more about the additional promotion (VanMeter *et al.*, 2018). Over 66% of customers in a poll in 2017 identified that they visit a food service business web and social media site before visiting the enterprise, and this does not apply to just the younger generations, as 53% of 56-65 year olds use the media. Further, 43% of Millennials interact with the menu online as a key part of the food and beverage experience (Thompson, 2017). It is clear that the use of this technology is a central aspect of the marketing activity and one that will only grow further.

Restaurant operators encourage their own staff to 'tweet', 'like' send 'streaks' and generally engage with the brand that they work for, with the purpose of increasing the business web presence and traffic. Never before has the worker become a branded employee, an advocate of the business to the extent which they are encouraged to be today. The engagement spills outside of the employees' paid hours, as the lines between work and leisure become further blurred.

Social media, and its multiple engagement, offer the opportunity to keep food service business at the forefront of a customer's mind and engage with the customer when they are not at the premises. It is the opportunity to talk and communicate with all your customers as you would normally do when they visit. The key is to engage and speak with them as customers and not to talk at them; it is all about having a conversation with the audience. The use of social media is no different (Olesen, 2018).

Online restaurant review sites

Web-based restaurant review sites are now common, and like reviews in traditional media, good reviews here play an important and powerful part in increasing trade. In an age when everything is online, the ratings of the critics, be they amateur or professional, have never been as important as they are today. The restauranteur has to answer critics in a way which is open and transparent for all.

The online critic sites are an area of growing importance. Food service businesses need to track their customers' voices. An internet search for online review sites will bring up many competing sites, and it can become a full-time job to monitor and responded to these. Popular websites that business should track include: Yelp, Google, TripAdvisor, Facebook, Foursquare, Yellowpages, Better Business Bureau BBB, Trust Pilot, Best Company; and dedicated restaurant review sites like Zomato, Opentable – the list is constantly being added to. The food service operator has the opportunity to respond in a constructive and positive way, building trust with its loyal customer base, while demonstrating to potential customers the integrity of the business.

There is concern that some food service operators are attempting to manipulate the online ratings through hiring reviewers to counter-posti negative comments. There are also examples of bogus reviewers who have critiqued a food service operation even before the establishment has opened! To counter this Tripadvisor, for example, place a 'redflag' against those it suspects are not genuine or created by the organisation.

The level of misinformation that is appearing online is having the effect that customers do not always believe what they read. While new sites are constantly popping up, the large majority of the consumers tend to migrate back to the large and well-established ones.

Developments of online feedback opportunities are generating a whole industry in monitoring customer feedback; online comments, posted by customers, and unfortunately also by malicious pranksters (trolls), are scanned by third party organisations on behalf of smaller food and beverage organisations. This can assist in protecting and enhancing the foods service provider's reputation.

Activity:

- Identify a local restaurant and review the social media interaction.

- What online presence do they have?

- What balance of positive to negative comments can you identify?

- How has the business responded to these?

Some of the benefits of using web-based media include:

- A way to distribute, promote, monitor and keep in touch with customers and potential customers.

- A more cost-effective media for many operators.

- More of a level playing field for independent operators against larger competitors.

Some challenges include:

- No strategic plans or rules can govern what happens externally.

- Operators constantly have to be there to interact and engage and as a result it can be extremely time consuming.

- For some consumers, very little information is considered to be private, therefore anything can be posted and they often expect operators to do the same.

- Operators can be unsure how to use these applications to their advantage, as they are very customer driven.

Essential considerations

- **Develop a robust social media policy:** Organisations need to have rules for the ways in which members of staff in the organisation engage with social media. This helps to present a consistent external image and also to prevent unauthorised posts or responses by staff.

- **Follow an agreed response protocol:** All responses should be in line with the organisation's standard response protocol. An example of a response protocol is illustrated in Figure 3.5. This is a simple example of a range of similar, and often more complex, response protocols, which are used by many organisations. It is also good advice for individuals.

- **Encourage more contributions:** Always do research before posting to ensure that all the facts are known, and encourage engagement by being positive and engaging with the community.

- **Review content:** Respond to posts promptly and efficiently. But always review content before posted. This is to avoid posting any content that is, for example, misspelt, incorrect, emotional, misrepresentative or liable.

- **Remember the legacy of content:** Once content is posted it will be seen immediately. It is also permanent. Even if it is deleted later it could still be seen through having been repeated or re-posted on other sites.

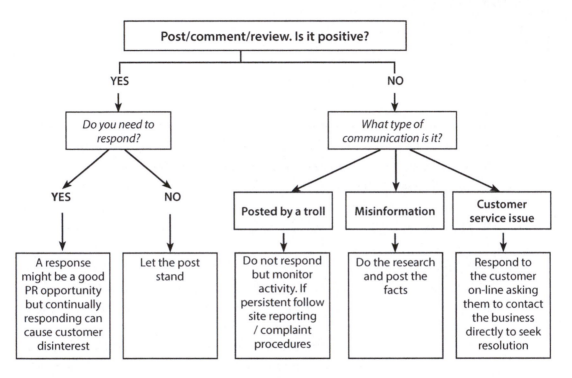

Figure 3.5: Example social media response protocol

Customer relationship management (CRM)

CRM is an essential tool for business to manage customers' contact information. These systems make it easier to manage customer relationships and retarget past customers to keep them engaged and returning.

CRM tools can also help segment customers into groups based on their previous interactions, membership of a loyalty programme or other demographic data. There are also free CRM tools such as MailChimp (https://mailchimp.com) and Hubspot (https://www.hubspot.com/products/crm).

CRM tools also provide a comprehensive way to monitor email campaign data, including email open rates, subscribes and unsubscribes. Some tools also have social media integrations to keep tabs on what people are saying about the business. See also sales and marketing performance indicators in Appendix A, page 339.

Activity:

Choose two food and beverage and using the various social media platforms such as Twitter and Instagram.

■   Analyse how they use social media to promote their business.

■   To what extent to you consider their social media presence effective, and will it increase business?

■   What do you consider to be customers' perception of the business from their social media presence?

■   What would you do, if anything, to improve it?

■ Estimating profitability

Estimating profitability is a case of budgeting costs and sales. How these budgets might be set is addressed in Chapter 9, page 263. When launching new products, and changing existing ones, the art of predicting outcomes is extremely imprecise. The methods used can however be very sophisticated. Some operators will measure the size of their selected target and segmented market, apply usage or uptake measures between competing products and multiply the resultant numbers of customers by an estimated average spend per head. This may be performed for each hour, day and month to produce the sales budget. Applying 'profitability on sales percentage' approach will determine the budgeted profit. However, the measures used cannot be guaranteed to be correct, and therefore best and worst scenarios should be considered.

Break-even analysis

One of the most common tools used in estimating potential profitability is break even analysis. This is used identify at what point all costs are covered and actual cash profit is being made. It is also used to indicate what the profitability levels (or losses) might be for various levels of sales. The analysis can also be based on the number of customers, if an average sales per head figure has been estimated.

An simple example of a break-even analysis chart is show in Figure 3.6. This figure illustrates the principle of break-even analysis in that:

■   **Fixed costs,** such as rent, rates and insurance premiums, remain constant and have to be paid even if there is no business.

■   **Variable costs,** such as meal ingredient and beverage costs, increase as the level of business increases.

■   **Semi-variable costs** (sometimes called stepped costs) are those where there is not a direct relationship between the level of business and the variable costs. This is where the costs are increased, for example, by employing another member of staff, but the profit to meet that extra cost will not be achieved until the sales have increased. (For simplicity of presentation, Figure 3.6 shows variable costs and semi-variable costs linked together)

■ **Total costs** are the fixed costs plus the variable costs.

■ **Total sales** is the total cash revenue.

■ **Break-even point** is where the sales revenue exactly equals the total costs; below that point the sales are not covering the costs and the business is making a nett loss.

■ **Net profit** is sales less total costs. As the level of custom increases above the break-even point, then the net profit also increases.

■ **Level of safety** – as the proportion of variable costs becomes greater than the fixed costs, this increases what is known as the 'level of safety' for the business.

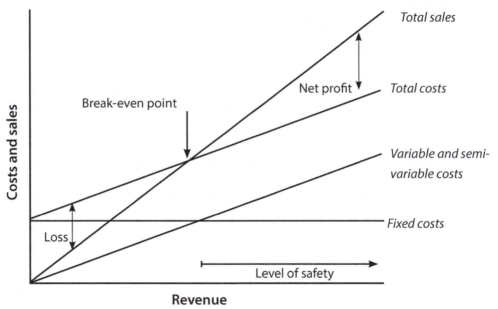

Figure 3.6: Break-even analysis chart

Lowering the break-even point

To increase the potential cash profit, the break-even point would have to be reached earlier. There are four ways this can be achieved:

■ Reduce the fixed costs

■ Reduce the variable costs

■ Increase prices

■ Increase sales

In general though, it is a combination of these approaches that can result in achieving greater cash net profit.

It is still an estimate

Although estimating profitability is valuable, it is still an estimate. The actual outcomes are usually different from those expected. However estimating profitability will at least give some indication as to what might happen. It also means that the progress after launch can be evaluated against the estimates and corrective action taken as necessary. (Chapter 9 explores the relationship between revenue, costs, and profits in more detail.)

■ Planning the product launch

Planning the product launch is an operational as well as a promotional issue. Operationally, the new food and beverage product will need testing. This will involve staff scheduling and training, specifying and sourcing the necessary ingredients and equipment and if possible testing full-scale production. If a full-scale test production run is not possible, perhaps due to cost restraints, a reduced-scale test should be performed. There will always be elements of the product that will not work entirely as planned, and finding out about these before the product launch enables these elements to be rectified. Not being able to deliver the product as promoted will result in consumers' expectations not being met, and this could negatively affect the market segment's uptake of the product. It is also worth remembering that customers seem to remember bad experiences more than good ones.

The launch of a new product gives rise to promotional opportunities. Special sessions can be organised by offering the product free, or at reduced prices, to selected groups on a one-off basis, thus gaining good public relations exposure. These events are often referred to 'shake out events' or 'soft openings'. They can be a good operational test of the product without the repercussions of not meeting customers' expectations, and place of the system under strain to test that all process and procedures work. Special offers can also be introduced to initially attract customers to the product, such as two items for the price of one (also referred to as Buy One, Get One Free – BOGOF), or free bottles of wine with a meal. However, special consideration must be given to the market segment's perception of the promotion, as free offers or reduced prices may not project the required image.

The timing of the product launch is also an important consideration. There are two issues regarding timing; one is getting the time right, and the other is having enough time available to get the product right. Getting the time right involves choosing a launch date that provides the best advantage to the operator. This will mean investigating the possibility of other events, which are going on at the same time and which may detract from or enhance the product launch. If demand is expected to fluctuate, and demand for food and beverage products does fluctuate between time of day, week, month and year, the planned launch time should be set to take this into account. It may be appropriate to launch the product before a busy period, in order to be able to build up to full capacity. Operations which do not give themselves enough time to develop and launch their product can find themselves offering products which are not successful, and the time available to develop a product may often be seen as insufficient. However if the product is not ready to be introduced in time, it is probably worth considering delaying the launch rather than offering a sub-standard product.

■ Offering the product and appraising performance

Offering the product and appraising performance are about putting the plan into action and monitoring the result. Chapter 9 details approaches to operations performance appraisal and to product performance appraisal.

3.4 Sales promotion

Once a product is launched, the volume of business has to be maintained and increased. Sales promotion is about offering short-term incentives, which are designed to change the buying habits of customers and increase the revenue of the operation (Kotler *et al.*, 2016). In order to do this sales promotions are geared to directly encourage the customer to purchase, often through short-term improvements in the cost–value ratio.

Sales promotions as a marketing tool require planning, monitoring and careful evaluation, so that mistakes are not repeated but successes are, and that these are then built upon. Additionally by their very nature, sales promotions are designed to attract attention and stimulate additional demand; consequently the operation must be prepared and have organisational operational plans to meet the additional sales that the promotion is likely to generate.

Sales promotions are oriented toward changing the customer's short-term purchasing behaviour through, for example:

- Increasing average spend and therefore sales revenue
- Invigorating slow-moving product(s)
- Promoting a new menu, product or product range
- Stimulating impulse purchasing
- Amalgamating items for sale
- Attracting attention and increased trade to the business for specific days, weeks or months and also during quite period of the day
- Promoting the celebration of special event(s)
- Increasing loyalty
- Establishing or enhancing awareness in existing and potential customers' minds of the business and its products
- Stimulating purchasing by communication of product/business features and benefits

- Informing in order to entice business
- Improving the product and service profile.

The essential feature of sales promotions is to move, or incentivise, the sale of the product today, or for a specific period of time, as a temporary measure to increase trade. For example this can be achieved through offering additional value, financial inducement to purchase and try, and advertising campaigns. Sales promotions can also be linked to public relations and sponsorship strategies.

Examples of tactical approaches that can be used to help to maintain and increased sales are:

- **Ensure menus and beverages lists are informative and that pricing is clear:** minimum and service charges should be easily identified and the inclusion of charges, which customers can view as sneaky, such as a cover charge, should be carefully considered.

- **Never discount:** as a general approach, discounting does not make good business sense. Once customers get used to the discounted price, it is difficult to then justify why the full price should be paid later for the same product.

- **Package:** instead of discounting. Offer a deal if the customer fulfils specific conditions, such as buying a certain number of products at the same time or over a period of time, with the promise of a future discounted product once the conditions have been satisfied. Other examples include offering set menus at a reduced price; including potatoes and vegetables with a dish, or a drink within the price of a meal.

- **Create special promotions:** such as specially priced seasonal menus; menus with wine flights, and time-based offers to encourage trade during slow periods, or for example, including additional elements at specific times, or pre- and post-theatre deals

- **Have well-trained, organised and knowledgeable staff:** leading to an increase in the perceived level of the service and consistent standards of operation. Staff should be always ready to answer customers' questions, not only about the food and drink but also about the local area. They should also be able to contribute to positive selling (upselling)

- **Have standard customer procedures:** and always enforce them. These are essential, for example, for customer dress requirements; mobile phone usage; maximum group size; minimum age; alcohol over consumption; efficient complaint handling; dealing properly with customers with additional needs (such as disability or dietary requirements); and minimum levels of acceptable customer behaviour.

- **Seek customer loyalty:** there are many ways of encouraging loyalty. Examples are: having good records of regular customers and targeting them with special promotions; giving vouchers each time a meal is taken so that a free course or drink can be gained once a certain number are collected; having a paid-for loyalty scheme where customers register, pay a fee and then are entitled to regular benefits, or promoting special offers through on-line booking systems, such as that operated by Opentable (www.opentable.com).

- **Seek customer feedback and act upon it:** use a variety of methods and always follow up, especially on bad feedback. When responding to complaints, customers don't want platitudes, they want to know that something will be done so that it will not be the same when they visit again. And if necessary offer refunds, not future promises of discounts or free meals.

- **Concentrate on promoting value:** anything that assists in customers perceiving that they are receiving increased value for money can be beneficial to the business. This can be things such as including potatoes and vegetables with the price of a dish, or including a drink (also see the notes in Chapter 2 on price, cost, worth and value, page 39).

- **Maximise cash gross profit:** in order for the business to survive, it is the *cash* gross profit that is important, not slavishly trying to achieve a *target percentage* gross profit. In order words, sales promotion needs to be targeted to encourage the highest revenue and also the highest cash gross profit contribution. (For further notes on cash gross profit, see Chapter 9.)

- **Reposition the product:** this is about reviewing the market(s) being targeted and the product connection with the customer. Often this is a result of a downturn or a change in business from the customers that have traditionally been coming to the operation. If there are clear sign of these changes then it is time to reconsider the product on offer.

See also, Chapter 2, 'Concept development', Chapter 9 'Appraising Performance', and Chapter 10 'Marking Strategic Decisions'.

Activity:

Identify two similar food and beverage operations:

- For each operation identify which of the tactics listed above are being utilised. There is likely to be a number operating at any one time.

- Consider to what extent the operation needs to reposition the product.

Merchandising

Merchandising is encouraging sales along with the aim of increasing the spend per head. It is mainly about the displaying of products in such a way that it stimulates interest and entices the customer to purchase. The basis of it is often associated with heightening the beliefs, attitudes, ideas and other meaningful values adopted by customers. In food and beverage operations merchandising is about helping customers interpret and evaluate what is being sold through a variety of verbal and non-verbal reassurances of the quality of the offering. All of this has to be consistent with the expectations the intended market might have, especially where in attempting to be competitive, the food service operation is increasing the likelihood of increasing competition from rivals.

The aims of merchandising are to:

- Identify real opportunities to promote sales
- Recognise and promote customer benefits
- Maximise the value and sales, and
- Appeal to the senses, and the customer's identification of 'self'.

The four principal ways of achieving this are through:

1 Starting to appeal to more customers
2 Charging existing customers more money
3 Spurring existing customers to spend more money
4 Investing what is sold with clearly expressed benefit(s) – thus enhancing perceived value.

In order to be able to adopt any of these approaches the food and beverage operation needs to attract customers to the business, encourage them to spend and also to encourage repeat business.

Merchandising can be most effective where it is based on a genuine understanding of customer needs. Merchandising, which is empathetic towards (in sympathy with) the customer, is based on having an awareness and understanding of the emotions and feelings of other individuals.

The aim of merchandising is to identify a range of opportunities to promote sales, maximise volume and revenue. If customer-contact personnel are involved in conceiving approaches to merchandising, such approaches will be better targeted as they will utilise the in-depth knowledge that these staff have of their customers and of their specific needs and desires. Merchandising techniques developed in this way can provide 'targeted' quality products, which are more likely to lead to total satisfaction and repeat business.

In effect, operations are then able to recognise and promote specific customer benefits from a position of in-depth knowledge. In empathetic merchandising the operation is more able to target the merchandising to communicate social and economic status and worth, group affinity and distinction, symbolic association, self-image, and shared value. Table 3.4 provides a summary of merchandising approaches and possible sample outcomes.

Table 3.4: Merchandising activities and sample outcomes

Merchandising activities	Sample outcomes
Marketing	Identifies demand with the ultimate aim of expanding the customer base, and creating and keeping customers.
Advertising	Attracts the customer through visual merchandising, sensory merchandising and service merchandising.
Selling	Through point-of-sale materials and active promotion of product.
Profitability	Ensures business success and strengthens and prolongs the lifecycle of the business.
Perception, experience and mood – staff recognition of immediate needs through reading the customer	Recognition that no two people are the same and perceive a stimulus differently at differing times.
Using design	Builds strong emotional and psychological links between the business environment and the customer.
Personality – traits, behaviours and experiences making the customer distinctive and unique	Recognition of customer traits or characteristics reflected back ensuring the customer realises they are in the right environment.
Emotional value and connectivity	Ensures customers are valued and have an orientation with the business's success.
Customer satisfaction and self-actualisation need	Ensures the continuation of the process and meets the customers' esteem needs (rising from notions of 'wise choice' and other positive character elements).

Menu and beverage list merchandising

The menu and beverage lists are vitally important sales tools. They are the key means of communication to the customer. Menu and beverage list merchandising is concerned with the way in which the menu and beverage lists can be utilised most efficiently as catalysts for optimising sales. It is necessary therefore for all menus and beverage lists to be correct against a checklist of operational compatibility, overall design and layout, clarity of expression, legibility, size, cleanliness and of course legality.

For example, within these principles the application of merchandising can be used towards a signature dishes. These are ones that represents the values of the food service operation and which are slightly different to what any other operation offers. These can be, for example, based on:

- A personal favourite of the chef/owner/restaurant manager.
- A local speciality.
- Larger portion dishes, such as giant steaks.
- A method of serving a dish, such as a sizzler platter, carved at the table, or flambé.
- A wide range of relishes, such has having 26 types of mustard.
- Product specialities such as cheeses, sausages or wines.
- A range of dishes on a theme, such as a platter of five desserts.

These offers can then be merchandised in number of ways for example internally through tent cards, key positions in the centre of the menu and externally built into the promotional campaign, on social media, in the local newspaper, leaflets and 'A' frame boards outside of the premises.

Creative merchandising

Displaying products in an effort to enhance sales applies as much to food and beverage operations as it does to general retail operations. The illuminated fascias above fast food service counters, which graphically exhibit the menu, illustrate this well. However it is equally important in, for example, fine dining restaurants to set the scene with display materials. These can include own brand merchandising, such as, champagne, wines, or the chef's own chocolate truffles, sauces, preserves, etc. Merchandising stimuli for food service operations can include:

- Aromas
- Audio visual displays
- Bulletin/blackboards/floor stands
- Directional signs
- Display cards/brochures
- Displays of food and drinks
  - Trolleys (sweet, liqueurs etc.)
  - Buffets/salad bars
  - Self-service counters – bar displays, flambé work, etc.
- Drink mats and placemats
- Facia boards
- Illuminated panels
- Other customers' food/drink
- Posters
- Production areas being able to be seen
- Tent cards, and
- Using service storage, for instance in wine racks, as part of the design concept.

Merchandising should not be difficult. In promoting sales, the basis of the promotion should be on providing customers with well-researched quality products which will potentially match their perceived value of those products and their need for them. The quality for the merchandising can also be used to set the food service operation apart from others..

Merchandising the core business values

Consumer interest in food products, preparation, sustainability and ethics has created new merchandising opportunities. These core values can be communicated to the customer through newsletters linked to offers, special product offers linked to sustainability as a demonstration of the corporate social responsibility (CSR) credentials. Examples of these are:

- The use of terms such as 'craft' and 'artisan'.
- Promoting the sustainability of food and beverage products.
- Concentrating on ethical sourcing.
- Featuring local sourcing of products and local seasonal foods.
- Ensuring the authenticity of products.
- Providing kitchen tours, 'visit our suppliers' and cooking lessons.
- Avoiding food waste.

■ Personnel selling

For sales promotions activities to succeed they must supported by the well-developed personal selling skills of the staff. If training includes the examination of the profiling of the operation's target groups of customers then staff will be aware of:

- The nature of the demand being met
- The people and organisations buying the product
- The frequency of their custom
- Their use of other businesses and why
- Their use of disposable income
- Their desire to express their unique identity, and
- Their desire for greater variety tailored to their individual needs.

Personal selling refers specifically to the ability of the staff in a food and beverage operation to contribute to the promotion of sales. This is especially important where specific promotions are being undertaken. The promise of a particular type of menu or drink, a special deal or the availability of a particular service can often be devalued by the inability of the staff to fulfil the requirements as promised. It is therefore important to involve service staff in the formulation of offers and to ensure that briefing and training are given so that the customer can actually experience what has been promised.

What staff need to know

There is an old adage which says: "If you can tell well you can sell well". Members of staff always feel more confident in personal selling if they have knowledge about the products and services on offer. Examples of the type of information staff will need to know include:

- A description of what the food is, including ingredients and cooking methods
- Names and descriptions of wines and other drinks
- An explanation of how the food, drinks or wines are to be served, together with accompaniments
- Where the produce comes from
- What the animals are fed on
- Where the fish are caught
- Where the fruit and vegetables are grown
- How the produce is delivered

- How food and drinks is stored
- The origins of wines and other drinks
- The specialities of the establishment and their origins
- The local area
- Menu symbols and their meaning; such as organic, fair trade, red tractor, heart foundation and vegetarian society
- Cultural traditions and differences, and
- Up-to-date information on different dietary requirements and allergens.

Enhancing knowledge

There are many ways of providing opportunities for enhancing the product knowledge for service staff. These include:

- Arranging for staff visits to suppliers
- Arranging visits to other establishments
- Seeking out supplier information
- Ensuring that staff taste products;
- Arranging for staff to visit local trade fairs
- Involving staff in the formulation of sales promotion activities, and
- Organising regular training and briefing sessions for staff.

Contributing to sales promotion

To contribute successfully to personal selling, service staff should be able to:

- Ensure any special promotions are known about and that customers receive what is being promised
- Describe the food, wines and drinks on offer in an informative and appealing way, that makes the product sound interesting and desirable
- Advise customers on food and drink matching
- Use opportunities to promote specific items or deals when seeking orders from customers
- Seek information from customers in a way that promotes sales, e.g., rather than asking *if* a dessert is required, ask *which* dessert they would like to have
- Use opportunities for the sales of additional items such as extra garnishes, special sauces or accompanying drinks, such as a dessert wine with a sweet course – this is often called *up-selling*
- Respect cultural differences
- Provide a competent service, and
- Seek customers' feedback on the food, drinks and the service.

Ability in personal selling is essential for all successful food and beverage operations, and ultimately the survival of the business. The contribution of service staff to the meal experience is vital. They contribute to the customers' perception of value for money, hygiene and cleanliness, the level of service and the atmosphere that the customer experiences. Good food and beverage service staff therefore must have a detailed knowledge of the food and beverages on offer, be technically competent, have well developed interpersonal skills and be able to work as part of a team.

For further information on marking and sales promotion see for example, Armstrong *et al.* (2016), Kotler *et al.* (2016), and Palmer (2014).

3.5   The consumer–product relationship as a dynamic process

Issues surrounding the consumer-product relationship have been explored in Chapter 2 and further extended in this chapter. Although presented and discussed primarily as a sequence (see Figure 2.2, page 36), the process of developing a consumer–product relationship is dynamic and organic, and also continuous. As consumers' needs, wants and demands change, and as the competition increases and technology offers new opportunities, managing the process of creating a consumer–product relationship is also about managing change.

Various frameworks have been suggested to help to develop and evaluate the consumer–product relationship. These may be viewed as tools to be applied as required, but they need to be applied continuously. Food and beverage operations will often engage in different stages of developing a consumer–product relationship at the same time. Market research should be an ongoing commitment; generating ideas and concepts should be built into the management of an operation; and searches for new and developing market segments is a major management responsibility. With so many business environment variables which are continually changing, including the operator's own personal and business objectives, it can be seen how promoting the status quo and relying on consumers to remain fixed over time is a very dangerous assumption. As product and business life cycles continue to shrink, the importance of managing these changes in order to defend against threats and respond to opportunities, is increased.

Managing change effectively and profitably in a food and beverage environment is as complex and as difficult as in any other type of business. In order to really embrace change there must be a management vision of where they want to be. Its focus will be satisfying the consumers of the food and beverage product. Management's first commitment is to communicate this vision with their staff, for without members of staff who are convinced of the need to change, and of the need to do things differently, the vision will not happen. Managing relationships within food and beverage operations, between groups of personnel, will play an ever-increasing role for management in the successful development of, or changing the consumer–product relationships.

For further information on marketing and sales see for example Bowie *et al.* (2016), Hooley *et al.* (2016) and Kotler *et al.* (2016).

3.6   References and additional reading

Armstrong, G., Kotler, P. and Opresnik, M. (2016) *Marketing an Introduction*, Harlow: Pearson.

Bitner, M. J. (1992) Servicescapes: The impact of physical surroundings on customers and employees, *Journal of Marketing*, **56**(2), 57-71.

Bowie, D. Buttle, F., Brookes, M. and Mariussen, A. (2016) *Hospitality Marketing,* 3rd edn, Oxford: Routledge.

British Standards Institution (BSI) at www.bsigroup.com (accessed January 2019).

BuzzTalk Blog, (2012), Electronic word of mouth presents a window of opportunity for businesses, www.buzztalkmonitor.com/blog/bid/233669/Electronic-Word-Of-Mouth-presents-a-window-of-opportunity-for-businesses (Accessed January 2019).

Campbell-Smith, G. (1967) *Marketing of the Meal Experience: A Fundamental Approach*, Guilford: University of Surrey.

Cousins, J., Lillicrap D. and Weekes, S. (2014b) *Food and Beverage Service*, 9th edn, London: Hodder Education.

Diefendorff, J. M, Croyle, M. H. and Gosserand, R. H. (2005) The dimensionality and antecedents of emotional labour strategies, *Journal of Vocational Behaviour*, **66**(2), 339-357.

EFQM (European Foundation for Quality Management) at www.efqm.org (accessed December 2018).

Grandey, A., Diefendorff, J. and Rupp, D. (2013) *Emotional Labour in the 21st Century: Diverse perspectives on the psychology of emotional regulation at work.* New York: Routledge.

Grandey, A. A. and Gabriel, A. (2015) Emotional labour at a crossroads: Where do we go from here? *Annual Review of Organisational Psychology and Organizational Behaviour,* at www.researchgate.net/publication/265547029_Emotional_labor_at_a_crossroads_Where_do_we_go_from_here Advance online publication (accessed January 2019).

Guerrier, Y. and Adib, A. (2001) Emotional labour and the blurring of work and leisure: A study of tour reps, London: Work Employment and Society Conference.

Gustafsson, I B, et al. (2006) The Five Aspects Meal Model: a tool for developing meal services in restaurants, *Journal of Foodservice*, **17**(2), 84–93.

Harvey, G, Vachhani, S J and Williams, K. (2014) Working out: Aesthetic labour, affect and the fitness industry personal trainer. *Leisure Studies*, **33** (5), 454-470.

Hochschild, A. R. (1983) *The Managed Heart*, Berkley CA: University of California Press.

Hochschild, A. R. (2003) Afterword to the twentieth anniversary edition. In: *The Managed Heart*, London: University of California, 199-207.

Hooley,G., Piercy, N., Nicoulaud, B. and Rudd, J.M. (2016) *Marketing Strategy and Competitive Positioning*, 5th edn, Harlow: Pearson.

Hospitality Assured, at www.hospitalityassured.com (accessed January 2019).

Hubspot at www.hubspot.com/products/crm (accessed January 2019).

Jones, P. (ed.) (1988) *Food Service Operations*, London: Cassell.

Jones, P. (ed.) (1994) *The Management of Food-service Operations*, London: Cassell.

Kotler, P., Bowen, J., Makens, J. and Balogau, S. (2013) *Marketing for Hospitality and Tourism*, Harlow: Pearson Education.

Kotler, P., Keller, K., Brady, M. Goodman, M. and Hansen, T. (2016) *Marketing Management*, 3rd edition, Harlow: Pearson Education.

Line, N., Hanks, L. and Kim, W.G. (2018), An expanded servicescape framework as the driver of place attachment and word of mouth, *Journal of Hospitality & Tourism Research*, **42** (3), 476-499.

MailChimp at: https://mailchimp.com (accessed January 2019).

Martin, W. (1986) Defining what quality service is for you, *Cornell Hotel and Restaurant Administration Quarterly*, **27**(1) , 32–38.

Mooney, L. (2016) The disadvantages of word of mouth advertising, smallbusiness.chron.com/disadvantages-word-mouth-advertising-26133.html (Accessed December 2018).

Olesen, C. (2018) Social media marketing for restaurants: the basics, www.lyfemarketing.com (Accessed December 2018).

Opentable at www.opentable.com (Accessed January 2019).

Palmer, A. (2014) *Principles of Services Marketing*, 7th edn, London: McGraw Hill.

Pettinger, L. (2004) Brand culture and branded workers: Service work and aesthetic labour in fashion retail. *Consumption Markets Culture*, **7** (2), 165-184.

Pizam, A. and Tasci, A. (2019), 'Experiencescape: expanding the concept of servicescape with a multi-stakeholder and multi-disciplinary approach', International Journal of Hospitality Management, Vol. 76, pp. 25-37. Qualman, E. (2012) *Socialnomics: How Social Media Transforms the Way we Live and do Business*, New Jersey: Wiley and Sons.

Soares, A. (2003) Tears at work; gender, interaction, and emotional labour, *Department of Organisation and Human Resources*, 2 (Spring), 36-44.

Thompson, H. (2017) Social media for restaurants is not just for young people, says poll, available at:www.bighospitality.co.uk/Article/2017/03/29/Social-media-restaurants-not-just-for-young-Millennials-says-poll (Accessed January 2019).

VanMeter,R., Syrdal, H. A., Powell-Mantel, S., Grisaffe, D. B. and Nesson E.T. (2018). Don`t just 'like' me, promote me: how attainment and attitude influence brand related behaviors on social media, *Journal of Interactive Marketing*, **43**(1), 83-97.

Warhurst, C. (2015) Service Economy in: *The Wiley Blackwell Encyclopaedia of Consumption and Consumer Studies*, Cook, D.T. and Ryan, M.J. Eds. London, Wiley Blackwell.

Warhurst, C. and Nickson, D. (2001) *Looking Good, Sounding Right; Style Counselling in the New Economy*, London: The Industrial Society.

Warhurst, C., Nickson, D., Witz, A. and Cullen, A. M. (2000) Aesthetic labour in interactive service work: Some case study evidence from the 'new' Glasgow. *Service Industries Journal*, **20** (3), 1-18.

Wong, A. and Mei, O. (1999) Analysing service quality in the hospitality industry, *Managing Service Quality: An international journal*, **9** (2), 136-143.

Wood, R. (2000) How important is the meal experience? Choices, menus and dining environments, in: Wood, R (ed.). *Strategic Questions in Food and Beverage Management*, Oxford: Butterworth Heinemann, 28-47.

Wood, R. (2013) *Key Concepts in Hospitality Management.* 1st ed., London: Sage.

4 Operational areas, equipment and staffing

Aim

To outline key considerations in the planning, design, equipping and staffing of food service operations.

Objectives

The chapter is intended to support you in:

- Developing a systematic approach to the planning, designing, equipping and staffing of food service operations

- Identifying the factors to be taken into account when making operational choices

- Ensuring compliance with health and safety requirements.

4.1   Key influences

Creating new operations, or renovating existing ones, means being involved in developing new concepts or rethinking old ones. This can include activities such as developing new menus, beverage lists and rethinking approaches to production and service, as well as concepts and design ideas which can be innovative and creative in approach, or follow a tried and proven delivery format. This in turn leads to reconsidering plant, and equipment such as crockery, glassware and cutlery, through to staff uniforms, and so on.

Other trends in restaurant design have included the opening up of the kitchen to be viewed by the customer, as part of the total dining experience, with some fine dining restaurants offering the opportunity to sit at the chef's table as part of the meal experience, a reorientation of the role of the chef as they become part of the customer dining interaction. There are also the minimalistic New York loft style restaurants. Traditional plates have been replaced by food presentation on wooden boards, glass plates, marble squares and slate, which can offer novel service concepts, and for some, a unique and exciting customer experience, but for others an unnecessary move away from traditional approaches to presentation.

It is important to be abreast of new food service approaches. It is the innovator who is able to capture the new market share, but the earlier adopter can capitalise on it and bring it to market before the product life cycle wanes.

Because of recent successes, and the pressure of industry competitiveness, further developments are now far less likely to be hindered by tradition. The boundaries of food service delivery and service are constantly being pushed in the search for the next competitive edge in the meal experience offer. Yet within this changing world order of creative and innovative food offers, traditionalism in service standards remains. It is for the food and beverage manager to know the market they are aiming for and the food service organisation's place within it.

However, there can also be pitfalls. New operations can fail simply because the spend on the interior design is far in excess of what the business will ever recoup, or the business does not attract sufficient custom because the design concept is not harmonised with effective staffing and menu and beverage list design. It is clearly a conundrum which needs to be carefully considered and the economics planned, if success is to be achieved.

There is a tangible relationship between the nature of the market, the type of demand being met and the budget available. In a competitive market unless the operation is unique, it has to be more attractive: customers need a reason for coming to a particular operation rather than to another offering a similar product.

Activity:

■ Identify four key recent innovations in food service operations.

■ Consider what you think the long-term effect of these innovations might have on the food service industry in general.

4.2   A systematic approach

The systematic approach to designing, planning, equipping and staffing a food service operation includes giving consideration to a wide variety of factors. These can be grouped under six broad headings:

■ The market needs

■ Operational needs

- Connectivity
- Space allocation and requirements
- Finance availability
- Sustainability
- Hygiene, health, safety and security.

The market needs

As a customer driven service business, it is the identification of the market needs that shapes the concept design and hence the operational needs. The needs of the market, or rather the need of the establishment to provide products to meet the determined market needs, may be ascertained by working through the first three stages of the food service cycle (see Chapter 1, page 3). These are:

1 **Consumer and the market** – which identifies the potential market for the business and the customer needs.

2 **Policy and objectives** – which identifies the policies, principles and business objectives that the operation is intended to serve.

3 **Customer service specification** – which identifies the type, range and scale of the food and beverage services to be provided.

Giving consideration to and making decisions within the first three stages of the food service cycle, (much of which has been discussed in Chapters 1 to 3), a framework will have been established. Within this framework, systematic consideration can be given to the planning and design of the facilities and determining the plant, equipment, and staffing required.

Operational needs

Included in the consideration of the planning and design of facilities and the staffing of the operation, is the determination of the various operational methods that will be used. These include:

- Receiving and storage methods
- Production systems and methods
- Service system and methods
- Dining arrangements
- Clearing methods
- Dishwashing methods
- Control methods
- Disposal of waste and waste products.

The movement of food and beverages through a food service operation should follow a logical linear sequence starting with receiving and storage functions and continuing through to the disposal of waste products and waste (see Figure 4.1).

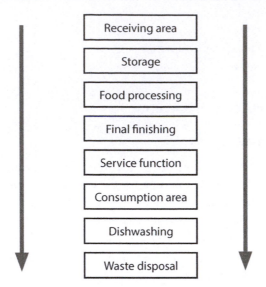

Figure 4.1: The flow of materials and staff

Operation aspects also include consideration of, and establishing, food and beverage control systems. This involves many different areas and individuals within a food service facility. Specific areas that should be looked at, and control procedures that should be established include:

- Cash control
- Sales analysis
- Control of the customers' bills and receipts
- Food production forecasting
- Control over the various storage areas, including refrigeration
- Purchasing and receiving control
- Standard recipes, recipe costing, portion control, and
- Quality control process of materials, facilities and staff.

Planning for these control mechanisms before the project has been completed, or even before it is under construction, is highly recommended. Operators significantly increase their chances for success when all of these areas have been critically examined and sufficient controls have been established. The consideration of operational aspects also needs to take into account the customer usage of food and beverage service areas. This will include issues such as access to the premises, and facilities such as toilets, and cover the needs of the disabled and of children.

Connectivity

The food service operation of the future will be fully internet integrated. Ubiquitous connectivity is at the heart of the operation, linking items of equipment to the internet and to each other. All types of interactions can be considered from ordering food, advising on and directly aiding cooking, minimising food waste, through to stock management and menu planning.

The integrated operation has the possibility to share information directly with suppliers. Linkages will create self-ordering systems, demand variance data and perhaps customer comments on the produce supplied. This will bring greater control for suppliers and will also be driven by the need for local produce and reducing food miles.

Food service operations are fast becoming centres of advanced innovation in the digital age. The applications of mobile, cloud, sensors and other smart technologies are changing operations to become more responsible and intelligent. These new technologies will contribute to food and beverage savings, while leveraging big data analytics. These innovations not only improve production processes but contribute towards solving global issues such as food waste, improve traceability, transparency and provide information about food safety and quality. Smart meters can help to reduce costs, for example, food and beverage wastage tracking systems provide a way to monitor and track the waste and provide information on which action can be taken to reduce costs.

■ Space allocation and requirements

Taking into account the considerations outlined above, Table 4.1 gives a rough guide to the space allocation required for different types of food service operations.

Table 4.1: Space allocations for food service operations

Meals	Square metres per meal served/hour		
	Up to 200	200–500	500+
Cafeteria	0.45–0.70	0.35–0.45	0.25–0.35
Hotels	0.35–1.60	0.35–0.70	0.35–0.45
Restaurants	0.35–0.90	0.35–0.45	0.30–0.35

Fast food outlets

The average size of most fast food outlets is currently around 1000–1500 m²

Restaurant and other dining areas

(NB Space allocation includes sideboards, aisles, etc.)

Style	Space per cover (m²)
Traditional restaurant	1
Banqueting	0.9
High-class restaurants	2

(NB For safety reasons all aisles should be 1 metre wide)

Food production areas	Space per cover (m²)
Up to l00 covers	0.5
100–1000	0.3–0.4
1000 or more	0.25

Source: developed from *Croner's Catering,* 1999

■ Finance availability

The main financial objectives of the operations will have been considered under stage two of the catering cycle (policy and objectives). Under this stage the finance available will have been determined and consideration will have to be given to:

- The cost of the space to be used
- The purchasing policies, e.g. buying equipment, leasing equipment, lease/ rental, new or used, and
- The expected life of the operation in terms of the product life cycle and therefore the expected life of the equipment.

■ Sustainability

Commitment to sustainable practices is imperative for competitiveness. It can not only reduce the carbon footprint but also increase the operational profitability. Sustainability and ethical practice are factors which many customers now consider is making decisions on where to eat out.

When designing or refurbishing premises, and when selecting equipment, careful evaluation of potential energy and water saving should be a part of each business's cost-saving, sustainability and corporate social responsibility (CSR) strategy. This should also cover the longer-term use of the premises and equipment. Apart from improved environmental credentials and a positive perception of the business, there is potential for increased energy savings. Food service operations can use two to five times more energy per square metre than other commercial buildings. Investing in energy efficiency is one of the best ways to protect a business from rising energy costs. Any sustainability programme has to be aimed at encouraging reduction, reuse and recycling, sometimes known as R^3.

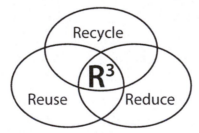

Figure 4.2: R^3 – Reduce, Reuse, Recycle (Source: developed from CESA, 2009)

An important factor in sustainability is the commitment to recycle. It makes both environmental and economic sense. With a recycling programme, a food-service operation can help divert many tons of material away from landfill and save the cost of waste disposal.

Conducting an energy audit can help to identify where energy consumption is inefficient and optimise it around the kitchen. This will be able to provide operation, equipment, energy, and water saving recommendations to reduce your consumption cost and protect the environment.

To back up the corporate social responsibility strategy, it is valuable to have an environmental policy. This can help to reinforce the responsibility of the team to be aware that from arriving at the beginning of their shift to leaving the work place, their actions will have a direct impact on the environment, the social responsibility charter and the profit of the organisation. Figure 4.3 gives an example of an Environmental Policy, which can be adapted for use in any hospitality business.

Environmental policy

The company recognizes its responsibilities to reduce its impact on the environment as part of national and international efforts to stem the continued risk of global warming.

We aim to:

- Operate in a sustainable way by minimizing the use of resources, including energy and water, and by using sustainable resources wherever possible.
- Purchase our food and ingredients from sustainable and local sources wherever possible, and to do our utmost to use seasonable food in our kitchens.
- Minimize kitchen waste and to recycle wherever possible.
- Harness the latest energy saving ideas and technology
- Improve the energy efficiency of all its properties whilst maintaining their character.

We recognise that much can be done through effective management, sub-meter monitoring and energy control and will work with all staff to support the aims of this policy.

This policy will form the basis of actions which will lead to reduced risk of polluting incidents, full legal compliance and better support for a sustainable future. This is expected by our customers, our staff and everyone associated with our business.

Alongside our commitment to this policy, the company recognises the need to meet the expectations of customers. This will include levels of comfort, hospitality and service.

Chief Executive: _____   Date: _____

Figure 4.3: Example environmental policy

Hygiene, health, safety and security

The design of food service facilities must at all stages reflect the need for safe and hygienic working practices. The early involvement of the local Environmental Health Officer (EHO) will reduce the risk of costly later amendments, bearing in mind the legal powers of the EHO to close catering premises considered unfit for food production. Similarly the local fire officer should be consulted prior to any significant alterations or changes of use. Security must also be taken into account in the design process to allow for the protection of the premises, stock, equipment, cash, data and of course people (staff and customers).

Legislation covers a wide range of topics, including: controlling and reducing outbreaks of food poisoning, training of all food handlers, preventing contamination of food, equipment and premises, provision of clean water, sanitary facilities and washing facilities, registration of premises and vehicles, content and labelling of food, including allergen information, preventing the manufacture and sale of any food that could cause illness or injury, and monitoring of food imports.

■ Using consultants

Many food service operations employ consultants, such as members of the Food Service Consultant Society International (FCSI, www.fcsi.org). Consultants can be either design or management consultants and some are both. They can support the layout and design of the premises and its plant and equipment, though to the development of menus and beverage lists, as well as marketing the business. Consultants are also be used to ensure legal compliance. For further information on facilities management see, for example, Stipanuck (2015).

4.3   Health and safety

The dual responsibility of employers and employees at work is to ensure that the premises and equipment are safe and that they are kept safe so as to prevent accidents to staff or others.

■ Developing a positive health, safety and hygiene culture

It is an important function of management to develop a culture of safety. Good management involves stimulating staff interest and motivating them to set goals to achieve the highest standards of hygiene and safety within the organisation.

A positive safety culture establishes health and safety systems; achieving the culture requires time and effort from management. Management must be caring, committed and well organised. Identifying named individuals who are competent to guide company policy and having knowledgeable staff who can contribute to the business through health and safety committees is essential. A summary of an approach to the development of a health and safety culture is illustrated in Figure 4.4.

Figure 4.4: Developing a health and safety culture

Developing health and safety policies

Management are required to develop workable policies, which address real workplace issues that are of practical use and are tailored to the operation and processes. Health and safety policies should lead to the identification of all potential hazards found within the business and attempt to deal with them, reducing the risk of injury *in so far as is reasonably practicable*. There is, therefore, an inseparable link between policy and risk assessment, the first stage of development of a comprehensive health and safety policy.

The policy sets down a commitment by the company, organisation or operation to encourage food hygiene practices within the organisation. These must be seen as laying down clear guidelines and objectives for management and staff. Some of these policies have been modelled closely on health and safety lines giving a detailed set of broad objectives with guidance in relation to particular processes. Emphasis must be on clear accurate guidance to ensure that members of the staff comply and that all who work for the organisation accept the policy. Some establishments ask staff to sign a form to indicate that they understand the policy and that they mean to comply with its objectives to maintain high standards of hygiene. Failure to comply, once signed, may lead to disciplinary action. The success of the policy must be judged on the commitment of the workforce, therefore before formulating any document it is advisable to consult with staff. It is important that any policy is simple to understand and is practical to operate.

Health and safety committees

Health and safety involves everyone in the food service operation from goods inwards to final product to service. In order to focus attention on the subject and to maintain a continued interest throughout the workforce it is advisable to set up a committee. Such a committee comprises those who have immediate responsibility for maintaining hygiene standards, quality control, production, service, training, etc. Staff representatives from various areas should be involved. Members should be changed from time to time to avoid complacency and to maintain interest.

Food hygiene audits

Food hygiene audits are intended to record deficiencies and areas for improvement and to monitor performance at certain points. These may be linked to any quality assurance (including ISO9001) criteria. The audit usually requires a suitably qualified person to carry out an in-depth inspection of the premises, plant and practices. The report is presented to management and includes observations and makes recommendations.

Many food service establishments change their techniques and procedures of operation without being aware of hazards that are introduced. It is all too easy for people who are familiar with the operation to fail to see what to outsiders are obvious problem areas emerging. Buildings may also be suffering from wear and tear and lack of repair. Equipment may also need overhauling. Often a hygiene audit is the only way of looking critically at the environment and thus picking up the problem areas or practices.

The frequency of these audits may vary, depending on the type of premises. High-volume production will justify more frequent audits. Establishments processing high-risk fresh commodities will also require more frequent audits. All in-depth inspections require properly recorded documentation, which provide the basis for reports to go to the people who are able to take action. Otherwise their value is diminished. Reports should prioritise, to assist management in their decision-making, especially when financial implications have to be assessed and considered. Many companies and restaurant establishments now employ private independent companies to carry out food safety audits.

■ Essential considerations

Employers need to assess any hazards or risks and implement procedures to deal with any accidents. All employees should receive training in accident prevention. Safety signs must be used to inform and instruct people using the premises so as to prevent accidents, or what they must do in the event of an accident.

Risk assessment

Prevention of accidents and preventing food poisoning in food service establishments are essential, therefore it is necessary to assess any possible hazard or risk and decide what action is to be taken. The purpose of regularly assessing the possibility of risks and hazards is to prevent accidents. First it is necessary to monitor the situation to have regular and random checks to observe that the standards set are being complied with. It is essential that an investigation is made if any incidents or accidents occur. The investigation must aim to track down any defects in the system and proceed to remedy these at once. The outcome of the assessment is that potential hazards or risks can be classified under four levels:

1 Minimal risk – safe conditions with safety measures in place.

2 Some risk – acceptable risk; however, attention must be given to ensure safety measures operate.

3 Significant risk – where safety measures are not fully in operation, also includes foods most likely to cause food poisoning. Requires immediate attention.

4 Dangerous risk – requires the cessation of the process and/or discontinuing of the use of the equipment in the system and the complete checking and clearance before continuation.

Temperature control

Generally there are two important temperatures: 8°C and 63°C. Foods, which may be subject to microbiological multiplication, must be held at no higher than 8°C or no lower than 63°C. There are a few exceptions, which include foods in display. These foods can be displayed for up to four hours and must then be destroyed or chilled and not held again or served at room temperature. Low risk and preserved foods can be stored at ambient temperature. Food, which is served hot, should be held at over 63°C. Under Scottish regulations reheated food must attain a temperature of 82°C providing this does not adversely affect the quality of the food.

Control of substances hazardous to health (COSHH)

Substances dangerous to health are labelled very toxic, toxic harmful, irritant or corrosive. While only a small number of such chemicals are used in food service operations for cleaning, persons using such substances must be made aware of their correct use, proper dilution where appropriate and to wear protective goggles, gloves and face masks. Members of staff must be trained to take precautions and not to take risks.

Hazard analysis and critical control point (HACCP)

It is a legal requirement for food businesses to have a system based on the seven principles of HACCP. These identify, assess and monitor the critical control points in food production procedures, and ensure that corrective actions are put in place and the systems verified frequently, with accurate documentation available for inspection and review.

HACCP analysis critically examines each stage of food production through to the final product and the consumer, identifying any which may appear vulnerable in terms of introducing a hazard into the food. Once potential hazards in the processes have been identified, whether it is within the preparation, processing, storage or service, then particular attention must be given to either eliminating or minimising the hazard. One of the advantages of HACCP is that a multi-disciplinary team is involved, because it covers the wide range of activities associated with the food product. Staff must be trained in HACCP, and for the process to be successful they must have commitment.

HACCP can be adapted by all sectors of the food service industry. The process is not just confined to large operators. On introducing the HACCP process into food production the following elements have to be implemented:

■ A detailed flow chart needs to be drawn up showing the path of the food (including beverages) throughout the production process.

■ All production details need to be identified so that any special characteristics are noted that could become a cause for concern.

■ Each stage in the production must be carefully examined to see if there is the possibility that a hazard could occur. The risks are then recorded as high, medium or low. Monitoring controls are then implemented. In all cases records must be kept.

■ Taking food samples and bacterial swabs also help to complement the HACCP programme.

Examples of critical control points (CCPs) include:

- Inspection (including temperature checks) of goods on delivery and before use
- Separate storage and handling of ingredients and the finished product
- Correct temperature ranges for refrigerated and frozen goods
- Cleaning procedures for equipment and utensils
- Cross-contamination with other menu items in process
- Personal hygiene and health standards
- Proficiency in use and cleaning of equipment.

Maintaining HACCP requires:

- Monitoring the information (e.g. temperature record charts) and take effective action when appropriate
- Altering the HACCP system as necessary if any feature of ingredients, processes or environment changes
- Carrying out periodic checks to ensure the accuracy of any necessary instruments
- Periodic laboratory testing of the microbiological condition of raw materials, equipment environment and product should be made wherever possible
- Ensuring adequate personnel monitoring, training and retraining.

Activity:

- Design a hazard analysis critical control system for a high risk food ingredient.

Safer food, better business

As HACCP is a system principally designed for manufacturing it is seen by many food service operators as being too complex. Therefore, a simpler system was developed which takes a slightly different approach in that it takes a generic view of all operations in a kitchen, for example, temperature monitoring. **Safer Food Better Business** (SFBB) is a monitoring process which is based on the HACCP approach but looks at the many steps or individual sub-processes involved in getting all the supplies from the supplier, processing them and then getting them to the customer. At each point where a risk is identified a control measure needs to be designed, implemented and monitored. These may include:

- Examining sub-processes such as:

☐ Specification	☐ Preparation	☐ Serving
☐ Buying	☐ Cooking holding: hot or cold	☐ Waste disposal
☐ Receiving	☐ Re-heating	☐ Cleaning
☐ Storage		

- Identifying potential risks from:
  - ☐ Contamination
  - ☐ Temperature
  - ☐ Cross-contamination.

- Taking measures such as:
  - ☐ Supplier checks
  - ☐ Checks for condition
  - ☐ Temperature checks
  - ☐ Colour coding knives and boards.

The Safer Food Better Business system is based on the principles of HACCP but in an easy to understand format. It is divided into two parts. The first part is about safe methods, e.g. avoiding cross-contamination, personal hygiene, cleaning, chilling and cooking. The second part covers opening and closing checks, proving methods are safe, recording safe methods, training records, supervision, stock control and the selection of suppliers and contractors. The system also includes pre-printed pages and charts to enter the relevant information such as temperatures of individual dishes.

Free self-study packs are available for the needs of different food businesses and can be downloaded from the Food Standards Agency website at www.food.gov.uk/business-industry/sfbb.

Activity:

- For an operation of your choice, summarise the steps required under HACCP or the Safer Food Better Business system.

- Identify what you consider to be the most crucial steps in the process.

4.4 Food production areas and equipment

Factors that influence kitchen planning and design are:

- The size and extent of the menu and the market that it serves
- Services: gas, electricity and water
- Labour, level of skills of people
- Amount of capital expenditure, costs
- Use of prepared convenience food
- Types of equipment available
- Hygiene and food safety
- Design and décor
- Multi-usage requirements.

The size and space of the food production area should enable the staff to be able to work safely, efficiently, speedily and in comfort. The aim when planning a kitchen is for food to be prepared and served without waste of both time and effort. Therefore, layout design must consider working methods that improve productivity and utilize equipment to reduce labour.

The main considerations are:

- Ensuring an efficient workflow
- Providing adequate work space
- Creating suitable work sections
- Ensuring access to ancillary areas
- Determining number, type and size of equipment
- Ensuring ease of cleaning and disinfecting.

Food production areas must be also designed so that they can be easily managed. The management must have easy access to the areas under their control and have good visibility in the areas that have to be supervised.

Workflow

Food preparation rooms should be planned to allow a logical workflow. Food is processed through the premises from the point of delivery to the point of sale or service with the minimum of obstruction. The various processes should be separated as far as possible. Food intended for storage, preparation, production and service should flow in a uniform linear direction and not cross paths with waste food or refuse. The process should also be designed to reduce the potential for cross-contamination of food items. Staff time is valuable and a design that reduces wasteful journeys is both efficient and cost-effective, while staff members are required to parallel process items in their job role, there is the need to understand the potential cross-contamination issues that could occur if the linear workflow process is not followed.

Newly-built premises should comply fully with the requirements of the appropriate hygiene and safety legislation. Plans should be discussed with the Environmental Enforcement Officers, as it is much easier and cheaper to provide satisfactory surface finishes and facilities at the design stage rather than having to replace later.

The use of satisfactory building materials and a well-planned layout is also essential to achieve high standards of hygiene. Within the food production design there must also be adequate facilities for cleaning and disinfection of utensils and equipment.

For planning purposes stationary equipment must be sited to allow for the cleaning of wall and floor surfaces. Alternatively, the machines and equipment should be fixed firmly to the floor without a gap. However, the design must avoid narrow areas or angles in contact with the floor.

■ Work space

The size of the premises must be adequate to allow efficient operation and the site must be large enough to accommodate possible future expansion. Approximately 4.2 m² (45 sq ft) is required per person; too little space can cause staff to work in close proximity to stoves, steamers, cutting blades, mixers, etc. which creates the potential for accidents. Aisle space of approximately 1.37 m (4½ ft) is desirable as aisles must be adequate to enable staff to move safely.

Lighting

The working area must also be suitably lit. Premises should take full advantage of natural lighting through large, well-placed windows. In addition, efficient artificial lighting is always required in food production areas. Adequate lighting is also essential in passageways, storerooms, stairs and in areas outside the building where staff need to go, such as refuse areas and delivery bays. Wall and ceiling finishes should be chosen to enhance available light by using light-reflecting colours.

Ventilation

Adequate ventilation is essential in order to create a comfortable working environment. A kitchen will require approximately 20-30 changes per hour, depending on its production needs. Those with specialist equipment such as tandoori ovens, require 60 changes per hour. It is also possible to find 120 changes per hour in small low ceiling basement kitchens. Nearly all kitchens, therefore, require mechanical ventilation especially those in a basement or enclosed within a building.

Specialised ventilation systems are required for sources of heat, fumes or steam. These include hoods above the equipment to collect the fumes via a duct, which leads to the outside, with filter arrangements to arrest the majority of heavy materials, such as grease particles, before they go into the ducting.

Expert advice is always needed in deciding which type of ventilation is best suited for food service operation and especially food production areas.

■ Working sections

The size and style of the menu and the ability of the staff will determine the number of sections and layout that are necessary. A straight-line layout would be suitable for a snack bar while an island layout would be more suitable for an hotel restaurant. The use of coloured chopping boards, cloths and knife handles can assist in determining the role of areas as help to reduce cross contamination. For example: green for salads; blue for fish; red for raw meat; white for diary and brown for cooked meat.

The kitchen and food premises must also have adequate facilities for hand washing and drying in all areas of the kitchen where food processing, preparation and handling are carried out.

■ ## Access to ancillary areas

A good receiving area needs to be designed for bringing in supplies easily, with nearby storage facilities suitably sited for distribution of foods to preparation and production areas.

Refuse containers must be situated outside the building, preferably in a covered but not totally enclosed area. Refuse can be divided into two types:

■ Dry waste – paper, cardboard boxes

■ Wet waste – food and kitchen debris.

The best type of containers for wet waste are either metal or plastic bins with a tight-fitting lid that keeps out vermin and insects, and that can be washed out easily. In warmer climates where refuse collection is not always daily, these areas can also be refrigerated to reduce odours.

■ ## Type, amount and size of equipment

The type, amount and size of equipment will depend on the type of menu being provided. Not only should the equipment be suitably situated, but also the working height should be set to enable it to be used without causing excess fatigue. Large- and small-scale equipment is expensive, and due consideration needs to be given to the productivity of the appliance and its versatility in use. Kitchen equipment manufacturers can provide details relating to output and size but as with all sales, the claims they make will require verification before purchase, as part of a sound organisation purchasing policy.

The various preparation processes require different types of consideration depending on what food is involved. A vegetable preparation area means that water from the sinks and dirt from the vegetables are going to accumulate and therefore adequate facilities for drainage should be provided. On the other hand, pastry preparation entails mainly dry processes and a cool atmosphere, separate from the hot kitchen. Whatever the processes, there are certain basic rules that can be applied which not only make for easier working conditions, but which help to ensure that the food hygiene regulations are complied with.

Kitchens can be divided into sections, based on the production process:

Dry areas	Stores, storage
Wet areas	Fish preparation, vegetable preparation, butchery, cold preparation
Hot wet areas	Boiling, poaching, steaming
Equipment	Atmospheric steamers, pressure steamers, combination oven, bratt pans, steam-jacketed boilers
Hot dry areas	Frying, roasting, grilling
Equipment	Cool zone fryers, pressure fryers, bratt pans, roasting ovens, charcoal grills, salamanders, induction cookers, halogen cookers, microwave, cook and hold ovens

| **Dirty areas** | Refuse, pot wash areas, plate wash |
| *Equipment* | Compactors, refuse storage units, pot wash machines, dishwashers, glass washers |

Kitchens are becoming streamlined with operators looking for bespoke power solutions as energy efficiency is becoming a priority. Modern kitchens are changing from environments packed with many production components to carefully balanced solutions that optimise workflow, heat management, productivity and maintenance. Kitchens need to be adaptable, reliable, high performance hubs, capable of enhancing productivity and ensuring energy efficiency. One approach is to reduce the kitchen footprint at the point of delivery with the increased use of prepared and part-prepared food components.

Prepared foods will require different types of equipment and labour requirements compared with part-prepared food or raw state ingredients.

Prepared food examples:
- ☐ Sous-vide products
- ☐ Cook–chill
- ☐ Cook–freeze
- ☐ Prepared sweets.

Part prepared:
- ☐ Peeled and cut vegetables
- ☐ Convenience sauces and soups
- ☐ Portioned fish/meat.

Raw state:
- ☐ Unprepared vegetables
- ☐ Meat which requires butchering
- ☐ Fish requiring filleting and portioning.

Consideration must be given to the management policy on buying food products in the prepared, part-prepared or raw state, and in turn ensure design plans incorporate facilities that allow materials are to be handled effectively. For example, the purchase of raw ingredients requires space to ensure that raw storage can be accommodated and staff work space to ensure that basic preparation can be undertaken, before the product can be processed for cooking. For the food service organisation, the usage of part- and prepared products, enables a reduction in kitchen space and hence an increased restaurant and service space to be developed, increasing the sales revenue. Part-prepared and prepared food products also facilitate the de-skilling of the production worker's role and with it reduced wages and time spent on tasks. Labour is one of the highest costs in the operational delivery of the restaurant, and cost savings here has a significant impact on profitability. Within the kitchen and the craft skill of the chef, this approach to food production and service can become a contentious issue.

The final selection of equipment will be made after detailed consideration of:

■ The functions that will be carried out within the cooking area of the kitchen

■ The amount of equipment, which will depend upon the complexity of the menus offered

■ The quantity of meals served.

■ The policy of management in use of materials from the traditional kitchen to the use of prepared foods, chilled items, frozen foods, where the kitchen consists of a regeneration unit only.

Given, however, that a certain amount of equipment is required, the planner has the choice of a number of possible layouts, within the constraints of the building shape and size and the location of services. The most common are the island groupings, wall siting and the use of an L- or U-shaped layout and variations upon these basic themes.

■ Ease of cleaning and disinfecting

Small daily-use restaurant equipment, such as crockery, cutlery and glasses, are normally washed in a separate area from the kitchen utensils. With the restaurant dishwashing normally located close to the kitchen 'in' door as a server drop area, before the server moves to the kitchen food collection point 'pass' and back into the restaurant through the 'out' door. The dishwasher, dependent on the size of the operation, can be front-loaded similar to a domestic dishwasher, but with a faster wash speed; for larger throughput, a conveyor dishwasher is the norm.

Work areas must be planned so that medium scale kitchen equipment can be easily cleaned. Large static kitchen equipment has to be cleaned and sanitised in situ. It is standard practice to have deep cleaning rotas, or an overnight kitchen shutdown for large equipment cleaning, which also includes the kitchen walls, floor and ceiling. It is usual for a cleaning contract company to fulfill this specialist task for large food service organisations.

Equipment must also be designed, constructed finished and arranged so that it can be easily cleaned and disinfected, safely, thoroughly and rapidly, without the need for skilled fitters or specialised tools. Equipment such as gravity feed slicers, mixers, processors, etc. which do require dismantling for cleaning must be easy to take apart and reassemble. All edges must be smooth and rounded. Rough and sharp edges constitute a serious hazard to cleaners. If equipment is difficult to dismantle because of poor design and may result in a danger to operatives, it will mean that those responsible for cleaning will be reluctant to clean it. This results in a lowering of hygiene standards and possible health risks.

The buyer of the equipment should also observe that all joints and welds are smooth and that nuts, bolts and screw heads are absent from food contact surfaces. All hinges should be capable of being taken apart for cleaning. No crevices in fitting panels, open joints and rough seams should be present in the equipment, as they have a tendency to become filled with accumulations of food, grease and dirt, which in turn will support bacterial growth and may then provide a food source for pest infestation.

For a more detailed consideration of kitchen design see Foskett and Paskins (2016), Chapter 5.

Activity:

- For an operation of your choice, draw a map of the food production operation indicating the flow of materials, people and waste.

- Design a streamlined digital banquet kitchen suitable for serving 500 meals at any one time

---

4.5   Food and beverage service areas and equipment

Food and beverage service areas fall into two categories, those for customers and staff usage and those for staff usage only. Staff and customer usage areas include consumption areas such as dining areas and service areas such as in cafeterias, bars and the associated services. Staff areas include stillroom, wash-up, storage and cellar areas.

The general considerations for staff usage areas are:

- Appropriate siting and with logical layout of equipment
- Ease of delivery access
- Ease of service
- Ensuring hygiene, health and safety requirements are met
- Ease of cleaning
- Sufficient storage space for service equipment and food items
- Security.

The general considerations for areas used by both customers and staff include first the general considerations for staff-only areas as above and in addition also take into account the meal experience factor of atmosphere (see Chapter 3, page 61). This includes consideration of:

- Decor and lighting
- Heating and ventilation
- Noise, and
- The size and shape of the areas.

■   Decor and lighting

The general considerations on decor are:

- Appropriateness to the type and style of the operation
- Sufficient flexibility especially where the space has multi-usage, e.g. function rooms
- Functional reliability
- Ease of maintenance
- Industrial rather than domestic quality
- Ease of cleaning and general housekeeping needs.

Lighting, itself an architectural feature, is a pivotal ingredient in food service operational design. Contemporary lighting and colour designs tend towards a versatile system of lighting by which a food and beverage service area may have brighter lighting at lunchtime and a more diffused form of lighting in the evening. Lighting can create image, generate atmosphere and seamlessly communicate a marketing and merchandising message. In tandem it can determine quality, price, and speed of turnover. The principal rule in lighting provision is that it be neither too bright nor too dark. Brilliant lighting does not create comfortable or intimate surroundings, but can be deployed at times to encourage customers to move from the area or speed the service. Fast food operations deploy bright lights and primary colours to remove the feeling of relaxation – the critical success factor for fast food is high volume sales and customers lingering are effectively reducing turnover and hence productivity. Dim lighting limits sensory evaluation and may inhibit safe working practices. It can also be an advantage to be able to change the colour of the lights for special functions and today's technology enhances these possibilities.

■   Heating and ventilation

There are two dimensions to heating and lighting:

- The maintenance of a reasonable temperature
- The ventilation of the areas.

The temperature of food and beverage service areas will change depending on the volume of customers and how long they stay in an area. For every ten people this is equivalent to a 1 kw fire being turned on. Temperature control will therefore need to take this into account especially where customers are in dining areas for a long period such as in function operations. Temperature also has an actual and a perceived reality. Customers will have preferred locations depending on their perceptions of the heating; asking to sit by windows, for example, as this is con-sidered a cooler part of the room, or not by doors because of suspected draughts, or not near buffets because of the heat or cold. In all these examples the actual temperature may be the same as other areas of the room.

In areas where food and beverages are served there are inevitable smells, which come from these areas. It is a truism that a single food smell is generally liked, for example fresh coffee or freshly baked bread, but that a combination of food smells is usually unpleasant. Some restaurant environments however, utilise the smell of food and beverage effectively to promote customer comfort and promote sales as part of merchandising. In general though, food smells are best avoided and the ventilation systems should be able to take account of this requirement.

Ambient noise

Because of equipment movement and customer and staff conversation, food and beverage service areas can be noisy. The customer expectation is that generally the higher the service level and price, then the lower the noise level that will be tolerated. This is also affected by the time of day; for instance, breakfast can be more acceptably noisy than dinner. Care needs to be taken in the design and selection of materials and equipment in order to contain noise at appropriate and acceptable levels. Sound absorbing materials in walls, floors and ceilings can assist greatly. Acoustical materials for ceilings and walls are generally the largest target areas for noise control. The floor space is another major surface area which when carpeted actively controls noise. Window treatments and tabletop linen also absorb noise pollution.

Another issue is that of noise transmission from one area to another as in an adjacent bar, lounge and kitchen. Sound transmission should really be considered and alleviated at the planning phase; afterwards it is a matter of control and the effective use of acoustical materials. Background music systems can also cause problems. It is an area of great controversy with very clear views being expressed as to why background music systems can aid or hinder operations. In general, it depends on the particular style of operations and the image that the operation is trying to project. If background systems are to be used then it is worth investing in high-quality equipment. Having cheap and badly regulated equipment is both distressful and fatiguing for customers.

The size and shape of the areas

Not only do the size and shape of the room affect the customers' enjoyment of the meal but also in table service areas the location of the tables becomes important. Some issues to consider are:

- The location of tables in a food service area especially taking into account the needs of the single diner and couples
- Facing positions (e.g. not towards service areas, walls, doors, or too close to service stations)
- Access for those with disabilities
- Ease of workflow

- Evenness of temperature and ventilation (including avoiding air-conditioning, heating and extraction hot spots)
- Access to exits and toilets
- Avoiding being directly in the path of live or piped music systems.

■ Food and beverage service equipment

The general points to be considered when purchasing equipment for a food and beverage service area are:

- Flexibility of use
- Type of service being offered
- Type of customer and the nature of demand being met
- Design, shape, colour, and durability
- Ease of maintenance and replacement
- Stackability
- Costs and funds available
- Storage
- Rate of breakage, e.g. for crockery
- Psychological effect on customers, and
- Delivery time.

Furniture

Furniture must be chosen according to the needs of the establishment and the variation in human body dimensions. The type of operation being run determines the specific needs as far as the dining arrangements are concerned. A summary of possible dining arrangements is given in Table 4.2.

Table 4.2: Examples of dining arrangements

Type	Description
Loose random	Free-standing furniture positioned in no discernible pattern within a given area
Loose module	Free-standing furniture positioned within a given area to a predetermined pattern with or without the use of dividers to create smaller areas within a module
Booth	Fixed seating, usually high-backed, used to create secluded seating
High density	Furniture with minimum dimensions and usually fixed in positioned within a given area to create maximum seating capacity, e.g. for cafeterias
Module	Seating incorporates table and chairs constructed as one and may be fixed
In-situ	Customers served in areas not designed for service, e.g. in aircraft and hospital beds
Bar & lounge areas	Customers served in areas not conventionally designed for eating

In determining the specification for furniture for food service operation the following factors might be taken into account:

- Comfort
- Cost
- Design
- Durability
- Function
- Movability
- Multi-functionality
- Safety
- Structure and materials
- Storage capacity (if required).

Very often by using different materials, designs and finishes and by careful arrangement the atmosphere and appearance of the food and beverage service area can be changed to suit different occasions. Restaurant and bar furniture need careful consideration. It needs to reinforce the aesthetics, style and ambience of the business. The ergonomics have to be carefully considered. Furniture needs to be sturdy yet easily moved, versatile, durable, low maintenance and with a superior finish. Where possible prior to purchase, performance evaluation should be carried out. This should definitely be requested where consultants are employed.

Tables

Tables generally come in four shapes: round, oval, square and rectangular. An establishment may have a mixture of shapes to give variety, or tables of all one shape according to the shape of the room and the style of service being offered. These tables will seat two or four people and two tables may be pushed together to seat larger parties, luncheons, dinners, weddings, etc. By using extensions, a variety of shapes may be obtained allowing full use of the room and getting the maximum number of covers in the minimum space.

Chairs

Chairs come in an enormous range of designs, materials and colours to suit all situations and occasions. Because of the wide range of styles, the chairs vary in height and width, but as a guide, a chair seat is 46 cm (18 in) from the ground, the height from the ground to the top of the back is 1 m (39 in) and the depth from the front edge of the seat to the back of the chair is 46 cm (18 in).

Additional purchasing considerations are the size, height, shape and the variety of seating required – banquette, armchairs, straight-backed, action–backed and padded chairs, giving the customer a choice, and also including high chairs for toddlers and kiddy boosters or cushions for children. Care also needs to be taken in matching chairs and seating generally with table heights, especially where chairs and tables in both metric and imperial measurements are being used.

With seating requirements generally there is a relationship between comfort and the time the customer will tend to spend in the seat. Thus less comfortable but adequately functional seating tends to be used in fast service operations and in higher-level service areas more comfortable seating is provided. It is also true because of differences in physiology, women tend to sit up straighter for longer than men. Therefore chairs with arms are more useful in operations meeting the needs of a male-dominated clientele.

Consideration also needs to be given to the needs of children, people with disabilities and the manoeuvrability and stacking capability of seating especially for function operations.

Sideboards/workstations

The style and design of a sideboard or workstations vary from establishment to establishment. The majority of commercially available sideboards are insufficient in strength of construction, storage capability and worktop provision. It is now more usual for operations to design and build their own sideboards or workstations, often incorporating them as part of the design of the dining area.

Food and beverage service equipment

The general points to be considered when purchasing equipment for a food and beverage service area are:

- Flexibility of use
- Type of service being offered
- Type of customer and the nature of demand being met
- Design, shape, colour, and durability
- Ease of maintenance and replacement
- Costs and funds available
- Storage
- Rate of breakage, e.g. for crockery
- Psychological effect on customers, and
- Delivery time.

Trays

Trays are used throughout food service operations. Their use ranges from carrying equipment and food to service on a tray, as in hospital, airline and room service operations. Additional considerations in the purchase of trays include:

- Lightness and strength – trays should be able to be carried when fully loaded and not become misshapen when weight is placed upon them
- Stackability
- Heat resistance
- Ease of cleaning

- Resistance to slippage of items place on them
- Resistant to damage from spilt items or damp.

Linen

There are many qualities of linen in present-day use, from the finest Irish linen and cotton to synthetic materials such as nylon and viscose. The type of linen use would depend on the class of establishment, type of clientele and cost involved, and the style of menu and service to be offered. Operations need to make arrangement to ensure the availability of linen to meet operational requirements. Decisions need to be made on whether the operation should:

- Have an in-house laundry and its own linen
- Purchase own linen and use an off-site commercial laundry, or
- Have a linen rental or contract with an external commercial laundry.

Essentially it comes down to the requirements and size of the business or organisation and the capacity in terms of available space to site a laundry and available capital for initial steep outlay. If the business is part of a group, another option may well be to utilise a centralised laundry service for the group.

Crockery

When purchasing crockery, the key factors to consider are:

- Every item should have a complete cover of glaze to ensure a reasonable length of life.
- Items should have a rolled edge, which will give added reinforcement at the edge and reduce the possibility of chipping.
- The pattern should be under rather than on top of the glaze. However, this demands additional glaze and firing. Patterns on top of the glaze will wear and discolour very quickly. Therefore, although crockery with the pattern under the glaze is more expensive its life will be longer.

There are now many more manufacturers in the marketplace than ever before. Food service operations can now choose not simply in terms of durability, but with bespoke design, size, colour, weight and shape as just part of an overall package. There is a wide range of traditional items available and their exact sizes vary according to the manufacturer and the design produced. There is also increasing use of more modern service ware such as that made from glass or plastics and also in a variety of shapes other than rounds. When purchasing service ware key considerations are:

- The extent to which there is to be common usage of items thus reducing the level of stock, e.g. using one size of plate for fish and sweet courses or using one bowl for items such as soup, fruit and cereal.
- The extent to which different service areas and different service times might have different crockery. For example, different banqueting crockery from coffee shop crockery or larger cups for breakfast.

■ The extent to which the various crockery items should match. It has become quite common to have differing designs of crockery according to different types of dishes and also to mix complementary patterns.

Tableware

The term tableware traditionally covers:

■ Flatware; all forms of spoon and fork

■ Cutlery; knives and other cutting implements, and

■ Hollow-ware; any item made from silver, apart from flatware and cutlery, e.g. teapots, milk jugs, sugar basins, oval flats.

Although traditionally referred to separately as *flatware* and *cutlery*, the term most commonly used now is *cutlery*, which refers to both.

The majority of food service areas use either plated silverware or stainless steel. Plain cutlery and flatware are more popular than patterned for the simple reason that they are cheaper and easier to keep clean. General considerations for choosing a selection of tableware items also include the extent to which items will have more than one purpose. For example, using jugs for hot water, hot milk or cold milk or using standard ranges of cutlery such as sweet/soup spoons, and general-purpose knives and forks rather than having, say, separate fish knives and forks.

Glassware

Glass also contributes to the appearance of the table and the overall attraction of the room. There are many standard patterns available to the food service operator. Most manufacturers now supply hotel glassware in standard sizes for convenience of ordering, availability and quick delivery.

Except in certain speciality restaurants or high-class establishments, where either coloured glassware or cut glassware may be used, hotel glassware is usually plain.

A good wine glass should be plain and clear so the colour and brilliance of a wine can be clearly seen; it should have a stem for holding the wine glass so that the heat of one's hand does not affect the wine on tasting; there should be a slight incurving lip to help hold the aroma and it should be large enough to hold the particular wine being served.

Disposables

The main varieties of disposable available are often used in the following areas:

■ Storage and cooking purposes

■ Service of food and beverages, e.g. plates, knives, forks, cups

■ Decor – napkins, tablecloths, slipcloths, banquet roll, place-mats

■ Hygiene – wipes

- Clothing, e.g. aprons, chefs' hats, gloves
- Packaging – for marketing and presentation purposes.

A considerable advance in the range of disposable available has been the introduction of disposables whose approximation to crockery and tableware is very close. For instance, they may have a high quality, overall finish and a smooth hard white surface. The plates themselves are strong and rigid with no tendency to bend or buckle, and a plasticising ingredient ensures that they are grease and moisture proof, even against hot fat and gravy. Oval luncheon plate, snack trays and compartment plates are all available to the caterer.

Advantages of disposables include:

- Equipment and labour: disposables reduce the need for washing-up equipment, staff and materials.
- Hygiene: usage improves the standard of hygiene in an establishment.
- Capital: usage reduces the amount of capital investment.
- Cost: disposables are cheaper than hiring conventional equipment.

Disadvantages of disposables include:

- Acceptability: customer acceptability may be poor.
- Cost: disposables can be more expensive than some conventional equipment and more so because of increasing environmental concerns..
- Supply: there is heavy reliance on supply and delivery time.

■ Bar areas

There are certain essentials necessary in the planning of bars. These are outlined as follows:

- **Area**: The bar staff must be given sufficient area of space in which to work and move about. There should be a minimum of 1 m from the back of the bar counter to the storage shelves and display cabinets at the rear of the bar.
- **Layout**: Careful consideration must be given, in the initial planning, to the layout. Everything should be easily to hand so that the bar staff do not have to move about more than necessary.
- **Plumbing and power**: It is essential to have hot and cold running water for glass washing. Power is necessary to provide the effective working of cooling trays, refrigerators and ice-making machines.
- **Storage**: Adequate storage should be provided, in the form or shelves, cupboard and racks, for all the stock and equipment required.
- **Safety and hygiene**: Great care must be observed so that the materials used in the make-up of the bar are hygienic and safe. Flooring must be non-slip. The bar top should be of a material suited to the general decor that is hardwearing, easily wiped down and has no sharp edges. The bar top is usually of average working height – of at least 1 m (3 ft) and a width of 0.6 m (20 in).

■ Automatic vending

Vended goods have 24-hour availability and the units can be sited in a variety of locations. wherever required. The types of service available may be broken down into two main groups: namely services and facilities such as car parking, toilets, baggage store, or consumables such as hot and cold meal/snacks and beverages.

Within food service, automatic vending refers to the supply of a wide range of beverages, both hot and cold, through coin/token-operated machines. Vending machines used for food service operations include:

■ **Merchandiser**: Customers can view the products for sale, for example, confectionery machines. Can also be used for refrigerated drinks (bottles and cans) and pre-packaged meals and snacks as well as for hot meals and snacks through internal heating.

■ **Hot beverage vendor**: This mixes the powdered ingredients with hot water to produce the product.

■ **In-cup system**: Ingredients are already in individual cups to which hot water is added.

■ **Cold beverage vendor**: Post-mix syrup mixed with water (carbonated or non-carbonated).

■ **Micro-vend system**: Provides a range of hot or cold foods from which the customer may make a selection and heat in an accompanying microwave oven.

The numbers and types of machines required depends on their location, the type and number of people they are providing a service for, the cost factor and the variety of food and beverage items required.

The machines required might be installed either individually or in small groups, to supplement the conventional catering establishment or to cover a small-scale demand that does not warrant the expense of employing the extra labour and plant. The opposite to this would be the installation of a complete vending service where demand is highly volatile, space is limited and the use of staffed operations would be uneconomical.

Automatic vending machines are not self-cleaning, self-maintaining or self-filling. Therefore, regular service maintenance is required and should be guaranteed if the vending service is to run smoothly and without the problems of mechanical breakdown. The type of vending machine and the service demand upon it will help to determine the regularity of the service requirements. All vending machines come with instructions about cleaning, maintenance and stocking, which do need to be followed for the machines to perform at optimum efficiency levels.

For more information on food and beverage service areas and equipment see for example Cousins et al (2014).

Activity:

■ For a service operation of your choice, identify what you consider to be the key design concepts being used.

■ Discuss to what extent these design concepts tally with the furniture choices and service equipment being used.

4.6   Staff management considerations

How management deals with key staffing issues can significantly affect the success of any operation. Areas that to be addressed include:

■ Determining the amount of required labour

■ The establishment of employee work schedules

■ The determination of operating hours

■ Staffing patterns

■ The various benefits that will be offered to employees

■ The varying skill and knowledge levels that will exist among the employees

■ The level of supervision that will be required

■ Issues that are centred on the remuneration package.

Addressing these issues will help to determine the organisational structure of the operation and the kind of management team needed to operate the facility in an effective and efficient manner.

Many successful restaurants are owned and operated by one individual whose personality becomes a part of the customers' dining experience. On the other hand, the management of the food and beverage department of a large hotel, or the food service in a large hospital or university, may be under the control of more than one person and is usually part of a more complex organisational team. In these cases, the policies and procedures of the food service facility should be laid out in an operations manual, to assure consistent implementation of management policies.

The members of staff have a critical influence on the success of a food service business. Food service operation have a range of roles. These include staffing for:

■ Food production

■ Food service

■ Beverage service

■ Marketing

■ Sales promotion

■ Merchandising

- Financial and physical resource management
- People management.

The true strength of a food service operation is the opportunity for human inter-face and the quality of its people to maximise that opportunity. Although this might appear trite, achieving this requires a systematic and analytical approach. When selecting customer contact personnel, it is crucial to have people who are likely to be liked by customers and whose personal attributes include a positive attitude and a customer-oriented approach that fits with the values of the food service brand. Food service businesses solely investing in greater efficiencies and mechanistic interactions can sacrifice the invigorative energies required to sustain positive and rewarding relationships between staff and customers. The food service organisations which are most likely to succeed, are those whose staff are serving with authenticity. Within some high energy themed restaurants and bars, staff are recruited as they are willing to live the brand, while looking and sounding the part as aesthetic labourers.

Optimising human resources

The key selection attributes of enlightened food and beverage personnel are clear. What is needed is an intrinsic ability to help people; it is an inner genuineness, and an ability to respond to, and attempt to satisfy, the needs of others. Willingness to learn is also important, as is a sense of urgency.

People are a major resource and maximising the potential of this resource requires the management of staffing to be at the forefront of the organisation and not within the traditional personnel (or human resources) department. It should be as upfront in the requirements of a manager's responsibilities as are the other responsibilities for the operation: finance and sales and marketing.

More and more individuals are entering the industry with improved edu-cational qualifications, which is presenting its own challenges, but in order to achieve a positive outcome, people need to be challenged and motivated through opportunity. Compensation through rewards and recognition should support this approach. The quality of the human resources should be the businesses strength: the essence of the core competence.

The management of people is not, and should not be, primarily an admin-istrative function. Managing people, developing teams and individuals, are all activities that are integral parts of the management of operations.

Health, safety and security

There are common-law duties on employers, which are to:

- Select reasonably competent staff (or provide training to bring new recruits up to a reasonable standard of competence)
- Provide adequate materials required for the job
- Provide a safe system of working.

Employees may claim damages from the employer for any injury sustained as a result of any breach of these requirements.

In turn, members of staff have responsibilities to contribute to maintaining the health and safety requirements of the food service operation. The implications for staff are that they should:

- Understand the food hygiene regulations and that it is their responsibility to act within the bounds of these regulations
- Notify management of any major illnesses
- Perform duties in any area concerned with the handling of food in a hygienic manner, paying attention to food and hygiene regulations
- Wear uniforms and protective clothing as required
- Make themselves familiar with all escape routes and fire exits in the building
- Ensure that fire exits remain clear at all times
- Participate in fire evacuation drills and practices
- Take reasonable care for the health and safety of themselves and of others, and ensure that health and safety regulations are followed
- Report to heads of department or duty managers any hazards which may cause injury or ill-health to customers and/or staff.

Employers and members of staff also take steps to ensure security. Depending upon the nature of the establishment, the security measures that are laid down may vary considerably. Procedures should be known and understood by all members of staff and management. This often includes:

- Using identity badges
- Being observant and reporting 'suspicious' persons and/or packages
- Not discussing work duties with customers or outside the workplace
- Allowing for the searching of bags, packages and the person
- Ensuring external fire doors are kept shut but not locked;
- Maintaining procedures for handling keys and restricted access
- Specific procedures for handling cash and other payment systems
- Ensuring that all areas have been vacated before locking up
- Having procedures for dealing with a suspicious item or package
- Having procedures for dealing with a bomb threat
- Having well developed and rehearsed procedures for the evacuation of the premises.

Facilities for staff

Within the space allocation of the premises, provision must also be made for staff facilities. Good clean facilities for staff are essential, if they are to be encouraged to work cleanly and hygienically. If clean conditions are provided and kept clean for staff they will be encouraged to take ownership of the working practices necessary to provide an ideal hygienic working environment.

The staff facilities must be readily accessible to staff and while in smaller premises where only one or two are employed, a single lavatory may suffice, in larger premises involving numbers of employees, it will be necessary to have separate facilities for each sex, which should be situated at each floor level.

Adequate storage space must be provided for outdoor and other clothing and footwear not worn by the staff during working hours. These articles of clothing must not be stored in a food room and therefore, must be stored in separate lockers allocated to each member of staff. It is advisable that a separate room be designated as a cloakroom so that clothes can be stored conveniently. Adequate washing facilities should be provided in the cloakroom, to encourage staff to wash their hands frequently and to reinforce personal hygiene.

Staff organisation

Staff organisation in food and beverage operations is focused upon having sufficient trained and competent staff on duty to match the expected volume of customer demand.

The staffing required will be as much dependent on the nature of the various methods being adopted, e.g. food production method, service method, control method, as it is on determining the staffing levels to meet the expected volume of customer demand.

Customer demand, or throughput can be determined from sales records. There is clearly also a relationship between the volume of customers served and the length of time they stay on the premises. The time customers take in different types of operation varies. This can range from, for example, ten minutes in a cafeteria through to three hours in a fine dining restaurant.

Opening times are determined by the consideration of:

- Local competition
- Local attractions, e.g. theatre
- Location of the premises, e.g. city centre/country/suburb
- Catchment area
- Transport systems
- Staffing availability
- Volume of business
- Local tradition.

Customer throughput

Customer throughput can be calculated for different types of operation. Examples of how this can be determined for different types of operation are as follows:

Table and assisted service operations

Since all customers are usually seated in both table and assisted service methods, throughput can be estimated for new operations as the level of throughput will be limited by the length of seating time and the opening hours of the operation. For existing operations, sales records will provide a guide to potential throughput. Staffing for each service period can then be estimated and allocated to specific duties. Staffing will also need to be estimated for preparation before and for clearing following service. Thus a restaurant open for two and a half hours at lunchtime may require staff for up to five hours.To calculate the total staffing required:

1 Estimate the number of staff required for each range of duties per service period in one week.

2 Multiply the number of staff per service period by the number of hours to be worked in each period.

3 Divide total staff hours by full-time working week hours. This will give the full-time equivalent of number of staff required.

4 Mix full-time, part-time, casual, seasonal and temporary staff hours to cover all service periods.

5 Draw up staff rota which may need to be on two or three-week cycle to allow for days off, etc.

The number of staff to each service period can now be calculated and a rota drawn up. However the actual staffing levels for these types of operations are determined taking account of various ratios. This can be as covers per head, such as in determining the number of covers covered by a station in a restaurant, or revenue per head.

Cafeteria operations

There are five factors that influence potential throughput in cafeterias. These are:

- Service time: the time it takes each customer to pass along or by the counter and reach the till point
- Service period: the time the cafeteria is actually serving
- Till speed: the time it takes for customer to be billed and payment taken
- Eating/seating time
- Seating capacity.

The main criterion is seating capacity. The speed required in the queue is determined by the seating capacity and the average seating time. For example: a cafeteria with say, 186 seats and with a till speed of nine per minute, will take 20.66 minutes to fill the cafeteria. If the customers' seating time is 20 minutes, then the cafeteria will be filled just after the first customers are leaving. A faster till speed will mean that the last customer through the till will have nowhere to sit. Too slow a till speed will mean the cafeteria is not being fully utilised. For one till, four to six people per minute is a maximum.

Generally, if the seating time is greater than the service period then the actual number of seats will need to equal the total number of customers. If the seating time is less than the time it takes to serve all the customers then the number of seats may be less than the actual number of people to be served. However, the queue may need to be staggered to avoid excessive waiting before service.

The staffing levels will take account of the number of till points that need to be open as well as the level of food production, counter service, clearing and dishwashing required.

Single-point service operations

Customer throughput in single-point service operations may be taken from records of till transactions. Increases and decreases in the customer throughput are provided for by increasing or decreasing the number of till points that are open (or in the case of vending, additional machines). If seating areas are provided then similar calculations as for cafeterias can be carried out, assuming there is a known percentage of customers using the seating facility.

Again staffing levels will take account of the number of payment points that need to be open as well as the level of production, clearing and dishwashing required.

Specialised forms of service

For hospital and airline tray methods there is a capacity limitation. For other forms of specialised service methods there are records or estimates of potential take-up of services in specific locations, e.g. hotel rooms, lounges or home delivery.

■ Labour model software and lean management

Service operations need effective labour decision making. However, the complexity of calculating demand becomes less predictable as an organisation grows. There a need to capture data sets of demand linked to individual staff performance; data that can be analysed through demand and labour models, so as to optimise staff requirements.

Workforce modelling captures the complexity of the labour process involved in the operation and delivers complete data management decision making models with components which can include:

- **Identifying demand for workers** – by small units of time (generally 15 or 30 minutes)
- **Employee availability** – tracking of work hour contracts and limits on an individual
- **Employee preference** – tracking times and dates that employees wish to work to increase job satisfaction
- **Workflow management** – to automate any manual processes such as time off, shift swaps, creating work rotas

- **Productivity models** – create data that can be accessed on many dimensions simultaneously. For example, cost, overtime and employee satisfaction
- **Identify high performance staff** – across the operation and also those who require additional training.

Organising duties

All duties required within the food service operation can be broken down into a listing of tasks. These can then be rostered. The exact nature of a duty roster will vary with on the type of establishment, the duties to be performed, the number of staff required, having time off, and whether a split/straight shift is worked.

The purpose of the duty roster is to ensure that all the necessary duties are covered in order that efficient production and service may be carried out. There is an old adage that 'everyone's responsibility is no one's responsibility'. It is crucial therefore for food service operations that all the required duties are covered and that all managers, supervisors and staff are responsible and accountable for specific tasks.

It is also important that a high level of discipline is observed during service periods. Losing a grip on the flow of the food production and service through staff not knowing their responsibilities, or not carrying them out, or misguidedly trying to help others, can lead to chaos, which customers easily detect. Care also needs to be taken to ensure that plans are made for contingencies such as unexpected increases in business levels or shortages of staff.

Having properly detailed tasks and duty lists also provides the basis for staff training. Task and duty lists for each of the tasks and duties given are drawn up and these should identify standards to be achieved. These are often brought together in standards of performance manuals.

Staff training

It is essential that all managers, supervisor and members of staff fully understand their responsibilities, have been trained to carry out their duties and also know the standards of performance, which are expected of them. The basis for achieving this can be through having precise, agreed and written job descriptions. These are then backed up by agreed standards of performance manuals that are regularly reviewed and updated. And all of this is then reinforced through regular training and briefing sessions. The advantages of well-produced training programmes include:

- Clearer identified and specified responsibilities
- Compliance with required standards of performance
- Improved competence and confidence of staff
- More efficient, safe and hygienic working practices.

Activity:

For a food service sector of your choice:

■ Identify the key recruitment challenges facing food and beverage managers.

■ Identify how food and beverage managers can reduce the impact of these challenges.

■ Standards of performance

Essential to any food service business are the setting and maintenance of standards of performance. Many organisations have standards of performance manuals, often referred to as 'SOPs'. This term may be used to refer to the standards themselves or to the manuals that contain their details.

Setting standards of performance, and training staff to achieve the standards, needs to be supported by regular reviews of the extent to which the standards are being met. In addition there needs to be a continuous process for the review and development of the standards. An approach to developing and maintaining standards of performance relies on four key elements:

1 Standards of performance

2 Supporting reference materials

3 Regular standards audit, and

4 Continuous review and action planning.

These four elements are discussed below.

Developing standards of performance

There should be standards developed for all aspects of the operation.

Standard of performance for front of house include those for:

■ Professional service

■ Preparation for service

■ Greeting and seating

■ Service of wine and drinks

■ Service of food

■ Billing and payments

■ Stores management

■ Closing duties.

Standards of performance for food production include those for:

■ Professional service

■ Preparation for service

■ Service of food

- Stores management
- Clearing down duties.

In developing standards, it is always best to ensure that they are reviewed with the people who are actually responsible for implementing them. This can bring an element of realism into the process and encourage future commitment to the agreed standards.

As individual standards are agreed, under each of the aspects above, a 'standards of performance manual' can be created. Many standards of performance manuals are very bulky and highly detailed. This can have the effect of reducing their use and application. An alternative is to separate the standards or performance statements from the supporting detailed. Under this system, for each aspect, there would normally be:

- An overall statement of the standard
- Statements on how the standard is to be achieved
- Statement on how the standard is to be measured.

Service of food	
Standard: Promptly serve all food items at the correct temperature and in a friendly and professional manner.	
How to achieve the standard:	**How achievement is demonstrated:**
Set the correct cutlery for food items used	The correct cutlery is laid prior to the service of each course (for special parties the cutlery is pre-laid).
Serve food at the correct temperature	Hot meals are not left unattended for a long time on the pass or on the workstation.
Observe the agreed standards for food service	Each customer's order is matched with the meal served. Plated foods are served from the right hand side, where possible. Plates are all put on the table the way round the chef intended them to be seen. Accompaniments are served at the correct time.
Ensure that excellent customer care is offered during meal	Customer satisfaction is checked and corrective action is taken where necessary. Attentiveness to customer's requirements is maintained.
Carry out clearing duties without unnecessary intrusion to customers	Tables are cleared efficiently, using a tray as required. Clearing is carried out from the right side, where possible, checking with each person before removing items. Only safe quantities of equipment are carried at any time. Empty glasses are removed using trays, without handling the insides or rims of the glasses.

Figure 4.5: Example standard of performance statements for the service of food in a restaurant.

Figure 4.5 gives example standard of performance statements for the service of food in a table service restaurant. Standard of performance statements can be developed under all of the aspects listed above. In general there should be no more than one page for each aspect. This helps to ensure that the standards can regularly be referred to, and are used as the basis for induction and job training.

Supporting reference materials

As suggested above, standards of performance statements should be presented in a readily accessible format. For each of the aspects the statement of the standards should cover no more than about a page. These statements can then be referenced to a wide range of separate supporting information. This can be, for example, from text books, or on-line resources. The information can also be loaded onto tablets. The types of reference information might include:

Images and explanations of, for example:

- Uniform requirements
- Standard table lay-ups
- Set up of back of house areas
- Dishes on the menu
- Safety signs

Detailed procedures, for example, for:

- Accidents
- Safe handling
- Complaints
- People with additional needs
- Billing and payments

Up-to-date information on, for example:

- Health and safety
- Allergens
- Licencing

Standards audit

Once standards of performance are set, they need to be regularly monitored to ensure they are being consistently applied. There are a number of measurement tools an operation can use. One of the simplest approaches is to use a checklist to record if the standards are currently being met, and over time. Figure 4.6 presents an example of part of a simple audit record. This example is for the statements of performance for the 'service of food', as set out in Figure 4.5 above. The statements of performance under the measures 3, 4 and 5, could also be expanded to include all the statements about how achievement is being demonstrated.

Food and beverage service audit	Date: Auditor:		
Standard	Measure	Yes	No
Service of Food Promptly serve all food items at the correct temperature and in a friendly and professional manner.	The correct cutlery is set before food is served (pre-set for special parties)		
	Food is served at the correct temperature		
	Agreed standards are observed for food service		
	Excellent customer care is offered during the meal		
	Clearing duties are carried out without unnecessary intrusion to customers		

Figure 4.6: Example standard of performance audit for the service of food in a restaurant.

■ ## Standards review process

The results of the audits will lead to an identification of achievement of the standards as well as problems with the customer service. Problems need to be addressed and solutions found, including seeking customer feedback. As customers' needs change and as the operation changes, then standards also need to be reviewed.

The review of the standards should then lead to an action plan for future development. Figure 4.7 gives a simple outline of an action plan.

Standards of performance action plan					
Date From:			Date To:		
Standard	Areas for improvement	Actions to be taken	By who	By when	Achieved Yes/No

Figure 4.7: Example of a standards of performance action plan.

More information on reviewing the operation is given in Chapter 9, Section 9.5 Appraising the product.

For further information on human resource management in the hospitality, tourism and leisure industries, see, for example, Boella and Goss-Taylor (2013) and Horner (2017).

4.7   References and additional reading

Boella, M. and Goss-Taylor, S. (2013) *Human Resource Management in the Hospitality Industry: A Guide to Best Practice*, 9th edn, London: Routledge

Catering Equipment Distributors Association at https://ceda.co.uk (Assessed January 2019)

Catering Equipment Suppliers Association at www.cesa.org.uk (Accessed January 2019)

Cousins, J., Lillicrap, D. and Weekes, S. (2014) *Food and Beverage Service*, 9th ed. London: Hodder Education.

Croner's Catering (1999) – updating service, London: Croner Publications.

Food Service Consultant Society International (FCSI) at www.fcsi.org(accessed January 2019).

Food Standards Agency at www.food.gov.uk/business-industry/sfbb (accessed January 2019).

Foskett, D. and Paskins, P. (2016) *The Theory of Hospitality and Catering*, 13th ed; London: Hodder Education.

Graham, D. (2006) The re-orientation of the professional chef; an exploratory study, *International Journal of Management Cases*, **8** (2), 23-34.

Graham, D. (2016),Views from the open kitchen, *Hospitality Quarterly*. Institute of Hospitality, Autumn. p44-46.

Horner, S. (2017) *Talent Management in Hospitality and Tourism*, Oxford: Goodfellow Publishers.

Stipanuck, D. M. (2015) *Hospitality Facilities Management and Design*, 4th edn, MI: American Hotel and Motel Association.

5 Food production

Aim

To highlight the importance of sound menu planning and emphasise its role in the planning, implementation and management of food production systems.

Objectives

This chapter is intended to support you in:

- Identifying types of menus and the classic menu sequence
- Planning menus
- Identifying key influences on menus
- Managing food production as an operating system
- Managing volume within food production systems
- Developing and managing the purchasing function
- Developing and applying operational control procedures.

5.1   Types of menus

Menus may be divided into two main classes, traditionally called *à la carte* (from the card) and *table d'hôte* (table of the host). The key difference between these two is that the à la carte menu has dishes separately priced, whereas the table d'hôte menu has an inclusive price either for the whole meal or for a specified number of courses, for example, any two or any four courses. There are, however, usually choices within each course.

All menus, no matter how simple or complex, are based on the two basic menu classes of table d'hôte or à la carte. Some menus also offer combinations of these two classes, with a number of menu items being offered together at a set price and other menu items being priced separately.

The term *menu du jour* (French) or *menu del dia* (Spanish) is sometimes used instead of the term *table d'hôte menu*. Another menu term used is *carte du jour* (literally 'card of the day'), or 'menu of the day', which can also be a fixed meal with one or more courses for a set price. A *prix fixe* (fixed price) menu is similar. A 'tasting menu' (*menu degustation*) is a set meal with a range of courses (often between six and ten). These tasting menus are offered in restaurants where the chef provides a sample of the range of dishes available on the main menu. These tasting menus can also be offered with a flight (selection) of wines – a different wine for each course., with the chef coming to the customer's table to explain the production of the dish. For all menus the price of the meal might also include wine or other drinks.

In addition to menus for main meals, such as luncheon or dinner, there are also requirements for other types of menu such as all day menus, floor/room service menus, lounge service menus, hospital tray service menus, airline tray service menus and rail service menus and event menus.

■   Classic menu sequence

At the end of the 19th century, France, and later other countries, had adopted the style of service known as *service à la russe*. In this system, the courses in a meal are served one after the other. Previously there had been a style of service known as *service à la française* where meals consisted of two courses, each made up of a variety of dishes, anything from 10 to 40 in number. The first set of dishes were placed on the table before the diners entered – hence the word *entrée* – and, when consumed, these dishes were removed or relieved by another set of dishes – hence the words *relevé* or 'removes' (see the classic menu sequence below).

Over the last 100 or so years the sequence of the European menu had taken on a classical format of dishes. This format is used to lay out menus as well as to indicate the order of the various courses. Although the number of courses on a menu, and dishes within each course, will depend on the size and class of the establishment, most follow the classic sequence. This is given in Table 5.1.

Table 5.1: Classic menu sequence

1 Hors-d'oeuvres	Traditionally consisted of a variety of compound salads but now includes such items as pâtés, mousses, fruit, charcuterie and smoked fish.
2 Soups (*potages*)	Includes all soups, both hot and cold.
3 Egg dishes (*oeufs*)	There are a great number of egg dishes beyond the usual omelettes, but these have not retained their popularity on modern menus.
4 Pasta and rice (*farineux*)	Includes all pasta and rice dishes. Can be referred to as farinaceous dishes.
5 Fish (*poisson*)	Consists of fish dishes, both hot and cold. Fish dishes such as smoked salmon or seafood cocktails are mainly considered to be hors-d'oeuvres dishes and therefore would be served earlier in a meal.
6 Entrée	Entrées are generally small, well garnished dishes which come from the kitchen ready for service. They are usually accompanied by a rich sauce or gravy. Potatoes and vegetables are not usually served with this course if it is to be followed by a main course. If this is the main meat course then it is usual for potatoes and vegetables to also be offered. Examples of this type of dish are tournedos, noisettes, sweetbreads, garnished cutlets or filled vol-au-vent cases. Today these are usually on the menu as a main course
7 Sorbet	Traditionally sorbets (sometimes now called *granites*) were served to give a pause within a meal, allowing the palate to be refreshed. They are lightly frozen water ices, often based on un-sweetened fruit juice, and may be served with a spirit, liqueur or even Champagne poured over.
8 Relevé	Refers to the main roasts or other larger joints of meat, which would be served together with potatoes and vegetables. These are usually now on the menu as a main course and in some restaurants may be presented on a trolley and carved at the table.
9 Roast (*rôti*)	Traditionally refers to roasted game or poultry dishes. Again today are usually on the menu as a main course and in some restaurants may be on a trolley carved at the table
10 Vegetables (*légumes*)	Apart from vegetables served with the Relevé or Roast courses, certain vegetables (e.g. asparagus and artichokes) may be served as a separate course, although these types of dishes are now more commonly served as starters.
11 Salad (*salade*)	Often refers to a small plate of salad that is taken after a main course (or courses) and is quite often simply a green salad and dressing.
12 Cold buffet (*buffet froid*)	Includes a variety of cold meats and fish, cheese and egg items together with a range of salads and dressings.
13 Cheese (*fromage*)	Includes the range of cheeses and various accompaniments, including biscuits, breads, celery, grapes and apples. This course can also refer to cheese-based dishes such as soufflés.
14 Sweets (*entremets*)	Refers to both hot and cold desserts.
15 Savoury (*savoureux*)	Sometimes simple savouries, such as Welsh rarebit or other items on toast, or in pastry, or savoury soufflés, may be served at this stage.
16 Fruit (*dessert*)	Fresh fruit, nuts and sometimes includes candied fruits.
17 Beverages	Includes a wide range of beverages, including: tea, coffee (in both standard and de-caffeinated versions) and a range of other beverages such as tisanes, chocolate, milk drinks (hot or cold), and proprietary drinks such as Bovril or Horlicks.

5

Although beverages are listed in Table 5.1 to indicate the sequence for meals, beverages are not counted as a course as such and therefore should not be included when the number of courses for a meal is stated. Thus if a meal is stated as having four courses, this means that there are four food courses and that the beverages at the end are an addition to these. Additionally although the sequence outlined in Table 5.1 shows the cheese course after the main course and before the sweet course, the sweet course is still sometimes offered before the cheese course.

The classic menu sequence outlined in Table 5.1 is based on a logical process of taste sensations. This classic sequence also provides the guide for the compilation of both à la carte and table d'hôte menus, as is evident in many examples of modern menus. The sequence is also used as a guide for the compilation and determination of the order of courses for event and special party menus.

However, a number of courses are often now grouped together. At its most simple this might comprise:

- Starters – courses 1 to 4
- Main courses – courses 5, 6 and 8 to 12
- Sides – potatoes and vegetables and salads
- Afters – courses 13 to 16
- Beverages.

The modern European classic menu sequence outlined above is derived from traditional European (mainly Franco-Russian, Swiss and English) cuisine and service influences. The menu structure and menu sequence can change considerably within the various world cuisines. Menu terms are culturally bound and as a consequence also vary, for instance in the USA a main course is commonly called an entrée and sweets are commonly called dessert. The term 'dessert' is also now becoming more commonly used to denote sweets generally.

Many Western modern cuisine terms are derived from the classic European cuisine. French terms are used as they can be internationally applied and understood. The use of French terms is primarily because it was in France that cuisine terms were codified through, for instance, the development and publication of the *Le Répertoire de la Cuisine* (first published in 1914; current English edition: Saulnier, 2003). This is much the same as the use of Italian terms for music (musical terms being codified in Italy), French terms in ballet (dance terms being codified in France) and English being the international language for aviation traffic control. However, all cuisines have terms which are specific to the region or country of origin.

Breakfast menus

There are two main forms for breakfast menus. These are:

- **Continental breakfast** – traditionally consisted of hot croissant, brioche or toast, butter and preserves and coffee as the beverage. Now this tends to include a wider variety of choice, including cereals, fruits, juices, yoghurts, ham, cheese, assorted bread items and a wider selection of beverages.

- **Full breakfast** – may consist of from two or more courses and usually includes a cooked main course. Full breakfast menus have changed to include a much more varied choice of items. Customers expect to see such items as fresh fruit juices, fresh fruit, yoghurt, muesli, continental pastries, homemade preserves, low fat spreads, decaffeinated coffee and mineral waters. There is also a trend toward including a range of international breakfast dishes.

Many operations offer a buffet breakfast service, sometimes called American Breakfast. Buffet breakfasts are often offered and priced at three levels:

1   Continental: Including juices, bread items and beverages.

2   Cold buffet: Including those items of continental breakfast plus a selection of cold items from the buffet.

3   Full breakfast: Full selection from the buffet including hot cooked items.

Afternoon tea menus

Afternoon tea is served in many establishments and in a variety of forms. Afternoon tea may be classified into two main types: Full afternoon tea (often now simply called afternoon tea) and high tea. The key difference between these two types is that a high tea includes items such items as grills, toasted snacks, hot and cold fish and meat dishes, salads, cold sweets and ice creams.

Other types of menus

In addition to traditional defined meal types, different menus are required to meet a variety of different customer needs. These can include:

- **Special party or function menus:** These are set menus for banquets or functions of all kinds. (For more information see Chapter 8, *Events, conferencing and banqueting*.)

- **National or speciality menus:** These can be both table d'hôte or à la carte menus specialising in the food (or religion) of the country or in a specialised food itself.

- **Hospital menus:** These usually take the form of a menu card given to the patient the day before service so that his or her preferences can be ticked. Both National Health Service and private hospitals cater for vegetarians and also for religious requirements. In many cases a dietician is involved in menu compilation to ensure nothing is given to the patients that would be detrimental to their health. Usually hospital meals are of two or three courses.

- **Menus for people at work:** These are menus that are served to people at their place of work in a range of cuisines and service styles. Such menus vary in standard and extent from one employer to another.

- **Menus for children:** These should emphasise healthy eating through a balanced diet. Those areas with children of various cultural and religious backgrounds should also have menus that reflect this cultural diversity.

- **Floor/room service menus:** floor or room service menu requirement varies from basic tea and coffee making facilities in the room, and possibly a mini-bar, to vending machines on floors, or the service of a variety of meals served in rooms.

- **Lounge service menus:** lounge service may include the service of continental breakfast, morning coffee, luncheon snacks, afternoon tea, dinner or late evening snacks as well as alcoholic beverages.

- **Airline tray service menus:** on many short-haul routes, only snack-type meals or sandwiches and beverages are offered. For some operators the provision of food and beverages is provided for an additional charge to the customer. On long-haul flights, airlines provide a more extensive service of food and beverages. The airline will provide dishes to meet its passengers' particular needs, for example, meals that meet a range of dietary requirements.

- **Rail service menus:** food service on trains is provided on the move and away from the home base and suppliers. The logistics of providing on-train food service are therefore similar in organisation to off-premises catering.

Regardless of what categorization style is used, it is important for the customer to be able to easily and readily navigate the menu. Confusing or illogically organised menus will only challenge customers in making the product selection, and could potentially affect sales.

5.2   Menu planning

Compiling of the menu is one of the food service operator's most important jobs, whether it is for establishments in the profit sector, or for those working to a budget, such as hospitals, schools or other similar institutions in the cost sector. The menu is a central management document that directs and controls the food service operation. It establishes what is going to be purchased, the cost, what staff and other resources are required to be deployed and the types of service needed. In addition, the beverage offer, the decor, atmosphere, theme or logo and service system, etc. all revolve around the provision of the menu.

In highly branded restaurant operations, menus are often centrally created to ensure brand consistency and quality. In certain styles of operations chefs work continuously to create a range of new, innovative and creative dishes. These chefs are at times developing ground-breaking recipe research using new ingredients and new technologies. and in some instances these restaurants and the food they produce can be referred to as the fashion 'cat walk' of the hospitality industry. The manager has at times to manage those chefs who create dishes which can be at time lead to 'chefs' ego trips', dishes which are not perhaps commercially viable – it can be a delicate balance, to harness the creativity while ensuring commercialisation. There is no shortage in the industry in recipe and product development, especially in reformulating recipes to produce product with less salt, sugar, saturated fat, with less calories.

A new recipe comes from an idea, it is then tested, validated and launched. Ideas and new recipes must be based on a business opportunity that has been identified with a clear customer benefit.

While there are trends to seek out new things to eat, new ways of eating and dining in different places and environments, products clearly have to be developed with the sector in mind. All products and recipes have to be tested. It is an advantage if you can ask a group of customers to try out the dishes, in order to get valuable feedback. Further alterations to the dish or recipe are often needed before you go live on the menu.

Developing a menu policy

When compiling the menu for an operation it is necessary to consider the creation of a menu policy that will govern the approach to the composition of the menu. This policy will determine the methods the operation will take to:

- Establishing the essential and social needs of the customer
- Accurately predicting what the customer is likely to buy and how much he or she is going to spend
- Ensuring a means of communication with customers
- Purchasing and preparing raw materials to preset standards in accordance with purchasing specifications and forecasted demand
- Portion and cost the product in order to keep within company profitability objectives
- Effectively control the complete operation from purchase to service on the plate.

Key influences on the menus

Menus are the result of a combination of a number of factors. Menu content, traditionally based on classic cuisine, is continually being influenced by changes in consumer requirements and taste.

Foods and beverages range from being considered as providing essential provisioning and nourishment though to meeting the needs of lifestyle, status and citizenship (Gillespie, 2001).

The gastronomy of any location is the result of a complex interplay between two key things. These are:

1 **Gastro-geography** – determines how foods (and beverages), cooking methods, customs and eating habits are, and have been, influenced by climate, soil, crops, history, tradition, psychology, commerce and peoples.

2 **Gastro-history-** determines the influences of the places surrounding a location, and also those beyond, with which the peoples have been, and are, involved.

Thus cuisine and eating habits and traditions of any area are a result of the physical location and the socio/cultural, economic, political, legal, ecological and technological influences, and the related developments which have taken place, and are continuing to take place.

A useful reference source a wide variety of cuisine information is *Larousse Gastronomic* (2009). For discussions on food and drink in cultural contexts see, for example, Sloan (2013)

The key influences affecting customer demand include:

- The relationship between health and eating
- Dietary requirements
- Cultural and religious influences
- Vegetarianism
- Prominent chefs and media
- Trends, fads and fashions.
- Ethical influences

Health and eating

The key issue in the relationship between health and eating is having a healthy diet. This means eating a balanced diet, rather than viewing individual foods as somehow less or more healthy. The use of the word 'food' here also refers to beverages.

Customers are also becoming increasingly interested in food hygiene and food safety generally. There are also particular reactions to developments in food technology such as irradiation and genetically modified food commodities and how these technologies are being used. Some customers are seeking to avoid these foods and some operations are already using the avoidance of these as a marketing feature. Additionally the use of organic foods is often being promoted as naturally produced foods.

Dietary requirements

Customers may require a certain diet for a variety of medical reasons, including the prevention of allergic reactions. Such customers will need to know about the ingredients used in a dish as eating certain things may make them very ill and may even be fatal.

Although customers with dietary needs usually know what they can and cannot eat, it is important that when asked, for a server to able to accurately describe the dishes so that the customer can make the appropriate choice. The server should never guess and if in doubt, should seek further information from a supervisor/manager/chef. Some establishments that provide foods for vulnerable groups, such as young children, completely remove certain allergenic foods, like nuts, from their menus.

Allergens

It is a legal requirement for food businesses to provide information on 14 specified allergenic ingredients. This information can be provided in writing and/or orally. If information is provided orally, the food business needs to ensure that there is some form of written signage that is clearly visible, to indicate that allergen information is available from a member of staff. Systems should also be in place to ensure that, if requested, the information given orally is supported in a recorded form (in writing for example) to ensure consistency and accuracy. Many operations use matrix charts with allergens across the top and menu dishes down the side. The prevention of allergic reactions now has a similar legal status as food safety and the prevention of food poisoning. Measures taken to provide information about allergens and also measures in place to prevent cross-contamination of non-allergenic foods with allergens must now form part of the HACCP plan and be part of due diligence. Authorised officers now have similar powers to take action against breaches in the legislation as they have with other food safety non-compliance. More information on allergens can be obtained from the Food Standard Agency at www.food.gov.uk.

Food intolerances

Food intolerance is different from an allergy because it does not involve the immune system. Nevertheless, the symptoms can be significant in terms of causing illness, reactions and discomfort. Food intolerance is much more common than food allergies. The symptoms may take longer to develop – for example, gluten intolerance (coeliac disease) or lactose intolerance.

Cultural and religious dietary influences

Various faiths have differing requirements with regard to the dishes/ingredients that may be consumed, and these requirements often also cover preparation methods, cooking procedures and the equipment used.

Vegetarianism

Vegetarianism may derive from cultural, religious, moral or physiological considerations. There are also various forms of vegetarianism, which will affect the food that are eaten by difference customers. As always the customer is always the best person to check with if there is any doubt.

Prominent chefs and media

In recent years menu content has been greatly influenced by prominent chefs such as: Heston Blumenthal, Hélène Darroze, Angela Hartnett, James Martin, Anton Mosimann, Jamie Oliver, Gordon Ramsey, the Roux brothers and Michel Roux, to name but a few. There is also huge influence from the media generally, including social media, together with chef and cookery programmes.

Trends, fads and fashions

Like any other product, cuisine and menus are subject to trends, fads and fashions. These include things that appear, are widely adopted, and just as quickly disappear. Examples of these include: everything with a coulis; kiwi fruit, food being set on a bed of smears of various ingredients; foams; a rösti of potato or various other ingredients; shaved vegetables; everything with a jus (juice or gravy); roasted vegetables and food being served on a variety of non-traditional materials, such as slate or wood .

Cuisine trends included *nouvelle cuisine*, which in the 1970s initiated a new movement in terms of understanding of food and its ingredients from cuisine classic. From this other food production styles have since developed; for example, eclectic cuisine, fusion cookery and molecular gastronomy (Graham 2006).

Trends include the established range of technical innovations such as: cook-chill; cook-freeze, sous *vide*, and induction hobs as well as the introduction to the use of new equipment such as centrifuge machines, Pacojets, dehydrators, thermomixers and smoking machines, and the use of ingredients such as gums, alginates stabilisers, emulsifiers, and modified starches.

A clear distinction can also be drawn between culinary innovation, which leads to long lasting influence and adoption, and culinary fashion. *Nouvelle cuisine* was certainly a cuisine innovation. Its development and adoption was characterised by four key elements: initiation by established chefs; understanding and application of the broad range of sciences and technology; support and promotion from knowledgeable media; and taking a long time to become fully established. Using the same four factors, *slow food* (see page 142) can be identified as a trend but most fusion cuisines can be identified as fads (with the exception of those centred on one gastronomic tradition, such as Indian or French). Additionally, there are also developments in cuisine that are yet to be identified as either a trend or a fad. For example, *molecular gastronomy* was the name given to a series of international workshops on the physical and chemical aspects of cooking. The term had since become associated (although not originally intended to be) with a possible culinary movement. Eventually at best it may be seen to be an underpinning of genuine gastronomic development, or at worst a detour into showy gastronomic alchemy. (Cousins *et al.*, 2010)

Activity:

■ From the trade press identify four possible development in cuisine

■ For each other these determine whether they can be considered as a passing fashion or have the potential to be a lasting culinary trend.

Ethical considerations

Customers have become increasingly aware of ethical issues, such as:

- Ensuring sustainability of foods consumed
- Fair trade
- The acceptability or otherwise of genetically modified foods or irradiated foods
- Reducing food packaging and food waste, and
- Reducing the effects that food production and food transportation have on the environment generally.

The food that we eat, and how we eat it, is socially bound with the norms of our society. What is acceptable in the production of food for one consumer and the manner which it is produced, may be deemed unacceptable by others. Ethical sourcing of food for foodservice operations depends on the nature of the establishment and the power of the consumer demand. For some consumers, price matters and the production of food such as chicken in highly industrialised surrounds is deemed to be acceptable. Yet for others, high value food commodities used in some gourmet restaurants have products such as *foie gras*, which is a premium price and deemed to be ethically acceptable by some and not by others. The ethics of the food which we eat crosses social and cultural boundaries, and it is challenging to qualify a uniform position.

5

Activity:

- Research the food commodities foie gras, veal, caviar (and the corresponding sustainable equivalent)
- What is your view of the product production processes?
- As a caterer would you serve them as part of your Corporate Social Responsibility policy?
- To what extent do your own cultural and social values affect your views?

There is also a greater trend towards using more seasonal and locally sourced food and beverage items. Apart from ethical issues the quality, taste, freshness and nutritional value are all at their peak, and supplies are more plentiful and cheaper.

For food service businesses, the benefits can also include:

- Improved menu planning, as suppliers can give information in advance on what they are able to provide
- More reliable products and service, with greater flexibility to respond to customer needs

- Increased marketing opportunities through making a feature of using locally sourced food and beverage items and through special promotions related to local seasons and food and beverage specialities, and

- Support for training of staff from local suppliers.

Food provenance is also increasingly important to customers. Customers are now far more more interested in where and how food is grown, raised or reared, processed and transported. This has resulted in more interested in:

- Greater availability of fresh foods (as opposed to processed foods)

- Certified foods such as Red Tractor and RSPCA Assured (formally Freedom Foods) which guarantee food safety and higher standards of environmental performance and animal welfare.

Promoting local food and traditional regional cuisine is the Slow Food movement. Its goals of sustainable foods and promotion of local small businesses are also associated with a political agenda against globalization of agricultural products. It also seeks to raise strategic awareness about sustainability and social justice issues surrounding food and farming.

Examples of sources for more information are:

- Cert ID: www.cert.id.com

- Department for Environment, Food & Rural Affairs: www.defra.gov.uk

- Ethical Consumer: www.ethicalconsumer.org

- Fair Trade Foundation: www.fairtrade.org.uk

- Free Trade Agency: www.freetradeagency.co.uk

- Heart Foundation: www.bhf.org.uk

- Red Tractor: www.redtractor.org.uk

- RSPCA Assured: www.rspcaassured.org.uk

- Slow food Organisation: www.slowfood.org.uk

- Soil Association: www.soilassociation.org

- Vegetarian Society: www.vegsoc.org

Activity:

- Briefly describe what is meant by food provenance.

- Identify the key menu features you would propose for a restaurant of your choice, which intends to market itself as promoting local produce.

Essential considerations in menu planning

Prior to compiling menus there are a number of essential considerations. In addition to the key influences on menus, already identified above, they include:

- **Location of an establishment:** This location should allow easy access to both customers and suppliers as and when required. A difficult journey can be off-putting no matter how good the quality of food on offer and can affect repeat business and profitability. If the establishment is in an area noted for regional speciality foods or dishes, the inclusion of a selection of these on the menu can give extra menu appeal.

- **Competition in the locality:** It is important to be aware of what is offered by competitors, including their prices and particularly their quality. Knowing this information enables an establishment to make decision about how to compete with local competition.

- **Suitability of a particular establishment to a particular area:** A self-service restaurant situated in an affluent residential district, or a very expensive seafood restaurant in a rundown inner-city area may not be very successful. Anticipating and analysing the nature of demand that the operation is planning to appeal to will contribute to ensuring that the menu will be developed to satisfy, for example, office workers in the city, with a fast lunch service. Also opportunities may exist for outdoor catering.

- **Spending power of the customer:** A most important consideration is how much the potential customer is able and willing to pay. (Pricing methods were also considered in more detail in Chapter 3, page 59).

- **Customer requirements:** It is the customer not the food service operator who selects his or her menu, so the analysis of dish popularity is necessary and those dishes that are not popular should not stay on the menu. Customer demand must be considered and traditional dishes and modern trends in food fashions need to be taken into account.

- **Number of items and price range of menus:** It is essential to determine the range of dishes and whether table d'hôte or à la carte types of menus are to be offered. Decisions regarding the range of prices have to be made. A table d'hôte menu may be considered with an extra charge or supplement for more expensive dishes, or more than one table d'hôte menu of different prices may be more suitable.

- **Throughput:** If space is limited, or there are many customers (and control of the time the customer occupies the seat is needed) then the menu can be adjusted to increase turnover, e.g. more self-service items or quick preparation items, or separate service for beverages.

- **Space and equipment in the kitchen:** Both of these will influence the composition of the menu and production of dishes. The menu writer must be aware of any shortcomings or deficiencies in equipment and may be wary of offering dishes that are difficult to produce. Also, certain items of equipment should

5

not be overloaded by the menu requirements, e.g. salamanders, steamers, fritures (deep fat fryers).

- **Amount, availability and capability of labour:** The availability and capability of both the preparation and service staff must be considered when planning a menu. Enough able and willing staff, both in the kitchen and the restaurant, are necessary to achieve customer satisfaction with any menu.

- **Supplies and storage**: Menu planning is dependent on availability of supplies, that is, frequency of deliveries of the required amounts. Storage space and seasonal availability of foods need to be taken into account when planning menus.

- **Cost factor:** When an establishment is run for profit the menu is a crucial consideration; but, even when working to a budget, the menu is no less crucial. Costing is the crux of the success of compiling any menu.

- **Nutritional information:** there are various initiatives to encourage people to be aware of the relationship between health and diet and also to address the problems associated with obesity. These initiatives include providing the nutritional content information on menus.

■ Menu construction

Menus can be constructed daily or pre-planned and predesigned for a specific period. Menus can also be constructed to be continuously repeated, called cyclical menus.

Daily menus

These are menus that are constructed for the day and often are offered alongside an la carte menu. They can range from a single food dish of the day thorough to a multi-course menu as a complete set menu, or with selections under each course (table d'hôte menu).

Advantages:

- Uses availability of foods on the day
- Can incorporate dishes made up from foods with shorter shelf life or from foods left over which need to be sold off.
- Provides opportunity to offer special deals.
- Can allow for chef creativity and/or to try out new recipes.

Disadvantages:

- Relies on the ability of the chef.
- May not prove popular and thus create waste
- May cause disruption in the kitchen in using untried recipes.

Pre-planned and predesigned menus

These are often found in for instance function and event operations. Before selecting dishes the food service operator is able to consider what the customer likes and the effect of these dishes upon the meal as a whole.

Advantages:

- Menu construction can be well balanced in terms of texture, colour ingredients, temperature and structure
- Event managers can quote prices instantly to a customer.
- Availability of kitchen and service equipment and the capability of the service staff is already taken into account.
- Quality of food is likely to be higher if kitchen staff are preparing dishes that they are familiar with and have prepared a number of times before.

Disadvantages:

- Pre-planned and predesigned menus may be too limited to appeal to a wide range of customers.
- Job satisfaction for staff who have to prepare and serve the same menu repetitively.

Cyclical menus

These are menus that are compiled to cover a given period of time, i.e. one month or three months. They consist of a number of set menus for a particular operation. At the end of each period the menus can be used over again, thus limiting the need to keep compiling new ones.

Advantages of cyclical menus

- They save time by removing the daily or weekly task of compiling menus, although they may require slight alterations for the next period.
- They can cut down on the number of commodities held in stock and can assist in planning storage requirements.

Disadvantages

- Regular customers can get bored with the repetition of dishes.
- Limits taking advantage of good buys offered by suppliers on a daily or weekly basis.

Menu content and design

Apart from the traditional book-style, menus are now presented in a wide variety of ways. These include:

- Single laminated cards.
- Fold out cards with inserts from the size A5 and above.
- iPads and other forms of tablets (which can also allow customers explore the ingredients comprising the dishes and the drinks).

- Chalk boards / white boards.
- Printed signs, sometimes illuminated from behind.
- Projections onto table tops.

Design considerations of the menu include:

- Size and shape.
- Artwork/colour.
- Ease of handling.
- Logical flow of information.

Menus should include:

- Clear and accurate description of the dishes.
- Clear indication of pricing, including whether a service, or any other charge, is included or not.
- Dietary information, such as identifying low fat dishes, providing details on allergen content, as well as offering to cook foods plainly.
- Items or groups of items should bear names customers recognise and understand. If a name does not give the right connotation, additional descriptive copy may be necessary.

Use the menu strategically

The menu is a strategic marketing tool. Good design shows dedication and professionalism, and can positively impact the restaurant's bottom line. As menu development and the application of retailing principles to the menu (Lashley, 2009) have become common, the emphasis on the menu mix and the positioning of dishes, along with the description and in some cases an image, has become highly sophisticated. The approach of linking dish positioning, the movement of the customer's eye across the menu (see below) and increasing profitability through upselling, has been collectively termed *menu engineering* or *menu psychology* (see Menu engineering, Chapter 9 page 287).

When designing the menu consider:

- How much to invest.
- Layout and design.
- The competition, to analyse what is good about them and what is less attractive.
- How menu items and prices of the competition compare.
- The neighbourhood.
- What the restaurant can offer that other restaurants cannot.

Examples of how to enhance the selling properties of menu include:

- Making sure that the look and feel of the menu is in harmony with the overall design of the restaurant. A menu must be designed intelligently as an important part of the brand. It must reflect the restaurant's personality, showcasing the top dishes and excite the customers while helping to increase the profitability

- Highlighting customer's favourites with boxes, colours, and photos to draw attention to them.

- Placing the more profitable dishes in first and last position on the menu. People are more likely to remember the first and last items they see on the list.

- Keeping prices in the body of the description paragraph and remove the currency sign to avoid drawing attention to them.

- Evaluating the restaurant every six to twelve months and ensure changes are made to anything that may be affecting the success of the restaurant.

Eye gaze motion theory

Western studies (Miller and Pavesic 1996; Pavesic, 1999; Panitz, 2000; Yang, 2012) have identified that, culturally, menus are read in very similar manner, starting with the centre of the menu and then move to the upper right corner, upper left corner, bottom left corner, bottom right corner, then back to first eye focus, as depicted in Figure 5.1.

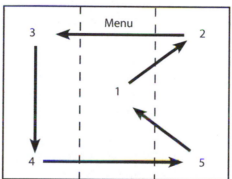

Figure 5.1: Eye gaze motion of a three-fold menu

The gaze model was introduced by Livingston (1978) who identified the key positions of the menu where customers generally focus their attention and view the most. This work was further extended by Panitz (2000). Further studies implied that the menu viewers read the menus as reading a book, from top to bottom and left to right. Generally, the principle still holds true and restaurateurs place higher-profit items in position one, often, with boxes and highlights (Yang, 2012).

Further work on cultural norms identified that Asian cultures (Choi, Lee, & Mok, 2010) gaze at the left-hand side rather than the right side and this represent the manner in which they have been taught to read, and more recently work has been undertaken on single, double and triple panel menus all with different results. The same principles of product layout and customers' selection of product have been applied to the layout of the back-bar products, shopping shelves displays and more recently a study of online menus and customer selection of the restaurant (McCarthy, Sasse, & Riegelsberger, 2004).

Activity:

■ Watch a friend read or flick through a magazine – note which side they read first.

■ Ask them why they read the magazine in the way they did.

■ Next time you dine out with friends observe their eye gaze on the menu.

Menu descriptions

A good description describes the dish accurately and succinctly. Most importantly, good descriptions need to tempt the customer, be vivid and appetising. So many restaurants simply do not get this right.

The description of the dish must include more than the ingredients. It needs to express the feelings that you want customers to experience, while listing any well-known brand name ingredients that may be included, with the indication that it is a registered brand name ®. Relevant terminology should be used, and geographical locations bring colour and conjure up well known associations. Descriptions must not be too long – say what needs to be said to set the menu item apart.

Menu copy should be set in a style of print that is easily readable and well-spaced. Mixing typefaces is often done to achieve emphasis; if overdone the overall concept is likely to look a mess and therefore unattractive to the eye. There are also simple ways to emphasise certain dishes, for example:

■ Draw a box around a group of items

■ Use typography that is different but easy to read

■ Use different colours or shading

■ Add a drawing around the items

■ Place an asterisk beside the item

Carefully devised descriptions can help to promote the individual dish, the menu generally and in turn the establishment. However, descriptions should describe the item realistically and not mislead the customer, as this has legal implications. Care should be taken therefore in the use of terms such as 'fresh', 'British' or 'organic', etc. and also cooking terms such as 'fried', 'roasted', etc. The description should always be a true one. For example, using the term 'home-made' indicates that the dish has been made at the premises; in the case of the term 'organic' it is only the food items that can be described as organic.

The use of icons or symbols to indicate the presence of allergens is permitted, as long as it is accompanied by words and numbers to ensure a uniform consumer understanding and to avoid misleading the consumer.

Food photography

All photographs need to remain consistent in style and presentation, otherwise they may appear inappropriate and negatively affect the feel of the menu. The image, once placed on the menu, then becomes the visual aid to represent the dish and if it is not presented in the same manner constitutes disappointment for the customer and potentially a breach of contract.

Food photography must be done professionally otherwise it can do more harm than good. If it cannot be done professionally it is best to not do it at all.

Prices and currency placement

Consider carefully where to put the actual prices. If prices appear in a column running alongside of the menu, customers may be inclined to compare items based solely on price and choose the cheapest item. This can be avoided by placing the price in the same line as the food and description. Another approach is to leave out the currency symbols, as you are allowing the customers to forget for a short while they are spending money, and in turn potentially spend more.

Mistakes in approaches to menu copy can include:

- Misalignment of brand and menu
- Descriptive copy is left out when it is required.
- Emphasis is lost because print size and style are not correctly used.
- Spelling errors
- Misused cuisine terms
- Listed meals which are not always available
- Missing translations for non-local language words or phrases
- Photos that do not reflect the actual food to be served
- Use of generic clip art

Being able to write interesting descriptive copy is a skill; a good menu designer is able to illuminate menu terms or specific culinary terms and in doing so is able to draw attention to them. Simplicity in menu copy enhances the communication process and enables better understanding. Always check the spelling and the descriptions, and if using words from other languages have a policy on accents: either none or all.

Some menus can be built around a general descriptive copy featuring the history of the establishment, or around the local area in which it is situated. Descriptive copy can alternatively be based on a speciality dish, which has significant cultural importance to the area or the establishment. In so doing, the description may to feature the person responsible for creating and preparing the dish, especially if the chef is reasonably well known and has appeared on national or local television or radio. The chef may have also had his/her recipes featured in the local press. This too may be included in the menu to create further interest.

5.3   Food production systems

A food production system has to be organised to produce the right quantity of food at the correct standard, for the required number of people, on time, using the resources of staff, equipment and materials effectively and efficiently.

As costs of space, equipment, fuel, maintenance and labour continue to rise, more thought and time have to be given to the planning of a production system and to kitchen design. Research is often lacking in this area of the food service industry, although research from equipment manufacturers concentrating on new technology is increasing.

The requirements of the production system have to be clearly matched to the type of food that is to be prepared, cooked and served, to the required market, and at the correct price. All allocation of space and the purchase of the different types of equipment have to be justified, and the organisation of the kitchen personnel also has to be planned at the same time.

Kitchen organisation

Escoffier is considered to be the founder of modern professional cookery and kitchen management. In 1902 he published *Le Guide Culinaire* (revised edition 2011). This brought together and codified the culinary traditions of the day and also set out the principles of kitchen management. For maximum efficiency, Escoffier organised the kitchen into a strict hierarchy. At the top is the executive chef, or *chef de cuisine*, who sets standards, manages costs, and directs kitchen work and training. The *sous chef* (or assistant head chef) oversees the food is preparation and presentation. Subordinate chefs are known as *chefs de partie*, and are each in charge of a kitchen section, assisted by *demi-chefs* and *commis* (apprentices). The number of section chefs depends on the size of the kitchen production. This includes *saucier* (sauces), *poissionier* (fish), *grillardin* (grilled items), *fritteurier* (fried items), *rotissier* (roasts), *garde manger* (cold food – sometime now called larder chef), *patissier* (pastries), and *chef tournant* (section relief chef). Initially the hierarchy of the kitchen brigade was widely adopted. Escoffier's division of labour system was introduced at a time when labour was cheap, skilled and plentiful and when menus were elaborate and labour intensive, and the kitchen a hidden world of work disengaged from the restaurant. Today labour and skills are in short supply, so many operations have been rationalised and redesigned to become more efficient and to deliver a more modern approach, together with encompassing different cooking styles and techniques.

Most food production operations now adopt a more simplified variation of Escoffier's kitchen brigade. The 'partie' system has also been developed further with many food production operations being based on the process approach, as opposed to the 'partie' (product approach) system. The process approach concentrates on the specific techniques and processes of food production. The system places importance on the identification of these common techniques and processes across the full range of required dishes. In developing the production system, groupings are not then based on the types of dishes or foods, which is the basis of the 'partie' system, but on the clustering of similar production techniques and processes which apply a range of common skills and encourage flexibility. Kitchens are becoming more streamlined, with reduced staffing, employing a greater level of technology to reduce labour costs and help to replace skill shortages.

Open kitchens and the chef's table

In line with the changing nature of food production systems and the growth in the interest of food, the kitchen vista has been transformed from the closed kitchen unseen by the customer. The new world of the open kitchen, where the chef and the kitchen space can be observed by the customer, creates a service vista which forms part of the innovative servicescape (Bitner, 1992 and Rosenbaum and Massiah, 2011). A restaurant offer that is designed to enhance the customer's sensory evaluation of the dining experience with the visual effects of watching the chef at work. Some operators have extended this further and developed the chef's table; a dining opportunity were the 'restaurant' table is actually located in the kitchen, often surrounding the customer in a glass 'cocoon' or 'table bubble'. These operations provide a unique experience for the customer as they observe the food being prepared, cooked and then served by the chef in conjunction with the waiting staff. The restaurant/kitchen design principles of this form of operation, has had a calming effect on the behaviour of the kitchen staff. As the old world of the aggressive macho-kitchen is positively dismantled, this kitchen re-orientation has also had the positive effect of attracting a higher proportion of female chefs.

The format of the restaurant with the open kitchen adds design of the concept, and by default, created the chef as an emotional and aesthetic labourer (Graham, 2015). The open kitchen work has added the dimension of employing staff who are"looking good, and sounding right" (Warhurst & Nickson, 2001; Williams & Connell, 2010) and how the physical traits of the individual are now commodified by the organisation to represent the values of the restaurant brand.

Food production systems

Food production is an operating system and can be managed through the application of the systems approach. A whole range of different cuisines fit neatly into this approach, because the key elements focus on the process, the way the food is prepared, processed (cooked) stored and served. Using this approach, food production systems may be identified using the input/process/output model of systems and the basic processes may be illustrated as in Figure 5.2.

Foods in	Storage	Preparation	Cooking	Holding	Regeneration	Presentation
Fresh	Ambient	Weigh/measure	Blanch	Chill	Regithermic	Bain-marie
Fresh cooked	Cool	Clear/open	Warm	Vacuum	Microwave	Service flats
Fresh prepared	Refrigerated	Chop/cut	Simmer	Freeze	Convection	Plates
Canned	Deep frozen	Combine/mix	Boil	Tray	Traditional	Bowls
Frozen	Dry store	Blend	Steam	Hot cupboard		Trays
Chilled		Shape/coat	Grill	Cold cupboard		Vending
Vacuum		Form	Sauté	Insulate		Buffet
Dehydrated			Brown	Ambient		Counter
Smoked			Bake			Trolley
Salted			Roast			Food dishes
Crystallised			Broil			Timbale
Acidified			Fry			
Pasteurised			Microwave			
Bottled			Water bath			
UHT						

Foods in ⟶ ——————————————— **Process** ——————————————→ **Foods out**

Figure 5.2: Input output process model for food production

Source: developed from the original work of Cousins and Foskett, 1989

The identification of the seven stages of food production in Figure 5.1 shows the types of **foods in,** the **processes** and the **foods out** or presentation stages. Using this approach a generic model of food production can be developed and this is shown in Figure 5.3.

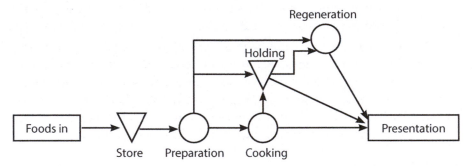

Figure 5.3: Generic model of the food production system

Source: based on the original by Cousins and Foskett, 1989

Developing this approach further nine standard food production methods can be identified and these are summarised Table 5.2. In practice food service operations often combine a number of these food production methods.

Table 5.2: Food production methods

Method	Description
Conventional	Term used to describe production utilising mainly fresh foods and traditional cooking methods
Convenience	Method of production utilising mainly convenience foods
Call order	Method where food is cooked to order either from customer (as in cafeterias) or from waiter. Production area is often open to customer area
Continuous flow	Method involving production line approach where different parts of the production process may be separated (e.g. fast food)
Centralised	Production not directly linked to service. Foods are 'held' and distributed to separate service areas
Cook-chill	Food production storage and regeneration method utilising principle of low temperature control to preserve qualities of processed foods
Cook-freeze	Production, storage and regeneration method utilising principle of freezing to control and preserve qualities of processed foods. Requires special processes to assist freezing
Sous vide	Method of production, storage and regeneration utilising principle of sealed vacuum to control and preserve the quality of processed foods
Assembly kitchen	A system based on accepting and incorporating the latest technological development in manufacturing and conservation of food products

5

■ Centralised production

Centralised production systems involve having a central food production kitchen where the bulk of foods are prepared, held and packaged and then transported to finishing kitchens where the final meals are produced ready for service. This can be in a single large-scale operation servicing various out-stations within the complex, or a separate food production facility proving food for a range of outlying operations, some distance away. The production is decoupled from the service kitchen and can be defined as an 'interrupted' catering system. The distance between the central kitchen and the satellite, or finishing kitchens, can vary. It can be localised in the case of a large conference hotel with multiple outlets, to that of a food manufacturer producing food (sometimes outsourced to a third party) for a large number of finishing kitchens, as for example in the case of brand restaurant operators. This can also apply to catering, where foods for inflight meals are created in central production kitchens and then transported to the aircraft for regeneration and finished on the aircraft.

■ Finishing kitchens

Finishing kitchens can consist of purpose-built regeneration equipment plus refrigerated storage. Additional equipment, such as a deep fat fryer for chips, boiling table for sauces and custards and pressure steamer for vegetables and so on can be added if required to give greater flexibility.

Where chilled food is produced to supply a service on the same premises, it is recommended that the meals should be supplied, stored and regenerated by exactly the same method as used for operations where the production unit and finishing kitchens are separated by some distance. Failure to adhere to just one procedure could result in disorganised production and reduce productivity. Once a decision is taken to sever production from service, this method should be followed throughout the system.

Considerations for adopting a centralised production system are based on:

- **Labour cost** – using staff more effectively and efficiently
- **Food costs** – greater control over wastage and portion sizes, linked to standardised recipes and standardised purchasing specifications
- **Equipment** – more use of technology.

The centralised system also relies on a range of technology for holding food for transportation. These include cook-chill, cook freeze, *sous vide,* Microsteam and water bath cookery, which are discussed in more detail below.

■ Cook-chill system

Cook-chill is a food service system based on the normal preparation and cooking of food followed by rapid chilling, storage in controlled low temperature conditions above freezing point, 0–3ºC and subsequently reheating immediately before consumption. The chilled food is regenerated in finishing kitchens, which require relatively low capital investment and minimum staff.

■ Cook-freeze system

Cook-freeze uses a production system similar to that used in cook-chill. However, the recipes have to be modified; enabling products to be freezer-stable and modified starches are used in sauces so that on reheating and regeneration the sauce does not separate. Blast freezers are used in place of blast chillers.

Overall benefits of cook-chill and cook-freeze

For the operation

- Good portion control and reduced waste
- Central purchasing – bulk-buying discounts
- Full utilisation of equipment and staff time
- Simplified delivery to units – less frequent
- No need to move hot food (EC regulations forbid the movement of hot foods unless the temperature is maintained over 65ºC (149ºF). Maintaining 65ºC is regarded as very difficult to achieve and high temperatures inevitably will be harmful to foods.)

For the customer

- Increased variety and selection
- Improved quality and maintained standards
- More nutritious foods
- Services can be maintained at all times, regardless of staff absences
- Smaller-capacity storage is required: 3–4 days' supply as opposed to up to 120 days
- Cooking techniques are unaltered (additives and revised recipes are needed for freezing)
- All foods can be chilled so the range of dishes is wider (some foods cannot be frozen). Cooked eggs, steaks and sauces such as hollandaise can be chilled (after some recipe modification where necessary)
- No system is too small to adapt to cook-chill.

Sous vide

Sous vide is a form of cook-chill: a combination of vacuum sealing in plastic pouches, cooking by steam and then rapidly cooling and chilling. The objective is to rationalise kitchen procedures without having a detrimental effect on the quality of individual dishes. Potential users are brasseries, wine bars, airlines, private hospitals and function food service operators seeking to provide top quality with portion convenience.

The advantages of the sous vide process

- Long shelf-life, up to 21 days if refrigerated
- Ability to produce meals in advance means better deployment of staff and skills
- Vacuum-packed foods can be mixed in cold store without the risk of cross-contamination
- Reduces labour costs at point of service
- Beneficial cooking effects on certain foods, especially moulded items and pates. Reduced weight loss on meat joints.
- Full flavour and texture are retained as food cooks in its own juices
- Economises on ingredients (less butter, marinade)
- Makes pre-cooking a possibility for à la carte menus
- Inexpensive regeneration
- Allows a small operation to set up bulk production
- Facilitates portion control and uniformity of standards
- Has a tenderising effect on tougher cuts of meat and matures game without dehydration.

Its disadvantages

- Extra cost of vacuum pouches and vacuum packing machine
- Unsuitable for some meats (for example, fillet steak) and vegetables which absorb colour
- All portions in a batch must be identically sized to ensure even results
- Most dishes require twice the conventional cooking time
- Unsuitable for large joints as chilling time exceeds 90 minutes
- Complete meals (for example, meat and two vegetables) not feasible – the meat component needs to be cooked and stored in separate bags
- Extremely tight management and hygiene controls are imperative
- Potentially adverse customer reaction (boil in the bag syndrome).

Microsteam technology

Used in food production for hospitals and schools, microsteam is a fast, healthy cooking system, which maintains the freshness of food using steam cooking. It enables nutritious meals to be available in minutes without the need for full kitchen back up. The vacuum-packed polymer packaging allows cooking to near perfection, resulting in maximum flavour and minimal nutritional loss.

The most important point about microsteaming is that it is not about reheating pre-cooked, but is about cooking the freshest ingredients from raw. The microsteam system is space saving.

Water bath cookery

Many chefs have adopted a technique of vacuum packing ingredients and cooking them at low temperatures in a water bath. This is a slow and gentle process. Moisture is not expelled and flavour is retained. Some meat is cooked from 6 to 46 hours at temperatures of 55–68°C.

Caution must be taken as this is not a *sous vide* system and environmental health officers like a minimum core temperature of 65°C for red meats and 80°C for poultry. Howeverm some harmful bacteria will survive or even grow at 50°C. It is strongly advised that if chefs use this system, there should be a regular system of food safety and analysis to establish the type of microbiological count.

Activity:

- Identify four examples of how the innovation in modern equipment has influenced menu design and culinary research in the last 5 years.

- Speculate on how innovation in modern equipment might continue to influence restaurant menu design in the future.

5.4   Volume in food production

The food production process may be seen in the general model for food production as was shown in Figure 5.3, page 152. That model identifies seven stages in the general food production process. These are:

1 Foods in

2 Storage

3 Preparation

4 Cooking

5 Holding

6 Regeneration

7 Presentation.

Each of these stages has an effect on the potential volume of the operation, and differing operations will route foods in different ways. The generic process was identified in Figure 5.3. This model can be adapted for all of the nine production processes identified in Table 5.2, page 153. For instance, a fast food process will flow from **foods in** to **store** to **preparation** or **cooking**, then to **holding** then to **presentation**. A cook-chill process will flow from **foods in** to **store** to **preparation** to **holding** or **cooking** then to **holding**, then to **regeneration** and then to **presentation**. However, for any food production system, it is difficult to determine the key process that limits the potential volume (Cousins, 1994), as each of the stages has a separate effect on the volume of food that is able to be processed at any time. The effects of each of the seven stages on volume of production are as follows:

1   Foods in

The availability of food and the frequency of delivery clearly have an impact on the maximum food volume of the operation. Greater and more frequent delivery opportunities increase the potential volume. In addition the variety of foods being bought, either in terms of food type or supplier source, will also affect food volume that can be processed.

2   Storage

The storage space and type of storage available determine the type of food that can be bought and the quantities that can be available at a given time. Capacity can be increased by altering the nature of foods being bought, for instance from fresh to convenience, and/or by increasing the delivery frequency.

3   Preparation

The extent to which food has to be prepared also impacts on volume. High preparation requirements increase the space and the layout required. This stage can be greatly affected by increasing the use of ready prepared foods and by the use of equipment for bulk preparation activities.

4 Cooking

The availability of cooking space and the time cooking takes can limit volume. Again this can be affected by variations in the needs for cooking and the type of cooking required. In addition the type of equipment used for the cooking processes can be altered to increase the volume of cooking that can be done at a given time.

5 Holding

Food volume is limited by the type and availability of holding space. Variations in the need for holding, in a given operation, can vary the potential food volume that can be processed.

6 Regeneration

This stage has similar characteristics to holding. However, the regeneration potential may not equal the full holding potential. High demand may exceed the ability of the operation to regenerate the volume of food required quickly enough.

7 Presentation

The food volume that can be handled at this stage is mostly determined by the speed of the service process. This assumes that a critical path analysis approach has been used to ensure that the full range of foods required at a given time is available at the same time.

Overall the need to meet the demands of the presentation stage is determined by the expected volume of business at a given time. Each of the previous stages, through the application of careful critical path analysis approaches, should be able to be planned and operated to meet the presentation demand.

5.5 Purchasing

Once a menu is planned, a number of activities must occur to bring it into reality. One of the first and most important stages is to purchase the food (also referred to as provisioning, or more often, procurement) and other items; and to receive the materials needed to produce the menu items. Skilful purchasing with good receiving procedures can do much to maximise the results of good menu planning. Six important steps must occur if purchasing and receiving functions are to be successful:

1 Know the market
2 Determine purchasing needs
3 Establish and use specifications
4 Design the purchase procedures
5 Ensure accurate receiving
6 Evaluate the purchasing task.

A market is a place in which ownership of commodity changes from one person to another. This could occur using the telephone, on a street corner, in a retail or wholesale establishment or at an auction. Since markets vary considerably, to do a good job of purchasing a buyer must know the characteristics of each market.

It is important also that the purchaser for a food service operation has knowledge of the items to be purchased. For example:

- Where they are grown
- Seasons of production
- Approximate costs
- Conditions of supply and demand
- Laws and regulations governing the market and the products
- Marketing agents and their services
- Processing
- Storage requirements
- Commodity and product, class and grade.

■ Classification of markets

The primary market

Raw materials may be purchased at the source of supply, the grower, producer or manufacturer or from central markets such as Smithfield, Covent Garden, or Nine Elms in London. Some establishments or large organisations will have a buyer who will buy directly from the primary markets. Also, a number of small establishments may adopt this method for some of their needs, i.e. the chef patron may buy his fish, meat and vegetables directly from the market.

The secondary market

Goods are bought wholesale from a distributor or middleman; the food service establishment will pay wholesale prices and obtain possible discounts.

The tertiary market

The retail or cash and carry warehouse is a method suitable for smaller companies. A current pass obtained from the warehouse is required in order to gain access. This method also requires the user to have his or her, own transport. Some cash and carry organisations require a VAT number before they will issue an authorised card. It is important to remember that there are the added costs of:

- Running the vehicle and petrol used, and
- The person's time for going to the warehouse.

Cash and carry can often be an impersonal way of buying as there are often no people to discuss quality and prices with.

Some large cash and carry operators will now deliver to the establishment.

◼ The buyer

The buyer is the key person who makes decisions regarding quality, amounts and price. The wisdom of the buyer's decisions will be reflected in the success or failure of the operation. The buyer must not only be knowledgeable about the products, but must have the necessary skills required in dealing with sales people, suppliers and other market agents. The buyer must also be prepared for hard and often aggressive negotiations.

Unscrupulous suppliers can also subject buyers to bribes and other inducements. Many suppliers will use pressure in order to get the buyer to purchase from specific sources. It is important to remember to treat the company's money as if it were your own. Use firm, friendly tactics and only socialise if it means that it will improve your buying position or benefit the company in some way. A buyer must always retain the right to be a free agent.

Buying demands integrity, maturity, bargaining skills and an even disposition. Buying associations have ethical codes to which members subscribe. They require a high standard of ethical relationship between buyer and seller.

A buyer must have knowledge of the internal organisation of the company, especially the operational needs, and be able to obtain the product needs at a competitive price. The buyer must also be acquainted with the procedures of production and how these items are going to be used in the production operations, in order that the right item is purchased. For example, the item required may not always be of prime quality; for example, tomatoes for soups and sauces, to be cost-effective, do not need to be grade A or class I. Another example is certain types of nuts which do not have to be whole prime quality nuts for certain pastry goods or salads. Therefore, to reduce costs it is better to purchase broken nuts.

A buyer must also know the storage requirements for each item and the space available, and the ability of the operation to finance special purchases in order to make good use of market conditions. For example, if there is a glut of fresh salmon at low cost, has the organisation the facility to make use of the extra salmon purchases? Is there sufficient freezer space? Can the chef make use of salmon, by creating a demand on the menu? The buyer must also have a knowledge of yield testing procedures and know how to work closely with the chef and food production team to establish a specification so the right item is obtained.

◼ Buying methods

These depend on the type of market and the kind of operation. Purchasing procedures are usually formal or informal. Both have advantages and disadvantages. Informal methods are suitable for casual buying, where the amount involved is not large and speed and simplicity are desirable. Formal contracts are best for large contracts for commodities purchased over a long period of time. Prices do not vary much during a year, once the basic price has been established. Using informal methods, prices and supply tend to fluctuate.

Informal buying

This usually involves oral negotiations, talking directly to salespeople, face to face or using the telephone. Informal methods vary according to market conditions and include:

■ *Quotation and order sheet method:* This uses a list of particular commodities always wanted in quantity and quality. Columns are provided to record prices from different suppliers. Prices are compared and orders given.

■ *Blank cheque method:* This is when there is an extreme shortage of a commodity or some other market condition exists where the buyer must get the commodity at any cost. This usually only operates in extreme circumstances.

■ *Cost plus method:* This is used when prices are not known or the market is unstable. Many suppliers like this arrangement, so that they do not have to add a safety factor to take care of risk, if commodities fluctuate considerably in price. They are free to buy at the most favourable price and then add on what they require to cover costs and give a profit. The amount over and above the cost paid for the item charged to the buyer is usually a standard percentage. Thus a supplier may buy fruit and vegetables and charge the buyer the price paid, plus 10%.

Formal buying

This is often referred to as competitive buying, giving suppliers written specifications and quantity needs. Negotiations are normally written. Methods are detailed as follows.

■ *Competitive bid method:* The sellers are invited to submit bids through written communications. The suppliers then send prices and other information on the commodities to the buyer. Bids are opened at a specified time to determine awards. Only those sellers able to meet the established purchase conditions of the buyer will be considered in awarding bids. The invitation to bid usually contains certain conditions. These will include:

  ☐ Terms of payment

  ☐ Discounts

  ☐ Method of delivery

  ☐ Invoice requirements.

■ **Negotiated method:** This is used when suppliers are hesitant to bid because of time restrictions, fluctuating market conditions, or a high perishability of the product. Negotiations may occur using the telephone and later confirmed in writing. Several suppliers are usually contacted to compare prices. This method is useful in that it allows competitive bidding while giving flexibility. When negotiating price or payment terms, it is important to know how much you spend with each supplier and the total value of goods actually received, as this improves your negotiating position .

5

- *Futures and contract method:* This is used by large organisations who have sufficient capital and staff to contract for future delivery of commodities at an established bid price. The advantage is that it ensures an adequate supply at an set price and avoids shortages and price fluctuations.

Selecting suppliers

Selecting suppliers is important in the purchasing process. First, consider how a supplier will be able to meet the needs of your operation. Consider:

- Price
- Delivery
- Quality/standards.

Information on suppliers can be obtained from other purchasers. Visits to suppliers' establishments are encouraged. When interviewing prospective suppliers, you need to question how reliable a supplier will be under competition and how stable under varying market conditions.

Suppliers are also selected on experience. A buyer soon gets to know the reliable ones. New suppliers are often tried and tested: some are retained. Considerations leading to a decision to continue to do business with a supplier include:

- If the supplier anticipates the needs of the organisation through monitoring market conditions and informing the company buyer of product and market information.
- Willingness to break quantities down as and when required rather than the buyer having to take a minimum quantity,which may be far more than the quantity required. For example if tomatoes are sold by the box as they would be in a primary market, the supplier agrees to break it down into a half box.
- Maintenance of adequate stocks to meet potential demand.
- Credit terms and discounts relevant to the buyer's business.
- Required access to premises and other delivery conditions such as timing.
- Potential for purchasing a wide range of products from one supplier that can lead to considerable savings.

Many suppliers now offer fresh fruit and vegetables, and part-prepared fresh vegetables. For example, peeled and turned potatoes, peeled and sliced carrots, prepared fresh beans. They may also offer a full range of frozen vegetables and speciality goods.

Three types of needs

In a food service operation there are three types of purchasing and stock needs:

- *Perishable:* Fresh fruit and vegetables, dairy products, meat and fish. Prices and suppliers may vary. Informal means of buying are frequently used. Perishables should be purchased to meet menu needs for a short period only.

- *Staple:* Supplies of canned, bottled, dehydrated, frozen products. Formal or informal purchasing can be used. Because items are staple and can be easily stored, bid buying is frequently used to take advantage of quantity price purchasing.

- *Daily use needs:* Daily use or contract items are delivered frequently on par stock basis. Stocks are kept up to the desired level and supply is automatic. Suppliers may be daily, several times a week, weekly or less often. Most items are perishable, therefore supplies must not be excessive, only sufficient to get through to the next delivery.

Quantity and quality

Determining quantity and quality of items to be purchased is important. This is based on the operational needs. The buyer checks out the market and looks for the best quality and best price. Delivery arrangements and other factors will be handled by the buyer. In smaller establishments the chef may also be the buyer.

When considering the quantity needed, certain factors should be known:

- The number of people to be served in a given period
- The sales history
- Portion sizes, determined from yield testing a standard portion control list drawn up by the chef and management teams.

Buyers need to know about food production, often to be able to decide how many portions a given size of order may yield. He/she must also understand the factors that can affect yields; for example cooking shrinkage may vary, causing problems in portion control and yield. Yield testing indicates the number of items or portions that can be obtained and helps to provide the information required for producing purchasing specifications. Yield testing should not be confused with product testing, which is concerned with the physical properties of the food texture, flavour and quality. In reality, tests are often carried out which combine both of these requirements.

The chef must inform the buyer of quantities. The buyer must also be aware of different packaging sizes, such as jars, bottles, cans and the yield from each package. There must be an indication of grades, styles, appearance, composition, varieties and quality factors such as:

- Colour
- Texture
- Size
- Absence of defects
- Bruising
- Irregular shape
- Maturity.

The chef and management team should establish quality standards when the menu is planned. Menus and recipes are developed using standardised recipes that directly relate to the buying procedure and standard purchasing specifications.

■ The standard recipe

Standard recipes are a written formula for producing a food item of a specified quality and quantity for use in a particular establishment. It should show the precise quantities and qualities of the ingredients together with the sequence of preparation and service. It enables the establishment to have a greater control over cost and quantity.

The objective of the use of the standard recipe is to predetermine the following:

- The quantities and qualities of ingredients to be used, stating the precise purchase specification, for example, the weight, grade, class, origin etc.
- The yield obtained from a recipe. The yield is the usable proportion of the ingredients, or the number of portions that can be obtained, once the preparation has taken place.
- The food cost per person.
- The nutritional value of a particular dish. This is now becoming increasingly important as more and more customers are becoming increasingly aware of the importance of nutrition, calorific value and healthy eating.

And to facilitate:

- Menu planning
- Purchasing and internal requisitioning
- Food preparation and production
- Portion control.

In addition, the standard recipe will assist new staff in preparation and production of standard products – which can be facilitated by photographs or drawings illustrating the finished product. There are now high-end software packages which fully integrate front of house systems with recipe costing software with integrated purchasing systems. However these systems do not automatically cost recipes. The process is initially time consuming, but the automated benefits that follow allow for fast updates in costing and the generation of new dish items.

■ Standard purchasing specification

Purchasing specifications have two functions:

1 They communicate to a supplier what the specifier wishes to have supplied in terms of goods and service.

2 They provide criteria against which the goods and services actually supplied can be compared.

The main advantages of specification buying are:

- Drawing up the specifications requires careful thought and a review of the buyer's needs. This frequently results in a simplification of the variety of products purchased and often reveals the possibility of using less expensive commodities. Both factors result in economies.

- Buying according to specifications frequently induces more suppliers to bid on an order, because all suppliers know exactly what is wanted and that their chances are as good as those of other suppliers because they are bidding on identical items. This increased competition for the business often results in lower prices.

- Specifications ensure the identical nature of items purchased from one or two sources. When the purchaser has more than one supplier of an item, this identity is essential and specification buying is a virtual necessity.

- Purchasing to specifications gives the person receiving the order an exact standard against which to measure the incoming materials and results in accurate inspection and a uniform quality of commodities.

- If specification buying is combined with quality control on the part of the supplier, it may be possible for the buyer to save money by doing a less complete inspection.

- Specification buying is a necessary step towards industry-wide standardisation and standardisation programmes hold the promise of substantial savings.

The main disadvantages of buying by specifications are:

- It is not economical to prepare specifications for small-lot purchases. This rules out the possibility of specification buying for many items.

- Specification buying adds to the purchaser's responsibilities. They must be able to state precisely what they want and the supplier's obligations extend only to complying with those terms. If the product does not live up to expectations, the liability rests with the buyer.

- In specification buying, the cost of inspection is greater than in purchasing by brand-name where you are guaranteed a standard through experience. Items purchased to specification must be examined, whereas branded items need little more than a casual check and count.

- There is always the danger of becoming over-defined in preparing specifications and as a consequence, paying more than necessary for items.

- There is also a danger of assuming that after specifications are established, the characteristics of the item have been permanently set. Unless specifications are periodically reviewed, there is a chance that the buyer will lose out on product improvements.

The content of a specification varies according to whether it is written for a user, designer, manufacturer or seller. A simple item may only require a brief description, whereas in the case of a complex assembly, the specification will be a comprehensive document, perhaps running to several pages. It is also convenient to write them in a standard form. An example of information to be included is:

- *Definition of the item:* Care must be taken so that a common catering term used by the buyer means exactly the same thing to the supplier; for example, whole sirloin means with bone and strip loin, without the bone; washed and sliced potatoes means after they have been peeled and of a thickness of no more than the specification.

- *Grade or brand-name:* For example, apples – grade extra class, or Granny Smiths; Lea and Perrins Worcestershire Sauce; where available it should state the desired variety and next acceptable substitute.

- *Weight, size or count:* For example, pounds, kilos; A2s or A10s; lemons 120s, pineapples l2s. Counts vary from country to country; therefore desired country of origin should be quoted against the count and the substitute country with the alternative count noted.

- *Unit against which prices should be quoted:* For example, per pound, per case, per box, per sack, each.

- *Special notes for the commodity:* For example, for meat it could contain details of the preparation of a particular cut of meat, or details of special packaging and delivery requirements.

Centralised purchasing within a company operating a number of units

There are advantages for large organisations in establishing a specialist department through which all purchasing is channelled. These include:

- Economies of scale enabling the use of bargaining power and resources to achieve the best result for the business. This is achieved through a consolidation of quantities that can take place resulting in quality discounts. Suppliers dealing with a central purchasing department have the incentive of competing for the whole or a substantial proportion of the requirements of the organisation.

- Cheaper prices may result since the fixed overheads of the supplier can be spread over a longer production runs; however, as food is a perishable commodity this may not have a major impact. Specialist purchasing staff can be employed for each of the major categories of purchase. Cheaper prices may be achieved by going directly to the grower and not via the marketplace, e.g. buying the whole crop of one farm at a negotiated rate.

- Lower administrative costs apply; for example, it is cheaper to process one order for £10,000 than ten each of £1,000. The use of computerisation can be used to facilitate the collection, summary and analysis of data, which in turn can improve purchasing efficiency.

Advantages of the co-ordination of the purchasing activity:

- Uniform policies can be adopted.

- Uniform purchasing procedures can be followed.

- Standardisation is achieved by the use of company specifications.

- Back-up services, especially stock control, can be co-ordinated.

- Staff training and development can be undertaken on a smaller scale with better results.

- Research into sources, qualities and supplier performance can be achieved.

- It is more convenient for the supplier to approach a central purchasing department.

Advantages of the control of the purchasing activity:

- The performance of the purchasing department can be monitored by fixing objectives and comparing actual results with predetermined standards.

- Stock rotation is achieved and loss of wastage due to out-of-date stock can be minimised.

- Uniform pricing is achieved and assists in standard costings nationwide.

For purchasing, a combination of centralisation and decentralisation may apply. It could be said that the function of the purchasing administration is already done centrally under the purchasing director, but no physical purchasing is done at this level. It is necessary to have central administration to ensure the achievement of company purchasing standards.

However, it is possible for non-perishable goods and commodities with an extended shelf life, to be bought centrally and delivered to the unit on a weekly basis. This would improve the effectiveness of this area. But the perishable items, i.e. bakery goods, dairy produce, fresh meat and fish, fresh fruit and vegetables, would be purchased straight into the unit. Alternatively, there could be a system whereby the unit informs a central office, operated by purchasing specialists, of their requirements, who then place the order and organise delivery to the unit.

No matter which system is adopted, there is always a need for purchasing specifications to assist in the task. Even specialists with technical training need to know the standard that the company expects its suppliers to reach. A standard indicated in a specification lends itself to the ultimate standard which a company wants to achieve. Good specifications aimed at the right standard will ensure:

- Quality products

- Quality service

- Acceptable prices.

An important factor in finding suppliers interested in selling commodities to a specification prepared by a food service operator is that of the purchasing power of the food service operator. If a food service operator is large enough, he is able to influence the supply trade quite easily. The small food service operator has a problem of purchasing only what suppliers have readily available to sell, as he has only a low purchasing power. To find suppliers to prepare commodities to his specification is rare and if fortunate enough to find any interested, extremely costly. Sometimes the difficulty can be overcome by finding suppliers who are already producing an item for a larger concern to a similar specification and who therefore can accept a compromise that will go towards the needs of the small food service operator's specification.

5.6   Operational control

Food is expensive and efficient stock control levels are essential to help the profitability of the business. The main difficulties of controlling food stocks include:

- Food prices fluctuate because of inflation and falls in the demand and supply, through poor harvests, bad weather conditions, etc.
- Transport costs, which rise due to wage demands and cost of petrol.
- Fuel costs rise, which affects food companies' and producers' costs.
- Changes in approaches to government food subsidies.
- Changes in the amount demanded by the customer; increased advertising increases demand.
- Changes in taste and fashion influence demand from one produce to another.
- Media focus on certain products, which are labelled healthy and unhealthy, will affect demand, e.g. butter being high in saturated fats. Sunflower margarine is high in polyunsaturates.

Each establishment should devise its own control system to suit the needs of that establishment.

Factors that adversely affect the establishment of an efficient control system include:

- Regular changes in the menu
- Menus with a large number of dishes
- Dishes with a large number of ingredients
- Problems with assessing customer demand
- Difficulties in not adhering to or operating standardised recipes
- Raw materials purchased incorrectly.

Factors assisting in the establishment of an efficient control system include:

- Constant menu, e.g. McDonald's, Harvester
- Standardised recipes and purchasing specifications
- Menu with a limited number of dishes.

With some of all these factors present in a food service operation, stock control is often easier and costing more accurate.

The process for food production control can be summarised as shown in Figure 5.4, which shows it as a five-stage process. Each of these stages is considered in turn below.

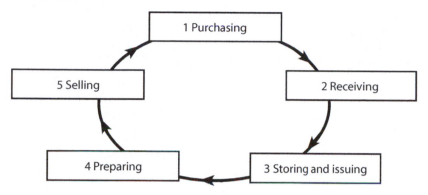

Figure 5.4: The food production control cycle of daily operation

Purchasing

Requisition and inventory control must be implemented. The purchasing transaction can be shown diagrammatically as in Figure 5.5. Control begins with the calculation of the amount and the writing of the specification. Orders are usually placed through a purchase order. This states the item or items required, amount, size, weight and other pertinent information.

All purchase orders have numbers so that they can be quickly identified. Only an authorised person should sign purchase orders. The individual issuing it normally holds one copy, one may go to the accounting department, and another to the receiving rooms. Copies are sent to the supplier. In some cases, it may be a requirement to have the purchase order signed and returned by an identified individual in the supplier's company, so it is then known that the order will be honoured.

Regular purchase orders are for one single order to be delivered at a specified date. 'Open delivery' purchase orders establish the purchase of items over a period of time. Items needed daily or weekly are often purchased by open delivery orders.

A purchase record may be maintained. This record may indicate what was ordered and from whom, as well as any other information that may be needed to be maintained. A purchase price record usually is maintained on cards to keep information on the price paid for a particular item.

Figure 5.5: Summary of the purchasing transaction

■   Receiving

Receiving practices vary with different organisations. The general principles of control are:

1   Check delivery note to see if the products delivered agree with it.

2   Inspect products/raw materials to determine if they are in agreement with the purchase order and specification.

3   Tag all meats with date of receipt, weight and other information needed to identify the delivery properly.

4   List all items received on the daily receiving report.

5   Accept the products/raw materials by signing the delivery note and returning the copy to the driver/delivery person.

6   Store or deliver to the correct place.

In large organisations, receiving is a specialised job. This job may be combined with the storeroom job. Authority and responsibility must be given to the individual receiving. This must include jurisdiction over those who help receive and store. The various approaches to receiving include:

- **Invoice receiving:** If the invoice accompanies the delivery with the delivery note, check the invoice against the delivery and check with the purchase order or the quotation and the order sheet, or other documents. Note any discrepancies. Check quality and quantity against documentation.

- **Blind check receiving:** For blind receiving, the clerk is given a blank invoice or purchase order listing the incoming products/raw materials. The quantities, quality, weights and prices are omitted. The receiving clerk must add these in when the products/raw materials are delivered. This enforces a formal checking system and not merely a glancing job to see if the goods agree with the figures on the invoice. The receiving clerk must weigh items to record their correct weight. A count is required in addition to a quality check. Another invoice with quantities, weights, quality and prices is sent to the finance office. This is checked against the invoice of the receiving clerk and the figures verified. Blind receiving is an accurate method of checking merchandise and verifying deliveries. It does take more time and costs more since it requires the clerk to prepare a complete record of all incoming products/raw materials.

- **Partial blind receiving:** This is a combination of invoice receiving and blind receiving. The receiving clerk has itemised purchase orders, delivery notes and invoices with the quantities omitted. When the goods, products and raw materials are checked, the quantity of each item is listed in the space provided. This is not as accurate as the previous method, but is faster and less costly. It is essential in both methods that the supplier's invoice does not accompany the goods, products or raw materials. If it does, the information on quantity must be omitted or made invisible by a blank area where such information would appear.

Good principles of receiving are important for control. These are:

1 Being ready and prepared for the delivery.
2 Checking the incoming goods thoroughly against the purchase order and the purchase specification. Open cases if they appear to be damaged or tampered with. Date all canned goods before storing.
3 Weigh items separately. When receiving bulk items, remove excess paper, ice, etc. before weighing
4 Weigh meats and tag them. The practice prevents disputes with the supplier about over- and under-weights. Tagging also reduces the chance of spoilage or excess weight loss. It also simplifies calculation of food costs, since a good record of meat withdrawals can be obtained from the tags taken from meat as it comes from the inventory.

Recording incoming deliveries is as important as checking quality and quantity. The form or style of doing this may vary but the intended principles are the same.

Activity:

- Identity four commodities: a fresh meat, a fresh fish, a fresh vegetable, and sugar.

- For each of these commodities identity and list the key stages from identifying the need for the commodity through to receiving and storage.

- Identify the critical point where control needs to be greater to ensure security of the commodity.

■ Storing and issuing

Raw materials should be stored correctly under the right conditions, temperature, etc. A method of pricing materials must be decided and one of the following should be adopted for charging food to the various departments. The cost of items does not remain fixed over time; over a period of one year a stores item may well have several prices. The establishment must decide which price to use:

- Actual purchase price
- Simple average weight
- Weighted average price
- Inflated price (price goes up after purchase), or
- Standard price (fixed price).

■ Stock control

A large catering operation needs two levels of stock control.

1 A card for each item stocked showing the stock level, purchases and issues.
2 A stock summary sheet which records the total holding at trading period end, along with item cost prices and total value.

Where a formal store system is in use, it is imperative that an accurate note is kept of all transfers out of the stores to work areas. This transfer note should contain the signatures of both the giver and receiver to ensure full responsibility and to reduce errors. The target for most types of catering operation should be that sufficient stock is held for not less than one week and not more than three weeks' trading.

Stock holding level is best expressed as a cash value of stocks at cost price. If stock consumption is £10,000 per week, then an ideal stock holding might be two weeks or £20,000. Stock value at the end of a trading period can be compared with the amount consumed during that period and adjustments can be made during the next trading period .

The stock level depends on several factors:

- The menu range

- The extent of the catering and hospitality services on offer
- The predictability of trading and forecasting
- Suppliers' distribution schedules – in remote locations this may be only once or twice a week
- Available storage space
- Product shelf life
- Cash and credit availability.

Remember to hold too much stock is wasteful of space and ties up money unnecessarily. However accurate holding levels are important. If there is a risk of running out of a commodity or ingredient, this could endanger the levels of sales.

Storekeeping

Keeping a properly run and efficient storeroom is essential in order to maintain the unified process of control throughout the establishment/organisation. A clean, orderly food store, run efficiently, is essential in any food service establishment for the following reasons:

- Stocks of food can be kept at a suitable level, so eliminating the risk of running out of any raw material.
- All food entering and leaving the stores can be properly checked; this helps to prevent wastage.
- A check can be kept on the percentage profit of each department of the establishment.

Preparing/production

This is an important stage of the control cycle. The cost of the food consumed depends on two factors:

1 The number of meals produced
2 The cost per meal.

In order to control food costs the operation must be able to:

- Control the number to be catered for, and
- Control the food cost per meal in advance of production and service by using system of pre-costing, using standardised recipes, indicating portion control.

Selling

In order to be able to sell well, it is necessary to be able to predict the volume of sales for a future period. In order to be of practical value the forecast must:

- Predict the total number of covers (customers)
- Predict the choice of menu items.

Therefore, it is important to:

■ Keep a record of the numbers of each dish sold from a menu

■ Work out the average spend per customer

■ Calculate the proportion, expressed as a percentage, of each dish sold in relation to total sales.

Forecasting is in two stages:

1 Initial forecasting – this is done once a week in respect of each day of the following week. It is based on sales histories, information related to advance bookings and current trends and when this has been completed, the predicted sales are converted into the food/ingredients requirements. Purchase orders are then prepared and sent to suppliers.

2 The final forecast – this normally takes place the day before the actual preparation and service of the food. This forecast must take into account the latest developments, e.g. the weather and any food that needs to be used up; if necessary suppliers' orders may need to be adjusted.

Sales forecasting is not a perfect method of prediction, but does help with production planning. Sales forecasting, however, is important when used in conjunction with cyclical menu planning.

■ Control and profitability

A summary of the key factors that will help the profitability of the food service operation is as follows:

■ Ensuring correct cooking of food to minimise portion loss

■ Efficient preparation of raw materials

■ Correct portion control

■ Minimising wastage, sufficient use of raw materials, utilising left-over food

■ Reducing theft

■ Accurate ordering procedures

■ Adequate checking procedures

■ Reference marks to standardised recipes and yield factors

■ Sufficient research into suppliers

■ Accurate forecasting

■ Sound menu planning.

5.7   References and additional reading

Bitner, M. J. (1992) Servicescapes: The impact of physical surroundings on customers and employees. *Journal of Marketing*, **56**(2), 57-71.

Cert ID at www.cert.id.com (accessed January 2019).

Choi, J., Lee, B. and Mok, J. (2010) An experiment on psychological gaze motion: A re-examination of item selection behaviour of restaurant customer, *Journal of Global Business and Technology*, **6**(1), 68-79.

Cousins, J and Foskett, D. (1989) Curriculum Development for Food Production Operations Teaching for the Hospitality Industry: A Systems Framework, *International Journal of Operations and Production Management*, **9**(5), 77-87.

Cousins, J. (1994) Managing capacity, in P. Jones (ed.), *The Management of Food-service Operations*, London: Cassell, pp. 174–187.

Cousins, J., O'Gorman, K. and Stierand, M. (2010) Molecular gastronomy: basis for a new culinary movement or modern-day alchemy?, *International Journal of Contemporary Hospitality Management*, **22**(3), 399–415.

Department for Environment, Food & Rural Affairs at www.defra.gov.uk (accessed January 2019).

Domene-Danes, M., (2013). El Bulli: 'Contemporary Intersections Between Food, Science, Art and Late Capitalism', BRAC - Barcelona Research Art Creation, 1(1).

Escoffier, A. (2011) *Le Guide Culinaire*, Translated by Cracknell H. and Kaufman R. Oxon: Routledge.

Ethical Consumer at www.ethicalconsumer.org (accessed January 2019).

Fair Trade Foundation at www.fairtrade.org.uk (accessed January 2019).

Food Standard Agency at www.food.gov.uk (accessed January 2019).

Foskett, D. and Paskins, P. (2016) *The Theory of Hospitality and Catering*, 13th ed; London: Hodder Education.

Free Trade Agency at www.freetradeagency.co.uk (accessed January 2019).

Gillespie, C. (2001) *European Gastronomy into the 21 Century*, Oxon: Routledge.

Graham, D., (2006a). The return of gueridon service, *Hospitality Review*, **8**(3), . 5-11.

Graham, D., (2015). The Chef as an Emotional and Aesthetic Labourer - an employee in transition, PhD study, Sheffield: Sheffield Hallam University.

Heart Foundation at www.bhf.org.uk (accessed January 2019).

Lashley, C., (2009). *Hospitality Retail Management*. Oxford: Butterworth-Heinemann.

Livingston, J.S. (1978) Menu design: For effective merchandising. *Cornell H&R Quarterly*, **19**(11), 38-46.

McCarthy, J. D., Sasse, M. A. and Riegelsberger, J., (2004). Could I have the menu please? An eye tracking study of design conventions. *People and Computers XVII — Designing for Society*.

5

Miller, J. and Pavesic, D. (1996) *Menu Pricing and Strategy* 4th edn. New York: John Wiley & Sons, Inc.

Panitz, B. (2000) Reading between the lines: The psychology of menu design, *Restaurants USA*. **8**, 81-87.

Pavesic, D. V. (1999) *Menu Pricing: 25 Keys to Profitable Success (Restaurant Manager's Pocket Handbook)*, New York: Lebhar-Friedman

Red Tractor at www.redtractor.org (accessed January 2019).

Robuchon, J., Montagné, P. and Larousse (2009) *Larousse Gastronomique*, London: Hamlin.

Rosenbaum, M. S and Massiah, C. (2011) An expanded servicescape perspective, *Journal of Service Management*, **22**(4), 471-490.

RSPCA at www.rspcaassured.org.uk (accessed January 2019).

Saulnier, L. (2003) *Le Répertoire de la Cuisine*, London: Barron's Educational Series

Sloan, D. (ed) (2013) *Food and Drink: The cultural context,* Oxford: Goodfellow Publishers.

Slow Food Organisation at www.slowfood.org.uk (accessed January 2019).

Soil Association at www.soilassociation.org (accessed January 2019).

Vegetarian Society at www.vegsoc.org (accessed January 2019).

Von Keitz, B. (1988) Eye movement research: Do consumers use information they are offered? *European Research*, **16**, 217-223.

Warhurst, C. and Nickson, D. (2001). *Looking Good, Sounding Right: Style Counselling in the New Economy*. London: The Industrial Society.

Warhurst, C. and Nickson, D. (2005) Becoming a class act? Reflections of aesthetic labour and routine interaction service. In: 23rd Annual Labour Process Conference: Strathclyde University.

Williams, C. L. and Connell, C., (2010). Looking good and sounding right': Aesthetic labor and social inequality in the retail industry. *Work and Occupations*, **37**(3), 349-377.

Yang, S. S.,(2012) Eye movements on restaurant menus: A revisitation on gaze motion and consumer scanpaths, *International Journal of Hospitality Management*, **31**(3), 1021-1029.

6 Beverage provision

Aim

To outline the key considerations for beverage provision within food service operations.

Objectives

This chapter is intended to support you in:

- Promoting safe, sensible drinking
- Identifying types of wine and drinks lists
- Developing and costing wine, drink and other beverage lists
- Developing skills in operating and managing the purchasing, storage and control of beverage stocks.

6.1 Safe, sensible drinking

There is increasing concern about higher levels of alcohol consumption and the health risks associated with it. Various initiatives are being tried such as improving information on labels, alcohol exclusion areas at certain times, restrictions on price promotions and also on licensing. Those who sell and serve alcoholic beverages, as well as being the subject of various licensing arrangements (see Chapter 1, page 28) are also being giving far greater encouragement to become more responsible.

The majority of the population drink alcohol for many reasons: to quench a thirst, as a relaxant or simply because it is enjoyable. A small amount of alcohol does no harm and can even be beneficial. However, the more you drink and the more frequently you drink, the greater the health risks.

Alcohol depresses the brain and nerve function, affecting a person's judgement, self-control and skills. The four general stages of becoming drunk are:

Stage 1: Happy (relaxed, talkative and sociable).

Stage 2: Excited (erratic and emotional; movement and thinking affected).

Stage 3: Confused (disorientated, loud, out of control).

Stage 4: Lethargic (unable to stand, talk or walk).

It is important that members of the service staff are aware of these stages so that potential problems can be identified and handled properly before they become more serious. This can include refusing to serve more alcohol to intoxicated persons, which is either required under the law or may be undertaken as a safety precaution – such as with people on aircraft.

◼ Alcoholic strength

The two main scales of measurement of alcoholic strength may be summarised as:

- ◼ OIML Scale (European): range 0% to 100% alcohol by volume (ABV).
- ◼ American Scale (USA): range 0° to 200°.

The Organisation Internationale Métrologie Légale (OIML) Scale, previously called Gay Lussac Scale, is equal to the percentage of alcohol by volume in the drink at 20°C. It is the universally accepted scale for the measurement of alcohol.

Table 6.1: Approximate alcoholic strength of drinks (OIML scale)

0%	Non-alcoholic
not more that 0.05%	Alcohol free
0.05–0.5%	De-alcoholised
0.5–1.2%	Low alcohol
1.2–5.5%	Reduced alcohol
3–6%	Beer, cider, FABs* and 'alcopops'** with any of these being up to 10%
8–15%	Wines, usually around 10–13%
14–22%	Fortified wines (liqueur wines) such as sherry and port, aromatised wines such as vermouth, vin doux naturels (such as Muscat de Beaumes-de-Venise) and Sake***
37.5–45%	Spirits, usually at 40%
17–55%	Liqueurs, very wide range

Notes

* FABs is a term used to describe flavoured alcoholic beverages, for example, Bacardi Breezer (5.4%).

** 'Alcopops' is a term used to describe manufactured flavoured drinks (generally sweet and fruity) which have had alcohol, such as gin, added to them. They are also known as alcoholic soft drinks or alcoholic lemonade. Usually 3.5 to 5% but can be up to 10%.

*** Sake is a strong (18%), slightly sweet, form of beer made from fermented rice.

The by volume measurement indicates the amount of pure alcohol in a liquid. Thus, in a liquid measured as 40% alcohol by volume, 40% of the contents will be pure alcohol. (Under the American Scale 80° (80 degrees proof) is equal to 40% ABV). The alcoholic content of drinks, by volume, is now almost always shown on the label. Table 6.1 gives the approximate alcoholic strength of a variety of drinks

Sensible limits

Not drinking alcohol cuts out any risk. However, medical opinion in the United Kingdom has set (in 2016) the limit at 14 units spread throughout the week for men and women (excluding pregnant women, where the advice is for no alcohol). Drinking in excess of these recommended limits is likely to be damaging to health. One unit of is equal to 10 millilitres (liquid) or 8 grams (weight) of alcohol. This is roughly equivalent to:

- Half a pint of ordinary beer or lager
- One glass of wine (125 ml)
- One glass of sherry (50 ml)
- One measure of vermouth or other apéritif (50 ml)
- One measure of spirits (25 ml).

However, it is also important to take into account:

- There are about 100 calories in a single unit of alcohol. The number of calories quickly adds up and can lead to weight gain. Replacing food with alcohol as a source of calories denies the body essential nutrients and vitamins.
- The number of units required to reach the maximum permitted levels for driving varies between individuals. Some alcohol remains in the bloodstream for up to 18 hours after consumption. This should be considered in relation to the legal limits for alcohol when driving. The legal limit in the UK is currently 80 milligrams of alcohol per 100 millilitres of blood or 35 micrograms per 100 millilitres of breath. The legal limit in Scotland is lower at 50 milligrams of alcohol per 100 millilitres of blood or 22 micrograms per 100 millilitres of breath.

Calculating alcohol intake

The amount of alcohol being consumed is a measure of both the strength of the alcoholic drink and the amount or volume of the drink being consumed.

To calculate the alcohol unit intake for wines:

Wine at a specific percentage of alcohol by volume multiplied by the amount in litres equals the units of alcohol per bottle. For example:

Wine at 12% alcohol by volume × 0.75 litre bottle = 9 units per 75 cl bottle.

Therefore this 75 cl bottle of wine will give 6 × 125 ml individual glasses of wine and each glass will therefore contain 1.5 units of alcohol (9 units in the whole bottle divided by the 6 glasses).

Other examples for calculating the alcohol unit intake for other drinks are:

Lager at 5% alcohol by volume × 0.50 litre measure = 2.5 units per measure.

Spirit at 40% alcohol by volume × 0.025 litre (25 ml) measure = 1 unit per measure.

Sherry at 18% alcohol by volume × 0.05 litre (50 ml) measure = 0.9 unit per measure.

(For further information on safe sensible drinking visit the *Drink Aware* website at www.drinkaware.co.uk)

6.2   Types of wine and drink lists

Wine and drinks lists are primarily a selling aid. The lists identify for the customer what is on offer, the price of the item and details such as the measure in which the item is to be sold.

As a general rule, all menu items should have identified pairing wines and other beverages. Staff will then be able to make recommendations as required and promote wine and other beverage sales.

Bar and cocktail lists

These may range from a basic standard list offering common everyday apéritifs, a selection of spirits with mixers, beers, wines by the glass and soft drinks together with a limited range of cocktails and non-alcoholic cocktails (often called mock-tails), to a very comprehensive list offering a wide choice in all areas.

When setting up a cocktail bar or preparing a bar and cocktail list, it is necessary to consider the availability of the specialised equipment, preparation requirements and stocks which are necessary for presentation including specialised glassware and garnishes, etc. Additionally in order to profit from yield management techniques, it is imperative that the majority of beverages have standard recipes and measures.

Apéritif lists

These can be combined with the restaurant wine list – although they are more frequently today presented as a separate apéritif list as are digestif and liqueur lists. For apéritif lists it is common to include lighter, drier styles in wines and fortified drinks although drinks with some acidity are useful to enhance appetite. The contents might include:

- Champagne – non-vintage, vintage, premier cuvées, Champagne rosé,
- Cocktails – such as Negroni, Manhattan, Aperol Spritz or Kir Royale
- Other sparkling wines, sparkling rosé
- Dry sherry – Fino, Manzanilla through to dry Oloroso
- Dry white wine – for example, Muscadet and New Zealand Sauvignon Blanc

- Lighter Mösel and Austrian wine styles
- Pineau des Charentes
- Ratafia
- Vermouths
- Bitters such as Campari
- White port
- Dry Marsala
- Tawny port (served chilled).

Restaurant wine lists

The wine list can be an extremely effective selling tool for a restaurant. Some establishments use their extensive and varied wine and drinks lists as a marketing tool to glean awards and further entice customers to a restaurant. Even Michelin Inspectors consider the variation and vintages of wine on offer and the standard of wine service when evaluating an establishment (Gil *et al.*, 2009). Customers can tell a lot about a restaurant from the content and presentation of the wine list. The list must inform, although too much information is just as bad as having none. Careful consideration also needs to be given to the extensiveness of the wine list as it can cost a vast amount of money to maintain.

Examples of types of wine list include:

- A full and very comprehensive list of wines from both New World and Old World countries, with emphasis on the classic areas such as Bordeaux/Burgundy plus a small selection from new, emerging wine regions;
- A middle of the road, traditional selection, e.g. some French, German, Italian together with some New World wines;
- A small selection of well-known or branded wines, or
- A prestige list predominantly with wines of one specific country.

Wines by the glass are increasing important to a restaurant or a bar offer. This can be a limited offer using a small number of bottles opened as required. More extensive offers use commercial preservation and storage systems.

Once a bottle is opened the wine can deteriorate quite quickly as it reacts with the air and oxidises. There are various methods of keeping wines once they have been opened. Some work by creating a vacuum within the bottle and then sealing the bottle with a removable closure, either manually or mechanically. Another system involves putting a layer of carbon dioxide gas (CO_2) on the surface of the wine, thus preventing air getting to it. Yet another system (Coravin) allows for the sampling the wine, or serving of wine by the glass, from closed bottles. A needle system, which goes through the cork, replaces the drawn wine with inert argon gas.

With the exception of sparkling wines, it is often better to serve the wine in a glass larger than the measure. This allows the aroma to develop in the glass and the wine to be better appreciated. Some fine dining establishments may serve wine in a glass designed specifically for the style of wine or grape variety they are serving to enhance the flavour experience further. Many establishments now also pour a measure of wine into a small carafe for the service of wine by the glass. This then allows the customer to pour the wine into their glass as required.

After-meal drinks lists (*digestifs*)

These are more frequently presented as a separate digestif or liqueur list. Digestif lists should comprise soothing, mellowing, heavier, sweeter and richer styles of beverages, for example:

- Really good sweet wines such as sweet German, Austrian, Loire and Jurançon wines can refresh the palate.
- Fortified wines such as port (vintage and LBV), sherry, madeira and marsala.
- Cognac, Armagnac and brandies and/or a specialist range of malt and 'older malt' whiskies.
- A range of liqueurs.
- A range of speciality liqueur/spirit coffees might also be included.

Banqueting, function and events wine lists

For banqueting, function and events wine lists:

1 The length of the list is generally according to size and style of operation.
2 There should be a range of prices from house wines to some fine wines to suit all customer preferences.
3 In some instances the banqueting department will draw wines from the restaurant wine list – this reduces the need for double stocking.
4 There is usually a selection of popular wine names/styles on offer.

Essentially operations try to achieve ease of availability, strong profit margin and high recognition. Some considerations in drawing up banqueting wine lists are:

- Ensuring that the list will allow suitable pairing with the menu(s) on offer – especially if there is a range of suggested standard menus.
- Because banqueting lists are often sent out months in advance of an event, care needs to be taken to ensure ongoing supplies.
- A disclaimer might be useful which advises that an alternative may be necessary, or substitutions may be made if the client does not request that wines be set aside for their event.
- Ensuring that the presentation of the sales mix data is able to distinguish between banqueting lists sales and from restaurant sales, as wines may appear to be performing more strongly simply through an order placed for a banquet.

■ ## Room service drinks list

These lists tend toward less formality. However:

- They usually offer a limited range of wines and other drinks although it can be helpful if the customers can purchase from the main lists if required.
- There may be a mini-bar/refreshment centre or choice from a standard bar list.
- In some instances a fixed stock in sealed decanters is provided for VIP customers.

■ ## Hot beverages

The three main hot beverages are teas, coffee and chocolate. With the growth of both independent and chain-store coffee shops, the consumer impetus is towards ever-higher standards of fresh preparation and an accelerating demand for more international styles. More recently far greater attention has been given to hot beverages with even the simplest of food service operations offering a broad range of teas, coffees and chocolate.

Coffee being offered includes filter, espresso, latté and cappuccino as standard. Single estate coffees are also entering the market with exceptional taste profiles and an emphasis on sourcing Fairtrade coffee is at the forefront. Various styles of iced coffee and cold brew are also becoming popular. Other offerings can also include traditionally made Turkish coffee. By far the most popular are the espresso-based coffees such as:

- *Ristretto* – intense form of espresso, often served with a glass of water in Europe
- *Caffè crème* – regular coffee prepared from fresh beans ground fresh for each cup, resulting in a thick cream coloured, moussy head
- *Espresso macchiato* – espresso spotted with a dollop of milk foam
- *Espresso con panna* – espresso with a dollop of whipped cream on top
- *Caffè latte* – shot of espresso plus hot steamed milk, with or without foam as desired
- *Flat white* – double shot of espresso topped with frothed milk which has been stirred together with the flat milk from the bottom of the jug, to create a creamy rather than frothy texture.

Teas offered can range from general basic teas to more specialise teas such as:

- *Assam* – full, rich and malty served at breakfast usually with milk
- *Darjeeling* – delicate and light usually served in the afternoon or evening with lemon or a touch of milk
- *Earl Grey* – blended Darjeeling and China teas scented with oil of bergamot. Served with lemon or a touch of milk
- *Jasmine* – fragrant and light green tea dried with jasmine blossom
- *Green* – an alternative to black tea as it contains a number of antioxidants.

6

- *Kenya* – refreshing and light tea served with milk
- *Lapsang Souchong* – smoky tarry highly aromatic tea, delicate on the palate with a rewarding acquired taste. Can be served with lemon
- *Sri Lanka* – golden tea from a Ceylon blend served with lemon or milk
- Iced teas may also be offered.

Prestige tea selections are also becoming more popular, and need better trained staff. The afternoon tea phenomenon has continued to develop with a much wide range of teas being available. In some establishments, expert 'tea sommeliers' are employed to ensure a high standard of tea service. Tea ceremonies are often performed tableside by infusing and blending teas and powders such as Matcha, which is a type of green tea, in front of the customers. A prestige tea selection will often include, for example: 1st flush Darjeeling, vintage white tea from hand rolled tips, and flowering teas.

Included under teas are also flavoured teas (tisanes) such as blackcurrant, cherry, etc.

Hot chocolate has become very popular. It may come sweetened or non-sweetened and as a powder or soluble granules and is mixed with hot water or hot milk. Whipped cream, from a whipped cream dispenser, marshmallows or a sprinkling of powdered chocolate may be added upon request.

Activity:

Taking into consideration expected clientele and price points, summarise the type of beverage list selection you would offer for a:

- Fine dining restaurant.
- Wedding venue.
- Chain style pizzeria.

Identify the key differences between them.

6.3   Developing wine and drink lists

Wine and drinks lists come in a variety of different styles usually reflecting the type of establishment. The factors affecting wine and drink lists are similar to those for menus (Chapter 5 , page 136). As well as taking those factors into account the compiling of wine and drink lists should also take account of:

- The overall presentation and style, including the colour scheme, being in keeping with the style of operation
- The size and shape of the list in order to make it easy to handle and use for both customers and staff and have the required durability

- Flexibility in design and construction so as to enable changes to be made as vintages change and for the inclusion of special promotions
- The length of time that the list will be in operation
- The overall design and legibility of the lists which can include illustrations, or inclusion of a contents page if the list is extensive
- Ensuring that the information included assists the customer as well as meeting legal requirements
- How decisions are to be made on the actual content of the list
- Considering the availability of supply, storage capacity and the capital investment required
- The inclusion of bin numbers which will simplify inventory and reordering for wine lists, so assisting both internal personnel and customers.
- The wine list must work in harmony with the main food menu. Wines should complement the food offerings with emphasis on particular wines if the restaurant has a specific theme, e.g. a seafood restaurant may serve a more extensive list of white wines.

The wine and drink lists are part of the expression or character of the operation. Some lists are now presented to the customer on tablets or other electronic devices. These can reduce printing costs and are easy to update. Presentational style can mark an operation as special, even though there may be very similar content to other operations within the local area. Poor presentation can adversely affect the customers' judgement of the business and the food and beverage product (also see information on menu design, Chapter 5, page 144).

Professionalism in beverage sales and service

The promotion of beverage sales has been greatly influenced by increasing professionalism in all aspects of beverage service.

For bar staff there are a range of qualifications, such as those provided by the British Institute of Innkeeeping (www.bii.org). Holders of liquor licences are also supported. In addition there are organisations such as the UK Bartenders Guild (ukbartendersguild.co.uk) and the International Bartenders Association (iba-world.com).

For sommeliers (or wine waiter or wine butlers) the two main qualifications are provided by the Court of Master Sommeliers (www.courtofmastersommeliers.org) and the Wine and Spirit Education Trust (www.wsetglobal.com). Competitions for sommeliers are run on a global basis (see for example the Association de la Sommellerie Internationale at www.sommellerie-internationale.com/en) and in the UK by the Academy of Food and Wine Service (www.afws.co.uk).

The promotions of other beverage, such as tea, are supported, for example, by the UK Tea and Infusions Association (www.tea.co.uk). With the increasing influence of the barista movement, the approach to coffee making, presentation and service has also become more far more professional with recognised qualifications. There are also international specialist coffee associations and internaltional competitions. Information on these can be found at websites such as World of Coffee Events, at www.worldcoffeeevents.org.

■ Contents of wine and drink lists

The contents of wine and drink lists are commonly listed in the order in which they may be consumed, for example:

1 Apéritifs – which alongside sparkling and still wines can include a range of aromatised wines, fortified wines and natural spring and mineral waters.

2 Cocktails and other mixed drinks (including non-alcoholic drinks).

3 Spirits and associated mixers such as aerated waters.

4 Wines – sparkling and still wines, alcohol-free, de-alcoholised and low-alcohol wines.

5 Beers, cider, perry and non-alcoholic drinks including natural spring and mineral waters, aerated waters, squashes, juices and syrups.

6 Digestifs – which as well as liqueurs may also include various spirits, such as brandy or a selection of eau de vie, malt whiskies, and also ports, other fortified wines, sweet table wines, and vin doux naturels.

7 Hot beverages including teas and speciality coffees.

■ Listing of wines

Wines are usually listed in three main ways:

- By place of origin (geographical)
- By type (sparkling, still), or
- By the grape variety.

Geographical listing for wines

The traditional approach is to list wines by geographical area. Within this approach the wines are presented country by country or region, such as for instance France, or Australia, and then area by area within that country. It is also usual to have the wines presented under each country, region or area with the white wines first, followed by the rosé wines and then the red wines. Using this approach, the listing of wines within a wine list might be:

1 Champagne and sparkling

2 France

3 Germany

4 Italy

5 Spain

6 Portugal

7 England

8 Other European wines

9 Australia

10 The Americas (Canada, USA and South America)

11 New Zealand

12 South Africa

13 Other world wines

14 House wines

Listing wines by type

A modern approach is to have wines listed by type:

- Sparkling wines
- White wines
- Rosé wines
- Red wines
- Dessert (sweet) wines.

The wines can then be listed under each type of wine in three main ways:

- Country by country
- Region by region (similar to the geographical listing described above)
- By the style of the wine.

If the wines are to be listed by type and by style, then the wines could be presented under the following headings:

- Sparkling wines
- Rosé wines
- White wines
  - ☐ crisp, zesty whites
  - ☐ grassy-fruity whites
  - ☐ rich, full-bodied whites
- Red wines
  - ☐ light, fruity reds
  - ☐ claret style reds
  - ☐ robust, herby-spicy reds.

To help the customer choose a wine and to enable staff to make recommendations, it is also useful for each of the groups of wines to be listed in order from the lighter wines to the fuller wines.

Listing wines by grape

If the wines are to be listed by grapes then one approach could be to list the grapes in alphabetical order as follows:

White grapes	Red grapes
Chardonnay	Cabernet Sauvignon
Chenin blanc	Gamay
Gewürztraminer	Malbec
Pinot Blanc	Merlot
Pinot Gris/Pinot Grigio	Pinot Noir
Riesling	Sangiovese
Sauvignon Blanc	Shiraz/Syrah
Sémillon	Tempranillo
Verdejo	Zinfandel
Other white grapes	Other red grapes

Under each heading the wines made with that grape are listed, as well as the principal blends that are made with that grape as the predominant grape. When the wines are listed under the headings 'Other white grapes' or 'Other red grapes', then the grape(s) of the wine should also be listed next to the name of the wine.

Again, to help the customer choose a wine and to aid staff in making recommendations, it is useful for each of the groups of wines to be listed in order from the lighter wines to the more full wines.

■ General information for wine and other drinks

It is usual to give information on wine and drink lists that help the customer in making decisions and also the staff in making recommendations. This information is shown below:

Wines

- ☐ Bin number
- ☐ Name of wine
- ☐ Country and area of origin
- ☐ Quality indication (e.g. AOC, Qmp etc.)
- ☐ Shipper
- ☐ Château/estate bottled
- ☐ Varietal (grape type(s))
- ☐ Vintage
- ☐ Alcoholic strength
- ☐ ½ bottle, bottle, magnum
- ☐ Price
- ☐ Supplier
- ☐ Descriptive notes as appropriate

Other drinks

- ☐ Type of drink, e.g. juices, whisky, gin, sherry
- ☐ Brand name if appropriate, e.g. Martini
- ☐ Style (sweet, dry, etc.)
- ☐ Description, e.g. for cocktails
- ☐ Alcoholic strength as appropriate
- ☐ Descriptive notes as appropriate

For more information on wine and food paring see, for example: www.matching-foodandwine.com, *The Essentials of Wine: with Food Pairing Techniques*, Laloganes (2008), and for detailed information on wine see, for example, *Larousse Wine*, Cobbold and Durand-Viel (2017) and *The Oxford Companion to Wine*, Robinson and Harding (2015).

Activity:

Many food service operations publish wine and drink lists on their websites.

■ Compare a number of on-line wine and drinks lists to identify the different ways they are presented.

6.4 Pricing of wines and drinks

Restaurant wine and drink pricing tends to be based on three basic methods of pricing:

■ **Cost plus pricing** – the selling price of a drink is determined by the addition of specific percentage, of the cost price, to the cost of the drink in order to achieve a predetermined percentage gross profit (gross profit = sales less the cost of sales). This makes more expensive wines and drinks far less attractive to customers. In practice, percentages are varied to achieve standard pricing for similar groups of products, e.g. all spirits or all minerals.

■ **Formula pricing** – the cost price of the wines and drinks is, for example, doubled and then a fixed cash amount is added. This approach to pricing may look more favourable for a higher quality wine.

■ **Rate of return** – the total costs of the business are determined for a given business level and from this the percentage of the cost price required to be added to the cost price is determined in order to ensure that the business will be viable.

■ **Market orientated** – the selling prices are determined by considering both what the customer is likely to pay as well as what others in similar operations, locally are charging. It is also worth considering that there is a certain naivety on the part of some consumers who expect restaurant prices to reflect those of the retail market.

In practice, a combination of these methods is used. For drinks other than wine, it is usual to find that similar products will have the same prices. This avoids each item having a different price and it makes it easier for staff to remember prices. In addition, the percentage of cost prices that is added will vary in order to achieve a balance of selling prices between various items. This is to ensure that the selling prices are in line with what the customer is likely to expect. Thus, lower-cost items such as minerals tend to have a higher percentage of the cost price added to them whereas higher-cost items such as spirits have a lower percentage of the cost price added.

6

For wines, the simple cost-plus approach to pricing (aiming for example for a gross profit of 66%) tends to be used. For example:

A wine with a cost price of £6 and a gross profit percentage of 66% added would be:

£6 x 0.66 = £3.96 + £6 = £9.96

There are also approaches are based on various formulas. One such formula approach is 'double the cost plus'. This takes the cost price of the wine, doubles it and then adds a fixed amount. For example:

A wine with a cost price of £6 doubled would be:

£12 plus £7.92 (66% of £12) = £19.92 Selling price

The difficulty with both cost-plus and any formula approach is that the higher quality wines have a disproportionately higher selling price that lower cost wines.

High selling prices, based on questionable levels of profit margins, do not encourage the sales of these higher priced wines. This then reduces the potential cash gross profit as customers will move to purchasing the lower cost wines with consequently lower cash profit.

An alternative approach to wine pricing can be based on gross profit cash contributions rather than slavishly seeking percentages. This approach uses a fixed mark-up. It recognises that the cash gross profit contribution derives from the total number of sales of an item multiplied by the cash profit that the item provides. Thus, the most profitable item is the one that gives the highest total cash contribution. Using this method, the selling prices for wines are determined by adding a fixed cash amount to the cost price. As a result the pricing of wines achieves a cash gross profit irrespective of the cost price of the wine. Often a banding system is used where the fixed amount is increased slightly the higher the cost price of the wine. With this approach, the higher-priced wines look more attractive to the customer. In the long run this approach tends to increase the cash gross profit through the increased sales of higher quality wines.

■ BYOB and corkage charges

Some establishments allow customers to 'bring your own bottle' (BYOB). This can be for various reasons including cases where the premises are unlicensed for the sale of alcoholic beverages. Other examples are where the operation is offering this as a special promotion or, for example, bistro operations that are located within wine stores. These operations then charge a set amount per bottle for allowing this and the operation will also provide the glassware for customers to use. This charge is known as a 'corkage charge'.

 Another example of where this can happen is for events. The organiser can negotiate with the venue to be able to supply their own wines and other alcoholic beverages. Again a set corkage charge is applied. This can be per bottle but more often now it is charged per person attending the event. The reason for this is because of the difficulties in determining exactly how many bottles have been brought to the venue and then how many bottles have actually been consumed.

Activity:

- Visit the websites of a number of wine and drink suppliers and look up prices of specific wines and other dinks.

- Compare supplier prices with those on different on-line wine and drink lists.

- Consider how do the price variables range in comparison to different types of establishment?

- Using the cost-plus approach to pricing calculate the selling price of the wines below from the cost price given with a 70% gross profit added:

  - Chardonnay - cost price £7.45

  - Pinot Noir - cost price £11.50

6.5   Purchasing

The objective of good purchasing is to achieve the right amount of stock, at the right quality, at the right level and at the right price. In contrast to food, beverages generally have longer shelf lives with the exception of cask and keg beers. However, all items do have a limited life although in the case of good wines this could be several decades.

Although longer shelf life will mean that greater stocks can be held, the cost of storage both in fuel and space costs has to be taken into account. In addition, the holding of high value stock ties up capital that could be used for other purposes. A basic rule of 'first in, first out' (FIFO) is good practice to follow with the stock rotation of most products.

For tied house premises, where the establishment is linked to a particular brewer, the sources for purchasing beverages are determined by the brewer. It is common for brewers to own or have links or associations with specific suppliers of spirits, minerals and other drinks. In these cases, the opportunities for selective purchasing are limited.

For free house premises, the establishment can determine whom they wish to buy from. Some considerations are as follows.

- **Using one main supplier** – The advantage is buying from one supplier rather than many, which reduces administrative costs. Deliveries will be regular and will cover all items. There are also additional benefits from the support that can be had from suppliers in producing wine and drinks lists and menu covers and from discounts that are available depending on amounts purchased. On the other hand, the range of beverages may be limiting in some way, thus reducing the potential range of beverages on offer in a particular establishment. In addition, using one main supplier can make the establishment overly dependent on that source.

■ **Using a variety of suppliers** – The establishment is able to take advantage of buying a particular range of beverages from suppliers whilst they are on offer and reduces dependency on any one particular source. It also means the establishment is more likely to benefit from special promotions or discounts at particular times and from differing sources. Potential disadvantages are that this approach increases the number of separate deliveries, increases paperwork and can lead to inconsistencies in the range of beverages on offer.

Generally, establishments use a combination of the two approaches above: on the one hand, using one main supplier but with additional purchases coming from other sources. Depending on the particular policy of the establishment, the buying of wines needs some further consideration. Buying wines for laying down and service at some future time can build up a good stock of fine wines which can, when sold, produce good profits. However, the downside is the initial capital required and storage costs together with the risks to the stock through spoilage and breakage that could be associated with this approach.

■ The costs of purchasing

There are three areas of cost associated with purchasing. These are:

1 The costs of acquisition:
   - ☐ Preliminary costs including, preparation and specifications, supplier selection and negotiation
   - ☐ Placement costs including order preparation, stationery, postage, telephone
   - ☐ Post-placement costs including order progressing, receipt of goods, inspection of goods, payment of invoices and other clerical controls.

2 The holding costs:
   - ☐ Financial costs, e.g. interest on capital tied up in inventory, cost of insurance
   - ☐ Losses through deterioration, pilferage
   - ☐ Storage costs including space, handling and inspection, stores lighting, heating/refrigeration, clerical costs, e.g. stores records and documentation

3 The cost of stockouts:
   - ☐ Cost of alternatives including buying at enhanced prices and or/using more expensive substitutes.

■ Determining stock levels

Stock levels may be determined by using past sales data. A useful formula is:

$$M = W (T+L) + S$$

Where:

M is the maximum stock
W the average usage rate
T the review period
L the lead time and

S the safety stock (buffer or minimum stock level).

An example using this formula could be:

W	=	24 bottles per week
T	=	4 weeks
L	=	1 week
S	=	1 week's usage, e.g. 24 bottles

Therefore:

$$M = W(T+L) + S$$
$$= 24(4+1) + 24$$
$$= 144 \text{ bottles}$$

Minimum stock (buffer or safety stock) may also be calculated as follows:

$$L \times W = 1 \times 24 = 24 \text{ bottles}$$

ROL (reorder level) may also be calculated as follows:

$$(W \times L) + S = (24 \times 1) + 24$$
$$= 48 \text{ bottles.}$$

Using this type of approach can enable operations to determine the appropriate stock holding to meet the needs of the establishment whilst at the same time minimising the amount of capital tied up in stock. Good stock control can be used to apply *just in time* approaches to stock holding (where suppliers are required to provide small lots of wine and drink supplies on demand), rather than stock levels being determined through *just in case* approaches (buying simply because it *might* be needed). There are also more sophisticated purchase management software solutions that can be used to digitally manage stock control with orders being processed and placed directly with suppliers according to sales figures.

6.6   Further consideration on wine provision

There are essentially two types of commercial wine cellar: the 'restaurant cellar' and 'long-term investment cellar', in some cases the two are combined.

Restaurant cellars usually stock three categories of wine:

- Inexpensive well-made wines for everyday casual consumption
- Moderately priced well-crafted wines from known producers
- Special occasion expensive wines from known producers such as premium older vintage and rarer vintages.

The centre of activity within the wine cellar will alter with the seasons. In winter months, investment in hearty reds matching heavier dishes produced during this period will increase. In warmer months it may be necessary to invest in more light wines, rosé and sparkling wines.

A long-term investment cellar ensures supply as well as value. It is often found in fine dining restaurants and hotels and incudes specific styles of wines (for laying down) whose value will potentially increase over time (a purchaser must also be aware it could potentially decrease in value). Although techniques in vinification (wine making) have changed enormously in the last two decades, proportionately in response to consumer demand for quicker maturing wines, great wines if stored correctly will have the potential to achieve more harmony over time, and, as other individuals consume these vintages prematurely the remaining stocks will increase their value. However high levels of capital invested in fine wines and spirits can seriously affect the cash flow of a business, so it is important for management to know what beverages to purchase and where and what optimum stock levels should be kept for the Purchasing wines

How wine will be purchased and from where will depend on the scale of the operation, the level of interest, purchasing freedom, specialisation, location and how much time can be devoted to sourcing wine. The range of options open to the food service operation is listed in Table 6.2.

Table 6.2: Sources for wine purchasing

Fine wine merchant/distributor	Most frequently used by establishments seeking best quality wines from well-known, well-established producers
(Branded) wine merchant/distributor	Most frequently used by small, medium and many large businesses
Wine division of a brewery company	Purchasers may be locked into purchasing only from a designated supplier
Direct from producer	Usually dependent on your proximity to producers and volume requirements. This option is useful for establishments wanting to offer 'own label' wine or beer giving personalised branding for the business
En primeur	Where ageing cellar space permits, this can prove profitable. See 'Brokers' below.
Wine retailers	Much less likely in larger establishments, but can be very effective for smaller operations, e.g. Majestic Wine
Wine clubs	Rarely used by larger businesses
Internet	Some good finds can be had; however, caution must be taken as there is an increase in fraudulent fine wines being sold online
Wine fair	Rarely used by the largest businesses. Good for the small and medium-sized business
Auction rooms	Good for small and medium-sized businesses
Brokers	Good for small, medium and large-sized businesses. The bulk of en primeur purchasing is now being managed through brokers
Tastings	Held by wine merchants and can invigorate sales as hoteliers and restaurateurs have ample opportunity to sample a broad range of wines

Many businesses will be purely interested in the price of specific wines. However the purchasing decisions will be better shaped if serious consideration is given to value for money and obtaining the return that an operation feels is justified for a particular outlay. Most suppliers do not surmise that operations select simply on price and operate with the understanding that there has to be a price–value balance.

Using merchants

Good merchants can steer buyers towards added value options but also assist in the composition of award-winning wine lists. Writing wine lists should be the merchants' main area of expertise, but the merchant should also be both food and marketplace aware. They should be able to propose the right level of wine list and the right quality of wine, which will be in keeping with the level of the establishment within the marketplace.

Larger hotels and restaurants tend to use more than one supplier and especially if they are part of a group, there may be one nominated supplier for the basic stock. The best merchants supply bespoke services for wine list printing and consultancy services in wine and these services are part of the merchant's main added value. They should be specialists in constructing wine lists, even to the extent of putting together a wine list with the wines from perhaps two other suppliers. Reputable wine merchants can also provide information suggesting food and wine combinations, but it should be remembered they are not absolute experts (no one is) as this is such a subjective area. The wine buyer must certainly be knowledgeable enough to detect bluffers and weaknesses/gaps in the merchant's knowledge or portfolio.

When a merchant is reviewing a list or suggesting a list to a client, they must be able to suggest wines for current drinking, and also be able to state clearly that 12 months from that period he/she will review the wines listed in terms of a development statement on the list. However, it may perhaps be more appropriate to change some of the wines completely at this stage. Wine merchants should also be able to undertake on-site promotions, and contribute to merchandising, training, tasting events, and be speakers at gastronomic events.

Many individuals agonise over the profitability of wine on their lists and many more get it completely wrong. The merchant can offer advice in this area if requested:

- The merchant can do many of the calculations, suggesting a total open margin, a total margin across the list and individual margins for each of the wines
- The merchant should also be able to give advice if the operation is perhaps a little too aggressive (greedy) in pricing some of the finer wines.

Maintaining the quality of wine stock

Wine is a living thing and the development of it must be periodically checked through systematic and regular tasting. This process is to ensure that wines are sold at their optimum condition and within expected the lifespan of the wine. In addition the wine waiter, or sommelier, must have an extensive knowledge of the contents of the wine list. He or she should also have a good knowledge of the characteristics of the different wines and other drinks offered. To develop these skills and knowledge a professional approach to tasting must be adopted. The tasting, or evaluation, of wine and other drinks is carried out to:

■ Develop learning from experience

■ Help in the assessment of the quality of a wine in terms of value (the balance between price and worth) when making purchasing decisions

■ Monitor the progress of a wine which is being stored, to determine the optimum selling time and as part of protecting the investment

■ Identify possible food matching

■ Assist in the description of a wine when explaining its qualities or deficiencies to customers

■ Provide a record of wines tasted, which also helps to reinforce the experience and the learning.

The professional tasting, or evaluation, of wines includes three key stages:

1 Recording the details of each individual wine

2 Looking at, smelling and tasting the wine

3 Recording the findings.

Whenever wine is being evaluated a written record must be kept. These notes should be made at each stage of the process; otherwise it is possible to become muddled and confused. The process of writing down the findings helps to reinforce the discipline of the approach and leads, over time, to the development of greater confidence and skill. This process also provides a record of wine tastings so that there can be greater confidence in the quality of the wines being sold. A cellar log is useful for recording these tastings; this can then be shared online with other wine professionals to compare tasting notes and experiences of certain wines, noting how well they are drinking at that point in time. There is also an ever-increasing range of smartphone applications that can take cellar notes with accompanying photographs to store and share tasting records.

6.7   Storage

The cellar is the focal point for the storage of alcoholic and non-alcoholic liquor. The key factors that will determine good cellar management are:

■ Good ventilation

■ High levels of cleanliness

■ Even temperatures of 13–15°C (55–59°F).

■ Avoidance of strong draughts, vibration, ultraviolet light and wide fluctuation of temperature should be avoided.

■ Storage of beers

For beers, good practices are:

- On delivery all casks should be placed immediately upon their stillions.
- Casks remaining on the floor should have the bung uppermost to withstand the pressure better.
- Ensuring the correct humidity.
- Spiling should take place to reduce any excess pressure in the cask.
- Tappings should be carried out 24 hours before a cask is required.
- Pipes and engines should be cleaned at regular intervals.
- Beer left in pipes after closing time should be drawn off.
- Returned beer should be filtered back into the cask from which it came.
- Care should be taken that the cellar is not overstocked.
- All spiles that are removed during service should be replaced after closing time.
- All cellar equipment should be kept scrupulously clean.
- Any ullage should be returned to the brewery as soon as possible.
- All beer lines should be cleaned weekly with diluted pipe-cleaning fluid and the cellar floor washed down weekly with a weak solution of chloride of lime (mild bleach).

■ Storage of wines

- A subterranean northerly aspect is ideal where possible.
- Excessive temperature variation should be avoided – a constant cool temperature of 7–12.5°C (45–55ºF) should be maintained which will assist the wines to develop gradually.
- Wine should be stored away from the likes of excessive heat, hot water pipes, heating plant or hot unit.
- Excessive dampness should also be avoided and a relative humidity of between 55–70% be maintained. Humidity assists in keeping the cork from drying out, but the very important labels require protecting in the cellar (ordinary hair spray will provide years of protection).
- Draughts and unwanted odours should be avoided, so the cellar should be clean and well ventilated.
- Fluorescent light (it does not give off heat) can be used in a cellar area. otherwise 20–40 watt maximum lighting should be used throughout. Wine can lose its colour followed by its flavour if exposed to too much light. Some wines are partially protected from light however, by their coloured glass bottles. Bright light however, especially sunlight or ultra-violet light should be avoided, especially with Champagne and Chardonnay.

- Table wines should be stored on their sides in bins so that the wine remains in contact with the cork. This keeps the cork expanded and prevents air from entering the wine – a disaster which quickly turns wine to vinegar.

White wines, sweet wines and Champagne are more fragile than reds. White, sparkling and rosé wines should be kept in the coolest part of the cellar and in bins nearest the ground (because warm air rises). Red wines are best stored in the upper bins.

Those red wines which are not filtered – in efforts to preserve their full flavour characteristics – are more likely to suffer from adverse cellarage. Syrah and Cabernet Sauvignon wines are more resilient than Pinot Noirs.

Special refrigerators or cooling cabinets can keep sparkling, white and rosé wines at serving temperature. These may be stationed in the dispense bar (a bar located between the cellar and the restaurant) to facilitate prompt service.

If fine wines cannot be cellared effectively in-house, location of the cellarage at a wine merchants should be considered. There are also self-storage systems around the UK, which provide temperature-controlled vault storage.

■ Storage of other drinks

Spirits, liqueurs, beers, squashes, juices and mineral waters are usually stored upright in their containers. For fortified wines, if screw caps are used the bottles can be stood upright. If with cork closures, lay the bottles on their sides, as for still and sparking wines. Cork stopper closures are generally used for sherries and some ports, which are also stored upright once opened. Vintage and crusted ports are stored horizontally but require time upright to allow sediment to settle at the bottom prior to decanting. Sherries rarely improve in bottle. Finos, Manzanillas and tawny ports are best consumed as soon as possible after purchase.

6.8 Beverage control

In any food service establishment where income is received from the sale of wine and other beverages, a system of control and costing must be put into operation. The system used will depend entirely on the policy of the establishment. Some or all of the books necessary, depending upon the requirements of the particular food service operation, are listed in Table 6.3 together with a statement of their purpose. Although referred to as books here, most modern-day systems are contained within one comprehensive digital solution. However, the basic processes are the same whatever the method being used to record the data.

Table 6.3: Examples of control books used in beverage control

Book	Used to record
Order book	Orders made to suppliers
Goods inwards/received book	Goods received from suppliers
Goods returned book	Goods that are sent back to suppliers
Returnable containers book	Returnable containers sent back to suppliers
Cellar stock ledger	Stock movement in and out of the cellar
Bin cards	Stock of individual lines in the cellar
Requisition book	Re-stocking orders for individual service areas
Daily consumption sheets	Usage of stock in individual service areas
Ullage book	Breakage, spillage and wastage
Off-sales book	Items sold at the off-sale prices
Transfers book	Movement of stock between different service areas

Analysing sales

In order to make decisions about the beverage provision over time there is a need to consider the analysis and evaluation of a number of factors. These include:

- Gross profit margin
- Beverage sales per customer
- Average number of bottles sold per customer
- Sales mix data such as how much white to red wine has been consumed as a percentage amount
- Assessing the average price per bottle sold per period
- Making stock considerations and changes to the lists based on popularity and profitability of items
- Logging requests for wines not on the list
- Monitoring the competition.

Chapters 9 considers in detail the whole range of issues involved with the appraisal of performance and making strategic decisions is considered in Chapter 10.

Determining the cost of beverage sales

The traditional approach to determining usage, or cost of sales, is to take the value of the opening stock, add to it the value of the purchases during the period and then deduct the value of the closing stock. This value is usually the cost price. For outlets with differing gross profit mark-ups, the issue to the various outlets are also costed at selling price to ensure that the revenue is reconciled with that expected from the issue records. This is a very laborious process.

An alternative method is as follows: the beverage stock of an establishment is located in two main areas, the cellar and the outlet or outlets. The outlet stock is usually set at a par level and returned to this level at a set time. This could be each day or each week. All that is really important, for control purposes, is the cost of actual sales. Therefore, only the cost of goods issued to the outlets needs to be calculated.

For the cellar, all that is really important is the physical stock. Its actual value is only required for the end-of-year accounts. If this is true then the stock control of the cellar can be undertaken as follows.

For each stock item, a bin card or entry in the stock book is drawn up including:

- Item – the name of the item
- Quantity – the stock unit, this could be a dozen, six or single
- Reorder level – the level of stock at which a new order is placed; this is predetermined for all items as is the quantity of the stock to be ordered
- Opening stock – in unit terms
- Deliveries – in unit terms
- Issues to outlets – in unit terms
- Closing stock – in unit terms
- Current cost price.

From this record for each trading period, the cost price of issues can be determined. This is the consumption as issued from the cellar to the outlets. In addition, stock levels can be first determined from the book and then physically checked against what is actually in the cellar. The advantage of this system is that it is only the cost of the issues that needs to be calculated.

For each bar or outlet, a similar system exists. There is a par stock and each day or week this is returned to the par levels. Over a period of time it will be found that the stock value of the outlet, at selling price, will be more or less constant. Thus the cost of goods issued to this outlet, at selling price, should equal revenue. This approach requires the predetermining of the stock levels, and the reorder levels, and ensuring that issues to the outlets within the operation are only in whole units (single, dozen etc.).

Activity:

Assuming the role of an Events Manager, you have an upcoming wedding for 100 guests.

- What quantities of Champagne/sparkling wine, white wine and red wine would you order? Give justifications for your calculations.

6.9   References and additional reading

Academy of Food and Wine Service at www.afws.co.uk (accessed December 2018).

Alcohol units and guidelines www.nhs.co.uk (accessed December 2018).

Association de la Sommellerie Internationale at www.sommellerie-internationale.com/en (accessed December 2018).

British Institute of Innkeeeping at www.bii.org (Accessed January 2019).

Cobbold, D, and Durand-Viel, S (2017) *Larousse Wine*, London: Hamlyn.

Coravin Inc. at www.coravin.co.uk (accessed December 2018).

Court of Master Sommeliers at www.courtofmastersommeliers.org (accessed December 2018).

Drink Aware at www.drinkaware.co.uk (accessed December 2018).

Imbibe at www.imbibemagazine.com (accessed December 2018).

International Bartenders Association at www.iba-world.com (accessed December 2018).

Gil, I., Berenguer, G. and Eugenia Ruiz, M. (2009) Wine list engineering: categorization of food and beverage outlets. *International Journal of Contemporary Hospitality Management*. **21**(1), 69-84.

Laloganes, J. (2008) *The Essentials of Wine: With Food Pairing Techniques*, London: Prentice Hall.

Robinson, J., and Harding, J (2015) *The Oxford Companion to Wine*, Oxford: Oxford University Press.

UK Bartenders Guild at ukbartendersguild.co.uk (accessed December 2018).

UK Tea and Infusions Association at www.tea.co.uk (accessed December 2018).

Matching Food and Wine at www.matchingfoodandwine.com (accessed December 2018).

Wine and Spirit Education Trust at www.wsetglobal.com (accessed January 2019).

World of Coffee Events at www.worldcoffeeevents.org (accessed December 2018).

6

7 Food and beverage service

Aim

To identify the key features of food and beverage service and their related management requirements.

Objectives

This chapter is intended to support you in:

- Developing your understanding of the service sequence and the service process
- Identifying and categorising food and beverage service methods
- Exploring the relationship between levels of customer service and resource productivity
- Developing approaches to the maintenance of good customer relations
- Dealing with the management of the volume in food and beverage service
- Managing the stages of the service sequence
- Controlling revenue.

7.1   The nature of food and beverage service

Food and beverage service is a difficult job. Whilst there have been changes in food and beverage service, with less emphasis on the high level technical skills (mistakenly bemoaned by some as deskilling) what wasn't initially being recognised was that other parts of the job are just as, if not more, important. The other thing that wasn't initially recognised was that the provision of high quality service was not confined to a particular type of restaurant and a particular type of service style. In other words excellence in food and beverage is not defined by the inclusion of a narrow range of high-level technical skills.

For food and beverage service the key requirements for staff are:

- Sound product knowledge
- Competence in technical skill
- Well-developed social skills
- The ability to work as part of a team.

Good food and beverage service is achieved where management continually reinforces and supports service staff in the maintenance of good standards of achievement in these aspects. Additionally the provision and maintenance of good service is primarily dependent on teamwork, not only among service staff but also amongst and between staff in other departments.

For managers within the food service operations, skills in marketing, staff management, team development, training, customer relations, financial management and operational management are necessary for the management of the service sequence and ultimately for the survival of the business.

7.2   Food and beverage service systems

Food and beverage service had traditionally been seen as a delivery system. However, as we saw in Chapter 1, food and beverage service actually consists of two separate systems, which are being managed at the same time. These are:

1   **The service sequence** – which is primarily concerned with the delivery of food and beverages to the customer

2   **The customer process** – which is concerned with the management of the experience the customer undertakes to be able to order, be served, consume and have the area cleared.

Separating the service process into two systems provides for a better understanding of the processes as well as providing an indication of the potential options for the organisation of food and beverage service.

■ The service sequence

The *service sequence* is essentially the bridge between the production system, beverage provision and the customer process (or customer experience). The service sequence may consist of eleven or more stages (Cousins *et al.* 2014a) as summarised in Table 7.1.

Table 7.1: Food and beverage service sequence

1 Preparation for service
2 Taking bookings
3 Greeting and seating/directing
4 Taking food and beverage orders
5 Serving of food
6 Serving beverages
7 Clearing during service
8 Billing
9 Dealing with payments
10 Dishwashing
11 Clearing following service

Within these stages, there are a variety of alternative ways of achieving the service. The choices on how the service sequence is designed, planned and controlled are made taking into account a number of organisational variables. These include:

■ Customer needs

■ Level of customer demand

■ The type and style of the food and beverage operation

■ The nature of the customers (non-captive, captive or semi-captive)

■ Prices to be charged

■ Production process

■ Volume of demand

■ Volume of throughput

■ Space available

■ Availability of staff

■ Opening hours

■ Booking requirements

■ Payment requirements, and

■ Legal requirements.

■ The customer process

If food and beverage service is viewed as primarily a delivery process, then the customer can often be seen as a passive recipient of the service. As a result, systems and procedures tend only to be designed from the delivery perspective. However, as discussed in Chapter 3, a customer service specification cannot be achieved if it does not take account of both the infrastructure supporting the specification as well as the ability to implement standards within the interactive phase.

If the whole issue of quality is to be taken seriously, then the customers' involvement in the process must be considered. Customers are not passive but provide the impetus for the operations in the first place. With casual dining becoming more prevalent, people now dine out regularly; therefore, customer demands and expectations have increased. In essence, the customer experience must be focussed on in more detail than ever before.

Activity:

Using your favourite food and beverage establishment as an example:

- Complete a 'virtual walk through' of the customer journey from entering the establishment to leaving it.
- Identify the key elements that make your visit there memorable.
- Identify the key elements that detract from your experience and could be improved.

If the delivery system, or service sequence view of food and beverage service is taken, fifteen or so food and beverage service methods can be identified. A casual consideration makes these various methods appears to be all different. However, when the analysis of service methods is viewed from the *customer process* perspective, i.e. looking at what the customer experience is, then five basic customer processes are identified. A summary of the five customer processes is shown in Table 7.2.

Table 7.2: Simple categorisation of the customer processes in food and beverage service

Service method	Service area	Ordering/ selection	Service	Dining/ consumption	Clearing
Table service	Customer enters and is seated	From menu	By staff to customer	At laid cover	By staff
Assisted service	Customer enters and is usually seated	From menu, buffet or passed trays	Combination of staff and customer	Usually at laid cover	By staff
Self-service	Customer enters	Customer selects items onto a tray	Customer carries	Dining area or take away	Various
Single point service	Customer enters	Orders at single point	Customer carries	Dining area or take away	Various
Specialised or in situ service	Where the customer is located	From menu or predetermined	Brought to the customer	Served where the customer is located	By staff or customer

Within this simple categorisation, all of the fifteen modern food and beverage service methods can then be grouped within the five customer processes. The details of these are:

A   **Table service**: the customer is served at a laid table. This type of service, which includes plated service (American) and silver service (English) is found in many types of restaurant, cafés and in banqueting. Other variations of table service include Guéridon service where food is served on to customer's plate at a side table or trolley; it may also include carving, jointing and fish filleting or the preparation of foods and flambage.

B   **Assisted service:** the customer is served part of the meal at a table and is required to obtain part through self-service from some form of display or buffet. This type of service is found in carvery type operations and is often used for meals such as breakfast in hotels. Many contemporary casual style chain restaurants have now adopted this style of service. It may also be used for functions.

C   **Self-service**: the customer is required to help him or herself from a buffet or counter. This type of service is found in cafeterias and canteens.

D   **Service at a single point**: the customer orders, pays and receives the food and beverages, at the same time, for instance at a counter, at a bar in licensed premises, in a fast food operation or at a vending machine.

E   **Specialised service or service *in situ*:** here the food and beverages are taken to and served where the customer is located. This includes tray service in hospitals or aircraft, trolley service on trains, home delivery, lounge and room service.

For detailed definitions of service methods please see Cousins et al. (2014) Food and Beverage Service 9th edition.

In the *customer processes* A to D, the customer comes to where the food and beverage service is offered and the service is provided in areas primarily designed for the purpose. However in the customer process E the customer receives the service in another location and in an area not primarily designed for the purpose.

With the exception of Group E, the *customer process* within each of the other four groups is similar for the different service methods that are found within each group. Additionally the skills, knowledge, tasks and duties required are similar within each group, with Group A being the most formal and Group D being more casual. Group E has a specialised set of requirements, which are different from those found in the other groups. To identify the commonality of tasks and duties, and therefore organisational needs as well as staff development needs, within each of the service method groups, the *service sequence* for each group can be examined in detail.

Viewing food and beverage service from the *customer process* approach on the one hand ensures a customer service-based perspective but on the other hand it also enables the management to consider alternatives. When deciding upon the service style to implement, it is imperative to seek the most efficient and effective style of service to meet both the needs of the business and the customer. This will effectively reduce labour costs and encourage staff to work more efficiently. It is possible, for instance, to alter the delivery of the service without essentially changing the customer process, by moving between the service methods within each of the first four groups. Thus within Group A, the change from full silver service to a plate service delivery system does not essentially alter the customer process. It will, however, affect the way the service sequence is organised and possibly the production system. On the other hand, changing between the service method groups will substantially change the customer process. If, for example, the service method changes from one in Group A to one in Group C, the effects on the requirements placed on the customer are very different, as can be appreciated from Table 7.2 above.

One further issue to come out of this analysis is to note, that apart from for fast food operations, there is no particular link between a specific service method and a specific food production method (for food production methods see Chapter 5). It is also possible that the food production and beverage provision may be separated from the service by distance or by time, or by both, as for example in off-premises catering.

The overriding factor throughout every service style is to achieve the satisfaction of the customer. This is the main objective and a business should aim to achieve this through delivering excellent service regardless of how formal or casual it may be.

7.3   Customer service vs resource productivity

On the one hand, a food and beverage operation is designed to provide customer services and on the other the achievement of profit is largely determined by the efficiency of the use of resources. Customer service can be defined (as discussed in Chapter 3), as being a combination of five characteristics. These were presented alongside the resources being managed, as shown again here in Figure 7.1.

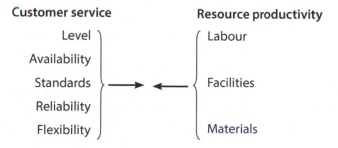

Figure 7.1: Customer service versus resource productivity

In determining the customer service specification for a particular operation, it is necessary to consider the effect that the achievement of the service specification will have on the productivity of the resources.

The effects of variation in the five customer service characteristics and the resource utilisation can be considered as follows:

- **Service level**: as the level of personal service increases, the labour costs will increase as the number of members of staff required will increase as well as the level of staff professionalism. Mealtimes are likely to become longer and therefore the potential capacity of the operation will reduce. In addition in the higher levels of food and beverage service, the equipment used tends to be of higher quality and the amount of equipment needed increases.

- **Availability of service**: increasing the availability of the service will potentially increase labour and material costs and will reduce the efficiency of the facilities used. In these cases it is necessary to endeavour to match the labour and materials being used to the expected volume of business which will vary over a given period.

- **Level of standards:** increasing the level of standards in the food and beverage operation will increase the cost of materials as better grade materials are used and increase the cost of labour as the level of staffing and the staffing professionalism will need to be higher. In addition, the provision of the facilities will have a higher cost again because of the higher grade of finishes being used.

- **Reliability of the service**: in order to ensure a high reliability in the provision of the service, again the labour and material costs will increase because, in order to protect the reliability of the product, it will be necessary to have a higher proportion of equipment, labour and materials available.

- **Flexibility of the service**: moving away from a limited standard range of products and services will increase material and labour costs and will reduce the efficiency of the facilities being used.

Reduced resource utilisation is often associated with the provision of a more individually tailored or personal service. There is therefore an expectation of a higher level of revenue being obtained from the higher prices that can be changed for the service. This higher level of revenue will compensate for the reduction in the efficiency of the use of the resources. A further development of this approach is that it is then potentially possible, through changes in the service process, to effect greater efficiency without fundamentally altering the customer process: moving from full silver service to plate service, for example.

On the other hand, and in all cases, the opposite of the examples given above will potentially increase the efficiency of the resources being used. This approach is often associated with more standardised levels of service together with reduced levels of personal service. Consequently this lower cost provision is then associated with potentially lower revenue due to lower prices being able to be charged. However lower cost provision and greater standardisation is also associated with potentially higher volumes of customers, so revenue matches the profit levels required by the operation.

In summary then, the development of the customer service specification should always take account of the five customer service characteristics identified above in order to be able to predetermine the level of resource utilisation and therefore the level of efficiency that is possible. This then also has implications for the revenue that will be required to meet the cost of the provision of the service. (Developed from the original text in Cousins, 1994.)

Activity:

Using the five customer service characteristics:

- Give three examples of different styles of food and beverage concepts.

- State how each operation has adapted the five characteristics to suit the provision.

7.4   Customer relations

The existence of good customer relations is as much a part of the food and beverage product as any other aspect. Developing and maintaining good customer relations can be achieved if people working in the food and beverage operation have:

- The ability to **recognise the symptoms** of a deterioration in customer relations
- The ability to **minimise the causes** of customer relations problems.

The **symptoms** of potential customer relations problems are:

- Increasing number of complaints generally
- Increasing number of complaints specifically about staff
- Increasing number of accidents
- Regular mistakes by staff in orders, etc.
- Customers arriving without previous bookings being noted
- Increases in breakages
- Shortages of equipment
- Arguments between staff
- Poor morale of staff
- High turnover of staff.

Minimising the causes of customer relations' problems is concerned with ensuring that the conditions members of staff work under are likely to support the maintenance of good standards of interpersonal skills. There are four requirements to be considered when attempting to achieve this:

- The existence of agreed procedures for dealing with a range of customer service issues
- The customer service specification being able to be supported by the physical capabilities of the operation
- The customer service specification being able to be supported by the technical, interpersonal skills, product knowledge and team working abilities of the staff
- The identification of the likely customer satisfaction or otherwise that customers are likely to receive from the food and beverage experience.

These four requirements are examined further below.

Agreed procedures

Example of situations where there is a need for agreed procedures are:

- Addressing customers
- Wrong orders
- Advising customer with dietary needs
- Complaints about food and beverage items or other matters
- Customer illness
- Enforcement of dress codes
- Emergencies such as power cuts, fire alarms and bomb threats
- Dealing with children (and lost children)
- Dealing with customers who have mobility, sight and communication difficulties
- Dealing with solo diners
- Unacceptable customer behaviour
- Lost property
- Alcohol over-consumption
- Enforcement of mobile phone and non-smoking codes including the non-use of e-cigarettes.
- Dealing with online feedback via social media or online review forums

Procedures for all these types of situations must be agreed and consistently applied by all staff. These procedures should then be reviewed and reconsidered on a regular basis as part of training sessions and staff feedback sessions.

Physical capabilities of the operation

Limitations in the physical capabilities of the operation to meet the requirements of the customer service specification will always be the cause of difficulties. This is why the customer service specification itself should only be agreed by taking account of the physical capabilities of the operation.

■ Abilities of the staff

Limitations in the capabilities of the staff to be able to support the intended customer service specification will also always be the cause of difficulties. Again there has to be a balance between the technical and interpersonal skills, product knowledge and teamworking capability of the staff and the requirements of the customer service specification. As well as interaction with customers, service staff also are interacting with staff outside of the service areas, e.g. kitchen staff, bill office staff, dispense bar staff, stillroom staff. It is important that the provision of the food and beverage product within an establishment is seen as a joint effort between all departments, with each department understanding the needs of the others in order to meet the customers' demands. If there is imbalance, then either the staff capabilities have to be modified or customer service specification altered so that the two are in harmony.

■ Customer satisfaction

The potential to achieve customer satisfaction should already have been built into the design of the product in order to ensure it meets the needs and expectations the customers have at the time. Knowing what the potential for customer satisfaction, or dissatisfaction, is from the food and beverage product can help to ensure that there are procedures in place for dealing with any difficulties that might arise.

7

Examples of incidents which can create dissatisfaction include:

- Wrong orders.
- Being sat in a restaurant right next to the only other table in the room.
- Wine and drinks being served after the food has been served.
- Being served by members of staff who do not know who had ordered what and do not know about what they are serving.
- Glasses being overfilled, together with incessant and unnecessary topping up of water or wine, especially when it is by any server who happens to be walking past the table
- Hot food being served on cold plates.
- Food being served on plates that are too large for the food, and for the place setting, or food being served on a variety of out of the ordinary surfaces or utensils.
- Waiting too long for cutlery to be provided or accompaniments to be served.
- Being given an inaccurate wait time for their food to be delivered.
- Being asked if everything is alright, often more than once, when just looking would provide the server with the answer to the question
- Staff chatting to each other when serving, or shouting over at another member of staff

- Rude, unhelpful and scruffy (including unkempt hair) staff.

- Having a disability and the service staff talking to a companion about them, rather than talking to them.

- Background music that is inappropriate, or too loud, or both.

- Being unable to attract a server's attention because no-one is watching the room, either because the members of staff are chatting in a group, or because there is no member of the staff in the room.

- Seeing poorly managed buffet displays: such as not kept stocked and tidy and having no regard for strict food stock rotation (fresh food being tipped on top of food already on display).

- Having to use dirty toilets and/or toilets that are not properly monitored and maintained.

- Other people's use of mobile phones.

In Chapter 1 (page 19) we identified that the potential dissatisfactions fall into two categories: those which are controllable by the establishment, such as scruffy, unhelpful staff, or cramped conditions; and those which are uncontrollable, such as behaviour of other customers, the weather, or transport problems. Being able to identify all of these possibilities will enable an operation to have procedure in place to deal with them when they occur.

See Chapter 9, page 294, for further information on reviewing performance and on obtaining customer feedback. Also see the notes on responding to social media issues in Chapter 3, page 76).

◼ Maintaining and enhancing customer relations

To minimise the potential for customer relations problems there has to be equal concern over the physical aspects of the service, the way in which the service is operated, and with the interpersonal interaction between customers and staff.

Maintaining good customer relations is essential for business survival. To help ensure good levels of customer relations are maintained, question to consider include:

- Are all managers and supervisors able to identify the symptoms of customer relations problems?

- Are all staff trained in the requirements of the job and is their ability regularly monitored?

- Are all staff aware of what is deemed as appropriate communication with customers? Is the emphasis in the work areas always put on the customer?

- What problems can be solved by physical changes to the operation?

- What problems exist because information to customers is insufficient other than that which can only be obtained from asking a member of staff?

- Are potential problems minimised by making arrangement in advance?

- Are there set procedures for a wide range of customer incidents?
- Are complaints always used as an opportunity to show real care for customers?
- Are all members of staff encouraged to identify and propose solutions for customer relations problems?
- **And, most important of all**: Do all supervisors and managers always observe the same service standards as those required from the members of staff?

■ Dealing with complaints

It is still a strange phenomenon in the hospitality industry that the response to complaints is often to just apologise. The customer actually wants:

- A clear indication that the complaint is understood
- An apology
- Things to be put right
- To be assured that steps are, have been, or are to be taken, to ensure such things do not happen again.
- To gain confidence that if they come back to the operation that things will have improved
- And importantly, that compensation will be offered if the customer has not received the service.

7.5   Managing volume

Business volume inevitably varies throughout any trading period whether this is a year, a month, a week or even an hour. Operating at under full capacity for any period can lead to a disproportionate increase in costs and therefore a reduction in the overall profit contribution. The management of food service operations therefore is also about matching the ability of the operations to provide services to the expected volume of demand.

Many large food and beverage service providers now use labour models and other software programmes to calculate and determine accurate staffing levels, using data from previous years and by observing trends in the marketplace. Consumer analytics can also be developed by looking at online records, restaurant app usage and customer profiles, in order to accurately observe customer behaviour and monitor increase or decline in business volume. These approaches reduce the likelihood of human error when managing volume and ensures the utilisation of labour is maximised at all times.

Kotler *et al.* (2013) identify specific dimensions that should be taken into account when considering the hospitality product (see Chapter 1, page 12). One of these dimensions is the 'perishability' of the product. This is a key dimension of the food and beverage product. It cannot be stored. For instance, seats in a restaurant, which are not sold at one mealtime, cannot be compensated for by additional sales at another time. In other words, the sale of food and beverage is limited by the capacity of the operation at the time. Therefore, in food and beverage operations, it is necessary to consider how the capacity of the operation for customer sales can be managed in order that the goals of the business may be achieved.

■ Measuring capacity

The capacity of a food and beverage operation is measured not only by considering the maximum capacity of customers at a given time but also the capacity that can be achieved over time. For example, a restaurant operation with a maximum seating of 100 covers can achieve a much higher actual capacity for a given meal period if the seats can be used more than once during the period. The potential for this will, however, vary according to the type of operation. A banqueting room, for example, can usually only be filled once during a meal period and therefore the size of the function in terms of covers served will determine the capacity achieved at that time. Fine dining restaurants now recognise the need to increase the dining room capacity within a service period and have begun to manage time slots giving the ability to re-use a table more than once in any given service. (For examples of how customer throughput can be determined for different types of operation, see Chapter 4, page 122).

■ Volume and service organisation

One of the key differences between the management of food and production and the management of food and beverage service is that as the volume of business increases, it requires fundamental alterations in the food production process, whereas the service process may simply be multiplied (Cousins, 1988). As the volume of food production increases, the way in which the production is organised has to change. This change can be either where the process is separated into various parts of the menu required, which is the basis of the 'partie' system, or where the production system is based on the type of processes being used. For food and beverage service, as the volume increases additional service is provided through, for instance, increasing the number of stations in a restaurant. This is much the same as the opening of additional checkouts in a supermarket or increasing the number of tellers available in a bank, as the level of demand increases.

Although in food service operations there is the possibility of changing the service methods, such changes are usually driven by needs to improve resource efficiency rather than by the need to provide for higher volumes of business. An example is breakfast service. This can be provided through conventional table service at any volume of business but the need to reduce costs, especially staff costs, is often the main reason behind moving to a buffet system.

■ Increasing throughput

There is a relationship between the volume of customers to be served and the length of time they stay on the premises. The time customers take in different types of operation varies. There are various norms, which exist for seating/consumption times. Examples of there times for various types of food service operation are given in Table 7.3.

Table 7.3: Seating/consumption times in various types of food service operation

Operation	Consumption time (minutes)
Restaurant	60–120
Carvery	45–90
Popular catering	30–60
Cafeteria	15–40
Wine bar	30–60
Pub (food)	30–60
Takeaway with seating	20–40
Fast food with seating	10–20

There is also a relationship between the potential volume of customers and the opening times of the operation. For example, in a full service restaurant, the seating time of customers might average one and a half hours. If the restaurant is open for four hours, then it might be possible to fill the operation twice. If, however, the opening hours were only two and a half hours, then this would not be possible.

Opening times are determined by the consideration of:

- Local competition
- Local attractions, such as a theatre
- Location of the premises, e.g. city centre/country/suburb
- Transport systems
- Staffing availability
- Volume of business anticipated
- Local tradition.

A way of increasing the potential volume of demand that can be accommodated is to consider ways of increasing the throughput of the number of customers. The desirability of this, and the extent to which it can be achieved, varies with the type of operation. Some approaches to increasing throughput might be as follows:

- **Review the service sequence steps:** Identify and review all the steps in the service sequence from welcoming customers, order taking, service of food and beverages, clearing, though to billing, payment and departure. Ensure there are set procedures for the individual parts of the service sequence, such as ensuring orders are taken within a specific time of the customer arriving. There may also be ways of combining various steps to increase efficiency, but at the same time not rushing the customers.

- **Turn tables:** This involves determining and allocating eating time limits for customers. Table turnaround systems are increasingly evident in food service operations. As customers have got used to this approach, the practice has become more prevalent, even in high end restaurant operations. However there are customers who can have seriously negative reactions to attempts to limit the length of the meal. This is especially so where the meal out is the sole purpose of a lunch or evening out. Bookings can be lost because of this. Clear communication with the customer is vital; pre-warning the customer of a time limit on the table can often mitigate a negative reaction. However it is wise to ensure that some flexibility remains in the system in order to allow for the customers who might accept this approach and those who won't.

- **Serve parts of the meal in separate areas:** Pre-meal drinks and order taking can be done in a bar or lounge area. This reduces the time required for the table. Similarly coffees and after dinner drinks can be offered to be served back in a bar or lounge area, in order to free up the dining table quicker.

- **Using both brighter lighting and less comfortable seating:** In appropriate settings, can have the effect of encouraging increased throughput.

- **Encouraging customers to share tables:** Although this can be a way of increasing customer throughput, the acceptability of this to customers substantially decreases in operations with higher levels of service and higher prices.

- **Ensure efficient clearing:** This will encourage further sales or discourage lingering. People feel uncomfortable being left sitting at an empty table or bar. This approach can also be adopted in lounge areas and for cafeterias.

- **Utilise new payment solutions:** Paying the bill is one of the biggest pain points in the customer process. Customers resent having to wait around for their bill. Emerging solutions such as contactless payment systems, using credit cards and debit cards, key fobs, smart cards, smartphones and other mobile devices can speed up the process for customers and allow staff to concentrate on providing great service.

Other approaches include limiting the need for increasing the throughput of customers, such as setting minimum charges for peak demand periods thus attempting to ensure maximum revenue from the customers who are being accommodated. Reduced menu alternatives with quick service promises can also be considered.

■ Limiting demand

Where the actual demand is significantly higher than the capacity of the operation, consideration must be given to methods of limiting the volume of demand. Depending on the type of operation, this issue varies in significance. An à la carte restaurant operating at a high customer service specification will tolerate fluctuations in demand and seek to ensure availability and flexibility to meet all the expected demand. Some restaurants offer an online booking service, which gives customers a clear idea of availability, however limited availability can sometimes increase demand further. On the other hand, a cafeteria operation will seek to maximise demand during the service period.

Limitations in demand can be achieved through pricing policies. In city-centre hotels for instance, the demand for full breakfast is limited in this way through disproportionately higher pricing for a full breakfast compared to other alternatives. Meal packaging is also a way of reducing the variations in the range of demand being met.

■ Using queues

In addition though, there is the use of queues to ensure that the operation is working to a full capacity. Examples of this approach are found in, for instance, fast food operations where although the queue is controlled by a time limit for the customers to queue, it does provide constant demand at the service point. Another example is, for instance, TGI Fridays, where the queue for food service is the central bar area. In this operation, the queue becomes part of the meal experience and also provides for revenue from the queue, through drink sales, while waiting for meal service. In managing the queue requirement there are a number of factors to be taken into account so that the process of waiting in the queue does not become a negative part of the service process from the customers' perspective. The factors, which affect customer satisfaction, and some of the actions that the food service operation can consider, are summarised in Table 7.4.

Table 7.4: Service considerations in minimising queuing dissatisfaction

Factor	Service consideration
Unfair versus a fair wait	Try to ensure that the wait the customer undertakes is perceived as fair; design queuing systems to ensure service to customers is strictly in the order of the queue
Uncomfortable versus a comfortable wait	Consider the impact of the waiting environment; seek to maintain a high level of comfort
Unexplained versus an explained wait	Provide reasonable explanations for the wait and update regularly; try to avoid the customers' seeing underused capacity
Unexpected versus an expected wait	Accept responsibility; provide reasonable explanations for the wait and update regularly
Unoccupied versus an occupied wait	Provide distractions, which either increase the effectiveness of the service sequence or involve the customer more in the service sequence
Initial versus a subsequent wait	Design the service sequence so that the customer has early contact with the servers; try to spread the total wait time across a number of the stages

Anxious versus calm wait	Assess the general level of anxiety of the customers; be aware of the need of customers for staff contact and reassurance
Individual versus a group waiting	Recognise that an individual waits feel longer than a group waiting; consider ways of ensuring that the wait is more pleasant through providing distraction
Valuable service versus less valuable service	Recognise that customers will wait longer the higher the perceived value of the service being offered; but still try to minimise the wait time
New or infrequent users versus regular users	Recognise that new or infrequent users will perceive that waiting times are longer than frequent users who will have become accustomed to waiting; always provide information and reassurance to all customers

Source: developed from proposals by Maister, 1985; Davis and Heineke, 1994; Cousins, 1994; and Jones and Peppiatt, 1996.

■ Banquet/function operations and capacity

In the organisation of banquet/function operations, there are special considerations in respect of capacity issues. Clearly the capacity of the function rooms will determine the maximum numbers that can be accommodated at a particular time. However, variations in the service methods and the dining layouts can alter both the maximum numbers which can be served and also the volume which can be achieved over time. Selling functions that are similar in service layout and method, for instance, can reduce the preparation for service and the clearing after service periods.

In addition, the capacity of function rooms is affected by the combination of the bookings taken. The taking of certain types of functions will reduce or preclude the taking of others. Noisy presentations will, for instance, limit the use of adjoining rooms. If the intention of the operation is to be flexible, then this is inevitable. If the operation wants to specialise (and therefore reduce the flexibility) it is possible to increase the volume throughout. This supposes however that the volume of business requiring more standardisation is available.

■ The complexity of managing capacity

Managing capacity in food and beverage operations is not a simple issue. The provision of food and beverages is highly complex with a variety of stages both in the production and the service processes, all of which have an effect on the volume of business that can be met. In addition, the limitations posed by the physical facilities are not always the key determinant of the potential capacity that can be achieved. In many cases the customer service specification will determine that inefficiency in the use of the facilities will be outweighed by the need to provide a certain level of service. In addition, the control of labour and material costs must be taken into account in determining the potential volume of business which can be handled within the predetermined customer service specification.

7.6   Managing the service sequence

In developing the customer service specification, the capability of the operation needs to be considered. Similarly, once the customer service specification has been determined, then the *service sequence* can be designed or redesigned and managed in order to ensure that the customer service specification is achieved. Aspects of the managing the service sequence are considered in the sections below.

■ The need for consistency

Within food and beverage service there are traditional ways of doing things that have become established over time. These are known as the 'service conventions' (Cousins *et al.* 2014a) and they have proved to be effective and efficient ways in which to carry out the service. Having agreed service conventions for the operation ensures standardisation in the service sequence and the customer process (see pages 204 and 205 for the definition of these terms), both for staff and for customers. These are often also used as the basis for the compilation of standards of performance manuals (SOPs). Examples of general conventions are given in Table 7.5.

Table 7.5: Examples of general conventions

General Requirements	Rationale
Work hygienically and safely.	For the protection of all staff and customers from harm and to avoid accidents.
Always work as part of a team.	To ensure a smooth, well organised and disciplined operation, all members of the team should be able to do their own job well and also able to contribute to team working, both within and between departments.
Pass other members of staff by moving to the right.	Having an establishment rule about each member of staff always moving to the right (or left) when trying to pass each other, saves time and avoids confusion and accidents.
Use checklists for all the tasks and dutires required.	Using checklists ensures that all the required tasks, are carried out in the same way, and that all the tasks are completed.

For food and beverage service to operate efficiently and smoothly, it is important that all members of the staff follow the same service conventions. Different establishments may adopt variations on the service conventions, but whatever service conventions are used it is essential that all members of staff follow the same ones. Otherwise the service will be inefficient and potentially chaotic. It will be an unpleasant experience for the staff working in the establishment and the customers will perceive that the operation is not coordinated and well managed.

■ Preparation for service

One of the preparatory tasks is the taking of bookings. Systems need to be developed to ensure that bookings are taken in a way that ensures the efficiency of the operation. This includes consideration of overbooking systems in operations where bookings are taken. There are, however, risks with this approach. It is also necessary to take into account the law on contract. Bookings for larger parties and events are discussed in Chapter 8.

Within the service areas, there are a variety of tasks and duties which need to be carried out to ensure that adequate preparation has been made for the expected volume of business and the type of service to be provided. These include:

- Housekeeping duties
- Setting out dining/consumption areas
- Preparing serving equipment, cutlery, crockery, glassware and disposable service ware
- Preparing linen
- Preparing counters and trolleys
- Stocking bar areas and stillroom areas
- Preparing and stocking workstations.

Examples of conventions when preparing for service are given in Table 7.6.

Table 7.6: Example of service conventions when preparing for service

Preparation tasks	Rationale
Prepare service areas in sequence.	Ensure service areas are laid out and housekeeping duties have been completed before the preparation for service begins. This can save time and unnecessary duplication of effort afterwards.
Place items on the table consistently.	Looks neat and presents a professional image. Make sure that any crested or patterned crockery or glassware is always placed the same way round on the table and that it is evenly spaced. Crests or badges are usually placed at the 12o'clock position.
Use trays.	Using trays is about efficiency. Smaller trays should always be used to carry equipment to and from tables. Larger trays are used to bring foods and beverage items to the service areas and to clear during and following service. Trays can also be used to serve plated foods from (or to clear plates onto) with service staff working as a pair.

Preparation for service should also include the briefing of staff to ensure that they have adequate knowledge of the product and about any specials, or particular customer requirements that are expected.

Taking food and beverage orders

Taking orders from customers for the food and drink they wish to have, takes time. Limiting the choice can reduce this time but this possibility depends on the particular operation. The order-taking process, though, is part of a longer process, which feeds information to the food production or bar areas and provides information for the billing method. Whatever type of system is used, whether manual or computer based, it will be derived from one of four basic order-taking methods. These are:

1 **Duplicate or triplicate manual checks**: One copy is used for billing purposes with the other being delivered to the kitchen. The server can retain a third copy as a record of the order and for use with order notation techniques (see under Order Taking in Table 7.7).

2 **Handheld or smartphone app ordering system**: whereby the order is taken at the table or prior to arrival on a handheld device or via a smartphone app which then electronically sends the order to directly to the kitchen or bar enabling the server to remain on the restaurant floor.

3 **Service with order**: taking order and serving to order, as used for example in bar service and take-away methods and also for self-service (where the customer self-selects from a counter).

4 **Pre-ordered**: individually, or for groups of people such as for events.

Even the most sophisticated electronic system is based upon either the triplicate or duplicate method. Checks can be written by staff on check pads or keyed in on handheld terminals. Customers can also hand write orders (as in some bar operations) or use electronic systems such as iPads. The order is then either communicated by hand to the food production or beverage provision areas, or, for computer-based systems, communicated electronically to visual display units (VDUs), or printout terminals, in those areas. There are also systems where the menu is projected onto tabletops enabling the seated customer to select their order from these interactive displays.

More recently, the introduction of mobile phone apps for food and beverage ordering allow customers to enter their orders, which are sent through the app to the kitchen or bar. The apps help to improve the speed of service, enabling more people to be served quickly. This also automates and improves the management processes. The potential downfalls of such automated kitchen ordering devices were original identified by William Whyte (1947) in his seminal piece work '*The Social Construction of the Restaurant*'. Where he identified the need for "meaning in interaction" between servers and production staff. Order messages cannot be effectivity communicated through technology, when requests deviated from the set process script. Staff can feel disengaged from the food service process and treated the customer as a commodity. Automation is an aid to the caterer, but not a substitute for interaction and its limitations need to be recognised.

Interestingly the use of such technology is being used by customers as a service USP or gimmick. Well-known public houses or bars in the UK are using bar service apps. The customer downloads the app onto their own device and while seated at the table can then order their drinks, pay for them and be served without moving from the table. People can also order remotely for their friends – or anyone – in the bar and many articles can be found in the press such as: www.independent.co.uk/life-style/food-and-drink/wetherspoons-pub-customers-order-pay-app-exploit-loop-free-drinks-alcohol-pints-beer-a7787466.html

Service conventions in order taking

When taking food and beverage orders staff need to follow the establishment service conventions to ensure efficiency and consistency. Examples of service conventions when taking orders, and the reasons for them, are given in Table 7.7.

Table 7.7: Examples of service conventions when taking food and beverage orders

Order taking	Rationale
Take food, wine and drink orders through the host of the table.	This is common courtesy. The host is usually the one paying so agreement always needs to be obtained for any items that are to be served. This will also save any disagreements about payments later.
Be able to explain to a customer what the food and beverage items are.	Customers like to know what they are eating and drinking. For some customers this is essential knowledge as there may be dietary requirements to be considered. Never attempt to bluff.
Use order notation techniques.	Using these techniques helps any server to identify which customer at the table is having a particular item of food or beverage. It saves servers having to shout the name of a dish at the table.
Always be aware of customers who may have additional needs.	Look out for, and be prepared to deal with, people with sight, hearing, mobility and communication difficulties. Also be prepared and be able to deal with children.
Be open-minded and non-judgemental towards customer differences.	This helps to demonstrate respect for cultural traditions and diversity in society.

In addition to the standard order-taking process, there is also a need to make provision for orders to cover specific incidents such as:

- **Follow on** – to indicate that one order has already been taken for that particular table or customer.
- **Supplement** - indicating that a portion of something is being ordered, which is additional to that which has already been served.
- **Return/Replacement** – for when a member of staff has ordered a wrong item and the order has to be sent back to the kitchen or bar and then be replaced.
- **Accidents** – for when an item has to be replaced because of, for example, the spillage of a drink. Usually this is also noted as a no-charge order.
- **No charge** – for when an item or meal is being given on a complimentary basis.

Within the order-taking procedure there are also many opportunities to the promotion of additional sales (sometimes referred to as up-selling) through exploiting the potential for personal selling by the service staff (for more information on personal selling, see pages 88 to 89).

■ The service of food and beverages

The various service methods available to the food service operator are listed in Table 7.2, page 205. The choice of service method will depend as much on the customer service specification as on the capability of the staff, the operation and the equipment available.

It is also essential that all staff follow the same service procedures to ensure consistency of service. Examples of service conventions, and the rationale for them, are given in Table 7.8

Table 7.8: Examples of service conventions for food and beverages

General service	Rationale
Serve cold food before hot food.	Avoids customers having hot food going cold whist waiting for cold items to be served. When the hot food is served the service is complete and customers can enjoy the meal without waiting for additional items to be served. For the same reason, accompaniments should be automatically offered and served at the same time as the food item.
Serve wine and other drinks before food.	Similar to the above. Customers will want to enjoy the wine or drinks with their meal. They will not want to wait for the wine and drink service, as their hot food goes cold.
Avoid stretching across customers.	Shows respect for personal physical space. If customers really have to be reached across then always use the arm furthest away from them. No one likes an elbow in their face. Also, no matter how clean the service staff are themselves, food and beverage smells do tend to cling to service uniforms.
Table service	
Place items on a table for the convenience of the customer.	Lower height items should be placed near to the customer and taller items behind or to the side of these. This makes items such as glassware, jugs or teapots easily accessible for the customer and helps to avoid accidents.
Start service from the right hand side of the host, with the host last.	Principal guests are usually seated on the right of a host. The service of the table starts by first serving the principal guest then moving anti-clockwise for plated service (clockwise for silver service) to each customer. This ensures that members of the serving staff are always walking forwards (and seeing where they are going) to serve the next person. The host is normally served last.
Serve women first.	This is sometimes done if it does not slow the service. However, there are potential cultural issue here. Particular care needs to be taken so as not to confuse things when the host is a woman. A host of either gender is still the host and should always be served last.
Silver serve food from the left hand side of a customer.	Ensures that the service dish is nearer the plate for ease of service and to prevent food being spilt onto the person. Customers can more easily see the food being served and make choices if necessary, and members of the service staff are also able to see and control what they are doing. Foods should always be placed consistently on each plate – otherwise it can just look a mess.

7

Use separate service gear for different food items.	Avoids different food items or sauces being transferred from one dish or plate to another and avoids messy presentation of foods on the customers' plates.
Serve plated foods from the right hand side of a customer.	Plates are placed in front of the customer with the right hand and the stack of other plated food is then behind the customer's chair in the left hand. If there is an accident, the plates held in the left hand will go onto the floor rather than over the customer. Plated foods should also be placed so that the food items are consistently in the same position for all customers, and as the chef had designed them to be presented.
Serve all beverages from the right hand side of a customer.	Glasses are placed on the right hand side of a cover and the service of beverages follows from this. For individual drinks and other beverages, the tray is held behind a customer's seat in the server's left hand. Other beverages such as coffee and tea are also served from the right. All beverages should also be cleared from the right.
Clear from the right hand side of a customer.	Plates can be removed from in front of the customer with the right hand and the stack of plates is then behind the customer's chair, in the server's left hand. If there is an accident, the plates held in the left hand will go onto the floor rather than over the customer. The exception to this is for side plates, which are on the left-hand side of the cover. These are more easily cleared from the left.
Separate the serving at table from food/ drink collection and sideboard/ workstation clearing.	Ensures that there is always someone in the room to attend to customers and to monitor the overall service, while others are bringing in food and beverage orders or clearing items away from the service stations. This approach also allows for the training of new staff and ensures that customer contact is primarily through experienced staff.

■ Billing

The various billing methods found in food service operations are as follows:

- ■ **Bill as check**: second copy of order used as bill
- ■ **Bill with order**: service to order and billing at same time, e.g. bar or takeaway methods
- ■ **Prepaid**: customer purchases ticket or card in advance either for specific meal or specific value. This can also include pre-loaded cash balances onto cards that can also be topped up.
- ■ **Voucher**: customer has credit issued by third party, e.g. tourist agency voucher for either specific meal or specific value
- ■ **No charge/ complimentary**: customer not paying
- ■ **Deferred**: refers to functions and events where bill paid by organiser.
- ■ **Account**: The total is added on to an existing account which will be invoiced at a later date.

The actual choice of billing method will be dependent on the type and style of the operation. However, the billing system is also part of a longer process linked first to the order-taking method and second to the revenue control procedures (see the notes on Revenue Control on page 226). In managing the billing method, it is necessary therefore to ensure that the method chosen supports both the order-taking method and the revenue control requirements.

Consideration also needs to be given to the use of electronic point of sale control (EPOS) systems and utilising new payment solutions such as contactless payment systems. The range of acceptable payment methods needs to be predetermined along with clarity on the level of discretion allowed to different individuals or groups of staff.

Clearing

The various clearing methods found in food service operations may be summarised as follows:

- **Manual 1**: the collection of soiled ware by waiting staff to dishwash area
- **Manual 2**: the collection and sorting to trolleys by operators for transportation to dishwash area
- **Semi-self-clear**: the placing of soiled ware by customers on strategically placed trolleys within dining area for removal by operators
- **Self-clear**: the placing of soiled ware by customers on conveyor or conveyorised tray collecting system for mechanical transportation to dish wash area
- **Self-clear and strip**: the placing of soiled ware into conveyorised dishwash baskets by customer for direct entry of baskets through dishwash.

The choice of clearing method, whether manual by staff or involving customers, will be dependent not only on the type of operation but also on the nature of the demand being met. In captive situations, for instance, it is possible to have greater customer involvement.

Again it is important that all staff follow the same establishment service conventions, such as those given in Table 7.5 and 7.7, to ensure consistency and efficiency.

Dishwashing

The capacity of the dishwashing system should always be greater than the operational maximum required. This is because slow dishwashing increases the amount of equipment required to be in use at a particular time and increases the storage space required in service areas.

The various dishwashing systems are as follows:

- **Manual**: manual washing by hand or brush machine of soiled ware
- **Semi-automatic**: manual loading by operators of dishwash machine
- **Automatic conveyor:** manual loading by operators of soiled ware in baskets mounted on conveyor for automatic transportation through dishwash machine

7

- **Flight conveyor:** manual loading by operators of soiled ware within pegs mounted on conveyor for automatic transportation through dishwasher.
- **Deferred wash:** the collection, stripping, sorting and stacking of ware by operators for transportation through dishwash at later stage.

Essentially, the potential volume that can be accommodated increases, as well as potential efficiency, from the manual method to the flight conveyor method, and the choice of method will be largely dependent on the scale of the operation. It is also often necessary to employ more than one method. The deferred wash system can be used as a cost-saving approach as wash-up staff do not have to be employed until the end of a service period especially when this is late at night.

Clearing following service

After the service periods, there are a variety of tasks and duties to be carried out partly to clear from the previous service and partly to prepare for the next. The efficient management of the clearing stage can have a dramatic impact on the potential reuse of an area.

Included in this stage of the service sequence is the requirement for the management of cleaning programmes. Detailed cleaning schedules need to be developed to ensure that all cleaning activities are coordinated. These can be daily, weekly, monthly and for other periods. Alongside these cleaning schedules, it is desirable to incorporate maintenance checks. These, together with the operation of cleaning schedules, can help to ensure that equipment and facilities are always available and in working order.

(More detailed information on the service sequence for differing service methods is set out in Cousins *et al.*, 2014b.)

7.7   Revenue control

Revenue control encompasses the sale of all food and beverage and is essential to ensure maximum return. Particular attention must be paid to the key factors influencing profitability. Crucial controls have to be assigned for the main factors affecting the revenue of the business, such as the menu, wine list and other beverages, the total volume of food and beverage sales, the sales mix, the average spend of customers in each selling outlet at different times of the day, the number of covers served and the gross profit margins.

The control system

The revenue control system should be simple and manageable and ensure control:

- At all locations of the operation where selling takes places, and
- For all items internally issued from the various departments.

With the aims of:

- Reducing pilfering
- Eradicating wastage
- Protecting revenue.

The type of control system varies with the size of the food service operation. There needs to be accountability for what has been served to the customer and payment for what has been issued from the kitchen or the bar. Accurate billing should be standard and the outcome should be that the system can provide a detailed breakdown of sales and revenue sources in order that adjustments and improvements may be made.

All staff handling cash and other payment methods should be adequately trained in the policies of the operation and the procedures to be followed with the aim of ensuring that revenue security is efficiently carried out at all times.

The systems that are used to support the various order taking and billing methods (see pages 220 and 224 respectively) are summarised below:

- **Manual systems:** using hand-written duplicate or triplicate checks for ordering from kitchen and bar and for informing the cashier. Often used with a cash till or cash register.

- **Pre-checking system:** orders are entered directly onto a keypad that then prints each order check with a duplicate and retains a record of all transactions. The keypad may be pre-set or pre-priced. This system may be found in many full-service restaurants and in popular catering.

- **Electronic cash registers:** allow for a wider range of functions including sales analysis. ECRs may be installed as standalone or linked systems. These systems are found in store restaurants, cafeterias and bars.

- **Electronic Point-of-sale control systems (EPOS):** have separate keypad terminals in the various service areas, which are linked to remote printers or visual display units (VDUs) in the kitchen, bar, etc. The terminals can be fixed or set in docking stations for hand-held use. In hotels, this equipment may also be linked to the hotel accounting systems. This system is also found in many modern restaurants.

- **Computerised systems:** enable several serving terminals, intelligent tills and remote printers to be controlled by a master unit compatible with standard computer hardware. Depending on software, the functions may also include a variety of performance measures such as planning and costing, sales analysis, gross profit reporting, stock control, re-ordering and forecasting, VAT returns, payroll, staff scheduling and account information. These systems are often found in hotels, fast food and chain restaurants.

- Smartphone app order and billing: sometimes referred to as Pin on Glass (PoG) whereby customers can remotely order and pay instantly through their smartphone, tablet or watches using restaurant apps or software such as Apple Pay.

7

- **Satellite stations:** remote terminals linked to a central processor to enable sales performance to be analysed (usually overnight) and reported back. These systems are found in fast food and chain restaurant operations.

Increasing development is taking place covering payments and point of sale systems. The introduction of Payment Services Directive (PSD2) is designed to promote payments innovation. It encourages faster payments systems and reduces the fees for processing payments. More information can be found on the Financial Conduct Authority website: www.fca.org.uk.

The more sophisticated the systems (point-of-sale, computerised and satellite) provide for increasingly efficient service at the point of sale, as well as improving the flow and quality of information to management for control purposes. The advantages vary from one system to another, but may be summarised as follows:

- **Fewer errors:** sales information entered will be more accurate because mistakes in the sequence of entries required for a particular transaction are not permitted. Automatic price look-up or pre-set keys are available rather than the potentially less reliable manual entry.

- **Faster processing:** transactions can be processed more quickly and this may be achieved by:
  - ☐ The automatic reading of price tags using a hand-held wand or moving the item over a fixed reader set in a counter top
  - ☐ Single key entry of prices, and
  - ☐ Eliminating any manual calculation or handwriting by the assistant

- **Training time:** may be reduced because many systems have a sequencing feature, which takes the user through each transaction step by step, giving instructions on a VDU.

- **Instant credit checking:** a customer's credit rating can be checked by having terminals compare the account number with a central computer file or through online connections to debit and credit card providers.

- **Detailed management information:** electronic systems provide more direct information, which improves both the detail and quality of computerised stock control and accounting systems and also makes them more economic for relatively small establishments.

- **Additional security features:** include such things as:
  - ☐ Locks which permit the ECR to be operated only by authorised personnel and totals that can only be altered and reset by supervisors and managers, and
  - ☐ Not disclosing at the end of the day the sum of the receipts that should be accounted for.

- **Advanced calculating facilities:** systems can be programmed to calculate the total price when a number of items of the same price are purchased, there are a number of items at various prices or if VAT has to be added.

- **Improved printouts:** in terms of quality and the amount of information contained on the customer's receipt. This may also include facilities where:
  - ☐ Receipts may be overprinted with sales and VAT
  - ☐ Both alphabetic and numeric information can be presented in black and white or colours, and
  - ☐ The receipt can contain the names of the goods purchased as well as, or instead of, a simple reference number.

- **Improved appearance:** modern systems are styled to fit in with the décor of present-day food service environments.

Individual operators will determine which system best suits their needs and gives them the information they require. Whatever revenue control system is used, it should be able to generate information for a variety of performance measures. These include:

- Reconciliation of total payments against orders served
- Average spend per head on food or beverages
- Average bill
- Sales mix data
- Consumer behaviour and analytics
- The use of loyalty cards
- Payment method breakdowns
- Seat turnover – the number of times a seat is used in a service period
- Sales per member of service staff
- Sales per period – can be monitored on an hourly basis such as in fastfood operations or in bar operations
- Sales per seat
- Sales per square metre or square foot.

The nature of, and the relationship between, revenue, costs and profits are explored in detail in Chapter 9, together with an examination of the various performance measures. A range of performance measures are detailed in Appendix A.

For more detail on consumer analytics see upserve.com/restaurant-insider/customer-analytics-restaurant-getting-pos/

Tips and service charges

Tipping for service varies across different cultures. Tipping practice in the UK is not as formalised as it is in other countries such as the United States of America. The average gratuity tends to vary between 10-15% in the UK whereas in the US it is normal for customers to add 18%-20% of the total bill. In Japanese dining culture it is seen as impolite to leave a tip. Other countries such as France and Australia tend to include a charge for the service within the listed prices (see for example, A Guide to Tipping at www.bbc.co.uk/newsbeat/article/38496354/tipping-a-guide-to-who-gets-what-and-how-much).

As consumers dine out more often now in the UK, the identification of good and bad customer service is easily recognised by savvy diners. Customer expectations have changed, which therefore place higher demands on service staff. However, tipping is an emotive and complex issue, which on one level is deemed as legitimate income, for others tax evasion, and to the customer as a way of rewarding the performance of staff.

In order to manage the tipping culture, many establishments in the UK have introduced a discretionary service charge which is added onto a bill and subsequently paid by the customer, or they can ask to have it removed. A service charge in the UK can typically be between 10-12.5%. Many consumers willingly pay a service charge with the understanding that the money will go directly to the staff as a tip, however, a service charge is not necessarily the same as a tip and businesses in the UK have no legal obligation to pay it to the staff and therefore some do not. Likewise, tips, service charge or cover charges cannot be used to make up an employee's pay to meet the National Minimum Wage. The UK Government has produced a Code of Best Practice to offer more guidance to business owners on how tipping protocols can be effectively managed and communicated to both staff and customers (www.gov.uk/tips-at-work).

Taxation of tips

All employees in the UK must pay tax on the gratuities they receive regardless of whether they are by credit card, cash or service charge. There are many ways a business can distribute tips. One of the most popular is a *tronc* system in which the tips are pooled together and shared equally amongst both the front and back of house staff. A tronc system is usually managed by one person who is referred to as the tronc master, with the amount due being paid directly into each employee's wage packet after tax.

Activity:

- What is your experience of receiving tips when at work – how was it organised?

- Compare the tronc system with the option of the individual server keeping the tips they earn. Which do you consider fairer?

- To what extend to you consider the issue of tips causes staffing problems?

■   Common malpractices

Although the aim of control systems is often to eliminate dishonesty, this cannot always be achieved. But the control systems can make it much more difficult. When designing control systems it is worth investigating possible malpractices.

Some of the common ones are listed in Table 7.9 together with advice on detection and a 1-3 rating of the difficulty of detection, with 3 being the hardest to detect.

Table 7.9: Examples of common malpractices in food and beverage operations

Malpractice	Detection	Rating
Dilution of liquor	A hydrometer will detect dilution, but a control test should also be performed from a new bottle as air temperature can affect the result. However this test is easy to make.	1
Short measures	Cocktails and other mixed beverages are vulnerable here. Can be checked at any time by Government enforcement officers i.e Trading Standards..	3
Overcharging of customers	Not easily checked in a busy bar or restaurant. If done frequently enough, the thief can end up with spare bottles or other items of unrecorded stock. Nowadays a receipt should always be proffered.	2
Undercharging of friends	Not easily checked in a busy bar or restaurant. If this appears to be taking place a careful watch is necessitated. General control procedures should detect this with checking systems and under due diligence a camera can be focused on cash registers.	3
Management pilferage	Difficult to detect as management have greater freedom of access. Missing produce/product can be written off as waste without ever being detected as pilferage. All management should have ledger accounts for all entertaining, comping and writing off. The existence of this type of control provides for open identification of potential abuse.	3
Kickbacks to managers	Here it is necessary to know what was purchased know what was bought, etc. Suppliers can make kickbacks directly to manager(s) ensuring the supplier(s) product is adopted above others. Free products, which could reduce operational costs, may be kept as incentive for buying goods from one supplier over another. Goods offered as 'incentive' may never actually arrive at the property and may be delivered to the member of staff or manager's home address. Kickbacks are always brought to light by lengthy and in-depth analysis.	3
Part-time banqueting personnel removing food, beverages and light equipment from the establishment	Utilise establishment security personnel to have a high profile presence and randomly search personnel. Provide clear polythene bags for all personal items brought into the premises, so as to be able to recognise the content on exiting the premises. In banqueting, for example, agreed limits of an average of 1/2 bottle per guest can still lead to whole bottles being misappropriated or creamed off the top. Corks could be counted back, although corks can also be stored and brought into the premises. Again, vigilance is important.	3
Cellar/stores personnel	Items can be booked out to bars and not be delivered. In this case they are lost at cost price. The blame can later be placed on the bars as having lost the items. Small and large amounts of food can also be lost through selling on to staff or others. Goods can be ordered as kickbacks and never recorded. Good control procedures should be able to detect this over time.	2

7

Cash registers taken off line	A register or point-of-sale machine may be taken off line, and assigned to only a couple of personnel to use. The server's sales can be tracked off line, albeit the machine is still tied into remote kitchen printers. Sales are recorded separately and the proceeds stolen by the member of staff or manager. This individual can make the adjustments the next day or at close of shift. Good control procedures and random checks can detect this over time.	2
Complimentary meals	Managers can void bills by using their management keys on point-of-sales machines. They can also give complimentary meals – often called 'comping'. Transactions can be voided or recorded as complimentary and the revenue stolen by the Manager. See possible approach to control under management pilferage above.	2
Utilising differentiated gross profit percentages	Items can be recorded as being sold in a department where the gross profit is lower than the department where the items are actually sold. E.g. optic liquor as off-licence liquor sales. Can be detected over time through control procedures and by examining sales patterns for anomalies.	3

Information on possible malpractices should also be shared through trade and professional association meetings so that up-to-date knowledge of potential malpractices can be obtained and monitored.

Activity:

■ Identify the key actions a manager can take in order to minimise the potential for malpractices.

7.8   References and additional reading

A Guide to Tipping at www.bbc.co.uk/newsbeat/article/38496354/tipping-a-guide-to-who-gets-what-and-how-much (accessed December 2018)

Cousins, J. (1988) Curriculum development in operational management teaching in catering education, in R. Johnson (ed.), *The Management of Service Operations*, Bedford: IFS Publications, pp. 437–459.

Cousins, J. (1994) Managing capacity, in P. Jones (ed.), *The Management of Food-service Operations*, London: Cassell, pp. 174–187.

Cousins, J., Lillicrap, D. and Weekes, S. (2014a) *Food and Beverage Service for Levels 1 and 2*, London: Hodder Education.

Cousins, J., Lillicrap D. and Weekes, S. (2014b) *Food and Beverage Service*, 9th edn, London: Hodder Education.

Cousins, J. and Weekes, S. (2018) Food and Beverage Service for the Level 2 Technical Certificate, London: Hodder Education.

Customer Analytics at https://upserve.com/restaurant-insider/customer-analytics-restaurant-getting-pos/ (accessed Devember 2018).

Davis, M.M. and Heineke, J. (1994) Understanding the roles of the customer and the operation for better queue management, *International Journal of Operations and Production Management* **14** (5), 21–34.

Financial Conduct Authority at www.fca.org.uk (accessed January 2019).

How To Use Restaurant Analytics From Your POS at https://upserve.com/restaurant-insider/customer-analytics-restaurant-getting-pos/ (accessed January 2019).

Jones, P. and Peppiatt, E. (1996) Managing perceptions of waiting times in service queues, *International Journal of Service Industry Management*, **7**(5), 47–61.

Kotler, P., Bowen, J., Makens, J. and Balogau, S. (2013) *Marketing for Hospitality and Tourism*, Harlow: Pearson Education.

Maister, D.H. (1985) The psychology of waiting lines, in Czepiel, J. A., Soloman, M. R. and Surprenant C. F. (eds), *The Service Encounter*, Lexington Books, Heath and Company, Lexington, MA, pp. 113 – 123.

Tips at work at www.gov.uk/tips-at-work (Accessed February 2019).

Wetherspoon's customers exploit loophole in pub's app to get free drinks at https://www.independent.co.uk/life-style/food-and-drink/wetherspoons-pub-customers-order-pay-app-exploit-loop-free-drinks-alcohol-pints-beer-a7787466.html (accessed January 2019).

Whyte, W. F. (1947) The social structure of the restaurant. *American Journal of Sociology*, **54**(4), 302-310.

7

8 Events, conferencing and banqueting

Aim

To provide an overview of the management and control of event operations.

Objectives

This chapter is intended to support you in:

■ Determining the size and scope of the events industry

■ Identifying the opportunities and challenges for operators

■ Maximising yield and profit through the application of strategic techniques

■ Identifying key organisational and staffing issues for events

■ Managing the event process.

8.1 Overview and structure of the events sector

An event is the planned management of an occasion that takes place between a space provider and a customer. The sector is commonly referred to as MICE (Meetings, Incentives, Conferences and Exhibitions) but other names used can include catering, events, conferences and banqueting. A list of event categories and examples is given in Table 8.1.

Table 8.1: Event categories and examples

Event catagory	Examples
Personal	Weddings, bar mitzvahs, anniversaries, birthdays
Local	Village fairs, community quiz nights, local drama clubs
Commercial	Conferences, exhibitions, trade shows, product launches
Fairs/festivals	Book fairs, carnivals
Public	Festivals, exhibitions, concerts, galas
Civic	Anzac Day celebrations
Special	National Day celebrations, cultural performances
Expositions	World Trade Expo, boat shows
Sporting	Dubai tennis open, Singapore grand prix
Global	Royal weddings, Live Aid
Mega/hallmark	Olympic, Paralympic Games and FIFA World Cup

In most cases the sector can be divided into two main groupings, conference and banqueting. Conference events focus on providing space for more formal business activities, whereas banquet events concentrate on activities for clients who wish to celebrate an occasion. Table 8.2 presents a comparison between the two types of event group and their characteristics. A more extensive description of event types is presented in Table 8.3.

8

Table 8.2: Comparison of conference and banqueting characteristics

Conference	Banqueting
Focus on conducting business or training	Focus on celebration and enjoyment
Emphasis on equipment and technology	Emphasis on food and beverage
Attendees tend to be from outside local area	Attendees tend to be from local vicinity
Lower staff to customer ratio	Higher staff to customer ratio
Booking lead times tend to be shorter	Booking lead times tend to be longer
Greater demand for accommodation	Less demand for accommodation
Duration can last from half a day to one week	Duration tends to last hours
Events tend to be less seasonal	Events tend to be more seasonal

Table 8.3: Examples of event types

Type	Description
Congress	Large assembly of individuals to convene or discuss business, culture, religion or another topic.
Exhibition/ trade fair	Large event attracting thousands of people. Targeting or promoting a specific sector of industry or consumer. Usually run over several days and can be open to the public, specify consumers only, or trade only.
Forum	Group of individuals discussing a specific topic or theme which in most cases would be led by a host who would channel discussions between a panel and the audience. Often held in an auditorium with microphones being moved around by assistants for the audience to ask questions.
Interview	Small meeting which maybe an employment or appraisal interview.
Lecture	Delivered by an expert to a large audience from a podium with the use of audio-visual equipment. Usually theatre style seating.
Meeting	A general term for a get-together of individuals with a common purpose.
Retreat	Normally in an out-of-town location and is organised by companies or associations for employees or members to meet for the purpose of team building, training, coaching or personal development.
Road show	Businesses or organisations delivering a series of presentations in multiple locations for the purpose of promoting and selling products or services.
Seminar	Similar to lecture but for smaller groups who actively participate on a particular theme or topic being explored. Interaction is the main objective of most seminars. Can also be part of a series located at different venues.
Workshop	Small groups are divided and work on specific problems, challenges or case studies.
Off-premises events	Off-premises events are delivered in another location away from the home base of the main business. These can be large of small events. Good logistical planning is essential and include activities such as: • Visit the site first and check the layout, design and access • Consider equipment, transport, fuel, water, holding equipment • Evaluate what utilities are available • If the event is outside ensure there is a backup plan in case of bad weather • Obtain insurance, licences and equipment • Draw up a plan of operations – what you need and when you need it.

Events can be provided either on or off the premises. On premise is where the event is held on the physical premises of the establishment or facility producing and serving the function. With off-premises, or outside catering, refers to food, beverage, equipment and servers being transported to a location such as offices, homes, boats or open spaces, etc. The event planner may provide anything from canapés and Champagne for a product launch to sit down banquets.

■ Size and scope of the industry

The events industry is a truly global industry with events being held each day around the world. Many major cities now feature large-scale conference and exhibition centres that host numerous events attracting local and international delegates. Events provide many benefits for destinations, which may include tourism, employment opportunities, publicity and financial growth. Table 8.4 shows top ranking countries for hosting meetings. In order to qualify for inclusion in the list, strict criteria of a minimum of 50 delegates attending the meetings, representing a variety of countries and lasting at least 3 days is adhered to.

Table 8.4: Ranking for top international meeting countries in 2017

	Country	No. of meetings
1	USA	941
2	Germany	682
3	United Kingdom	592
4	Spain	564
5	Italy	515
6	France	506
7	Japan	414
8	Canada	360
9	Netherlands	307
10	Austria	281

Source: International Congress and Convention Association, 2017

Examples of venues where events can be hosted include hotel function rooms, conference centres, community centres, restaurants, bars, church halls, academic institutions and community centres. The majority of space is multifunctional so can be used to accommodate different types of events. In most cases the venue will be responsible for the planning and delivery of the event. However, events can also be organised by event management companies (EMCs) or contract caterers. EMCs are professional groups or individuals that organize events on a contract basis on behalf of their clients. Some of the services provided by event management companies include:

- Concept development
- Planning the event theme and decor
- Marketing and advertising
- Ticketing
- Screening venues
- Risk assessment
- Contracting entertainers, speakers and other artists
- Dealing with caterers.

■ Appraisal of event management

There are many benefits for hospitality operators in hosting events, examples include:

- Better utilisation of space and resources
- Flexible options for space
- Potential to capitalise on annual and local events
- Showcase facilities to large numbers with potential for return business
- Additional revenue streams
- Greater opportunity to achieve customer satisfaction as pre-booked and therefore less opportunity for errors
- Savings through bulk food and beverage purchasing
- Less food waste due to fixed menu and numbers, and
- Reduced labour cost through using high quantity of part-time staff.

In addition to the many benefits of hosting events there are also challenges. Table 8.5 highlights some of these challenges and also provides potential solutions of how they may be managed.

Table 8.5: Hosting events: examples of challenges and potential solutions

Challenges	Potential solutions
Highly perishable product with pressure to fill space daily (for definition of perishability see Chapter 1, page 12)	Seek to maximise space utilisation through well-developed sales strategies and effective sales team
Competitive with many venue options	Conduct competitor analysis and differentiate
Large quantities of inventory and equipment to manage	Develop service standards, control, consider outsourcing equipment to reduce liabilities
Difficult to manage expectations of large numbers of customers	Conduct primary and secondary research with target markets to better meet their needs
Large events creates a challenge to manage satisfaction of all guests	Develop and implement quality controls, monitor customer satisfaction throughout
Often dependent on large quantities of casual labour	Selecting the right external agency, set strict criteria for casuals, develop close-knit team, induction and training 'treat as full-timers' (see also Table 8.11)
Heavily reliant on AV technology as part of event and access requested to advanced technologies such as virtual assistants using artificial intelligence, web casting and live streaming.	Outsource audiovisual (AV) provision an support to third-party specialist also providing technical support. . Invest in advanced technologies and up skill staff to support the use of these.
Many stakeholders in process	Select partners carefully, build relationships and treat well

Many hotel operations feature both restaurant and event space on the same premises. Table 8.6 presents a contrast of these two types of operation highlighting the impacts both can have on organisational profit. This table also indicates that event operations tend to yield more profit than restaurant operations.

Table 8.6: Contrast of restaurant and event operations

Restaurants	Events
Extensive list of menu items	Limited set menu
Uncertainty about which menu items will be selected	Minimal uncertainty – normally fixed menu
In most cases uncertainty about definite numbers that will visit restaurant	Minimal uncertainty – final numbers in most cases confirmed before event
Uncertainty about what time customers will arrive therefore difficult to schedule resources and staffing	Minimal uncertainty – customers arrive at prearranged time allowing better planning
Potential for food wastage due to difficulty in forecasting sales	Minimal food wastage as catered to confirmed numbers
Food production to consumption times shorter reducing time for quality control	Times longer allowing for a higher degree of quality control (e.g. cook–chill, cook–freeze)
Focus on fresh ingredients and which makes bulk ordering a challenge	Large customer numbers allow potential for bulk ordering and financial savings
Booking lead time times (if any) is shorter	Lead time is longer allowing for greater preparation of product and service
Difficult to practise yield management	Easier to practise yield management
Greater dependence on weather patterns	Less dependence on weather patterns
Simultaneous production/consumption provides challenges to standardise	Greater standardisation of product therefore less room for error
Combination of full and part-time labour	High percentage of part-time casual labour

8.2   Sales and marketing

Event space can range from a small social space in a church hall to a grand ballroom in a luxury hotel. Whatever the size of space it is a cost, and when it is not occupied it becomes an expense. It is therefore essential that event operators put in place clear strategies to ensure event space is sold as often as possible, achieving the greatest profit per square foot. Examples of some sales maximisation activities may include:

- Marketing of venue to different customer segments
- Maximising distribution channels and intermediaries
- Effective sales teams
- Event sales strategies.

■ Marketing a venue to different customer segments

Event operators have a diverse range of customer segments that they can target to fill their space. Table 8.7 shows a range of these segments and some of the potential opportunities they provide for venues.

Table 8.7: Examples of event segmentation

Segment or market	Opportunities
In-house customers	Customers visiting a hotel or other venue for another purpose should be made aware of event facilities available
Local businesses	Local businesses with no event facilities may require space for events
Local area residents	Local residents provide opportunities to cater for personal functions such as birthday parties, anniversaries and family get-togethers
Corporate companies	Large corporate companies often require space for business meetings, product launches and promotions and social functions
Charities or non-profit organisations	Providing event facilities to these organisations during low-demand periods can assist in raising the profile and image of the business
SMERF groups	Social, military, educational, religious and fraternal groups tend to be more price-sensitive, which can provide opportunities to sell event space during low-demand periods
Associations market	Many associations require event facilities to host meetings and other events
Incentives market	Incentives are in most cases organised by corporate companies to reward their employees who have achieved goals and sales targets
Exhibitions market	Generates revenue for hotels in terms of venue hire for using the function space and also potential to see accommodation and food and beverage services

■ Maximising distribution channels and intermediaries

Event operators can use a variety of intermediaries and distribution channels to maximise sales. Table 8.8 describes some examples of these channels.

Table 8.8: Examples of intermediaries and distribution channels

Example	Description
Company or department web pages	Allow clients to view details, availability and also has the potential for booking event rooms directly through on-line booking systems.
Central reservations system (CRS)	Some large hotel chains where event revenues account for a large proportion of the total business now operate a central reservations system solely for event reservations.
Event/meeting planners	Independent event management companies: either undertaking the entire organisation for a client or working on a commission basis, promoting specific venues and other services.
Destination management companies (DMC)	DMCs manage events (from small meetings to large incentive groups) on behalf of their clients. Hotels offer incentives to DMCs through commission on sales of accommodation and food and beverage commission, as encouragement for the DMC to promote the hotel.

Convention bureaus	Bureaus promote the destination rather than the hotel. In most cases they send international leads for conventions/exhibitions/conference to hotel partners, e.g. the Dubai Convention Bureau.
Web-based software for meeting/events	Examples of these companies include Cvent (www.cvent.com/uk), EMS (www.ems-events.co.uk(and Etouches at (try.etouches.com/event-management-software). They are used by meeting planners to send proposals to hotels and other venues.
Accommodation and meeting booking sites	There are a variety of search and booking sites such as HotelPlanner (www.hotelplanner.com) and Meetings.Com (www.meetings.com)

■ Effective sales teams

Different organisations will have different structures in relation to their sales teams. Smaller operations may just have co-ordinators who deal with incoming enquiries, whereas larger organisations will have larger teams with responsibility for different segments. What is important in a competitive marketplace is that sales should be proactive with sales personnel being allocated specific targets, given the right training and tools to meet these targets and monitored closely. It has the potential to achieve good results and sales incentives can be provided and rewarded accordingly. Sales personnel could be evaluated on the following criteria:

- Number of telephone calls made, prospects or leads
- Number of appointments, presentations or show-rounds made
- Through appointments, presentations or show-rounds, what was the amount of revenue generated through these conversions.

■ Event sales strategies

Due to the competitive nature of the sector, various techniques are recommended to fill conference and banquet space achieving the greatest financial return. Some approaches may include:

- Utilising efficient event-booking software
- Applying effective sales techniques
- Creating venue generated events
- Developing high quality event collateral.

8

Activity:

- Identify a range of innovative sales and marketing techniques that could be used by an events sales team to market an underused event space.

Event booking software

It is not enough to fill the event space with any customer, but to fill it with the right customer at the right price at the right time. In venues with large conference facilities a yield management technique is used to ensure the best financial return is achieved per room, per day. This is now commonly done with the use of automated room booking software. In addition, these systems can provide the venue with up-to-date information on function room availability, usage statistics, daily forecasts, actual yield per event and room set-up configurations.

Sales techniques

For those operations aiming to achieve a maximum yield on event bookings, Table 8.9 provides a list of possible techniques that can be adopted.

Table 8.9: Examples of event sales activities

Sales technique	Rationale
Forecasting high and low demand days for events throughout the year	Essential to be aware of when demand is high or low so that operators can set rates based on supply and demand and achieve the greatest yield per event booking.
Maintaining reservation records	Including records of booking enquiries, type of requests, cancellations, rejections and refusals. This can assist in budgeting and determining customer needs and potential demand for the next year.
Maintain past history records	Including booking behaviour, consumption preferences, delegate pick-up and shortages. This provides a more accurate estimate of their real potential when dealing with repeat bookings in the future.
Forecasting net yield per event booking	For operations with bedroom accommodation, when accepting event bookings consideration should also be give to potential for additional spend on food and beverage and room accommodation.
Booking pattern awareness	Keeping abreast of event booking patterns of target segments and market can assist operators to adjust marking approaches accordingly.
Future bookings	Operators should avoid confirming final details of bookings too far in advance as external changes can take place that could impact supply or demand, resulting in changes to costs.
Cancellations	Ensure cancellation procedures and controls are in place, including clear cancellation penalties.
Commissions for intermediaries	Consider methods of bookings and commissions paid to agents. Net yielded profit should always be calculated when dealing with intermediaries with the projected revenue minus fee.

Table 8.9 also indicates that it is important for event operators to be aware of high and low event demand days throughout the year as different approaches are needed at different times. Some high demand periods for operators may include:

- Weddings and other social occasions
- National and religious holidays

- Annual cultural events
- End of financial year.

When demand is **high** for events, operations *should not* consider:

- Accepting subsidised corporate account bookings
- Accepting bookings from low income groups or segments
- Consider letting out large meeting rooms too far in advance for non-bed-room-related business, as this may then turn away more lucrative residential business nearer the time.
- Offering discounts or promotions
- Providing any complimentary products or services
- Having any out of order rooms or refurbishments.

When demand is **low** for events, operations *should* consider:

- Offering promotions
- Never denying a booking if possible and be prepared to negotiate if necessary
- Creating venue generated events
- Providing upgrades
- Providing incentives for employees to maximise spend per head using positive selling techniques
- Providing familiarisation trips for potential clients
- Consider giving some space free to local communities. This could be an excellent way to introduce the facilities, provide good will, network with local business and provides the potential to secure future event bookings.
- Carrying out internal quality audits
- Carrying out deep cleaning and routine maintenance.

Other ideas to fill event space may include:

- Embracing social media and new technology to promote the venue and communicate to existing and potential customers (see also, Chapter 3, Table 3.3).
- Making the event venue 'more green' in its operation and develop a corporate social responsibility (CSR) policy. This can then be built into marketing literature and appeal to the 'sustainability sensitive' customer segments. See 'Greening of Events' on page 246.
- E-mail alerts at beginning of week to regular customers informing of room availability.
- When hosting residential conferences and exhibitions encourage and provide incentives for delegates to bring spouse or partners. This can result in additional spend by the partners in other outlets within the venue.
- Developing ways to reward loyal customers in a competitive marketplace, suing for example: complimentary accommodation, refreshments, gifts or discounts on future events.

8

Creating venue generated events

When event operators are faced with the challenge of having few bookings and empty capacity, they may attempt to create demand through developing own generated events. Event managers should create ideas that can be developed into own events (Davidson and Hyde, 2014). The following questions may be considered when generating ideas for creating events:

■ What is the event?

■ Who is it targeting?

■ How the target audience will be reached?

■ What costs are involved?

■ What are the forecasted revenues and potential profits?

■ How it will be evaluated?

Activity:

■ Compare and contrast the marketing mix of two events providers of your choice.

■ Identify how they compete with competitors on price, product, place and promotion?

Some ideas for own events may include wedding fairs, themed nights, guest speakers, wine clubs and tastings and cookery demonstrations. Figure 8.1 provides an example of the process for developing venue-generated events from idea to sale.

Figure 8.1: Venue generated events: the process

Event collateral

Marketing brochures are commonly used as a tool to advertise and promote the event facilities. These brochures can either be printed in the form of a folder, glossy flyer, supplied electronically on a compact disc or downloaded direct from the company website. The marketing information could include:

■ Logo of venue or establishment

■ Contact information (e.g. address, telephone, e-mail, website, Facebook or Twitter address).

■ Geographic map of location with road, rail and other transport links

■ An introduction to the venue (e.g. history, setting, atmosphere)

- Floor plans or blueprints of rooms detailing dimensions
- Details of different room set-up configurations, with numbers accommodated in various styles
- Professional photographs showcasing different events catered
- List of products and services offered (e.g. bedroom accommodation, car parking, leisure club, 24-hour security)
- Unique selling points of venue (e.g. award-winning chefs, professional service team, largest room in area, high-tech audio visual equipment, environmentally aware)
- Testimonials from satisfied customers and companies
- Examples of a range of menus for different events and prices
- Residential and non-residential delegate packages
- Prices of rooms and accommodation
- Classifications, star rating and awards.

Activity:

- Choose three events venues and evaluate their approach to events marketing. Is the necessary information readily available for potential clients? How could it be further improved?

- What advertising channels do they use and are they effective?

For more information on event creation see for example: Raj, Waaters and Rashid (2017) and Sharples *et al*. (2014).

Outsourcing and events

In the planning, preparation and delivery of the event, venues often need to outsource services and products with many different third parties to make the event a success. This may be done for several reasons including

- The venue prefers to outsource that specific product or service due to its specialisation, cost or convenience
- The customer has requested a specific external company to deliver a particular product or service, or
- The venue does not provide the particular product or service so needs to outsource.

Examples of third parties include suppliers of:

- Staffing (severs, bar staff, chefs, toastmaster etc.)
- Audio visual and lighting equipment
- Furniture (tables, chairs, dance floors)

8

- Decoration
- Marquees/tipis
- Linen
- Entertainers (disc jockeys, musicians, croupiers, children's entertainers)
- Professional caterers (for example kosher or halal caterers)
- Interpreters
- Transportation providers.

The outsourcing of services and products is a growing trend within hospitality. Some of the drivers of outsourcing are:

- Poor job markets
- Pressure to reduce costs
- Greater demand for quality
- Greater competition
- Fast growth of information technology.

Outsourcing of services is now being considered as a strategic move by organisations as it allows for greater specialisation, the ability to focus on core product and subsequently gain a competitive advantage.

White label events

Some events companies offer a 'white label' events service in which they sell an existing concept or event type to different companies, who will then re-brand with their own corporate branding. This is particularly useful for companies to use if planning time or resources are restricted, making it easier for businesses to use an event type that has been used previously and is proven to work.

White labelling also refers to a venue being asked to give no external indication of the organisers of an event or its purpose. They are either not referred to at all or are given a fictitious name. This is to ensure privacy for the event.

Greening of events

Sustainability is becoming a key focus of businesses across all industries including the events sector. This can often be referred to as 'greening of events'. Many businesses are adapting to calls for enhanced pro-environmental behaviour and find themselves becoming more accountable through their corporate social responsibility policies. The main purpose of 'greening' an event is to reduce energy and waste consumption. There are many drivers for companies taking the step to introduce more sustainable solutions. The key motivations can include increased competitive advantage, financial benefits, image enhancement and meeting the increased pressure from stakeholders (Crane and Matten, 2019).

Some considerations to make when planning an event to make it greener include:

- Eliminate the use of single-use plastics
- Use locally produced food
- Choose a venue in a central location with good public transport links
- Where possible avoid the printing of brochures/event materials
- Encourage visitors/guest to recycle ensuring appropriate waste bins are well-labelling

Further information on sustainability in the events sector see, for example, Seraphin and Nolan, 2018.

8.3   Staffing considerations

The organisational structure of event operations can differ depending on:

- Size of event operation
- Sales turnover
- Standards
- Management structure
- Geographic location of operation.

As events can be hosted in many different venues the internal structures can vary from a large sophisticated structure in a conference centre to a restaurant owner hosting an event in a small independent pizzeria. Regardless the structure, some of the main skills and qualities for any operator hosting an event are:

- Welcoming and friendly approach
- Good personal presentation
- Flexibility in accommodating customers' needs
- Ability to sell products and services to add value to the event
- Planning and co-ordination skills
- Visible to staff and existing and potential clients
- Hard working and creative.

A typical conference and banqueting operation in a four-star hotel is detailed in Figure 8.2. Table 8.10 then details some examples of the key positions and highlights some of their main responsibilities.

8

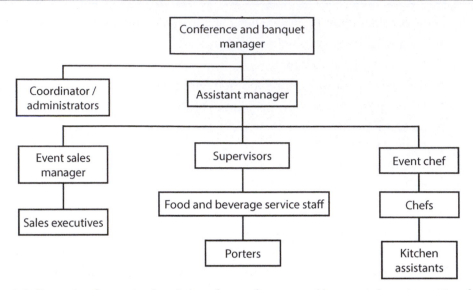

Figure 8.2: Example of organisational chart for conference and banquet department in a four-star hotel

Table 8.10: Examples of event staffing and responsibilities

Role	Responsibilities
Chef	Discuss event menu options with customers, create menus, food preparation and production
Supervisor	Oversee and supervise events, train employees, book casual employees, manage stocks, manage customers' expectations, monitor departmental performance standards
Sales manager	Create sales and marketing plan for events department, monitor the external environment, implement and monitor marketing plan, manage the sales and marketing team, set sales executives' targets and ensure maximum function room occupancy and rates are achieved, conduct market research within marketplace, develop promotions to increase demand
Sales executive	Conduct sales calls with event clients and prospects, make presentations, conduct show-rounds and follow up leads with prospective clients
Event coordinator	Take reservations and maintain the events diary, send out event brochures, marketing emails, create contracts and function/event schedules, liaise with departments when planning events
Servers	Set up events and carry out preparation tasks, serve customers, attend to customers' needs, break down rooms
Bar staff	Requisition beverages, carry out preparation tasks, serve customers, complete payment transactions if cash bar is operating
Porters	Transport and set up furniture and equipment, assist event servers, break down rooms, general cleaning

■ ## Agency staff

As the demand for events is very variable, it is common for event operators to use agency personnel as and when required. This allows for greater flexibility when staffing events and brings subsequent labour savings. However, using large quantities of casual labour can create challenges in their management. Table 8.11 details some of the potential challenges when using casual labour, also some impacts, solutions and suggestions on how to manage them. In event operations that use a large proportion of casual personnel, it is good practice to have a team of personnel from other departments who are trained in basic customer service and food and beverage service skills to assist if an emergency arises.

Table 8.11: Casual event personnel: potential challenges, impacts and solutions

Challenges	Potential impacts	Potential solutions
Many casual staff are transient and may not have the right skills	Service errors More responsibility on venue to train More monitoring required Greater potential for customer complaints	Provide job descriptions to agencies Consider using students from local hospitality schools, colleges or universities Inductions, training and detailed briefings
Different staff are supplied for events	Staff not aware of required standards Service inconsistencies More training required by venue Lack of team harmony Difficult to form a team	Try to use the same personnel each time, this will assist in building a team and greater efficiency will be achieved Provide standards of performance to agency to ensure the training of personnel. Only when potential staff demonstrated the required competence should they be supplied to venue.

For more information on staffing considerations generally see Chapter 4 and Cousins *et al.* (2014), Chapter 11, *Events*.

8.4 Costing considerations

The accurate costing of an event is crucial, with several aspects to consider when calculating the proposed selling price of an event or venue.

■ Fixed costs are those which are unchangeable regardless of the number of tickets sold or attendees. They can include staff overheads, utility costs and premises rent.

■ Variable costs will change with the number of attendees or tickets sold. Likewise, the cost of marketing, food and beverage costs will also vary accordingly

The cost of an event can be broken down into four main categories:

1 Operational or production costs – including hiring of event staff, construction, insurance and administration

2 Venue/site rental

8

3 Promotion – advertising, public relations and sales promotion

4 Talent – costs associated with entertainment

These four main categories can be further broken down into more specific detail when budgeting and costing as shown below in Figure 8.3.

Conference/Event Costing	Actual cost	Mark-up %	Variable (+or-)	Total	Profit
Event design/branding					
Utility overheads					
Envelopes and mailing					
Stationary/Brochures printing					
Breakfast per person					
Lunch p/p					
Dinner p/p					
Beverages p/p					
Flowers/candles					
Table/chair hire					
Linen hire					
Staff					
Photographer/videographer					
Audio-visual hire					
Entertainment					

Figure 8.3: Example conference and events budget template

Further detail on event costing can be found in Ferdinand and Kitchen (2016)

8.5   Managing the event process

All events, by definition, have a beginning and an end. (Getz, 2007). With each event, be it small or large, it is recommended that operators follow a series of key steps to ensure the event runs efficiently and profitably. The event process can be divided into three main stages that include the Pre-event, Event and Post-event. Each of the three stages then comprises of a set of tasks to ensure a successful event is achieved. This event process can be brought together as illustrated in as shown in Figure 8.4.

At each stage, event operators must put in place standards to ensure that both financial and quality control is achieved. Each of the three stages, and the tasks associated with them, are discussed below.

Stage	Task
Pre-event	1 Customer enquiry
	2 Event proposal
	3 Event contract
	4 Event order
Event	5 Event set-up
	6 Event quality
	7 Team briefing
	8 Customer welcome and service
Post-event	9 Event break-down
	10 Event billing
	11 Event evaluation

Figure 8.4: The event process

■ Pre-event

1 Customer enquiry

The enquiry is the initial stage of the event process. Prospective customers who require a venue for an event would in the first instance make contact with the venue by telephone, e-mail or via social media Most enquiries would be dealt with by an individual in the events office, or by the manager in a smaller independent operation. It is good practice for customers to have one point of contact from first visit through to the end of the event. This way, the communication between customer and event planner is enhanced. If the customer is dealing with different personnel throughout, miscommunication, delays and frustration may take place leading to dissatisfaction. First impressions matter, so it is imperative that a friendly, professional and helpful image is conveyed from the start. When enquiries are received, the initial details required by the venue from the prospect would be the type of event, date/s required and numbers attending. On obtaining this information the staff member would be able to determine if they can help the prospect with their enquiry. Most event offices would use a diary, usually computer based, to keep track of room bookings and availability throughout the year. Enquiries can be received from either intermediaries, prospective first time customers or returning customers.

Site visit

If the caller is a first-time customer and is local, it is good practice to invite them to the venue, as this is an opportunity to:

- Showcase the facilities
- Establish their specific needs for the event
- Build a rapport with the customer
- Recommend products and services.

When there are geographic restrictions and the customer is not able to view the venue they would in most cases be directed to the venue's website or sent marketing information with all the particular details.

Showcase facilities

As many cities have several venues offering event facilities, it is imperative that the appointment is well planned and executed. Where possible, it is good to invite the prospective client (also often simply referred to as the 'prospect') into the venue when rooms are already set up, as this allows them to get a better picture of the products and services available. Some event operations make it a standard to always have rooms set up for any viewings that may take place and that prospective clients, where possible, should not be shown empty rooms. Furthermore, if an appointment is made, every effort should be taken to ensure the rooms and surrounding facilities are clean and well presented. Poorly presented facilities can turn off prospective clients and lose business. Therefore, it must be seen as a sales opportunity right from the start.

If the venue is a smaller operation, photographs of past events can be a good way of displaying the type of events that can be delivered. Other approaches being used to showcase facilities include websites, electronic presentations or virtual tours presented on iPad type devices.

Establish the specific needs for the event

Be it over the telephone or during a visit, event staff members are required to ask many questions to obtain all the details and requirements for the event. To ensure that no question is forgotten, many establishments use a checklist or event booking form. Examples of details on a checklist may include:

- Organiser's contact details (telephone, mobile, e-mail), also Facebook and Twitter in some cases
- Type of event (conference, workshop, wedding reception, anniversary dinner)
- Theme (if any)
- Information on attendees (e.g. quantity, age, children, dietary requirements or food allergies)
- Food requirements (e.g. breakfast, lunch, dinner, snacks)
- Food service method (e.g. silver service, buffet, cocktail, family service)
- Beverage requirements (e.g. cash bar, host bar, wines, liqueurs)
- Chronology of events and times (e.g. arrival, breaks, meals, speeches, departure)
- Room set-up style (e.g. classroom, theatre, cocktail, banquet)
- Audio and visual requirements (e.g. projector, microphone, speaker, handheld PowerPoint presenter (controller) or laser pointer)
- Telecommunication requirements (e.g. conference call facilities, Wi-Fi)
- Equipment (e.g. staging, lighting, dance floor, podium)
- Decoration (e.g. linen, flowers, red carpet)

- Financial (e.g. customer's budget, deposit, payment method)
- Accommodation (e.g. room bookings, complimentary rooms)
- Other (e.g. car parking requirements, disability, deliveries, table plans, VIPs).

Recommend products and services

Another role during this enquiry stage is to recommend services and products that would add value to the customer's event. The staff member dealing with the enquiry should have a good knowledge of all services available and be able to advise, guide and up-sell whenever appropriate. Should a site visit take place it is good to involve key employees in the discussions. For example, when discussing a menu for a wedding, having a senior chef available to make suggestions and offer advice can be very helpful. A current trend is to become more client-centric, providing customers with exactly what they want from food to layout. Traditional marketing approaches tend to overload prospective customers with menus and packages. This has the potential to narrow the potential offer available to the customer and leaves little room for flexibility and scope.

Often a key requirement for event organisers is to be able to provide advice on event organisation, etiquette, order of precedence and standard customs and procedures. Publications such as the various Debrett guides are a valuable resource for venues. For more information see: *Debrett's Correct Form* (2017); *Debrett's Wedding Handbook* (2017) and *Debrett's A-Z of Modern Manners* (2018).

2 Event proposal

When all the information for the event has been gathered, the venue will create an event proposal to be sent to the client. This will present a complete breakdown of how the event will run and the proposed charge. It is common for clients to obtain several proposals from different venues to compare and contrast to get the best value. It is therefore essential that the proposal is prepared promptly, professionally and is competitively priced. A few days after sending out the proposal the venue should conduct a follow-up phone call to discuss and finalise the proposal with the client. It is common at this stage to change arrangements to suit the client and the final charge may also be negotiated and confirmed. It is the objective of the event planner at this time to close the sale and create an event contract.

3 Event contract

The contract is the formal agreement between the event planner and the client. The contract will state the event details, prices, deposits, terms and conditions, responsibilities and legal clauses. Two copies of the contract would in most cases be created which both the venue and the customer will sign. Once the signed contract has been received from the client an event order will then be created.

4 Event order

The event order, or function schedule, is an internal document and its purpose is to communicate details of the forthcoming event to the various internal parties, departments or personnel within the venue. It is prepared by the event coordinator and would be circulated, prior to the date of the event, to the different departments within the venue for their action or information. The different departmental managers are then required to familiarise themselves and their teams with the event, and action any specific details relating to their department. For example, if a particular wine is required for a forthcoming event, then the stores would order accordingly. Examples of departments that may receive a copy of the event order may include kitchen, restaurants, bar, stores, reception, maintenance, housekeeping and finance. For event operators that have events taking place most days, it is good practice to hold weekly meetings to run through the event orders for the forthcoming week. These meetings should consist of key staff members involved in the preparation and running of the events such as the event coordinator, events manager, supervisors and a senior chef. The purpose of the meeting is to finalise arrangements, check progress, identify any concerns, resolve problems, and identify areas overlooked and action points. As illustrated in Figure 8.5, the event order is a detailed breakdown of the event, what is happening, how and when.

Date: Tuesday 16 April 2019	**Customer**: Regency Electronics *SAMPLE*	
Event Type: Meeting	**Contact Details**: Miss Julie Parsons	
Time: 9am – 5pm	**Telephone**: xxx xxxx xxxx **Fax**: xxx xxxx xxxx **Email**: Julie.parsons@xxxxx.com	
Numbers: 120 Persons		
Timings	**Lunch menu**	**Room set-up and equipment**
9.00 – 9.15 Coffee/tea on Arrival	Carrot and Herb Soup	Theatre style with top table for 3 persons
11.00 – 11.15 Coffee/tea break with Pastries	Chicken Fillet with Broccoli and Sweetcorn in a Mushroom Sauce	Data projector and laptop
13.00 -Lunch in Restaurant	Selection of Desserts from Buffet	Table microphone and speakers
15.00–15.20 Afternoon Tea		TV and smartphone docking station
17.30 Finish	Tea or Coffee	3 Flip charts with paper & marker pens
Other Details		
Reception: Event to go on lobby notice board		
No seating plan for lunch – Plate service		
1 guest in wheelchair who will need assistance on arrival		
2 x gluten allergy		
Jugs of iced water on tables throughout meeting		

Figure 8.5: Example of an event order

■   The event

5 Event set-up

Each event needs to be set up for the event to take place. Some are small and require minimal preparation, but some are larger, for example a wedding, which requires meticulous pre-planning to ensure all the preparations are achieved within the deadline. For larger events, a project management or 'base plan' approach is an effective way of meeting the set-up objectives. Tasks are broken down into smaller chunks, allocated a time for completion and put in the correct order of priority. Another method is to have a countdown plan which details what tasks are required to be carried out, by whom, each day counting down to the event. These methods would be used as management tools to brief service personnel beforehand and to delegate tasks accordingly. It is the supervisor's responsibility to ensure that all tasks are achieved in the right time and as requested. For large events, pre-developed checklists are a good way of ensuring that all tasks have been completed and nothing has been forgotten. For example, forgetting to place champagne in the refrigerator for a large event could be disastrous. Whatever method is adopted, good planning is essential. As presented in Figure 8.6, a Gantt chart provide a visual presentation of the timings of different tasks.

	3pm	4pm	5pm	6pm	7pm	8pm	9pm	10pm	11pm
Table lay up	██	██							
AV testing	██	██							
Bar service			██	██	██	██	██	██	██
Meal service				██	██	██			
Speeches							██		
Entertainment								██	██
Staff briefing	██								

Figure 8.6: Example of a Gantt chart for an event

An important part of any event is the preparation. Typical tasks may include:

- Setting up tables, seating and side stations
- Laying tables for conferences (e.g. paper, pencils, glass, cordials)
- Laying tables for lunch or dinner
- Setting up front and back bars (e.g. glasses, beverages, accompaniments)
- Setting up of equipment (e.g. dance floors, projectors, staging), and
- General cleaning of the event area.

Room set-ups

Depending on the space available, there are a variety of room set-ups that event operators can use for events, as illustrated in Figure 8.7. When deciding on the most appropriate set up, consideration should be given to certain factors for example, objectives of event, atmosphere, numbers of people, room size, flow and time available. Some customers may on occasions pick room set-ups that would

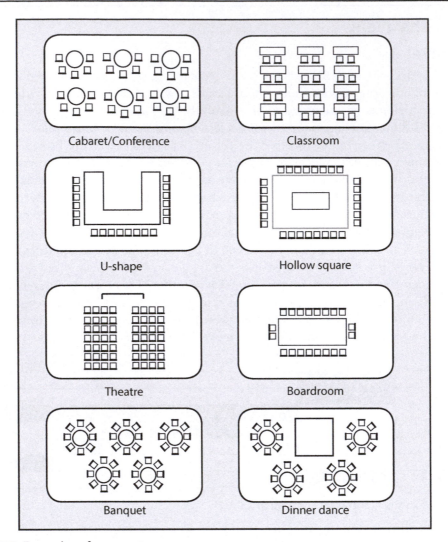

Figure 8.7: Examples of room setups

not be suitable so it is important for venues to guide the customer on the right set-up to achieve greatest customer satisfaction.

Seating plans

It is now common for seating plans to be produced in two main ways:

1 An alphabetical list of the people attending, giving an indication of the location where the person has been seated.

2 A listing of the people attending, showing all the people seated in the same location, or on a specific table.

Before the event, a copy of each of the two types of seating plans are made and these are checked with the organiser.

For further information on set-ups, see Cousins *et al.* (2014), Ch. 11, *Events*.

6 Event quality

It is important for event operators to plan well and implement the necessary quality controls to ensure customer satisfaction is met. However, with any event the venue is confronted with challenges that need to be overcome. Tables 8.12 and 8.13 highlight some of the challenges when dealing with banqueting and conference events coupled with some recommended solutions.

Table 8.12: Banqueting: Potential challenges and recommendations

Potential challenges	Example recommendations
Menu design – Ensure event menus are created considering the customer's needs and the operation's resource capabilities.	A pre-cook-off menu with chefs and client will provide an opportunity to improve quality and identify any operational challenges. Avoid attempting complex menus. Ensure allergen information is provided. Include at least one dish that is suitable for a range of dietary requirements
Food safety – When dealing with large numbers the importance of food hygiene becomes even more important.	Enforce HACCP procedures (see Chapter 4 page, 88) Prohibit customers bringing own food onto premises
Food quality – When dealing with large numbers it is a challenge to replicate the standard of fine dining, as time between plating and consumption may be longer.	Develop dish specifications Select dishes that fit well with holding processes. Ensure effective kitchen supervision to maintain quality control
Food timing – A challenge when catering to large numbers is ensuring prompt food service delivery.	Gain a clear understanding of the time available for the meal and select the most appropriate food service method.
Flow of service – Bottle-necks/ queuing can cause dissatisfaction for both customers/ service staff.	Ensure most appropriate service method is selected for numbers and space available.
Service quality – Future cost of dissatisfaction is always a concern when dealing with large quantities of guests.	Ensure service personnel are skilled Carry out thorough pre-service briefing Implement order of service Ensure effective supervision takes place
Diverse customer base – Events can be host to a diversity of guests with different dietary requirements.	During enquiry stage ask specific questions relating to demographic and potential dietary information of guests and recommend accordingly.
Intoxication – Over-consumption of alcohol can take place during some celebratory events.	Educate and train bar servers on sensible and responsible alcohol service to customers. Employ security for events where a large consumption of alcohol is forecasted (e.g. weddings, sports occasions) Conduct pre-event risk assessments
Event crisis planning – Even with pre-planning changes can take place outside the control of both the venue and the customer	Event operators and their management teams need to carry out crisis planning and attempt to predict uncertainties and how they can be minimised.

8

Table 8.13: Conferences: Potential challenges and recommendations

Potential challenges	Example recommendations
AV delivery –Hi-tech audiovisual equipment are susceptible to whistling and interference during usage.	Ensure a qualified AV technician is on standby for full duration equipment is being used.
Keeping up to date with information technology – Technology is changing daily and keeping abreast can be costly.	Outsource technology to external companies to achieve a good standard of IT and reduce departmental equipment expenses. Invest in staff training on emerging technologies to offer enhanced technical support to clients.
Multiple contractors – With large conferences there could be multiple external contractors involved in the set up of the event.	Establish early on from the client which contractors are being used and obtain contact numbers to coordinate set-up times accordingly.
Additional revenues – It is common for groups of delegates to unexpectedly stay after an event and use other facilities such as bars or restaurants.	To avoid the potential for poor service, maintain good customer history records of any groups that have done this in the past, as it could recur.

To help to improve and maintain quality, an event operation could apply to be accredited by a trade association, such as the UK Meetings Industry Association (MIA), which conducts independent assessments of event operations and awards them Entry, Silver and Gold levels. For more information on the MIA and the assessment criteria, visit www.mia-uk.org. In addition there are a wide range of potential industry awards.

For more information on quality management see Chapter 3, page 63.

7 Team briefing

Shortly before the event is due to commence a final briefing should always take place by the manager with the service team. A briefing may include :

■ The company, type of event and number of guests

■ How the event will run (e.g. chronology and timings of event)

■ Order of service for event

■ Communicate the details of organiser, host and any VIPs

■ Inform of any special requests

■ Allocation of tables to servers

■ Menu briefing by chef

■ Re-cap on any key standards.

8 Customer welcome and service

It is good practice when the guest arrives to run through the event order one final time. The reasons for this are:

■ It puts the customer at ease

■ It allows the customer to make any final last minute adjustments

- It eliminates any errors on behalf of the venue.

During the event a supervisor's key responsibilities might include:

- Delivery of the event as per the details stipulated on the event order
- Ensuring departmental service standards are maintained, sales are maximised and costs are minimised
- Being visible and accessible to organisers, guests and staff throughout event.

Post-event

9 Event break-down

At the end of the event employees will break down the event, which may include duties for example:

- Collapsing furniture and equipment
- Clearing tables
- Taking cutlery, crockery and glassware to stewarding
- Transferring soiled linen to laundry room
- General cleaning
- Re-setting for next day's event or show rounds.

10 Event billing

At the end of the event the organiser or host would sign the bill to confirm all charges (room, food, beverage, miscellaneous) are correct. This would either be settled immediately or invoiced to the company. For more information on billing see Chapter 7, page 224.

11 Event evaluation

It is essential with at the end of any event that an evaluation is conducted with both with the customer and the event team. In addition to speaking to the customer at the end of the event, customer feedback can also be organised with either a follow-up telephone call, e-mail or mail questionnaire. It does not matter which method is used as long as it is conducted. With the event team it is good practice to discuss and measure how the event performed against planned budget, event order and departmental service standards. Further identifying what worked well and what areas need to be improved in the event delivery. It is imperative that all feedback is disseminated and circulated to the relevant department heads and any evaluation paperwork should be placed on the customer's file for future action.

For further information on events management issues see, for example, Ferdinand and Kitchen, (2016) Shone, A. (2013) and Raj, Walters and Rashid (2017)

8.6   References and additional reading

Crane, A. and Matten, D. (2019) *Business Ethics: Managing Corporate Citizenship and Sustainability in the Age of Globalization* 5th edn, Oxford: Oxford University Press.

Cousins, J., Lillicrap D. and Weekes, S. (2014) *Food and Beverage Service*, 9th edn, London: Hodder Education.

CVent at www.cvent.com/uk (accessed January 2019).

Davidson, R. and Hyde, A. (2014) *Winning Meetings and Events for your Venue*, Oxford: Goodfellow Publishers Ltd.

Debrett's Correct Form (2017), Surrey: Debrett's Ltd.

Debrett's Wedding Handbook (2017), Surrey: Debrett's Ltd.

Debrett's A-Z of Modern Manners (2018), Surrey: Debrett's Ltd.

EMS at www.ems-events.co.uk (accessed January 2019).

Etouches at https://try.etouches.com/event-management-software (accessed January 2019).

Ferdinand, N. and Kitchen, P. (2016) *Events Management: An International Approach*, 2nd edition, London SAGE Publications Ltd.

Getz, D. (2007) *Event Studies: Theory, Research and Policy for Planned Events*, Oxford: Butterworth-Heinemann.

HotelPlanner at www.hotelplanner.com (accessed at December 2018).

International Congress and Convention Association at https://www.iccaworld.org (accessed at December 2018).

Meetings Industry Association at www.mia-uk.org (accessed January 2019).

Meetings.Com at www.meetings.com (accessed January 2019).

Raj, R., Walters, P. and Rashid T. (2017) *Events Management*, 3rd, New York: SAGE Publications Ltd.

Seraphin, H. and Nolan, E. Eds (2018) *Green Events and Green Tourism: An International Guide to Good Practice*, Oxford: Routledge.

Sharples, L., Crowther, P., May, D. and Orefice, C. (2014) *Strategic Event Creation*, Oxford: Goodfellow Publishers Ltd.

Shone, A. (2013) *Successful Event Management: A Practical Handbook* 4th edition, Andover: Cengage Learning.

9 Appraising performance

Aim

To identify and evaluate the techniques of measuring and appraising the performance of food and beverage operations.

Objectives

This chapter is intended to support you in:

- Considering the basis for performance appraisal

- Identifying the aspects of food service operations which are commonly appraised

- Developing skills in the application of a range of performance measures and appraisal techniques to revenue, costs and profits and the food and beverage product

- Determining the usefulness and limitations in the various quantitative and qualitative appraisal techniques and their application to food service operations.

9.1 Approaches to appraisal

In order to systematically appraise a food and beverage operation it is necessary to identify the component parts of an operation and appraise them separately before bringing them all together and appraising the operation as a whole. For a food and beverage operation the first component parts for performance appraisal are:

- Revenue
- Costs
- Profits
- The product.

The nature of revenue, costs and profits are complex. Each of these is considered in detail together with the approaches that might be used to appraise them. An identification of key points for each aspect is given at the end of the section where they are examined. The appraisal of the product is then considered taking account of the data, which the appraisal of the revenue, costs and the profits might provide.

The next stage, which is considered in Chapter 10, is to bring the various strands together in order to complete the appraisal of the operation as a whole and to make strategic decisions about the current and future operation and the business.

■ Fundamentals of appraisal

Appraisal is the action of placing a value on a measurement or collection of measurements. Those taken in a food and beverage operation are predominantly concerned with performance, and are therefore often referred to as 'performance measures'. They are also known as Key Performance Indicators (KPIs). However, a measure alone has no value. In order to be able to place a value on a performance measure, there will need to be an identified objective to measure it against. For example, an actual revenue measurement of £1200 has limited value until it is compared with a revenue objective of £1000. The revenue can then be appraised as surpassing the objective by £200, or 20%.

Other measurements and objectives are needed in order to explore or value the revenue measurement further. If cost objectives and actual costs are known, it is possible to explore or value the revenue measurement in a more meaningful way, i.e. the amount of profit (or loss) can be measured. Subsequently a profit objective can also be applied and a further value placed on the achievements of the operation.

In order to begin to appraise a food and beverage operation it is therefore a prerequisite to identify the goals and objectives of the operation. Knowing the operation's goals and objectives will enable the appraiser to focus on those parts of the operation which most significantly impact on the achievement of the goals and identified objectives.

In Chapter 2 we identified that:

- **Goals**, or aims, are the broad intentions of an organisation.
- **Objectives** are the measurable outcomes, which will indicate the progress being made by an organisation towards meeting its specific goals.

Operational appraisal then is concerned with measuring achievement against the objectives.

There may however be circumstances where the operation's objectives are not clear. In these situations it will be necessary for the appraiser to take a proactive role. This proactive role will vary depending on the responsibilities of the appraiser. For example:

- Area managers, managers, department heads and others with responsibility for revenue, costs, profits and product quality, who are unclear as to their objectives, need to be proactive by consulting with other members of their organisation (usually their immediate line manager), in an attempt to establish what the objectives are.

- An owner-operator with no clear objectives should consider what their objectives are. This can either be done by the owner or can be done in consultation with others: the staff and/or a consultant, for example.

The formulation of objectives is an important part of any business in order to try and ensure that resources are being directed efficiently and that the goals will be met. As objectives are dynamic and vary according to circumstances, the setting and revising of them is a continuous process. Appraisal is part of this process as it measures the extent to which the objectives are being met. The resultant appraisal will help in confirming or revising the appropriate goals for the organisation, which in turn will lead to the setting, or revising of the organisation's objectives.

The basis for effective operational appraisal

Effective appraisal can only be achieved if there are established objectives for the food and beverage operation. These objectives are usually in the form of budgets and statements of other standards, against which actual performance can be measured and appraised. The time and resources devoted to identifying, establishing and communicating objectives will vary between operations, depending on the perceived importance of this process. In operations where the objectives are not clear, staff and management should be proactive in order to identify and establish what their objectives actually are.

Budgets

Some of the measurable objectives of a food and beverage operation are commonly expressed in the form of 'budgets'. Examples of measurable 'budget' objectives are revenue, costs, profits, average spend per head, number of customers. These are used in a number of ways:

- Budget objectives are compared to actual performance and therefore help to appraise that actual performance, e.g. revenue budgets.

- They can help effect control over the operation, e.g. cost budgets.

- They can help to predict the future, e.g. cash flow and profit forecast budgets.

Operators will mainly use budgets to assist in making reasoned and objective evaluation of the performance of the operation, so that informed decisions can be made regarding their business. However, budgets can be used for other reasons.

Budgets are often thought to act as a motivator. Sometimes the ability to achieve the budget is related to remuneration and bonuses, or if budgets are not met employment of those thought to be responsible may be terminated. This 'stick and carrot' use of budgets can act as a motivator if the budgets are perceived to be achievable. Conversely they can act as a demotivator if they are perceived to be unobtainable.

In order for budgets to be perceived as a motivating factor, they should be set with the agreement of all the participating parties. In large organisations, budgets are agreed between layers of the organisation, for example between the board of directors and the operations director, then the operations director and the regional managers, and so on until agreement between the unit managers and the department heads. In smaller and owner-operated food and beverage operations this agreement between the parties is potentially easier to achieve.

Even with such a consultative approach to budget setting it is still possible for there to be conflict, with one side wishing to increase budget sales and reduce budget costs (often the position of the higher-layer manager, the budget setter), while the other party is trying to reduce budget sales and increase budget costs (often the position of the lower-layer manager, the budget taker).

Nevertheless, however they are set, it is still possible that budgets may be ill conceived and badly or falsely communicated. If the desired operational objective is to be identified through the budget, then the setting of the budget itself should be examined for its possible limitations, and how these limitations might affect the use of budgets as an appraisal or valuation of the actual achievement.

In summary then:

- Budgets which are set in measurable and achievable terms, and which need to be achieved in order that the organisation can realise its goals, are true objectives.

- Budgets, which are set as intentions for the organisation with little relationship with the goals of the organisation, are not true objectives. These are merely broad intentions, which are being used for other purposes, such as being the basis for determining bonus payments for managers.

In measuring performance against budgets, it is worth first considering the true nature of the budgets as this will then determine the extent to which the performance appraisal is in fact a measure of the effectiveness of the organisation in meeting its goals.

Performance against budget

Approaches to measuring and evaluating revenue, cost and profits are discussed in more detail below, and the formulae used to measure operational performance are listed in Appendix A. Examples of calculations are given in Appendix B. The example exercise in Appendix C illustrates the process for calculating a variety of performance measures and their evaluation. This exercise especially includes the calculation of variance against budget; a concept which is often misinterpreted.

For an operation with budget revenue of £300 and a budget cash gross profit of £195, the budgeted percentage gross profit will be 65% (£195 ÷ £300 x 100). If on review it is found that the actual revenue is £200 and the cash gross profit is £110, this will give the gross profit percentage of 55%. This outcome is likely to be reported as 10% drop in gross profit (65% less 55%). This is not a true interpretation. For any measurement of performance against budget, it is the actual cash amounts that must be compared and measured. Using the figures above:

- The percentage variance on revenue is the difference between the actual cash revenue and the budget revenue, as a percentage of the budget revenue. So the variance is calculated as: £200 – £300 ÷ £300 x 100. This equals –33.3%. So there has been a 33.3% drop in revenue.

- The percentage variance on gross profit is the difference between the actual cash gross profit and the budgeted cash gross profit, as a percentage of the cash budget. So here the variance is calculated as: £110 – £195 ÷ £195 x 100. This equals – 43.5%. So there has been a 43.5% drop in gross profit.

For further reading on essential financial techniques see, for example, Burgess (2014).

Standards

Other measurable objectives of a food and beverage operation are often expressed as standards. Examples of measurable standards are: portioning, purchasing specifications, staff uniform, temperature, time. These standards are seen to be useful to operators in a similar way to budgets:

- Standards are compared to actual performance and therefore help to appraise that actual performance, e.g. portioning.

- Standards help effect control over specific parts of the operation, e.g. staff uniform and hygiene.

- Standards can contribute to ensuring a consistent product, e.g. the same service, meals and atmosphere, at all times and in all locations.

Some operators will write these standards down in the form of standards of performance manuals or training manuals, with many national branded food service operations being extremely detailed in their approaches. The manuals will attempt to prescribe precisely each task and duty to be performed, often supported by the use of diagrams, photographs and videos. These manuals are generally used for three main purposes:

1 Manuals can provide a way for management to communicate the prescribed performance of various tasks and duties necessary to produce and control their product.

2 Manuals help to ensure consistency of product throughout all the food and beverage operations in a group or chain.

3 Manuals can act as a set of objectives against which to appraise performance.

As with budgets, not all food and beverage operations will have written-down standards, and similarly, operators and managers should be proactive in trying

9

to identify and establish what these standards are. In general terms, the existence of agreed standards makes a valuable contribution to the maintenance of consistent product delivery for an operation.(Standards of performance manuals are discussed in Chapter 4, Page 126).

We have already drawn a distinction, in Chapter 3, page 65, between different types of standards. Product quality (in terms of technical standards) and service quality (in terms of service standards) are by their very nature different. Technical standards can be identified, measured and compared. Also procedural service standards can often be usefully identified. Service though is highly varied and there is some doubt as the extent to which it is possible to prescribe useful service standards beyond defining a relaxed framework (especially for convivial standards) or whether it is in fact, for some operations, desirable at all.

For further information on restaurant cost control see, for example, Dobson and Hayes (2015).

9.2   Appraising revenue

Food and beverage operators view revenue as perhaps the most important measure in the operation. Revenue is also called turnover, and is often quoted as a measure of the size of a business; but high revenue does not necessarily equate with high success. Operations with high revenue can and do fail. However to be successful, revenue is a prerequisite, and most operators would put revenue achievement at the top of their list of objectives.

Revenue is a consequence of two variables: price and volume. Changes in either one or both of these variables will affect the level of revenue over time. Table 9.1 demonstrates how changes in the price and/or volume variables can affect the revenue.

Table 9.1: Effects of price and volume on revenue

Example	Covers/volume	Selling price (£)	Revenue (£)
1	100	10.00	1000.00
2	120	10.00	1200.00
3	120	9.00	1080.00
4	100	12.00	1200.00
5	80	15.00	1200.00
6	120	12.00	1440.00
7	80	10.00	800.00
8	80	9.00	720.00
9	100	9.00	900.00
10	80	11.00	880.00
11	110	9.00	990.00

In the examples given in Table 9.1:

- Example 1 is the starting-point or base line.
- Examples 2–6 show revenue increasing.
- Examples 7–11 show revenue decreasing.
- Examples 3 and 5 produce increased revenue even though one of the variables has decreased.
- Examples 10 and 11 produce decreased revenue even though one of the variables has increased.

In order to appraise the revenue of an operation over time it will therefore be necessary to collect information on both the price and the volume variables.

Most food and beverage operations will measure volume by the number of customers served. In a table-service restaurant operation this is a fairly simple matter of referring to copy customer invoices, kitchen order checks or electronic data collection from the cash register. In a counter-service food and beverage operation it is not so easy to know the actual number of customers that have been served, and therefore the number of transactions may be recorded, e.g. in a fast food store. In some food and beverage operations it is not seen as necessary to know the actual number of customers or the actual number of transactions, e.g. in a ba r. In this situation the revenue is still a product of the price and the volume, but it will not be possible to identify the reasons for any revenue variations so accurately.

The prices of an operation can be taken from the menus, wine and drinks lists and other methods of 'product offer' communication. However, price can also be measured by how much a customer is actually spending. Many operations use 'average spend per head' (ASPH), or 'average check', as a way of determining the price variable.

Using price and volume data

If an operation knows its total revenue and the number of customers or number of checks over a specific period, then it is possible to calculate the ASPH and the average check figures. For example:

If:

Total revenue (£)	1000
Total number of customers	500
Total number of transactions	100

Then:

ASPH	= £2.00	(total revenue divided by the number of customers)
Average check	= £10.00	(total revenue divided by the number of transactions)
Average group size	= 5	(total number of customers served divided by the number of transactions)

This example also shows the calculation used to determine the average size of a group of customers. This can be useful information. Knowing that larger or smaller groups of customers make up a significant part of the market can help in the planning of the restaurant and kitchen layout for example, or to focus advertising and promotion.

Interpreting calculations

An ASPH or average check amount can be misleading because 'averages' do not give the whole picture. An ASPH of £12.50 could be the result of all customers spending £12.50; or half the customers spending £6.25 and the other half spending £18.75. The same misinterpretation can be applied to the average group size measure, and also to for instance, the average number of customers per hour/day/week. Infinite combinations are possible and it is therefore important to take into account the limitations of averages.

It is often useful to generate figures that show the ASPH for different quartiles. This will give information on, for instance how many customers are spending within the highest quartile (25% of spend), the bottom quartile and the middle two. This can also be useful over specific service times such as main meal times where minimum charges can be introduced to force up the level of the ASPH.

Additionally these measurements and others are seen to be more useful when they are used for cross-sectional and time-series analyses.

- **Cross-sectional analysis:** This is to (a) compare one section of an operation with another section of the same operation, or (b) compare one operation or part of an operation with another in the same or similar sector of the food and beverage operations business. For example, comparing the revenue of one steak house restaurant with another in the same chain, or comparing the revenue of one fast food chain with the revenue of another.

- **Time-series analysis:** This is to compare a measure over a period of time; for example, comparing the revenue of a unit for one week with the revenue of the same unit for the previous week or with the revenue from the same week one year ago. Comparing present with past performance helps place some value on the revenue measure, although it is important to take into account any circumstances that may have changed.

Taking account of price changes and inflation

When comparing revenue for different trading periods it is important to take account of price changes and inflation in order to get a truer picture of the performance of the operation.

For example: A restaurant that had a revenue of £100,000 in year one and a revenue of £120,000 in year two, is seen to have increased its revenue by £20,000 or 20%. Let us assume that the number of customers has remained static and that prices were increased by 10% (In this particular example we will assume that the current rate of inflation was 10%, although this by itself may not be the only reason why prices might be increased or changed.) Taking into account the price rise it might be said that the value of the increased revenue is not £20,000 but only £10,000. In general terms one would have expected the restaurant to increase its revenue to £110,000 in the second year just to remain at the same revenue level, i.e. £100,000 plus the rate of inflation/rate of price increase at 10% (£10,000) would be £110,000. Although the restaurant had an actual revenue of £120,000 taking account of the effect of inflation will mean that revenue has only increased by £10,000 or 9.1% in real terms. (To take account of inflation the revenue should have been £110,000. Actual revenue was £120,000, the percentage increase is therefore 9.1% [£10,000/£110,000 × 100].)

When comparing revenue for different time periods, it is therefore important to know if price rises and/or inflation have been taken into account.

■ Comparing like with like

Revenue comparisons between food and beverage units should also be made with some caution and in relation to the circumstances. Two roadside restaurants in the same chain will have identical menus and prices, and may even have the same seating capacity, but their revenues may be different. This difference in revenue will still be a product of the volume and price variables, but factors outside the control of the unit management, such as location and spending power of their market, will affect revenue levels, and therefore the revenue budgets need to allow for these differences. Revenue comparisons between food and beverage businesses also need to be made with caution because the objectives and/or costs of the two businesses may be different. The performance of any operation therefore cannot be made using revenue alone.

In order to try and make effective comparisons between food and beverage operations other forms of revenue measurements can be made. Revenue per customer/seat/square metre/staff member, etc. can be measured and compared to similar operations. These measures can also be performed over time on the same business or unit. The real question when these types of measurements and comparisons are made is: 'Are they useful?' It is not always clear if these measurements and comparisons will be useful until they are actually measured and compared. If the time and data are available to make these types of detailed measures and comparisons, then it may be worth doing.

■ Comparison over time

Perhaps the most useful form of revenue appraisal is over time. Average spend per head, average revenue per customer, number of customers, revenue per member of staff, revenue per square metre, etc. can all be measured on an ongoing basis and compared. It will therefore be possible to identify changes and maybe trends, and if any significant changes in these measures are noticed, remedial action can be taken.

When comparing over time, comparisons are often made between the same periods of different years for example January this year with January last year. This can have problems. The number of Sundays for instance can have an effect on the potential of the business let alone the actual achievement. The operations may be closed on a Sunday. Bank holidays can also be at different times or the year, as well as various festivals. For this reason rolling totals of 12 months are often used. Thus the total revenue and other measures at the end of January are the totals for the 12 months to date. These are then compared to the total revenue and other measures for the 12 months up to the end of December. This type of comparison over time gives a far better indication of actual trends than simply taking a comparison of month to month.

Key points of revenue appraisal

- Revenue is a product of price and volume. An appraisal of revenue will need to take account of changes in both of these variables.
- Averages of price, volume and revenue do not always accurately reflect the complete situation and are prone to misinterpretation.
- Inflation and/or price rises need to be taken into account when comparing different trading periods.
- Different businesses/operations/units may have different objectives and direct comparisons may not be comparing like with like.
- Comparison over time can be useful but it is worth considering with rolling 12-month totals which provide a more useful basis for determining true trends and performance.
- Revenue cannot be fully appraised without reference to other operational variables, such as cost and profit.

9.3 Appraising costs

As important as revenue is for the operation to obtain, costs are seen as the most important for the operation to control. Costs are usually divided into fixed, variable and semi-variable costs:

- **Fixed** costs remain constant over a set period of time even though the level of business fluctuates, e.g. rent, rates and insurance premiums.
- **Variable** costs are proportional to the level of business, e.g. meal ingredient costs and beverage costs.
- **Semi-variable** costs are part fixed and part variable, e.g. staff and fuel. There will be a minimum number of staff needed all the time and the cost will then increase as the business increases. There will be similarly there will be a minimum level of fuel cost all the time and again the cost will increase as the business increases.

However, it is more important to know how and why any costs are incurred, and how to measure them accurately, than to argue if they are fixed, variable or semi-variable.

Most **fixed costs** (and some **variable costs**) can be negotiated with the supplier. These include thigs such as rent, insurance and even interest rates (the cost of borrowing money). Once the costs of these services are established, they are then fixed for the duration of the contract period, although interest rates and some other costs can fluctuate often.

Variable costs and **semi-variable** costs can be appraised in absolute terms, but are more commonly appraised as a proportion of revenue. Putting aside the fixed part of the semi-variable costs, (e.g. standing charge for electricity), these variable costs are proportional to the volume of business and therefore revenue. A food and beverage operation will measure these costs as a percentage of revenue, usually on a weekly basis. Costs of food, beverage, staff, linen, disposables, marketing, maintenance and other variable costs can be, and commonly are, measured as a percentage of revenue.

■ Identifying and measuring costs

Appraising fixed and variable costs objectively can be performed as follows:

A cross-sectional analysis

This can be performed by comparing the costs incurred by one food and beverage operation with similar types of food and beverage operations, thereby allowing a 'value for money' appraisal to be performed. Publications such as Keynote and Mintel reports and trade magazines such as *The Caterer*, *Restaurant Magazine* and others, provide useful information in this area, so that comparisons can be made. However, the cost structures of food and beverage operations can vary in a way which makes comparisons difficult. For example, one restaurant may be owned and operated by a family partnership that owns the premises outright (the debt having been paid off over a long period of time), while another restaurant is paying high rent or interest charges. The fixed costs of these two similar restaurants will be very different, resulting in a much lower break-even point (the point at which the operation starts making a profit, see Chapter 3, page 77) for the restaurant with the lower fixed costs. These cost structures are often seen to change over the life cycles of most businesses.

Relating one cost to other costs

Costs are almost certain to increase in absolute terms year on year, due to inflation and/or the changing cost structure of the business, but by appraising costs as a proportion of total costs, or as a proportion of total revenue, a comparative measure can be established. For example, if the fixed costs in year one are 25% of total costs and 7% of total sales, and in year two are 30 and 9% respectively, then a relative dimension is added to cost appraisal. These changes in costs can be calculated to provide a relative measure, which helps in their appraisal. This relative measure is sometimes miscalculated, as there may be confusion as to how percentage changes are measured. Table 9.2 gives an example of how these measurements are made.

A time-series analysis

Comparing costs over a period of time, usually year on year, is the basis for this type of analysis. The absolute and the percentage change in these costs can be measured and a comparison made with the previous year's changes. One common budget or standard objective measure in these circumstances is the current rate of inflation or retail price index. Changes in staff costs (rates of pay) are often related and calculated in this way. However, if some costs are seen to rise significantly more or less than the current rate of inflation, or significantly more or less than in previous years, consideration should be given to changing the operating systems of the food and beverage business to take advantage of, or counter, this changing cost structure. Changing from electricity to gas or changing from silver service to buffet service, in order to reduce fuel or staff costs, would be examples of changing operating systems in order to reduce these costs in real and proportional terms.

Again in this approach it is often that comparisons are made between the same periods of different years. As was considered under revenue appraisal in Section 9.2, page 247, approaching comparisons in this way can have problems. Therefore consideration should also be given to the comparison of rolling 12-month totals over time.

Table 9.2: Calculation of change in costs and revenue

Costs / revenues	£
Last period costs	1,000
Present period costs	1,200
Last period revenue	10,000
Present period revenue	11,000
Absolute change in cost	200
Percentages	**%**
Percentage change in absolute cost	20.00
Last period costs as a percentage of revenue	10.00
Present period costs as a percentage of revenue	10.90
Change in cost as a percentage of revenue	9.00

The example given in Table 9.2 indicates how the percentage change in absolute terms is calculated by dividing the difference between the costs in this period and the period before (£1200 – £1000 = £200), by the original or last period's cost (£1000), and multiplying by 100:

$$\frac{1200 - 1000}{1000} \times 100 = 20\%$$

Costs can be said to have risen 20% in absolute terms. However, as a percentage of revenue, costs have been seen to rise from 10 to 10.9%. The percentage change in these cost percentages is calculated as follows:

$$\frac{10.9 - 10}{10} \times 100 = 9\%$$

The percentage change in costs as a percentage of revenue is 9%. The percentage change between 10 and 10.9% is not 0.9%. It is critically important to know the difference between these measurements, 20% being the absolute cost change percentage, and 9% being the relative change in the cost as a percentage of the revenue. It might perhaps be more accurate to say that costs have risen by 9% (relative to revenue) than by 20% (in absolute terms).

If the figures here were representing rolling 12-month totals the same issues would apply. However using a 12-month rolling total gives a truer indication of trends and how the operation is actually doing over time. It is a far better indicator and worth considering.

■ Industry norms

There is no one standard or budget percentage for the various costs. Food costs of between 20% and 60% are often quoted as acceptable for particular types of operation, as are staff costs of between 11% and 35% and marketing costs of between 1% and 2%. Some examples of food, liquor and labour costs for different types of operation are given in Table 9.3. However, these figures should only be used as a guide because the actual percentage of the cost will vary depending on the specific objectives of the food and beverage operation.

Table 9.3: Examples of food, liquor and labour cost percentages for differing types of food service operation

Type of operation	Example food cost (%)	Example liquor cost (%)	Example labour cost (%)
Public house	40–60	45–60	15–30
Restaurant	30–50	35–55	25–35
Banqueting	30–45	30–45	18–32
Fast food	20–35	–	11–18
Popular catering	30–45	45–60	15–35
Wine bar	50–60	45–55	12–22

It might be assumed that some sectors of the industry will share similar cost percentages, but there is no evidence to support this assumption. An up-market restaurant with an average spend per head of around £70–100 may have the same food cost percentage as a roadside food and beverage operation with an average spend per head of around £9. The two operations may also have very similar staff cost percentages. Conversely, two very similar operations may have widely differing cost percentages, for example staff cost percentages being low, say 15% of total revenue in an operation run and staffed by a family, and being say, 25% of total revenue in an operation which hires staff on the open market. Small family businesses like restaurants and take-aways can have low barriers to entry, and because of the family interest are willing to work long hours at rates of pay below what is acceptable to others, resulting in much lower staff cost percentages.

In some sectors of the food service industry, the market is becoming much more competitive and more concentrated in the hands of the large operators. For example, in retail food service, prime high street sites have become prohibitively expensive to all but those who can significantly reduce costs and afford the highly expensive mass advertising campaigns and premium rents. The barriers to entry in this 'retail food service' market are becoming higher and therefore restricting the smaller and family-run operations.

This move towards an oligopolistic industry structure is also found in 'contract', 'outside' and 'transport food service operations', and cost percentage comparisons between them can be made. The chain, or group, food and beverage operations place great value on reducing costs and cost percentages as this is seen as leading to greater profits, and opportunities for a greater market share than their rivals through more competitive pricing. In this highly competitive market, economies of scale, especially in distribution, purchasing and marketing costs, provide advantages over the smaller operator. A greater investment in new technology also provides opportunities to develop more efficient and cheaper operating systems. These large operators see their actual survival as dependent upon their ability to reduce and control their costs, and therefore the value placed on cost comparisons between them is high.

■ Apportioning costs

In order to understand the cost structure of a food and beverage operation it is necessary to know why the various costs are incurred, and which costs can, or should be, attributed to the various parts of the operation. As the product is made up from a number of factors comprising the meal experience (see Chapter 3, page 45), and is therefore not homogeneous – because different customers purchase and value different parts of the experience – apportioning costs requires the identification of the component parts of the product.

Costs are often identified as being either direct or indirect:

■ **Direct costs**, by definition, can be apportioned directly to the various parts of the menu and drinks list. The ingredient costs of a meal or drink may be calculated accurately and the direct cost for each item on the food and drinks list identified. The use of standard recipes and tailor-made spreadsheets is common among large operators in identifying and measuring these costs.

■ **Indirect costs,** which comprise almost all the other costs beside the ingredient costs, are much more difficult to apportion. Examples of these indirect costs are: staff, linen, maintenance, cleaning materials, marketing, management, administration, rent, rates, fixtures, fittings, equipment, insurance, training and fuel.

An additional consideration in dealing with indirect costs is the proper apportioning of a range of costs that are often ignored; or rather simply absorbed without any proper accounting of them. Examples of these costs include: staff and management feeding costs; special promotions that reduce selling prices; 'comping' (providing food and beverages for free or at a discount); managers' allowances and entertaining of existing or potential clients. If these costs are not properly accounted for, then the expected actual revenue for the departments providing the services is reduced. As a consequence, this is unfair to those departments, as the true gross profit figures for the departments will also be reduced. In all cases these types of costs should be charged to internal accounts such as, for example: employment costs; marketing and promotion costs; 'comping' costs, and managers' accounts. This process ensures that the expected revenue, and consequently the gross profits of the different departments, is accurately measured. The costs are also then recognised and recorded as costs to the business as a whole. In addition, and importantly, it ensures that the levels of these costs are properly measured and consequently are able to be properly controlled.

In order to overcome the problem of measuring how much of the indirect costs should be apportioned to the individual menu and drinks list items, the costs are commonly apportioned as a percentage of the selling price. This proportion is usually identified as the proportion of the total individual cost to total revenue, for example, for staff costs this might be:

Total food revenue	= £1000.00
Total staff costs	= £300.00
Staff cost	= 30%
Individual menu item selling price	= £1.25
Apportioned staff cost at 30%	= £0.375

All other indirect costs are often calculated and apportioned in this way, or they can be formed into groups such as overheads e.g. rent and rates, or operational expenses, e.g. linen and cleaning materials. Which of these costs are included in these different groupings will vary from operation to operation. Many will simply group all these indirect costs together under 'overheads'; such apportioning is calculated as follows:

Total food and beverage sales	= £1000.00
Total overheads	= £120.00
Overhead cost	= 12%
Individual menu or drinks list item selling price	= £1.25
Apportioned overhead cost at 12%	= £0.15

Although this is an uncomplicated way to apportion costs, it is clearly not accurate. If total staff costs are 30% of total revenue, it does not necessarily follow that all menu and wine list items have a labour element of 30% of their selling prices. It is the processes the various ingredients undergo which determine the labour cost, and as various ingredients undergo different processes – some highly skilled and time consuming, others simple and quick – the labour costs for individual menu and drinks list items are quite different. The same inaccuracy is inherent in apportioning other indirect costs. It is for these reasons that in food service operations only the material costs (food and drink) are directly related to revenue. This is the basis of a gross profit calculation for all food service operations. All other costs are treated as being incurred by the operation as a whole. This is the basis for determining net profit. The appraisal of profits is discussed further below.

Key points of cost appraisal

- The cost structures of food and beverage operations vary, and change over time.
- Costs can be measured in absolute terms or as percentages of total costs and revenue.
- Changes in the proportional relationship between costs can be measured, helping to identify opportunities for increased efficiency through changing the operating systems.
- Proportional relationships between costs and inflation also need to be taken into account.
- Cross-sectional and time-series analyses can be used to appraise costs.
- Rolling 12-month totals can provide a useful basis for determining true trends and performance.
- Increased competition among food and beverage operators is leading towards an oligopolistic market in some sectors, creating a situation where operators with the lowest costs are perceived as having a key advantage.
- Identifying and allocating direct costs is relatively straightforward, but methods for identifying and allocating indirect costs need to be considered carefully.

9.4 Appraising profits

Profits (or losses) are the difference between revenue and costs and appraising profit requires the identification of the relationship between the revenue and the costs. The profit and loss account of an operation summarises the result of this relationship. Table 9.4 gives an example of a simple profit and loss account.

Table 9.4: Example of simple profit and loss account

Item		£
Income/revenue		1000
Direct costs/ingredient costs	300	
Staff costs	250	
Operating costs	100	
Overheads	150	
Total costs		800
Profit		200

In the example given in Table 9.4 the profit is £200, but this does not necessarily tell the whole story. Because profitability is expressed in many different ways, and as food and beverage operators use these ways differently, it is important to clarify which costs have, or have not, been included in the profit measure.

Profitability measures

The main profitability measures are:

- **Gross profit** (GP) in food and beverage operations is the difference between the selling price or revenue, and the cost of the food or drink ingredients. Examples are given in Table 9.5.

Table 9.5: Comparison of gross profits

	Individual item examples				Whole operation example	
	Burger	£	Soup	£		£
Income	Selling price	3.50	Selling price	1.75	Food and beverage revenue	1000
Expenditure	Food cost	1.49	Food cost	0.34	Food costs	170
					Drink costs	130
Total costs		1.49		0.34		300
Gross profit		2.01		1.41		700

- **Gross profit percentage** (GP%) is the gross profit measured as a percentage of the selling price or revenue. The GP% for the burger example is 57.4, the GP% for the soup is 80.6, and the GP% for the operation example is 70. Food and beverage operations use this measure extensively but it is important to recognise that a higher GP% does not always mean a higher GP. The soup has a higher GP% at 80.6 than the beefburger at 57.4, but the soup is less profitable in absolute or cash terms with a lower GP – at £1.41 – than the beefburger at £2.01.

- **Operating profit** is measured in different ways by food and beverage operators, but its common usage would be that profit which has been derived solely from the operation, and excluding any profit that might have been made from selling land or buildings for example, which may have been owned by the business. Again, it is necessary to establish if any such 'non-operational' profits have been included in this measure before it can be appraised. It is also necessary to establish if overhead costs have been deducted.

- **Operating profit percentage** is the operating profit measured as a percentage of revenue. As with gross profit percentages, a higher operating profit percentage does not always mean a higher operating profit; Table 9.6 gives two examples. Operation A has a higher operating profit percentage at 20% than operation B at 15%, but operation B has made a higher operating profit at £300 than operation A at £200.

Table 9.6: Comparison of operating profits

	Operation A	Operation B
Revenue	£ 1,000	£ 2,000
Operating costs*	£ 800	£ 1,700
Operating profit	£ 200	£ 300
Operating profit %	20%	15%

* These costs will include ingredient costs and staff costs, but might not include overheads, therefore the extent to which the other costs might have been included needs to be established

- **Net profit** is usually the measure where all costs have been deducted from the revenue, including the overheads. However, it is possible that not all costs have been deducted. Sometimes the cost of interest payments, loan repayments and dividends will not have been deducted, and again care must be taken to check this.

- **Net profit percentage** is the net profit measured as a percentage of revenue. Again a higher net profit percentage does not always mean a higher net profit.

- **Net operating profit**, **net operating profit percentage**, both before and after tax and/or dividends, are examples of other measures which are used. Again, it is necessary to check which costs have or have not been deducted, and to appreciate the difference between a percentage measure and an absolute measure.

- **Departmental and unit profit**: these are measures that are used to identify the profitability of individual departments or units within a food and beverage operation. Some costs can be directly attributed to a department or unit, such as the cost of staff who only work in that section, and food and drink costs, but other costs such as rates and rent may be more difficult to apportion accurately.

- **Yield profitability** measures are used mainly to measure the profitability of the beverage side of a food and beverage operation, although it can also be applied to the food side. Table 9.7 shows how yield is calculated.

Table 9.7: Yield comparisons

	Operation A	Operation B
Total beverage revenue or yield	£ 1,000	£ 1,000
Total selling price of beverage consumed	£ 960	£ 1,050
Yield percentage	104%	95.2%

At the end of each period, usually a week or month, the amount of beverage stock consumed is identified for each beverage item held in stock. In order to produce the yield figure, the selling price of each of the beverage items – taken from the price list/wine list – is multiplied by the units of that beverage item consumed. This yield is then measured as a percentage of the actual revenue.

In **operation A** the yield was 104%. This can happen because, for example:

☐ Drinks have been mixed, as in a cocktail, which realises a greater revenue than the sum of the parts that have been used to create the mixture.

☐ Customers have been overcharged or short-changed.

☐ Customers have been given short measures.

☐ The yield measure has been miscalculated.

☐ Wastage has not been as high as expected.

In **operation B** the yield was 95.2%. This can happen because, for example:

☐ Wastage or ullage has occurred

☐ Customers have been undercharged

☐ Customers have been given a larger measure than necessary

☐ All the revenue has not been received

☐ The measure has been miscalculated.

Measuring the yield percentage therefore allows an appraisal of that operation's efficiency in delivering the product and also receiving the correct revenue.

Whichever profitability measures are used it is critical to know which costs have been included in the calculations, how they were apportioned and which costs may still have to be deducted. When this has been established it is then possible to appraise profitability in both absolute and relative terms.

Before going on to consider the nature of profit in more detail it may be worth summarising the relationship between revenue, costs and profits for a food service operation. This summary is given in Figure 9.1.

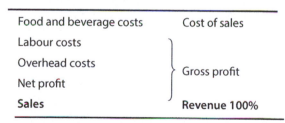

Figure 9.1: Summary of the relationship between revenue, costs and profits in food service operations

Thus in food service operations:

■ **Revenue** (or sales) is most often counted as 100% and percentages for costs are always determined on this basis, i.e. as a percentage of sales.

- **Gross profit** is total sales less cost of sales (or material costs – for food and beverages) and again the gross profit percentage[1] is determined as a percentage of sales.
- **Net profit** is revenue less cost of sales, overheads and labour costs. Again net profit percentage and the percentage of overheads and labour are all calculated as a percentage of sales.

Examples of operational calculations, which include an illustration of the relationship between revenue, costs and profits, based on the matrix shown in Figure 9.1, are given at Appendix B.

■ Exploring gross profit

Gross Profit percentage (GP%) is widely considered to be the most important profitability measure. In most food and beverage operations this is measured weekly although it can be measured as often as is required as long as there are the resources available.

GP% is a simple measure of efficiency but it is important not to confuse efficiency with profitability. On many occasions an efficient operation is also a profitable one but this is not always the case. Food and beverage operations purchase ingredients that are processed into a consumable meal or drink. This process is in fact adding value to the raw ingredients, and the extent to which value is added is a measure of that operation's efficiency at achieving this conversion process.

An operation which converts a £2 ingredient cost into an £8 meal or drink might be said to be 400% efficient (£8 – the price, divided by £2 – the cost), and an operation which converts a £1 ingredient cost into a £5 meal or drink can be said to be 500% efficient. The second example is more efficient (500 compared to 400%) but is less profitable (£4 compared to £6).

An operation that has poor purchasing resulting in higher ingredient costs, poor storage resulting in wastage, poor security resulting in pilferage, poor production resulting in high wastage, poor portioning resulting in larger portions than specified and poor pricing resulting in lower revenue, will have a lower GP% than the same operation which improves on these poor performances. In larger food service organisations the unit and departmental manager is seen to have an influence over how these activities are performed and as such the GP% is thought to measure a particular manager's performance. However it is not usually the case that the unit or departmental manager has any influence over the price, this being determined higher up the organisation, and on many occasions they will not have an influence over the purchasing because specified suppliers and negotiated prices are again determined higher up the organisation.

The actual GP% figure against which a manager's performance is measured will also be set higher up the organisation. In a chain operation these GP%s will

---

1 For kitchen operations the gross profit percentage is sometimes referred to as kitchen percentage or kitchen profit.

be set for each individual operation based on the sales mix of the menu and beverage lists. This sales mix – the amount sold of each menu and beverage list item – will vary from operation to operation depending on the customer profile and the selling techniques of the staff.

The manager can influence the selling techniques of the staff, but the manager usually has little influence over the customer profile. Perhaps the most influential factor over customer profile, especially in chain operations, is location. Bearing in mind these factors, an operation will be allocated a suitable GP% to obtain. Achieving this prescribed GP% is seen to be a good performance while not achieving it is seen to be a poor performance.

One way in which to decide upon the prescribed GP% is to run a particular unit or department over a period of time and take an average of the actual GP%s achieved. In reality GP%s are often set with reference to a desired efficiency level based on what is thought to be achievable (see also potential profitability, p. 283). This GP% is also seen to change as new menus are introduced.

An important factor which influences the introduction of new menus is the opportunity to increase the operation's efficiency and therefore new menus may often come with a higher GP% to obtain. In these situations a chain operation usually pilots the new menus in specifically selected units in order to obtain customer feedback and establish the new efficiency and profitability measure. This measure is then applied to the rest of the group's operations with slight variations for different customer profiles, as these will affect the sales mix of the individual units.

Having established the required GP%, the departmental or unit manager is then measured against the ability to achieve it. The dilemma with this measurement is that it measures a percentage not an absolute figure. Percentages are not cash and cannot be banked. A higher than required GP% will not necessarily realise a higher than required GP if the required revenue is not achieved (see Table 9.8).

Table 9.8: Comparison of GP in relation to revenue

	Operation A	Operation B
Required revenue (£)	1,000	1,000
Actual revenue (£)	900	1,100
GP percentage required (%)	65	65
GP percentage achieved (%)	66	64
GP required (£)	650	650
GP received (£)	594	704

- **Operation A** has a higher GP% than required at 66 (good management?) but only achieves a GP of £594, £56 below that required, because sales have not achieved their target (perhaps out of the control of the operation?).
- **Operation B** achieves a GP% below that which is required at 64 (bad management?) – but achieves a GP of £704, £54 above that required, because sales have exceeded the target (again, perhaps out of the control of the operation?).

In this example operation A could be said to be more efficient than operation B, but operation B is more profitable than operation A.

The example given in Table 9.8 indicates the reason why GP% is often more highly valued than GP itself. The GP% as a measure of efficiency will allow for variations of revenue. If operation A had achieved its GP% of 65, its actual GP would have been £584, and although this is below the required GP of £650 the operation can still be viewed as adding value or operating efficiently. The fact that the sales are £100 under that which is required may not be directly under the influence of the manager. Indeed, it is normal for sales to fluctuate due to the inaccuracies of budgeting and predicting the future. Therefore, by measuring GP%, allowances for these sales fluctuations are made. The same reasoning is applied to operation B. Sales are above the required or budgeted amount, but if the operation was running as efficiently as required and achieved its GP% of 65, the actual GP would have been £715, £11 more than actually achieved.

■ The tyranny of gross profit percentages

Many departmental and unit managers will perceive the achievement of the GP% as more important than the achievement of the budgeted revenue. As explained earlier in this chapter, revenue budgets may be seen as being too high for the unit to obtain and that even if the revenue budgets are achieved this may only mean that they are set higher next year. However, if the GP% is regularly achieved, the manager can state that the operation is being run efficiently. This thinking takes place at all the operational levels within a food and beverage operation. Regional managers and directors should be more concerned with cash profits rather than with percentage profits, but at the operational level the percentage values of the profits are more highly valued, often because more senior managers also attach to much value to them.

The reason for this anomaly is because the GP% measure is seen as a measure for controlling the efficiency of the management and staff rather than addressing profitability. As it is used as a control method, opportunities exist to exploit the system to the detriment of cash profit. Table 9.9 gives an example.

Table 9.9: Comparison of GP cash and GP percentage

Menu items	GP (£)	GP (%)	Selling price (£)
Beef	6.00	50	12.00
Fish	3.50	70	5.00
Chicken	4.50	75	6.00
Lamb	5.20	65	8.00

In the theoretical situation in Table 9.9 the two menu items that might be likely to be identified by the managers for positive selling would be the fish and chicken because they yielded a higher GP% than the beef and lamb. By selling these items the manager would be aiming to achieve as high as possible a GP% for the individual sale of a menu item, which would in turn contribute positively to the achievement of the required GP% for the whole operation. If, in this situation, the required GP% was 68%, the fish and the chicken sales would shift the balance of GP% achievement towards this goal, but any sales of beef and lamb would shift this balance away from the goal. The manager is motivated by an efficiency control mechanism towards achieving a required profit percentage.

However a more profit-focused examination of Table 9.9 reveals that it is not the fish and the chicken that are the most profitable items in cash terms. With GPs of £3.50 and £4.50 respectively they are considerably less profitable than the beef and the lamb at £6.00 and £5.20. A positive selling policy promoting the sales of the beef and the lamb would realise greater cash gross profits than the one promoting the fish and the chicken. However, because GP% is the control measure, the operation is seen to place more value on percentage profitability rather than cash profitability with the result of a decrease in cash profit. The fact that a control measure, which is so widely used in the food service industry, should have this effect (or at least the possibility of this effect) should be of serious concern to all food service operators.

Potential gross profit and potential gross percentage

Some food and beverage operations attempt to avoid the situation described above by the use of a further measure, which is termed potential profitability.

With the increasing introduction of computerised tills and control systems some operators calculate the cash GP and GP% that an operation should have achieved in theory for a particular time period. The ingredient cost and price of each menu or beverage item have already been entered into the till system which then automatically records the number of sales of these particular items, and thus a theoretical cash GP and GP% are calculated.

Recording such data is not new – computerised stock control systems are the main application of such systems – but not all operators are aware that this data can be converted into meaningful sales mix analysis information, of which potential cash GP and GP% are but two examples. Table 9.10 gives an example of a calculation for potential cash GP and GP%.

Table 9.10: Example of a calculation for potential cash GP and GP%

Menu items	Cost (£)	Price (£)	No. sold	Revenue (£)	GP (£)	GP (%)
Beef	6.00	12.00	100	1,200	600	50
Fish	1.50	5.00	150	750	525	70
Chicken	1.50	6.00	130	780	585	75
Lamb	2.80	8.00	70	560	364	65
Totals			450	3,290	2,074	63

Each of the four menu items in Table 9.10 is seen to be achieving a different cash GP and GP%. After totalling, the revenue is £3,290, and the potential cash GP and GP% are calculated at £2,075 and 63% respectively. This potential cash GP and GP% are what the operation should achieve with this particular sales mix. However, if the sales mix were to change from one period to another for any number of reasons (for example: changes in number of customers, increase in party bookings, changes in positive selling routines), then the potential cash GP and GP% may also change. Using the example of Table 9.10, with an increase in the number of fish dishes sold and a decrease in the number of beef dishes sold, while the total number of covers served remains the same, there is a lower potential (and hence achievable) cash GP even though the GP% has increased. Table 9.11 shows the new potential measures to be £1949 and 66% respectively.

Table 9.11: Effect of changed sales mix

Menu items	Cost (£)	Price (£)	No. sold	Revenue (£)	GP (£)	GP (%)
Beef	6.00	12.00	50	600	300	50
Fish	1.50	5.00	200	1,000	700	70
Chicken	1.50	6.00	130	780	585	75
Lamb	2.80	8.00	70	560	364	65
Totals			450	2,940	1,949	66

In operations where potential case cash GP and GP% are calculated it is possible to measure the operation's performance against that which was actually achievable in relation to the sales mix for that particular period. In the two examples above it is seen that although the operation in Table 9.11 produces a potential GP% of 66 (a potential cash GP of £1949), it is not as profitable as the operation in Table 9.10, which only produces a potential GP% of 63 (but a potential cash GP of £2075, which is £126 more). Operations that calculate potential cash GP and GP% are therefore more able to measure the operation's efficiency in relation to a changing sales mix. This method of calculating potential cash GP and GP% not only continues to take account of changing sales levels but also changes in the sales mix, and as such can be seen as a much fairer way of measuring an operation's performance. More importantly, however, is the change in emphasis of this control and performance measure away from purely measuring GP% and towards measuring actual cash GP. Thus, taking potential GP% and cash GP into account shifts the appraisal of profit towards cash actually received and away from percentages.

However, in operations where potential GP% is calculated, there is evidence that there is a third GP% which is used to measure and control performance, namely a desired GP%. This desired GP% is set at a level that the operator would like to achieve, in much the same way as the GP% is set in operations where they do not calculate potential GP%. An example of how this might work in practice for a particular time period is:

Potential GP%	69
Actual GP% achieved	68.5
Desired GP%	70

In the example above the operator has set a desired GP% of 70. This is the GP% that the operator wants to achieve. From the actual sales mix for that period it was only possible to achieve a GP% of 69 – the potential GP% – and a GP% of 68.5 was actually obtained. The value placed on this performance might therefore be as follows:

- The unit was unable to achieve the GP% desired by the operator. This is a result of the sales mix and may have happened because waiting staff were unable to sell the required high GP% menu and beverage list items.

- However, the unit was also unable to achieve the potential GP%, which is a measure of their inefficiency to add the required value.

Calculating potential GP% and cash GP, and using them to help appraise food and beverage operations, still allows for fluctuations of revenue – the reason why GP% is used as the main performance measure – but moves the consideration of value in the direction of GP cash and away from GP%. That many food service operators do not calculate potential GP% and cash GP, even though they already have the technology to do so, means that they are potentially reducing their ability to maximise cash profitability.

Sales mix analysis

Sales mix analyses methods involve identifying the sales relationship between the various menu and beverage list items. By far the most common application of these analyses is to determine the relationship of item numbers sold, i.e. a popularity index. A simple beverage list example is shown in Table 9.12.

Table 9.12: Sales mix example for beverages

Item	Number sold	Percentage of total
Champagne	20	10
Rhône wines	50	25
Loire wines	70	35
Bordeaux wines	60	30
Total	200	100

From the information shown in Table 9.12 it can be observed that Loire wines represent 35% of the total wine sales and as such are the most popular customer purchase. Bordeaux wines are the next most popular at 30%. Rhône wines at 25% are the third most popular and champagne at 10% is the least popular customer purchase.

Many operators use the identification and ranking of item popularity to assist with the compilation of new menus and beverage lists. In its most simplistic form the least popular item or items are removed from the listing although this is not always the case. In Table 9.12 it would worth retaining champagne on the wine list because customers expect to be able to purchase it when required, albeit infrequently. Champagne on the wine list will also contribute to the customers' perception of the operation's image.

However, popularity should not be confused with profitability. There is a relationship between popularity and profitability but the most popular selling item is not necessarily the most profitable. In order to examine this relationship it is important to identify which type of profit should be measured. As this is a relationship between individual menu and wine list items, the requirement is that the profit measure must also relate to these individual items. Apportioning costs to individual food and beverage items is difficult. How much of the electricity expenses should be apportioned to each item for example? The same difficulty is experienced when attempting to apportion labour costs. However, direct ingredient costs can be apportioned which will result in a measure of GP for each individual item. A relationship between popularity and GP is illustrated in Table 9.13.

Table 9.13: Example of profitability calculations

Item	GP (%)	No. Sold	Percentage of no. sold	Total GP (£)	Percentage of total GP
Standard burger	0.90	650	31.2	585.00	23.8
4oz burger	1.20	540	25.9	648.00	26.4
Standard cheeseburger	1.08	320	15.3	345.00	14.1
4oz cheeseburger	1.40	290	13.9	406.00	16.5
Double burger	1.65	285	13.7	470.25	19.2
Totals		2,085	100.00	2,454.85	100.00

From Table 9.13 it is possible to compare a popularity ranking with a profitability ranking, as shown in Table 9.14. The profitability ranking is clearly different from the popularity ranking, enabling a more focused valuation of the sales mix in relation to how much the individual menu items contribute – at a GP level – to operational profitability.

Table 9.14: Example of popularity and profitability rankings

Popularity ranking	Percentage of no. sold	Profitability ranking	Percentage of total GP
Standard burger	31.2	4oz burger	26.4
4oz burger	25.9	Standard burger	23.8
Standard cheeseburger	15.3	Double burger	19.2
4oz cheeseburger	13.9	4oz cheeseburger	16.5
Double burger	13.7	Standard cheeseburger	14.1

These techniques can have an element of sophistication; for example, linking with the amount of stock being held relative to its profitability, and consideration of a new menu item also relative to its potential profitability. All the various sales mix analysis techniques can categorise the individual menu and wine list items and suggest strategies for each category. These strategies are designed to improve profitability but there is evidence that the techniques themselves can be too complex and unproven to be assigned any value by many operations in the food service industry.

■ Menu engineering

One popular approach to sales analysis, which had gained some popularity, is the technique known as 'menu engineering'. This is a technique of menu analysis that uses two key factors of performance in the sales of individual menu items: the popularity and the GP cash contribution of each item. The analysis results in each menu item fitting into one of four categories: Stars, Plowhorses, Puzzles and Dogs. The advantage of this approach is that it provides a simple way of graphically indicating the relative cash contribution position of individual items on a matrix as illustrated in Figure 9.2.

Cash gross profit contribution

	Low	*High*
High	**Plowhorses** Items of high popularity but with low cash GP contribution	**Stars** Items of high popularity and also high cash GP contribution
Low	**Dogs** Items of low popularity and with low cash GP contribution	**Puzzles** Items of low popularity but with high cash GP contribution

Percentage of total sales (popularity)

Figure 9.2: Menu engineering matrix

Source: Adapted from Kasavana and Smith, 1982

There are a variety of computer-based packages that will automatically generate the categorisation, or some development of it, usually using data directly from the electronic point-of-sale control systems.

To determine the position of an item, two things need to be calculated. These are:

■ The cash GP category

■ The sales percentage category.

The cash GP category for any menu item is calculated by reference to the weighted average cash GP. Menu items with a cash GP which is the same as or higher than the average are classified as high GP items. Those with lower than the average cash GP are classified as low cash GP items. The average also provides the position of the line separating Plowhorses and Dogs from Stars and Puzzles.

The sales percentage category (popularity) for an item is determined in relation to the menu average taking into account an additional factor. With a menu consisting of ten items one might expect, other things being equal, that each item would account for 10% of the menu mix (total sales). Any item, which reached at least 10% of the total menu items sold, would therefore be classified as enjoying high popularity. Similarly any item, which did not achieve the rightful share of 10%, would be categorised as having a low popularity. With this approach half of the menu items would tend to be shown as being below average in terms of their popularity. This outcome would potentially result in frequent revisions of the composition of the menu. It is for this reason that Kasavana and Smith (1982) recommended the use of a 70% formula. Under this approach, all items, which reach at least 70% of their rightful share of the menu mix, are categorised as enjoying high popularity. For example, where a menu consists of say 20 items, any item that reached 3.5% or more of the menu mix (70% of 5%) would be regarded as enjoying high popularity. While there is no convincing theoretical support for choosing the 70% figure rather than some other percentage, common sense and experience tends to suggest that there is merit in this approach.

Interpreting the categories

There is a different basic strategy that can be considered for items that fall into each of the four categories of the matrix:

■ **Stars**: High popularity / high profit. There are the most popular items, which may be able to yield even higher cash GP contributions by careful price increases or through cost reduction. High visibility is maintained on the menu and standards for the dishes should be strictly controlled to ensure constancy of the item for the customer, which in turn can encourage further sales.

■ **Plowhorses**:High popularity / low profit. These again are solid sellers, which may also be able to yield greater cash GP contributions through marginal cost reduction. Lower menu visibility than Stars is usually recommended.

■ **Puzzles**: Low popularity / high profit. These are exactly what they are called. Items such as, for instance, flambé dishes or a particular restaurant speciality can add an attraction in terms of drawing in customers, even though the sales of these items may be low. Depending on the particular item, different strategies might be considered, ranging from accepting the current position because of the added attraction that they provide or increasing the price further.

■ **Dogs**: Low popularity / low profit. These are the worst items on a menu. The first reaction is to remove them. An alternative, however, is to consider adding them to another item as part of a special deal. For instance, adding them in a meal package to a Star may have the effect of lifting the sales of the Dog item and may provide a relatively low-cost way of adding special promotions to the menu.

Some potential limitations

Elasticity of demand

One of the practical difficulties with price level adjustment is not knowing enough about the 'elasticity of demand'. The effect of demand (number of covers) of any one change in the general level of menu prices is usually uncertain. Also, what applies to one menu item equally applies to the menu as a whole. There is an additional problem of 'cross-elasticity of demand' where the change in demand for one commodity is directly affected by a change in price of another. Even less is known about the cross-elasticity of demand for individual menu items than the elasticity of demand for the menu as a whole. Any benefit arising from an adjustment in the price of one item may therefore be offset by resultant changes in the demand for another item. Price level adjustments must therefore be underpinned by a lot of common sense, experience and knowledge of the particular circumstances of the operation.

Labour intensity

In menu engineering the most critical element is cash gross profit. While this may be important the aspect of labour intensity cannot be ignored. The cash GP on a flambé dish for example may be higher than on a simpler dessert, however, when the costs of labour are taken into account – especially at peak periods – it may well be that the simpler dessert is the more profitable overall.

Shelf life

The food cost of an item used to determine the cash GP may not take account of cost increases which are the result of food wastage through spoilage, especially at slack times.

Fluctuations in demand

Another factor is the consistency of the buying of the consumer. The approach assumes that changes can be made in the promotion of various items and that this will be reflected in the buying behaviour of the customer. The approach will work well where the potential buying pattern of the consumer is fairly similar over long periods. However, where the customers are continually changing, as for instance in the restaurant of an hotel, popularity and profitability can become more affected by changes in the nature of the customer and the resultant change in demand rather than as a result of the operation attempting to manipulate the sales mix.

Further applications

While this technique is presented here related to menu food items the same technique can also be applied to wine and drink lists. It is interesting to note, for example, that in many instances the house wine, although having the highest gross profit percentage contribution, often makes a relatively low contribution to the cash gross profit. Additionally, the principles of the technique underpin the approaches to the selling of hotel rooms and the rates that may be charged, now known as 'yield management'.

It is clear however that although there are some difficulties, benefits can arise since the menu engineering approach requires the following:

■ Planning for continuous control of cash GP

■ Giving prominence to, and controlling the determinants of, menu profitability; i.e. the number of items sold, the cash GP per item and the overall composition of the menu

■ Application of an analytical approach recognising that menu items belong to distinctly dissimilar groups, which have different characteristics and which require different handling in the context of cash gross profit control.

■ Exploring net profit and operating profit

These profitability measures are used to evaluate more fully the efficiency of a food and beverage operation to add value, because they take account of all or most of the costs incurred by the business. The relationship between costs and revenue to produce net operating profit is not as directly proportional as the GP measure and it is more difficult therefore to identify the relationship between an individual menu and wine list item and total net operating profit.

The main relationship for total net operating profit appears to be with total sales revenue. This relationship is twofold. As a percentage measure it values an operation's efficiency at adding value. As an absolute measure it values a specific amount of residual utility – usually in cash – which has been derived from an absolute revenue. As has been noted, a high percentage measure may be of less residual utility – cash – than a lower measure. However, as long as the measures are calculated using the same criteria, i.e. they use the same revenue and costs measures, they can be compared. This comparison can help appraise an operation's performance. Table 9.15 gives examples of net operating profit measures.

Table 9.15: Comparison of net operating profit

	Actual: Year one		Year two		Year three		Budget for: Year three	
	(£ 000s)	(%)	(£ 000s)	(%)	(£ 000s)	(%)	(£ 000s)	(%)
Unit A								
Sales	1,500		1,600		1,700		1,800	
Net op profit	150	10	155	9.70	145	8.53	180	10
Unit B								
Sales	700		750		800		900	
Net operating profit	70	10	75	10	67.5	8.44	90	10

In the example in Table 9.15 all the measures have been made using the same criteria, year on year, and for both units. An appraisal of the operation's performance, as individual one-off food and beverage unit, might be as follows.

Unit A

- Sales have increased by £100,000 year-on-year representing a percentage increase year-on-year of 6.67% and 6.25%, and overall by 13.3%. Sales for year three are also up £100,000 but 5.55% under budget.

- Net operating profit increased 3.33% by £5,000 in the year two and decreased 6.45% by £10,000 in year three. Net operating for year three is £35,000 and 19.44% under budget.

- Net operating profit as a percentage of sales has declined from 10 to 9.7 to 8.53% compared with a required level in year three of 10%.

Unit B

- Sales have increased by £50,000 year on year representing a percentage increase year on year of 7.14 and 6.67%, and overall by 14.3%. Sales for year three are also up £50,000 but are 11.11% under budget.

- Net operating profit increased 7.14% by £5,000 in year two and decreased 10% by £7,500 in year three. Net operating profit for year three is also £22,500 down and 25% under budget. From year one to year three net operating profit declined by 3.57% (£70,000 to £67,500).

- Net operating profit as a percentage of sales (10%) was maintained in year three but has declined to 8.44% in year three.

The evaluation above identifies the differences between absolute figures and the differences between percentages. This may appear at times to be fairly tortuous, especially when all the changes are presented together. In reality more value may be placed upon certain measurements than others, depending on the message to be communicated, and not all the measurements will be communicated at the same time.

Using the examples above it could be said that sales have increased in Unit A by over 6% each year, but this says nothing about net operating profit being almost 20% under budget. This is why it is so important to question the presentation of the information that is provided. When it is stated that sales have increased by over 6% each year, the immediate response should be to ask for other performance measures, in this case profit both in percentage and in cash terms. Questioning is crucial in order to fully appraise an operation. And again it is important to remember that it is only cash, and not percentages, that can be banked.

■ Industry norms

Many might argue that further value can be placed upon the information in Table 9.15 by comparing the performance of these operations with an industry norm, i.e. a measure which suggests a performance generally found and therefore expected within the industry. There are however two key difficulties in this approach:

1 Food service operations must be categorised into industry sectors before an average or mean net/operating profit can be calculated for that sector. It is possible to categorise food service operations but no two operations are the same (even chain operations differ), and each will probably have different objectives resulting in different values being placed upon their profitability.

2 The environment in which food and beverage operations operate is dynamic. This environment relates to: consumer behaviour and social/cultural changes; the financial market; the national and international economic position; and political issues and legislation. Different operations will react to these continuing changes in different ways resulting in differing valuations of profitability. The norm therefore may be seen as an arbitrary measure.

The effects of inflation

Inflation is another consideration, which may be taken into account, as it is a measure of the usually upward movement of prices across a range of commodities and services. For example, if net/operating profit had increased by 10% over the last 12 months, and inflation had been 5% over the last 12 months, it might be considered that in real terms profitability is up only 5% (10% profitability improvement minus 5% inflation). This will be an important consideration for those managing, owning and directing food and beverage operations in the appraisal of profitability. In addition, company taxation and dividends are also an important consideration and will affect profitability.

Stakeholder interests

As in any appraisal of performance, the important consideration in making any comparison is the value of the information to the stakeholders, i.e. those with a vested or invested interest in the business. An understanding of the stakeholder interests can make the appraisal of the operation more objective and of more value.

Key points of profit appraisal

- It is always necessary to be clear how any profit measure is arrived at and ensure that any comparisons made are like with like.
- Profitability measures themselves have no value. It is only when they are appraised against an objective that they may have value attached to them.
- Setting the objective, norm and/or budget is difficult and sometimes results in subjective judgements.
- Sales mix analysis is important in determining the difference between the popularity and profitability of items.
- Gross profit percentages are used as a measure of efficiency but this is not the same as measuring profitability.

- Profit percentages are often used, as the basis for comparison but cash profit contribution is what the operation should be seeking to achieve.

- Comparison with industry norms can be useful, if applied with caution, especially to chain operations.

- Comparison over time can be useful with rolling 12-month totals providing a useful basis for determining true trends and performance.

- Considering profitability must take account of the needs and interests of the operation's various stakeholders.

For further information on profit planning see, for example, Harris (2013).

Activity:

- Review the formulas for the performance measures (KPIs) listed in Appendix A.

- Work through the calculations exercise set out in Appendix B.

- Undertake the exercise on trading results comparison and evaluation set out in Appendix C.

9.5   Appraising the product

It is clearly good business sense to monitor level of satisfaction that customers have with the current customer service specification. This is especially important in relation to changing customer needs. Objective product appraisal will help in determining the extent to which the customer service specification is matching, and continuing to match, both the operator's and the customers' expectations.

We saw, in Chapter 3, a six-stage process for an integrated approach to service quality management. This process was summarised in the Figure 3.4, page 70. Stages four and five of the process require the monitoring of the operational aspects (technical and procedural standards) and the monitoring of customer satisfaction. The undertaking of these two stages in tandem will provide the information on the product of the operation, which will identify the need for changes that might be necessary to the customer service specification.

Single unit and/or owner-operated food and beverage operations often adopt a fairly subjective and intuitive approach to product appraisal. However this does not mean that it cannot be as, or even more, effective than a structured and objective one. This subjective and intuitive approach may be more efficient for a single operation that does not have to appraise and control its product over a multi-unit structure. Also, although it is highly dependent on the integrity and skills of its management and staff, there is really no problem if the customers also have the same subjective values and perceptions. It is this intuitive response to customer needs that enables some single food and beverage operations to be highly successful.

Chain operations usually lead the field in this area. With their branded products it is necessary to effect tight control over the customer service specification. Appraising and controlling revenue and costs are systemised through budgeting, and standardised procedures. Appraising and controlling the product are also effected through the use of standardised procedures, including the use of standards of performance manuals. Many of these approaches are also adaptable and useful to a single food service operation.

■ Approaches to product appraisal

Customer satisfaction questionnaires

Customer satisfaction questionnaires are often found in hospitality operations and/or sent to customers after they have experienced the product. The forms usually ask for some rating of the experience with details ranging from factors such as warmth of greeting to value for menu and also likelihood of recommending the operation to someone else. Whilst these types of forms can be very useful from a public relations point of view they often provide little in the way of useful objective measurement of the achievement of the customer service specification.

Complaint monitoring

The monitoring of complaints (and compliments) can assist in measuring the achievement of customer satisfaction and the achievement of various aspects of the customer service specification. The effectiveness of this process though is very dependent on being able to determine if the complaint is in fact a result of not meeting the customer service specification. It is quite possible that complaints will come from those whose expectations are higher than the intended customer service specification or that the complaints are unjustified or the result of some other dissatisfaction, which is not in the control of the operation in the first place.

Staff focus group sessions

The running of staff focus groups can provide a valuable review process for operations, especially when independent people lead these sessions. Opportunities can be taken to review the customer service specification against the experience of the staff who have to operate as part of it. Reports from the service staff can provide a springboard from which to go back through the design of the original customer service specification and to identify where changes can and need to be made.

Mystery shopper

A mystery shopper is an unidentified customer who tests the services of the organisation. This individual will check that standards are maintained. The mystery shopper will work to a brief and check list (basically a diagnostic tool). Some will also be involved in benchmarking competitors. Mystery shoppers are not expert; they need by necessity to remain customers. The individual shoppers tend then not to be professionals, although the companies behind them are.

Process reviewer

The process reviewer differs from a mystery shopper in that the process review is employed to identify problems and also opportunities for improvement. This approach can also be adapted for use in making comparisons with competitors. The process reviewer will more than likely be an internal reviewer (a member of staff) who will also signal training needs. Reviews are primarily concerned with checking if the right things are being done.

Quality auditor

Quality auditors are usually independent people who are concerned with checking on the standards at every stage to ensure conformance to procedures. An audit can also test hypotheses or substantiate hunches about organisational service efficiency and effectiveness. The auditor offers independent evaluation of facility and service quality to determine fitness for use and conformance to customer service specifications. The auditor will both observe and participate in the customer experience. Audits tend to be consumer oriented and usually provide a wealth of detail on the operation as well as comparisons with competitor achievement.

Quality standards analyst

The quality standards analyst (QSA) is a professional, with hospitality industry experience, generally brought in by senior management. The analyst will undertake a planned and systematic examination of the quality system and its implementation and determine the adequacy of the system and conformance to it. This individual will also look at all quality related aspects of the business. As well as producing a standard report, the analyst will ensure that the report is more qualitative in nature, than a quality auditor's report, which is usually more quantitative. This is also similar to the *Hospitality Assured* programme of the Institute of Hospitality (previously referred to in Chapter 3, page 68).

The basis of many of these approaches is often a checklist of aspects, with some operations having identified and specified over 150 aspects. This list will contain aspects covering such areas as:

- The words, demeanour and body language of the welcome
- The information and selling routine
- The time taken to deliver each menu and beverage list item ordered
- The taste, colour, texture, temperature and presentation of menu and beverage items
- The presentation of the bill and concluding routine.

Once the customer service specification has been evaluated both in terms of the operational aspects (technical and procedural standards) and the level of customer satisfaction, an appraisal can also take place in non-customer areas. This part of the appraisal can cover such areas as:

- Temperature and stocking levels in the fridges and freezers

- Cleanliness, security and safety of all areas
- Current data collection and collation up to date.

Once this product audit has been completed the results are often calculated as a percentage of the possible achievement. Each operation will, or should have, already determined the level of achievement required. Where the level of achievement is unacceptable this then leads to resources being concentrated to rectify specific underperformances (or non-compliance with the customer service specification). This process is dynamic, and as changes are made to the product, so the customer service specification is modified.

■ Using product appraisal data

The various processes outlined above will produce a variety of data about the operation. This can be used to review, and alter where necessary, the customer service specification.

However within the data there will also be information that may provide for a broader range of possibilities. Better use of the data can provide for a far more qualitative, and therefore richer, analysis of the information, which leads to be better understanding of the operation.

The data can be used to generate information on what is important to the customer and how the operation is achieving those things, is capable of achieving those things and also if the staff share the same view on what is important. Considering these various aspects is the basis of some of the thinking behind the 'SERVQUAL' approaches (as discussed in, for instance, in Bowie and Buttle, 2016; Johnston *et al.*, 2012 and Parker 2018). These authors also detail a range of other approaches to measuring operations performance.

Approaches can also be apprised and extended into other examples of useful comparison matrices. Three of these are presented and explained below.

Customer importance/Operational achievement

This two-by-two matrix considers all the aspects of the customer service specification and is used to indicate the level of importance the customer attaches to them, against the level of the achievement of the operation in meeting these requirements. Placing the various aspects on the matrix can be useful in determining and planning what action should be taken. The matrix, which has four positions, is shown in Figure 9.3.

- **Position 1 – High Importance and High Achievement**

   The first priority of any operation is to maintain these aspects. This is always true as taking action on other positions before these are attended to could potentially endanger achievements in this position. Action should only be taken in the remaining three positions if the operation can be sure that aspects already in this position can be maintained.

Operational achievement

Figure 9.3: Customer importance/Operational achievement matrix

- **Position 2 – High Importance and Low Achievement**

  The second priority is to examine and take action on these aspects. It is clear that the customer places a high importance on these aspects and therefore action taken on them can lead to quick returns in improved customer satisfaction levels. Action to be taken here can be a mixture of reviewing equipment appropriateness and stock levels as well as staff training and development.

- **Position 3 – Low Importance and High Achievement**

  Aspects that appear in this position are always a puzzle. There is something being achieved but it is not of great importance to the customer. Aspects here can be combined with aspects in box 2 above so that possible trade-offs can be achieved. Offering the customer high achievement in something else could in some way compensate for things, which are of high importance, but which are not currently being fully achieved. Offering a fast business lunch option could, for instance, potentially compensate for a limited range menu.

- **Position 4 – Low Importance and Low Achievement**

  The initial response to aspects that appear here is to leave them. Yes they are of low priority but customer needs change and these factors do need to be monitored. Long-term lack of achievement could lead to possible future customer dissatisfaction with another aspect of the service.

Customer importance/Operational capability

This two by two matrix considers aspects of the customer service specification and is used to indicate the level of importance that the customers attach to them against the extent to which the operation is actually capable of achieving them. Placing the various aspects on the matrix can be useful in determining and planning what action should be taken. The matrix, which has four positions, is shown in Figure 9.4

Figure 9.4: Customer importance/Operational capability matrix

- **Position 1 – High Importance and High Capability**

  Again the first priority for action in any operation is to maintain these aspects. This is always true. Taking action to improve capability elsewhere could potentially endanger achievements in this position. Action should only be taken in the remaining three positions if the operation can be sure that aspects already in this position can be maintained.

- **Position 2 – High Importance and Low Capability**

  The second priority is to examine and take action on these aspects. It is clear that the customer places a high impotence on these aspects and therefore again action taken on them will lead to quick returns in improved customer satisfaction levels. The action taken however may also mean that the customer service specification is changed and that the customer is advised more clearly that the operation is not able to offer particular aspect.

- **Position 3 – Low Importance and High Capability**

  Aspects that appear in this position are again a puzzle. There is something that the operation is capable of achieving but it is not currently of great importance to the customer. Again, aspects here can be combined with aspects in box 2 above so that possible trade offs can be achieved. Additionally a feature and benefit can be made of this particular aspect so that customer satisfaction can be improved through an impression being given of greater added value.

- **Position 4 – Low Importance and Low Capability**

  The initial response to aspects that appear here is again to leave them. The priority for action planning may be low but again customer needs change and these factors do need to be monitored. Long-term lack of capability could lead to possible future customer dissatisfaction either with another aspect of the service or with the operation not being able to respond to future priorities that customers may have.

Customer importance/Staff importance

This matrix considers aspects of the customer service specification and the level of importance the customer attaches to them against the extent to which the same aspects are important to the staff. Again, placing the various aspects on the matrix can be useful in determining and planning what action should be taken. The matrix has four positions and is shown in Figure 9.5.

Figure 9.5: Customer Importance/Staff Importance matrix

- **Position 1 – High Customer Importance and High Staff Importance**

  The first priority again of any operation is to maintain these aspects. This is again always true. Strengthening the capability of staff and rewarding their achievement of these aspects will reinforce their importance for staff and the operation as a whole. Again it is important to focus on these aspects first as taking action to balance things up elsewhere could potentially endanger achievements in this position. However, action should only be taken in the remaining three positions if the operation can be sure that aspects already in this position can be maintained.

- **Position 2 – High Customer Importance and Low Staff Importance**

  The second priority is to examine and take action on these aspects. It is clear that the customer places a high impotence on these aspects and therefore again action taken on them will lead to quick returns in improved customer satisfaction levels. However there could be a variety of reasons why staff may not consider these aspects as important. These may range from difficulties that the staff encounter in providing a particular type of service, such as equipment shortages, to a lack of competence or confidence. Action taken here then should be well considered, although clearly the intention is that the staff should share the same value as the customers in the importance attached to a particular aspect of the customer service specification.

- **Position 3 – Low Customer Importance and High Staff Importance**

   Aspects that appear in this position are again a puzzle. These are things that the staff think are important to achieve but which are not currently of great importance to the customer. This can have serious consequences for an operation. If the members of staff believe that they have capabilities that the customer and the establishment do not value, or that they do not in effect share the same values as the customer in relation to the customer service specification, then it does raise obvious questions about the suitability of the staff in the first place. Difficulties here can also be affecting the problems being identified by aspects in box 2 above. Trade-offs are not really possible. The aspects that are of importance to the customers must be reflected in the importance attached to them by staff, otherwise the customer service specification cannot be achieved.

- **Position 4 – Low Customer Importance and Low Staff Importance**

   The initial response to aspects that appear here is again to leave them. The priority, for action planning purposes, may be low but again customer needs change and these factors do need to be monitored. Therefore there is some merit in increasing the awareness of staff about these aspects so that they are able to monitor possible changes over time in the customers' priorities.

   The use of the three approaches exampled above can be complex and sophisticated, using well-designed questionnaires and external consultants to provide greater objectivity. However ,these approaches can also be used simply and productively as, for example, a basis for conducting staff focus groups or as a basis for team development sessions.

Activity:

For a food service operation of your choice identify:

- Expectations which are important to the customer.

- The extent to which the operation is meeting the customer expectations.

- The extent to which the operation can meet the additional customer expectations.

- Potential difference between the customer expectations and the apparent importance given to them by the staff of the operation.

This chapter has considered the different aspects of appraising performance. To support this Appendix A gives a listing and explanation of the most common operation ratios and KPIs. Chapter 10 builds on this chapter by looking at approaches to marking strategic decisions. The financial ratios identified in Chapter 10 are also listed and explained Appendix A (page 339).

9.6 References and additional reading

Adams, D. (2019) *Management Accounting for the Hospitality, Tourism and Leisure Industries, A Strategic Approach*, 3rd edn. Oxford: Goodfellow Publishers.

Bowie, D. Buttle, F., Brookes, M. and Mariussen, A. (2016) *Hospitality Marketing,* 3rd edn, Oxford: Routledge.

Burgess, C. (2014) *Essential Financial Techniques for Hospitality Managers, A practical approach*, 2nd edn. Oxford: Goodfellow Publishers.

Dobson, L and Hayes, D. (2015) *Food and Beverage Cost Control*, 6th edition, Oxford: John Wiley & Sons.

Harris, P. (2013) *Profit Planning for Hospitality and Tourism*, extended 3rd edition, Oxford: Goodfellows Publishers.

Hospitality Assured at: www.hospitalityassured.com (accessed January 2019).

Johnston, R., Clark, G. and Shulver, M. (2012) *Service Operations Management: Improving Service Delivery*, 4th edn, Harlow: Pearson.

Kasavana, M. and Smith, D. (1982) *Menu Engineering: a Practical Guide to Menu Analysis*, Lansing, MI: Hospitality Publications.

Keynote at www.keynote.co.uk (Accessed January 2019).

Mintel at www.mintel.com (Accessed January 2019.)

Parker, D. (2018) *Service Operations Management: The Total Experience*, 2nd edn, Cheltenham: Edward Elgar Publishing Ltd.

Pizam, A., Shapoval, V. and Ellis, T. (2016), Customer satisfaction and its measurement in hospitality enterprises: A revisit and update, *International Journal of Contemporary Hospitality Management*, **28** (1), 2-35.

Restaurant Magazine at www.bighospitality.co.uk/Info/Restaurant (accessed January 2019).

The Caterer at www.thecaterer.com (Accessed January 2019).

9

10 Making strategic decisions

Aim

To identify and review approaches to strategic decision-making.

Objectives

This chapter is intended to support you in:

■ Identifying the components of strategic planning as a systematic process

■ Identifying and applying approaches to business analysis and evaluation

■ Developing a balanced approached to performance measurement and strategic planning

■ Selecting and applying strategic planning techniques and approaches appropriate to food service operations.

10.1 The origins of strategy

Assessing the achievement of an organisation against its aims and within the business environment leads to the requirement to consider making strategic decisions about the current operation and the future of the organisation.

Strategy is the means by which organisations attempt to achieve their objectives. In most organisations there is likely to be a complex set of stakeholders concerned to influence the objectives and hence the strategy of the organisation. Rather than be too concerned about the right definition of strategy it is useful to develop an understanding of what different writers or speakers mean by strategy, i.e. what are the underlying concepts that they are trying to get across?

As a working definition for the purposes of this book, let us propose that strategic decisions are:

- Major decisions that affect the direction to which an organisation, or part of an organisation, is committed for the next few years
- Decisions which involve a significant commitment of resources
- Decisions which involve complex situations at corporate, business unit and operational level which may affect and be affected by many parts of the organisation.

Within this context there are a number of terms often used in relation to strategic decision-making. These include:

- **Vision**: conceptual or imagined view of the organisation as it might be in the future.
- **Mission**: fundamental purpose of an organisation, which is intended to lead it towards its vision.
- **Policy**: set of ground rules and criteria to be applied when making decisions.
- **Goals/Aim**s: broad intentions of the organisation.
- **Strategy**: means by which the organisation tries to fulfil its mission.
- **Objectives**: measurable statements of what must be achieved as part of the strategy in order for the goals/aims to be realised.
- **Tactics**: decisions and actions intended to achieve short-term objectives.

These terms may also be see as being presented in a hierarchy. Thus, **policies** are derived from thinking about the **vision** and the **mission** of the organisation, and **objectives** are determined in order to ensure that the **goals/aims** of the organisation are achieved. The interpretation of these terms can however vary depending on where and how they are being used. The establishment of goals and objectives for an operation have previously been discussed in Chapter 2, page 47. Examples of tactics for sale promotion are discussed in Chapter 3, page 80.

Levels of strategy

It is now widely recognised that strategy making should take place at different levels of the organisation. It is also common practice to identify three levels of strategy: corporate, business unit and operational levels:

1   **Corporate strategy** includes the plans for the strategic direction of the enterprise and how this is to be achieved.

2   **Business strategy** is developed for the business unit whether this be a single establishment or a division of a company.

3   **Operations strategy** includes the product, market, and functional and departmental plans.

10

The part of the organisation where the responsibility will lie for these different levels will vary from organisation to organisation. In a small company the business unit will also be the corporate level and operational level; but in a larger organisation the levels can be separated with different managers at each level. How the three levels of strategy relate can be indicated as in Figure 10.1.

Figure 10.1: The three levels of strategy and the relationship between them

The strategies at the various levels in an organisation clearly need to be consistent. However this does not mean that they have to be common or the same. The appropriate business and operational strategies for a national food service company may not need to be the same in each of the locations it is operating in (for example, resort, city centre, tourist area, transportation). It is also worth reminding ourselves that any food service operation is not necessarily in one market. The same unit could, for instance, be in the restaurant, licensed trade, banqueting, conference, business and leisure markets. In short, different approaches may be required for different customer groups or more appropriately the different types of demand, which the operation is designed to satisfy.

10.2 Assessing current performance

In the same way as we identified three levels for considering strategy it is also common to use the same three levels when considering the performance of the current operation as a whole. These levels are:

1 **Corporate** – which is considering the strategic direction of the operation and how this is being achieved?

2 **Business** – which is considering the performance of the enterprise in terms of profitability, competitiveness and other business measures

3 **Operational** – which includes day-to-day sales and the way the product is provided and promoted

In a single business unit these three levels are operating together. In a larger enterprise different members of staff and management may undertake the responsibilities for each of these levels separately.

It can be useful though, to consider any enterprise having these three levels. It makes for the consideration of any matters at any of the three levels not as independent issues but within the context of the organisation as a whole. Thus operational issues and decisions made about them are set within the business requirements and also then within the contribution that is being made to the corporate direction of the enterprise.

Operations are not an end in themselves: decisions made to correct underperformance or over performance at the operational level have to take account of the business implications and the strategic direction required. It may well be that operational underperformance or over-performance is a result of changes in the business environment and this should be identified before any corrective action is taken, otherwise this can lead to an effort potentially frustrated and at worst, resources wasted. Equally corporate and business decisions must take account of the operational capability of the operation in achieving them. The need for a balanced approached is further discussed in Section 10.5, page 321.

When and how

Decisions need to be made on when the appraisal of the whole operation should take place and how such an appraisal should be performed.

- **When** the appraisal takes place will depend upon the constraints and opportunities perceived by the enterprise, and the rate of change in these issues. Although formal performance appraisal can normally be undertaken half-yearly or yearly, it is often the case, especially within a fast-changing business environment, that the process would be more organic, with the formal processes being used to confirm the action, which may have already been taken.

- **How** such an appraisal is structured will affect the outcome of the appraisal process and the value placed upon it. It can be helpful to separate the appraisal of the whole operation into three main activities:
  - ☐ Quantitative analysis
  - ☐ Business environment appraisal
  - ☐ Qualitative evaluation.

These three areas are interdependent, but it can be useful to consider them separately before considering the interrelationship between them and subsequently the processes for making strategic decisions. Taking this approach helps to separate out what can be potentially overwhelming sets of data.

Quantitative analysis

An analysis of financial and other quantitative data relating to a specific food service organisation is useful because undertaking it can:

- Enable a study of trends and progress over a number of years
- Enable comparisons with the competition and the industry as a whole

- Reveal lost profit and growth potential
- Point the way forward by identifying areas needing improvement. This is especially the case when the organisation is not performing well compared to major competitors and/or within the industry as a whole
- Identify and emphasise possible danger areas.

Much of Chapter 9 was concerned with identifying techniques for quantitative operational appraisal. Alongside the operational ratios should also be considered other financial ratios. Ratio analysis is extensively used to assess the financial position of a company. It is aimed at characterising the company in a few basic areas affecting its financial standing. There are many ways of grouping operational and financial ratios and formulae. These are the main categories for most of the common formulae:

- Operational ratios
- Activity ratios
- Profitability ratios
- Liquidity ratio
- Gearing ratios
- Stock market ratios.

Each of the common ratios, and the formulas and explanations of what the individual ratio can indicate, are detailed under these six headings in Appendix A. As there are several formulae in each category, this can make this type of analysis seem complicated. However, the operational ratios summarised in Appendix A have already been considered in depth in Chapter 9. Many of the rest of these ratios are calculated at either the business or corporate level in the organisation.

In order to interpret fully the meaning of a ratio, it is necessary to have some basis of comparison. For operational ratios, there will usually be internal budgets and objectives against which to measure them. To illustrate this further an example of budget and trading results comparison and evaluation is detailed in Appendix C.

Operational ratios can also have more general values based on traditional experience and industry norms. Many of the rest of the ratios also have such values. For instance generally desirable figures for liquidity are a liquidity ratio of 2 and an acid test of 1. Such absolute figures are difficult to justify completely and relative figures are therefore often used with respect to the industry average or close competitors. When considering the share prices of a company, for example, it is usual to compare the company's share price with other companies' share prices within the sector and to compare it against the Stock Market FTSE 100.

No single figure provides sufficient information for evaluating the operational and business performance and also the financial health of the enterprise. Reasoned judgements as to the financial standing of the company will involve groups of calculations being undertaken. The important point is that this analysis, taken as a whole, is what needs to be considered not any particular figure.

Skills in quantitative analysis and evaluation are an essential part of food and beverage management. This is because quantitative analysis and evaluation of the operation:

- Are essential parts of performance appraisal, alongside other analytical tools
- Need to be considered over time in order to compare how they vary year on year and where possible how they compare with the average of the industry.

Generating quantitative data provides a useful background for appraising the performance of the organisation; but care needs to be taken when the results are being interpreted:

- The view that is being provided is based on historical data. It does not automatically imply that the trend identified will continue into the future.
- At best, average ratios provide a guideline to existing proportions that are representative in a given industry.

Additionally a number of different ratios need to be calculated before any conclusions should be drawn:

- Ratios should be used as an additional tool to back up issues identified in another area of analysis.
- The evaluation of the ratios is more important than the figures themselves.

For more information on the use of performance measures, see, for example, Harris (2013).

Activity:

Obtain the annual report of two food service companies.

- Review formulas for the performance measure listed in Appendix A.
- Compare and contrast the financial performance of the two business.
- Identify which of the business you consider to be more viable in the longer term , giving your reasons for your decision.

10

Business environment appraisal

Appraising the business environment enables a food and beverage operation to understand how it relates to the current business environment, how the business environment is changing, and facilitates an objective view of the future. Appraising the business environment also includes an examination of the competition and the threats to the operation, which competitors may pose.

The range of resources apportioned to this activity can vary, with large operators employing economists and strategic directors, and small operators often relying on instinct and intuition. For the hospitality industry there are a range of professional sources of information that regularly provide opportunities for sharing information and gaining insights into changes in the business environment.

These include the professional and trade bodies and the trade press. There are also several techniques available to assist in the appraisal of the business environments, which are covered in detail in a variety of texts and publications. The two main ones are PESTLE and Porter's Five Forces.

PESTLE

The PESTLE framework (as discussed in detail in Chapter 1, pages 18 to 22) is widely used to classify potential influences on the future of the business. The PESTLE (Political, Economic, Social, Technological, Legal and Ecological) analysis, when carried out well, is a sophisticated approach, which provides for a fairly wide and deep evaluation of the current and potential macro-business environment.

Porter's Five Forces

As well as the macro-business environment, the micro-business environment should also be considered. Porter (2004a, 2004b) proposes that competitiveness within an industry can be determined by reference to Five Forces. The famous Five Forces model is shown in Figure 10.2.

Figure 10.2: The Five Competitive Forces

Source: adapted from the original in Porter, 2004a

The central force is the **rivalry amongst existing firms** competing in the same industry. But the strength of the model is that it includes four other competitive forces that influence the attractiveness and profitability of the industry. These are:

- The threat of **new entrants** and how easily they can break into the market.
- The bargaining power that can be exerted on the industry by its **buyers.**

- The bargaining power that can be exerted on the industry by its **suppliers.**
- The extent to which **substitute products** can take over from the existing industry.

These five forces represent the industry environment and the extent and strength of these forces determine the attractiveness of the industry. Of crucial importance is recognising that both direct competitors and the nature and strength of the competitive forces change with time and sometimes very suddenly. These changes within the micro-business environment can be provoked by changes in the PESTLE factors of the macro-business environment.

Using the Five Forces model

The use of the Five Forces model provides for the systematic review of the organisation's competitive position at both corporate and business levels. The model helps to focus attention not only on direct competitors but also on substitutes. For example, better transport systems, which directly reduce the demand for overnight accommodation, are a clear, but not immediately obvious, example of a substitute for accommodation services.

Porter's full diagram of the Five Forces is shown in Figure 10.3 (page 308). Here are added practical determinants of the relative power of each of the Five Forces. From this full version of Porter's diagram, it can be seen that many of the determinants are themselves determined either by PESTLE factors or, very importantly, by factors that the organisation can itself directly influence by changing its strategies at business or operational level.

The **industry competitors** are those organisations that a food service business identifies as being in direct competition and the **rivalry among existing firms** is the level of competition that exists between the existing operations.

Potential entrants are the new organisations, which may threaten the business of existing organisations within the market. The **barriers to entry** into the market are the factors that might deter new operations. These include:

- Capital cost of entry (for example plant and equipment).
- Cost disadvantages such as licence requirements or adverse government policy.
- Entrenched customer loyalty to existing organisations.
- Economies of scale achieved by existing large businesses.

Buyers are the customers of the food service operation. Buyers can have varying degrees of power. A strong **bargaining power of buyers** will make it easier for buyers to attempt to force down prices whilst at the same time require better quality. Buyers will also tend to play off different food service operations against each other. The influence of buyers is greater if, for instance, they are large in terms of volume of business or spend, or if the market is highly competitive.

10

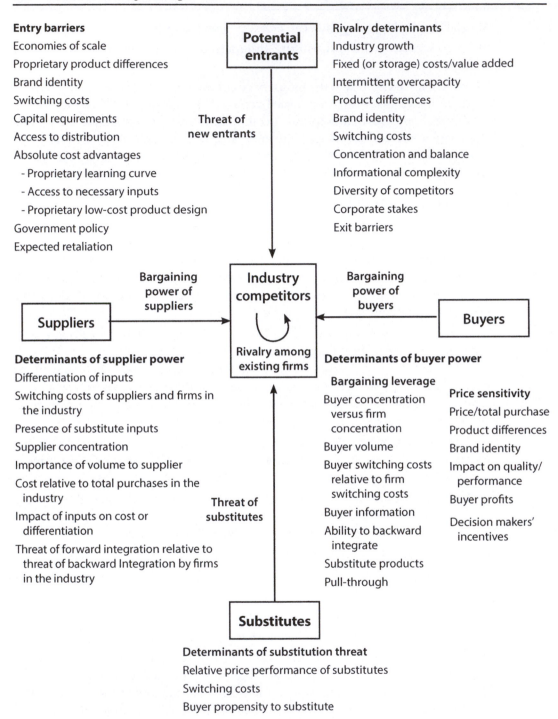

Entry barriers
Economies of scale
Proprietary product differences
Brand identity
Switching costs
Capital requirements
Access to distribution
Absolute cost advantages
  - Proprietary learning curve
  - Access to necessary inputs
  - Proprietary low-cost product design
Government policy
Expected retaliation

Potential entrants

Threat of new entrants

Rivalry determinants
Industry growth
Fixed (or storage) costs/value added
Intermittent overcapacity
Product differences
Brand identity
Switching costs
Concentration and balance
Informational complexity
Diversity of competitors
Corporate stakes
Exit barriers

Bargaining power of suppliers

Industry competitors

Bargaining power of buyers

Suppliers

Rivalry among existing firms

Buyers

Determinants of supplier power
Differentiation of inputs
Switching costs of suppliers and firms in the industry
Presence of substitute inputs
Supplier concentration
Importance of volume to supplier
Cost relative to total purchases in the industry
Impact of inputs on cost or differentiation
Threat of forward integration relative to threat of backward Integration by firms in the industry

Threat of substitutes

Determinants of buyer power

Bargaining leverage
Buyer concentration versus firm concentration
Buyer volume
Buyer switching costs relative to firm switching costs
Buyer information
Ability to backward integrate
Substitute products
Pull-through

Price sensitivity
Price/total purchase
Product differences
Brand identity
Impact on quality/performance
Buyer profits
Decision makers' incentives

Substitutes

Determinants of substitution threat
Relative price performance of substitutes
Switching costs
Buyer propensity to substitute

Figure 10.3: Full diagram of Porter's Five Forces Model
Source: developed from Porter, 2004b

Suppliers provide the materials and other stocks for the business. The **bargaining power of suppliers** tends to be powerful where, for instance:

- They are integrated – operate as a cartel
- They are suppliers of small organisations with essential materials
- Their groups of products are integrated, e.g. brewer who is also a wine merchant; or
- They integrate forward, e.g. a wine supplier which also operates wine bars.

Substitutes are those alternative products which the buyers might choose instead of the food service operations product. This is complex. For a food service operation, the nature of demand being met will be a key **determinant of the substitution threat.** Food service operations that are linked to another activity, such as retail or leisure, will be highly dependent on the customer carrying out the first activity. There are many alternative or substitute activities to retail or leisure pursuits that the customer might choose. This will then affect demand for the food service product. Even where this is not the case, substitutes for food service operations are also other types of food service operation that might not be seen initially as in direct competition; for instance, a customer choosing a McDonald's rather than choosing a fine dining restaurant.

Activity:

- Choose a single independent restaurant and identify how each of the Five Forces could affect the business.

- Choose a chain restaurant group and identify how each of the Five Forces could affect the business.

- Consider any key similarities and key differences in the way each the Five Forces affects each type of business.

Organisations always need to be aware that existing or potential competitors will also be modifying their strategies to attempt to be more competitive. In turn, many of these possible changes to strategy, or changes to the relative competitiveness of an industry, are caused by changes to PESTLE factors. Gaining an understanding of the macro-industry environment and the competitiveness within an industry (micro-business environment) can inform a food service organisation about how their strategies can be managed in order to be successful.

Using the Five Forces and PESTLE, or other analysis techniques, is a learning process, which will strengthen the organisation by making possible a more focused appraisal of how the food and beverage operation complements and matches, the business environment in which it operates. The value placed upon any of the analysis tools by food service operators will depend upon their skills and objectives. To ignore these approaches is unwise; to include them in appraising an operation's performance, no matter how modestly, is good business sense.

10

■ Qualitative evaluation

In many ways the qualitative evaluation of an operation is on the one hand the hardest to achieve well but on the other hand potentially the most rewarding. It is about getting to the heart of the reasons for the success of the operation and for considering how to maintain and develop it further.

Section 9.5, *Appraising the product*, details various approaches to qualitative analysis on which to make judgements about the extent to which the organisation is achieving its customer service specification. We have also considered the various approaches to quantitative analysis (page 305 to 307) and to appraising the business environment. In all cases, any qualitative evaluation needs to be considered taking account of the current and future business needs as well as being supported by data. We have already identified that:

- Quantitative assessment should be used as an additional tool to back up issues identified in another area of analysis

- The evaluation of the quantitative analysis is more important than the figures themselves.

Qualitative evaluation takes account of the quantitative analysis and also the appraisal of the external business environment. The outcomes of qualitative evaluation are informed views being taken on, for example, the extent to which:

- The customer service specification is appropriate to meet the current and intended customer demand, or are some parts of the specification higher than required and others insufficient

- The customer service specification can be simplified to make it easier to provide, or to make it more cost effective and reliable

- The service is consistent and reliable and whether that is a major selling point

- Processes and procedures are competitive with those of competitors and if not knowing why not

- All the aspects of quality control and quality assurance of the food and beverages being sold and the service of them are being controlled

- The equipment is at the standard required (both in capability and stock level terms) to meet the customer service specification and what equipment will have to be improved or replaced

- Members of staff are well selected, up to the job and supported by sufficient training

- Members of staff are paid well enough and are motivated to contribute to the fulfilment of the customer service specification

- Staff suggestions are listened to in order to consider changes to the range of products on offer

- The organisation has the ability to maintain the current customer service specification and the ability to respond to change.

Attempting to develop views on these types of issues can illuminate other issues such as the effectiveness of the customer service specification in meeting what the customer wants, and also what staff and managers understand the competitors are about to do.

The data that will be generated from the quantitative analysis, and the appraisal of the business environment will have already generated a variety of possible actions to be taken. Action will be as much dependent on the needs of the operation as it will on determining the effectiveness of the operation in meeting current and future business demands.

■ Using the food service cycle as an analysis tool

A systematic way of approaching the appraisal of the operation is to use the food service cycle as an analysis tool. The cycle can be used as a dynamic model. Figure 10.4 gives the eight stages of the cycle (which we first saw in Chapter 1, page 3) and indicates the issues that could be considered under each stage.

The food service cycle	Issues to be considered in appraising the operation
1 The consumer and the market	Changes in the markets served by the operation and changes in the consumer needs.
2 Policy and objectives	The level of achievement in meeting the objectives of the operation and the extent to which the goals and the vision are being realised.
3 Customer service specification	The appropriateness of the existing menu and beverage lists and other services in meeting the customer needs, and the extent to which the existing customer service specification is sustainable.
4 Facilities	The effectiveness of the planning and design and operational capability of the facilities, plant and equipment to support the customer service specification.
5 Purchasing	The effectiveness of the purchasing, storage and control methods to meet the operational requirements.
6 Production and service	The effectiveness of the food production and food and beverage service methods, and the efficiency and appropriateness in the use of the resources being applied to them (including staffing), in order to support the customer service specification.
7 Control of costs and revenue	The extent to which revenue and the costs of materials, labour and overheads have been controlled, and the appropriateness of the methods adopted to meet operational requirements.
8 Monitoring of customer satisfaction	The effectiveness of the methods used to monitor the level of customer satisfaction and the extent to which the customer satisfaction has been achieved.

Figure 10.4: The food service cycle as an analysis tool

10

There are two dimensions to using the food service cycle in this way:

■ By using the food service cycle to present the information that has been generated, it will help to organise what is known about the operation and its performance, but more importantly it will also help to identify where there are gaps in the information and where additional information might be required to make the evaluation more complete.

■ Viewing the operation within the cycle will help to identify operational strengths and weaknesses. Within the cycle any difficulties, which are identified in one area of the cycle, will cause difficulties in the elements of the cycle that follow. For instance, difficulties with purchasing will then have had effects on production and service, and control. Similarly the difficulties experienced under one stage of the cycle will often have their causes in the stages that precede it.

The food service cycle helps in considering the operation as a whole i.e. as an operating system. Approaching the analysis and evaluation of the operation using the food service cycle will also help to determine the limitations of the information that is known, which will then lead to better evaluation of the operation and its performance.

The true causes of difficulties in any of the eight stages and the implications of them can be more easily and accurately identified. In operations the causes of difficulties in one stage are often one or two stages before that stage, rather than necessarily being in that stage it self. For instance, difficulties with food and beverage service can often be because of equipment shortages, stock outs, incorrect pricing information etc. rather than being a result of difficulties directly associated with the service. Similarly, difficulties identified in one stage will also have knock on effects on the stages that follow. Being able to identify and understand these various interrelationships will mean that decisions on operational changes will only be considered after finding the true cause of any difficulties, and taking account of the effects of any proposed changes might have throughout the operation as a whole.

Activity:

For a food service operation of your choice:

■ Use the eight stages of the food service cycle as a basis for an analysis of the operation.

■ Draw conclusion about the extent to which the operation is being successful under each of the eight stages.

■ Identify what action (if any) you think the operation may need to take.

External comparison

The current performance of the operation will have been compared with performance in the past and also against the current goals and objectives of the organisation. This can then also be extended to making comparisons with other organisations. This is sometimes called **benchmarking**.

Benchmarking is a process of making comparisons with the performance indicators of other food service operations, and then also making comparisons with the performance indicators of organisations in similar types of operations, but in different industries, to see the how the organisation compares with best practice. This process could involve undertaking comparisons using many of the ratios which are given in Appendix A as well as, for instance, complaint levels, or stock handling, or energy saving, or staff turnover in other service operations. There can be useful lessons to be learnt if the organisation does not compare well. For food service operators, there is also the Best Practice Forum – further information can be obtained at www.bestpracticeforum.org.

In the same way as the food service cycle can used as a basis for investigating the internal operation (see Figure 10.4), it can also be used as a basis for comparisons with other operations. Information gathered about competitors' operations can be organised and examined in a similar way to information about the internal operation. This helps to make the comparison more systematic and objective.

Additionally in the past few years there has been an increased interest in **performance indicators** in both the public and private sectors. These are often fairly simple quantitative measures such as:

- Time to answer the telephone
- Time to respond to a 999 call
- Percentage of trains arriving on time, or
- Percentage of patients on a hospital waiting list for more than two years.

They might also be more specific or detailed, such as those widely used in hospitality industry. The industry uses quantitative measures such as:

- Average sales per sales person
- Gross profit percentages
- Seat turnover, or
- Energy efficiency measures.

Although few people would disagree with the need to assess efficiency and effectiveness in order to improve efficiency whilst maintaining standards, the use of performance indicators can have drawbacks such as:

- The concentration on quantitative measures tends to draw too much attention to that which can easily be measured, rather than considering the much richer concepts of service and quality that are much more difficult to measure.

10

- Performance indicators measure behaviour, but they also have the tendency to change behaviour; people start to work to satisfy the indicator rather than the requirements of the customers.
- Some of the indicators are prone to being manipulated in order to give the impression of a higher quality than is actually being achieved.

More recently, for the hospitality industry in the UK, under the aegis of the Institute of Hospitality, an accreditation programme has been developed which is based on quality management assessment systems that also take into account a measure of the reality of customer service. This is the Hospitality Assured programme – more information on this can be obtained at www.hospitalityassured.com.

Whatever approaches are considered and used, the question always needs to be asked as to whether any organisation should actually be doing the things that the performance indicators are measuring. Many people work extremely hard doing jobs that either do not need doing or do not need doing in that way. Instead of asking questions such as how can things be done better, at lower cost or faster, it is often better to first ask 'Why do we do what we do at all?'

Effective qualitative evaluation is the essence of successful food and beverage management. It is systematic, in that it is supported by data, but it also allows for appropriate professional judgement to be applied. Well done it can ensure that valuable resources are not wasted on making the operation comply with a customer service specification that either is no longer relevant to customer demand or no longer able to be achieved by the physical capabilities of the operation, by its staff or both. Overall, the food and beverage manager's job is to ensure that the right questions are being asked, not to provide all the right answers.

10.3 Assessing organisational capability

Any food service organisation should be in a position to assess its strengths and weaknesses and determine what it sees as its core competencies. Many of the existing strengths and weaknesses, which already exist within the operation, are as result of linkages between different activities and the consistency of the operational strategies. It can therefore often be shown that:

- Better training of staff tends to result in better service
- Early attention to problems may avoid expensive compensation later
- Greater prevention of problems reduces unexpected demands
- Better design leads to lower service costs
- Liaison between departments allows for better planning, reduced costs and improved customer service.

One way of exploring these issues further is to consider **resource analysis**. This is concerned with:

- Identifying the strengths and weaknesses of the organisation's resources in meeting the requirements of the current strategies
- Identifying how the current resources could meet the needs of possible changes in the business environment and therefore customer demand
- Identifying what changes would need to be made to the current resources in order for the organisation to meet future and competitive demands.

There are a variety of methods for carrying out a resource analysis. Some organisations go through very formal processes, whilst others have a more informal approach. Whichever way it is done, it is important that, once carried out, it is continuously updated. One approach to resources analysis, based on approaches to resource audit put forward by Johnson *et al.* (2017), is outlined as follows:

1 Carry out a value chain analysis:
   - To look at how effectively and efficiently all the resources are being used in each stage of the operation.
   - To look at how effectively the resources are contributing to meeting the goals and objectives of the organisation
   - To develop and use measures for the control of resources.

(The value chain includes all the stages of the operation. For food service operations the various stages and interrelationships are indicated in Chapter 1, Figure 1.4, page 7).

2 Draw comparisons:
   - With past performance of the organisation
   - With norms in the industry
   - With best practice in similar activities in other types of organisation.

3 Assess balance within the organisation:
   - Analyse the range of products that are offered and make decisions about the appropriateness of them in meeting current demand
   - Analyse the skills/personalities of the staff involved in order to determine to extent to which they complement the requirements of the customer service specification
   - Analyse the flexibility of the organisation in meeting the range of current demand
   - Analyse the capability of the resources of the operation in order to determine the extent to which the operation is able to meet the demands of potential future demand.

Undertaking these activities should lead to the identification of key issues which will enable the identification of the:

- Strengths and weaknesses of the operation
- Core competencies of the operation (what do we do and how good at it are we? And then: what could we do and how good at it could we be?).

10

Such an audit should enable the organisation to assess its current and potential strategic capability. The development of the strategies for the organisation can then take into account:

- The current and potential strategic capability of the organisation
- The opportunities and threats it faces
- An identification of the future resources and capabilities required to implement an adopted strategy successfully.

Strategic analysis, planning and implementation are a continuum, not as a sequence. Therefore equally there may need to be modifications to the existing strategies to take account of the strengths and weaknesses of the existing resources, as well as also ensuring that plans are considered which will develop the resources so as to be able to implement future strategies.

For more information on value chain analysis also see Parker (2018).

10.4 Strategic analysis and planning

Strategic analysis and planning of the organisation is concerned with attempting to identify:

- Its strengths and weaknesses
- The opportunities and threats facing it at the time.

Most writers on strategic management argue that the task of managers is to develop strategies which:

- Use the organisation's strengths to capitalise on external opportunities or counter threats.
- Seek to alleviate the organisation's weaknesses.

This is in an effort to achieve the organisation's goals and objectives and hence satisfy its stakeholders. Strategy formulation is thus an interplay between internal strengths and weaknesses, external opportunities and threats, and stakeholders' expectations.

SWOT analysis is useful to the food and beverage operator because it allows a focused identification and evaluation of the issues that affect the operation. Strengths and weaknesses are usually internal to the operation and might include such items as the product, staffing, management and the effectiveness of the operating systems. Opportunities and threats are usually external to the business and might include such items as the existing and potential customer needs, interest rates, demographic changes, infrastructure developments and national and local economic outlooks.

Strategic management then can be considered to be a process aimed at managing the interface between the external environment (the opportunities and threats) and the internal capabilities (the strengths and weaknesses) of the organisation.

■ Using SWOT analysis

SWOT analysis can be used in considering the organisation and the business environment in which it operates and as a basis for developing strategy in line with its mission. It can be a very powerful and effective tool because it has the great benefit of conceptual simplicity. The idea of identifying what you are good at, and where you are weak, is very simple. But in practice different managers have different perceptions of the strengths and weaknesses of the same organisation. The same is true of opportunities and threats.

However, the conceptual simplicity of SWOT allows it to be used very creatively. It can bring into the open conflicts of perception and test assumptions. Used well, it can cut through internal politics and its use and application need not be threatening.

SWOT analysis is often used to portray a simple snapshot of the business at a specific point. But the real purpose of the SWOT analysis is far more useful than that. It provides the basis for determining what decisions need to be taken.

Using SWOT analysis in practice

Strategy should be related to the external environment and the internal resources and capabilities of the organisation, not made in a vacuum. Similarly, the separate components of a SWOT analysis should not be considered in isolation as can be seen in the extended SWOT matrix shown in Figure 10.3.

		Strengths	**Weaknesses**
		List of strengths	List of weaknesses
Opportunities	List of opportunities	**Box 1** Strengths to make use of opportunities	**Box 2** Weaknesses which prevent the exploitation of opportunities
Threats	List of threats	**Box 3** Strengths to counter threats	**Box 4** Weaknesses which prevent the countering of threats

Figure 10.5: SWOT Matrix

An organisation may have resources that give it strengths to take advantage of opportunities in the external environment (Box 1) or that can be used to reduce the effect of the threats (Box 3). Alternatively, external opportunities and threats may cause an organisation to examine current weaknesses (Boxes 2 and 4) and eradicate these so that it can take advantage of opportunities or counter potential threats. In some situations, an organisation can use existing or newly developed strengths to benefit from new opportunities (Box 1).

To use this as a process tool, specific opportunities and threats need to be listed to see how each of these links to the strengths and weaknesses of the organisation. This helps in making decisions on the actions that need to be taken. Similarly, an organisation can list individual strengths and weaknesses and see how these relate to the potential opportunities and threats. It is also useful to match these against the needs of the existing markets, the potential markets and also to those of competitors.

◼ The need for constant monitoring

Business generally is going through a period of rapid change, which is turbulent and uncertain, not developmental or evolutionary. In this situation, it is not enough simply to monitor periodically the factors that in the past have indicated opportunities and threats. Rather, food service organisations need to be constantly on the lookout for new issues and new developments, which may have a radical effect on the business environment, and on the actions of competitors both of which may have an affect on the business that the food service organisation is in.

The annual event of monitoring 'key variables' in readiness for an update of the annual plan, or budget, may be too infrequent; an important opportunity may be missed or a dangerous threat may become a reality. Even if a threat is recognised, the organisation may not be able to adapt in time.

Monitoring can also be more difficult because many opportunities and threats are not easily recognisable. A development in an obscure area of technology may have effects on a wide variety of sectors of the economy that few, if any, people recognise at the outset, as with Twitter, for example. The developments, which may ultimately have a high impact on a business, do not often happen in an area that directly affects a particular organisation, but to businesses three or four positions up or downstream. For example changes in the use of specific packaging materials not only affect the manufacturers of the packaging materials but also the wholesalers and then the food service operation, which subsequently retails the products.

In such a situation there can be an in-built pressure to collect more and more data on an ever-increasing number of factors to try to make the future more certain. This can be counter-productive and cause data overload or 'paralysis by analysis'. There are more data available but less information than before.

◼ Assessing for now and the future

The assessment of strengths and weaknesses cannot stand still. It is a continuous process. Strategic capability needs to be assessed, not just for now but also for the future. As time passes the current strategy will have developed and been modified and also the external business environment is likely to have changed. This in turn will lead to the need to modify strategies in the light of these changes.

There is then a continuous interplay between formulation, implementation and assessment of SWOT analysis now and in the future. The process of assessing current strengths and weaknesses should be part of this process. They should be assessed not only in terms of their appropriateness now but also for the future. It works in many ways:

- What possible external changes might make a current strength into a weakness or vice versa?
- How can a current strength be used to explore a future opportunity?
- How can a strength be developed further to be of greater benefit in the future?

The other issue that needs to be faced is where changes are required and where the resource capabilities of the operation are unable to meet them.

As the market, competition and the business environment change over time, so there will need to be changes in the core competencies of the organisation. A current core competence that gives a food service operation an edge over competitors may become commonplace amongst competitors in a few years. Thus any organisation need to be continually developing its core competencies so as to be better prepared to face the future.

Activity:

- Carry out a SWOT analysis for an operation of your choice.

- From your analysis, identify:

  - ☐ Strengths the operation has to be able to make use of opportunities

  - ☐ Weaknesses which might prevent the exploitation of opportunities

  - ☐ Strengths which enable the operation to counter threats

  - ☐ Weaknesses which might prevent the countering of threats

- From the results, identify key steps the operation might need to consider to make its position stronger.

10.5 The need for a balanced approach

When reviewing business performance, there is a tendency for senior managers to be mainly concerned with financial performance indicators, such as costs and profits. At the operations level the main concern is with operational issues, such as staffing, stock control and efficiency. This difference in focus also leads to a difference in both the activities of those involved and in the language they use to talk about the business performance. Middle managers have traditionally tried to bridge the gaps between these two groups (Johnston *et al.*, 2017).

10

In addition to the financial and operational considerations, a business must also take account of external factors (stakeholders and customers), and the need to ensure the organisation can meet current and future demands (development and learning).

Traditionally the four perspectives were considered in different ways by the different parts of an organisation hierarchy. For any business there is a need for a balanced approach which incorporates the aspects that the different levels are considering. There are now a number of frameworks for achieving this, with the best known being the Balanced Scorecard (a term first coined by Kaplan and Norton, 1996). This framework incorporates performance measurement from four perspectives.

- **Developmental** – organisational capacity, knowledge and innovation
- **Operational** – efficiency
- **External** – stakeholder and customer satisfaction
- **Financial** – performance and financial management

The Balanced Scorecard

The Balanced Scorecard encourages a more integrated approach to performance measurement and strategic planning, where all levels of an organisation are contributing to the future success of the business through each level looking beyond their traditional focus.

The balanced approach aims to ensure that an organisation is not managed and developed by merely looking at the **Results** (External and Financial measures). It recognises that organisations also need to know how the **Internal Drivers** (Developmental and Operational measures) are contributing to those **Results** (Johnston *et al.* 2012). Figure 10.6 identifies the four measurement perspectives and indicates the relationship between them.

Figure 10.6: The four types of performance measures

Source: Developed from Johnston *et al.*, 2012

Using the Balanced Scorecard, as a framework for performance measurement and strategic planning, helps organisations to:

- Translate the mission statement into operational terms
- Consider more than just financial outcomes
- Look at causes, not just effects
- Ensure a consistency of vision, and
- Identify areas for improvement.

The approach can also be:

- Developed for corporate, unit and operation levels, and
- Modified to suit individual operations.

However, there are some potential limitations. For example, organisation can:

- Assume the measures being monitored are the correct ones.
- Rely too much on benchmarks that the organisation itself has identified.

The process

In order to implement the Balanced Scorecard for specific businesses, operations, departments or groups of staff, management have to:

- Translate the vision into operational terms
- Communicate and form linkages between management, operations and customers
- Identify what, when and how to measure performance
- Identify realistic and appropriate targets
- Generate and analyse the data
- Provide feedback, and
- Learn from the experience.

For each quadrant of the scorecard, it is necessary to determine the performance indicators by answering the questions:

- What is to be measured?
- What the target or benchmark to be achieved?
- How is it going to be measured?

There should always be a mix of reference points for measures, from both internal and external sources. These include, for example, internally set goals and targets together with external industry benchmarks. Table 10.1 identifies examples of performance measures for each of the four quadrants of the Balanced Scorecard.

Care has to be taken to ensure that what is measured, and the unit of measurement, are relevant to the individual business needs. It is also important to distinguish between measurements which are based on fact (objective) and those which are based on opinion (subjective). Appraisal and decision making should always be supported by facts.

Further information on the Balanced Scorecard see, for example, Johnston *et al.* (2012) and the website of the Balanced Scorecard Institute:http:// www.balanced-scorecard.org.

10

Table 10.1: Examples of performance indicators for the four perspectives of the Balanced Scorecard

Internal Drivers	Results
Developmental Training and development needs and opportunities Staff flexibility / adaptability Staff availability Staff turnover Plant and equipment needs and capabilities	**External** Market share Stakeholder evaluations Customer satisfaction records Customer loyalty Repeat custom Customer profile changes Complaints
Operational Customer service specification Sales mix / Menu mix Speed of order to delivery Dish specifications Plate waste records HACCP Operational performance measures such as average spend per head	**Financial** Return on investment Cash flow Return on capital employed Earnings per share Turnover £ Gross Margin % Nett margin %

Note: (A detailed listing of operational and financial measures is given in Appendix A).

10.6 The basis of strategy

One of the most influential concepts in the development of strategic thinking in the last decade has been that of generic strategies. Michael Porter (2004a) proposes that there are three basic ways by which organisations can achieve a 'sustainable competitive advantage' over its rivals. These are the 'generic strategies' of:

- **Cost leadership**: whereby the organisation sets out to be the lowest cost producer in its industry.

- **Differentiation**: a strategy based on enhancements to products which are valued by customers and for which the customer will be prepared to pay higher prices in order to obtain unique benefits.

- **Focus**: where the organisation chooses a narrow competitive scope; that is, it selects a particular segment or group of segments of the market that it can serve exclusively well. There are two variants of this strategy:

  □ A focus based on cost whereby the organisation seeks a cost advantage in its chosen segment

  □ A focus which is based on achieving differentiation in that segment.

Porter argues that for an organisation to be successful over the long term it must be very clear which of the generic strategies it is following. Such a choice then informs all strategic decisions that must be made.

A development of Porter's approaches has been the **Strategy Clock** (Johnson *et al.*, 2008 and 2017). This has eight different strategy options (rather than Porter's four) and these are based on combinations of price (low to high) and perceived added value (low to high). It attempts to ensure coherence of strategy across different resources in the organisation, and links the use of resources to customer requirements.

	Needs/risks	
1 Low cost to the customer/ low added value	Likely to be segment specific	**Low cost**
2 Low cost to the customer	Risk of price war and low margins/need to be low operating cost leader	
3 Hybrid	Low cost base and reinvestment in low cost and differentiation	
4 Differentiation - without price premium	Perceived added value by user, yielding market share benefits	**Differentiation**
- with price premium	Perceived added value sufficient to bear price premium	
5 Focussed differentiation	Perceived added value to a particular segment, warranting price premium	
6 Increased cost/standard value	Higher margins if competitors do not follow/ risk of losing market share	**Likely failure**
7 Increased cost/low value	Only feasible in monopoly situation	
8 Low value/standard cost	Loss of market share	

Figure 10.7: The strategy clock. Based on Johnson *et al.*, 2008 and 2017

The Strategy Clock takes a customer perspective on strategy by plotting perceived added value against price. These are both factors external to the organisation that relate to how customers make their purchasing decisions. However a modification to this model is proposed in that the horizontal axis should more appropriately be the 'cost to the customer' rather than simply being the price (in cash terms), as in the Johnson *et al.* model. This issue has been discussed (in Chapter 2, page 39), where we indicated that **value** in a food service operation is more likely to be measured by the customer as the relationship between **worth** and the **total cost to the customer**. This 'cost to the customer' included, for instance, the lost opportunity of being somewhere else, travel costs, the possibility of disagreeable company, poor service, poor food, etc.

Taking account of this modification, the Strategy Clock, as shown in Figure 10.7, illustrates that the strategic routes indicated by the positions 1 to 5 inclusive, can be sustainable strategies and that the strategic routes indicated by positions 6, 7 and 8 are destined for failure.

Developing this further, the strategic basis of each of the eight routes may be summarised as in Figure 10.8. From this figure it can be seen that:

- Strategic routes 1 and 2 are strategies that are aimed at achieving sales through being of low cost to the customer.
- Strategic route 3 is a hybrid.
- Strategic route 4 and 5 are about being different from competitors.
- Strategic routes 6, 7 and 8 offer a mixture of high cost to the customer and low perceived added value and therefore all of these are likely to be unsuccessful strategies, which will ultimately lead to the failure of the business.

Using this application of the Strategy Clock for considering the strategic route for food service operations may at first appear simple. However, the nature of any food and beverage product is that it may simultaneously be aimed at meeting a wide variety of different types of demand. This is both in terms of the types of demand being met by one particular part of the product as well as by the nature of a food service operation, for instance, offering a range of products, e.g. breakfast service, morning coffee, business lunches, afternoon teas, family meals, special diet provision, pre-theatre meals, evenings out, post-theatre meals, special parties, functions and also retail merchandise and parking services. It is therefore quite likely that any operation will need to split the product(s) down and consider the types of demand being met and then place each of these products separately on the Strategy Clock.

Activity:

For each of the eight strategic routes the Strategic Clock:

- Identify one food service business that fits into each of the routes.

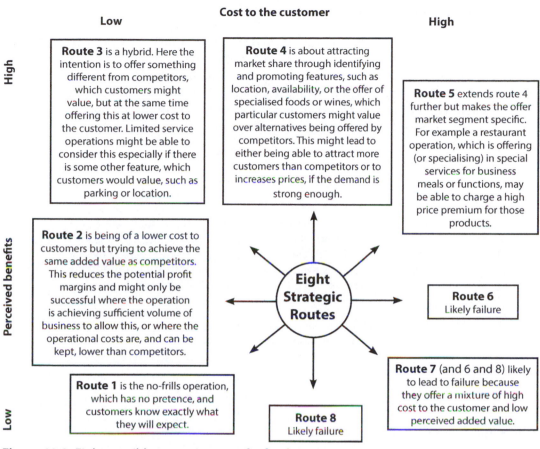

Figure 10.8: Eight possible strategic routes for food service operations

Source: Developed from Johnson *et al.* 2008 and 2017.

10.7 Strategic direction

Various approaches exist to assist in determining strategic choices for an organisation. Examples of these include:

- Growth Share Matrix (Boston Consulting Group (BCG) matrix; also referred to as BCG-matrix or Boston matrix) which helps to consider the portfolio of products.

- Life cycle analysis which helps to identify when products are likely to decline or need to be refreshed.

- Ansoff Growth Matrix which interrelates the products and the markets and helps to determine the strategic options for the business.

10

■   Product portfolio

The Boston Consulting Group's Product Portfolio Matrix (as discussed in Johnson *et al.*, 2017) balances off relative market share (relative to the competition) and market growth. This matrix is mainly valuable when considering products. Individual products can be placed onto the matrix alongside competitors to determine the relative market share. Figure 10.9 identifies the four quadrants of the matrix and give an indication of the actions that can be taken.

Market share

	High	Low
High	**Stars** Products in high growth markets and have relatively high share of that market. Stars generate the highest amounts of profit. Important to protect and invest to become Cash cows.	**Question Marks** Consume resources and generate little in return. They absorb most profit as attempts are made to increase market share. Some will move to star position and others need to be discarded.
Low	**Cash cows** Products with a high share of a slow growth market. Cash cows generate more profit than is invested in them. Keep them for the time being but review regularly.	**Dogs** Do not generate profit and tend to absorb it. Aim to get rid of these products.

(Market growth — vertical axis label, High to Low)

Figure 10.9: Market growth /share matrix

Source: based on 'BCG Classics Revisited: The Growth Share Matrix'

It is important to seek to maintain a balance in the product portfolio. The funds generated by Cash Cows are used to turn Question Marks (also known Problem Children) into Stars, which then may eventually become Cash Cows. As some of the Question Marks will become Dogs, there always needs to be a larger contribution from the successful products to compensate for failures.

Like any business model, the matrix can has its drawbacks. There is an assumption that higher rates of profit are directly related to high rates of market share. This is not always the case. Market share may be gained but the cost of development needs to be covered,

■   Life cycle analysis

Life cycle analysis is an approach that attempts to consider what strategies might be appropriate taking account of the position of the product in the product life cycle and also the competitive position of an organisation. The approach can be used to identify possible strategies that might be considered. For instance a strong competitive position in a mature market indicates that possible strategies might be to aim to attain cost leadership, to renew the product, to aim for a focussed strategy or to seek to differentiate the product (see, for example, Bowie and Buttle, 2016 and Kotler *et al.*, 2013).

The main usefulness of this approach is that it can be used to establish the suitability of particular strategies in relation to the stage of industry maturity and the organisation's competitive position. In life cycle analysis, as in the other approaches, determining the stage in the product life cycle of the particular hospitality product is necessary in order to assess the appropriateness of current strategies or to consider future ones. However, identifying the position of the various hospitality products can be difficult.

The hospitality industry provides products that are already well established alongside some products that are newly launched and others that are at the end of their life cycle. Bowie and Buttle (2016), identify four stages of the product life cycle: introduction, growth, maturity and decline as illustrated in Figure 10.10.

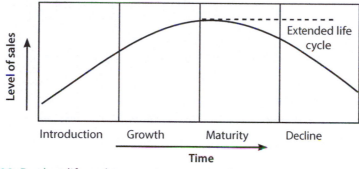

Figure 10.10: Product life cycle

As well as presenting this classic view of the product life cycle Bowie and Buttle (2016) also identify two specific, and for the food service industry very important, variants:

- The first is the *fad* product life cycle, which is characterised by rapid growth matched by equally dramatic collapse. Certain types of restaurants or discos might fall into this type of life cycle.

- The second variant is the *long* or *extended* product life cycle. This cycle is characterised by an extended maturity phase, which implies high consumer repurchase levels, with little loss of sales to other competitors. Some products of the hospitality industry can fall into this type of life cycle. Examples are some fashionable luxury restaurants and five-star hotels, essential function food service outlets, life style products such as holidays and a wide variety of other products that have been revamped and re-launched.

In many cases the food service product which is being considered will be positioned in the extended life cycle phase. Therefore, the main strategies required are primarily those that are mainly aimed at:

- Increasing customer loyalty
- Investing to maintain customer service and improve perceived value, and

■ Developing and extending existing sales through repackaging and re-launching the product.

When considering the complexity of the food service product and endeavouring to determine the position of the particular product in the product life cycle, and within the various standard strategic direction models, it is worth taking account of these two variants in particular, as these will significantly change the interpretation of some of the more standard strategic direction models.

Activity:

■ Identify, with reasons for your choice, a food service concept that is in each of the stages of the product life cycle:
   ☐ Introduction
   ☐ Growth
   ☐ Maturity
   ☐ Decline

■ Identify, with reasons for your choice, a food service concept that is in the:
   ☐ Fad product life cycle
   ☐ Extended product life cycle

■ Strategic options

The Ansoff Growth Matrix (Ansoff, 1988 and also discussed in Johnson *et al.*, 2017) interrelates the product and the market, each of which will vary depending upon whether we are dealing with new or old products or markets or both, as illustrated in Figure 10.11. So, for example, if the current product range is being provided within existing markets the organisation needs to have a clear market penetration strategy. If the products are current, but are being offered within the new markets, then a market development strategy will be required. If the organisation has developed new products that it aims to sell within a new market the strategy needed will be diversification orientated.

		Products	
		Present	New
Markets	Present	Do nothing Withdraw Consolidate Market penetration	Product development
	New	Market development	Related diversification Unrelated diversification

Figure 10.11: Ansoff's Growth Matrix with alternative strategies/directions

The strategic options identified within the matrix are explained below:

- **Do nothing:** a 'no change' strategy can be wrongly perceived as 'no strategy'. If there are no foreseen internal and external environmental changes the organisation may choose to take a conscious decision to continue with the strategies currently being undertaken. A positive decision to retain the business in its present market is a perfectly logical one. To stand still in a dynamic environment might be considered as moving backward, but changing strategies in an unchanging environment may be quite inappropriate. Generally though, unless an organisation's environment is very stable, this is unlikely to be a viable option. However this option should always be considered as it provides a valuable comparator when considering other different options.

- **Withdrawal**: there may be circumstances in which it might make sense to withdraw from a particular activity in a particular market, especially if continuation is no longer profitable or viable. For a single food service operator this is often that hardest decision to have to make.

- **Consolidate**: this implies taking action to retain existing market shares. In growth markets this will lead to increased sales. In mature or declining markets actions such as improved service or quality, or reduced costs may be required.

- **Market penetration**: this is a strategy of attempting to increase market share. This is likely to be easier in growth markets. In mature or declining markets, competitors are likely to react to competitive moves (for example, lowering prices, increasing advertising, improving quality and so on) to steal their business.

- **Product development**: this involves offering new products to existing markets. A decision to develop new products may be based on an identified customer need, which is currently not being met, or be derived from technological advancements. New product development always carries an element of risk as many new products do not achieve required levels of profitability and may lose money.

- **Market development**: this involves taking existing products into new markets. These may be new market segments, new uses of existing products, or new geographic markets. Penetrating new markets is risky as it represents a move into the unknown.

- **Diversification**: although this term is often used fairly loosely, here it is used in the sense of offering new products to new markets. There are two types of diversification: related and unrelated.

  - ☐ **Related diversification**: where the development is broadly within the same industry. This can further be classified as:

    - ❖ Backward integration, which is a move into an activity that is already an input into the food service organisation's existing operations (i.e.

backwards in the supply chain, further away from the customers, such as a restaurant having interests in a farm).

❖ Forward integration, which is a move into an activity which is an output of the organisation's existing operations (that is, forward in the supply chain, nearer to the consumer. This is difficult as many food service operations are already at the end of the supply chain. However it can include activities such as joining marketing consortia).

❖ Horizontal integration, which is a move into a competitive or complementary activity, such as a restaurant linking with leisure attraction or being located within an hotel.

☐ **Unrelated diversification**: where the development is outside the industry in which the organisation currently operates. This can be for instance a food service operation also being in the car trade.

Diversification in any form is doubly risky as it involves both products and markets of which the organisation has no experience. Nonetheless, the attraction of diversification is often irresistible for organisations apparently offering possible opportunities to control supply (backwards integration), control markets (forward integration), spread risk (particularly in unrelated diversification), utilise under-employed capacity or cash, and so on.

Particularly alluring is the prospect of **synergy** whereby two or more activities complement each other to the extent that the whole is greater than the sum of the parts. This concept that 2 + 2 = 5 is often put forward as the reason for diversification, but in many cases it has proved very difficult to achieve in practice.

When applying this matrix – or more importantly the thinking behind it – an organisation can consider the possible options it could adopt in each of the four segments of the alternative strategic directions in the matrix in Figure 10.11 and then appraise each of these for suitability, for and against.

This approach requires the process to be undertaken systematically in order to answer a variety of questions as follows:

Present market, present products

What would be the implications of doing nothing? Is withdrawal feasible? What would consolidation or market penetration mean for the organisation?

Present market, new product

This presents much scope for creative powers. What sort of new product could be developed for the present market? The environmental analysis (see page 307) and SWOT analysis (see page 319) could give some clues here.

New market, present products

This requires a reassessment of the strengths of the products. Has the organisation really considered fully the scope for entering into new markets?

New markets, new products

Here there is a need to control imagination. Diversification may look superficially attractive, but there are a host of potential dangers and risks. Decisions of this nature tend to involve a considerable outlay. This is particularly true of unrelated diversification. What special skills can the organisation bring which will promise success in new and unfamiliar markets? Unless these can be identified then it would be better to forget it.

Activity:

Obtain a major company report.

- Identify what strategic choices have been made and why.

- Consider the extent to you consider the strategic choices appropriate and why.

10.8 Strategic means

Through the use of the various approaches put forward by Johnson *et al.* (2017 and Ansoff (1988), various strategic options can be identified. Strategic direction can be implemented through three basic means: internal development, acquisition (external) development and through joint ventures. Each of these three options is considered below:

- ## Internal development

This is also referred to as 'organic growth'. It depends on the organisation using its own competencies and resources to put its strategy into effect. The advantages are that the organisation can build and develop the required skills and knowledge without encountering the cultural problems often associated with developments involving other organisations. Internal development also enables developmental costs to be spread over a longer period. In many food service operations internal development is the only realistic option. Its major disadvantage is the length of time that may be required, to develop new products, acquire new skills and gain access to the new markets, which a particular strategic direction might imply.

- ## Mergers and acquisitions

Acquisition has proved a particularly attractive means of moving quickly in a chosen strategic direction although this has mainly been related to larger organisations. The ownership structures of UK and American companies have made this a common means of achieving fast and very visible strategic action for many organisations.

The reasons for acquisition vary. Rapid entry to particular markets, immediately increased market share, cost savings through rationalisation, balance sheet

10

improvements or other financial reasons including more favourable tax treatment, may all play a part. Potential problems for acquiring firms usually arise from not knowing exactly what is being bought. Many factors do not emerge until after acquisition.

Mergers differ from acquisitions only in the sense that the coming together is voluntary, although it may be as a result of competitive pressures. Mergers and acquisitions are often justified on grounds of potential synergies although these often prove difficult to actually realise. However, the biggest problems usually arise post merger or acquisition when cultural differences between the two organisations emerge. When combined with political activity these often cost more in terms of time and resource to resolve than originally envisaged.

Joint development

These are becoming both increasingly varied and popular. They arise where an organisation recognises the need to work with one or more outside organisations to achieve its strategy. It may be a need to share costs, or scarce resources, knowledge or skills or regulatory or legal constraints, which lead to the need for joint development. Such arrangements include joint ventures, marketing consortia, franchising, business networks, strategic alliances, subcontracting and so on. Issues to be considered include how to manage relationships between the organisations, and also identifying when the arrangement should be ended and how.

10.9 Evaluation criteria

Clearly it is possible to think of many different options for any food service organisation given its position in the business environment at a particular point in time. Making choices about which of these alternatives will best help the organisation to achieve its strategic objectives requires some criteria against which to evaluate the various possible alternatives. What specific criteria will be used will depend on how success is to be measured in the organisation. However Johnson *et al.* (2017) suggest that it can be helpful to consider the **suitability**, **feasibility** and **acceptability** of any given option.

Assessing suitability

Consideration of suitability can be based on assessments of whether the option:

- Exploits the core competencies of the foodservice organisation
- Seizes opportunities presented to the food service organisation by changes in the business environmental and counters any threats which the organisation may be facing, or
- Meets the expectations of key organisational stakeholders.

These considerations are not necessarily mutually exclusive but there may be conflict within and between them. This goes back to the previous discussion in this chapter on the basis of strategy.

It may be useful to consider the issues, which can arise, using three different approaches. Again these are not mutually exclusive, and each one may offer new insights into the options being evaluated:

■ **Strategic logic:** this is the rational/economic approach primarily concerned with matching an organisation's core competencies with the business environment (and in particular the market) it faces. Such an approach draws heavily on the various models of strategic analysis mentioned here and elsewhere . These include, for example: Porter's competitive advantage concepts (page 308), Five Forces (page 309), the Strategy Clock of Johnson *et al.* (page 325), Ansoff's matrix (page 330), together with life cycle analysis (page 328), and synergy (page 332).

■ **Cultural fit:** this approach attempts to assess the extent to which an option fits the prevailing culture and the political realities in the organisation. If a proposed strategy is likely to be rejected by key players in the organisation or runs counter to the prevalent organisational thinking, it is likely to run into difficulties during implementation no matter how logical it may appear from an economic perspective. This raises the issue of whether an organisational culture can be changed to suit an apparently desirable strategy or whether strategy should be driven from the existing culture.

■ **Research evidence:** it may be quite reasonable to ask why, with so much research being carried out by businesses and academics over many years, it is necessary to approach each strategic decision as if it were unique. It can be argued that any such decision will indeed be unique, but any decision-making can be usefully informed by past experience of other such similar decisions. Monitoring the trade and business press, networking through professional trade bodies and associations, taking the advice of consultants and generally reading the business literature, can prove very rewarding.

Assessing feasibility

Feasibility is concerned with whether the food service organisation can actually put the strategy into operation. In other words: does the organisation have the resources, such as finance, skills, equipment and the technology, to support the strategic choices being made? Of particular concern should be the assessment of:

■ **Funding:** any strategy is likely to require capital investment. A cash flow forecast is vital to assess both the amounts and timing of the investment and the returns from the project.

■ **Break even:** it is essential to assess the volume of sales required to achieve the required return from any strategy. It is then possible to assess the resource implications of such a volume and whether in fact it is possible to achieve such a level of sales.

- **Resource implications**: this is a detailed assessment of the physical and human resources required to achieve the strategy. If there is a shortfall between existing and required resources the organisation will need to determine how this can be met in the time-scales and within the costs assumed by the proposal.

Assessing acceptability

The key issue in assessing acceptability is an understanding of stakeholder expectations. These may well vary between different stakeholder groups. Of particular interest to many key stakeholders (particularly managers, owners and providers of finance) will be an assessment of the potential financial returns and risks from any particular proposal.

Financial return can be assessed using payback or discounted cash flow (DCF) investment appraisal methods. Cost/benefit analysis is widely used in the public sector, where the analyses of profit is inappropriate or too narrow a measure. Cost/benefit analysis attempts to put a financial value on all costs and benefits including intangibles.

Financial risk can also be assessed through calculating the projected financial ratios that adopting a specific strategy would imply. Important factors are gearing ratios (increased gearing through increased borrowing exposes a company to greater risk) and liquidity ratios (lowering the liquidity ratios increases financial risk). (See Appendix A for a listing of key financial ratios). Another useful approach is to use sensitivity analysis, particularly by using spreadsheet packages, to pose various 'what if?' questions. These approaches enable owners and managers to assess the impact of changes in interest rates, capacity, utilisation, market shares and so on, on the financial projection for a possible strategy.

■ Strategy and organisational types

If the approaches to strategic management were (or could be) undertaken in a wholly scientific way, decisions would only be rational and objective. But organisations are complex and the culture and power that exists in and around one will substantially affect the actual decisions that are made. Some of this will be reflected in, and thus determined by, the nature of the objectives of the organisation.

We saw in Chapter 2 that organisational goals tend to be derived from a mixture of economic, managerial and social factors. It can be useful to consider the type of organisation that the food service operation might be, as this will substantially affect the specific approaches that will be adopted and the nature of the strategic decisions that will be made. The nature of any organisation is created through a complex interplay between the various stakeholders involved and the level of power that they can exert. Individual owner-operated food service businesses will often predominately reflect the nature of the owner, as the owner is likely to hold the most power. In larger organisations the number of stakeholders that are involved will increase, and with this the predominance of power may shift to, for instance, shareholders, or strong groups of customers.

Considering organisations from this perspective can help to indicate why, for instance, similar food service businesses facing similar business environments, might make quite different strategic decisions. The actual decisions about the strategic approaches adopted, the strategic direction of an organisation, the basis of strategy and the ways in which strategies will be achieved, are likely to depend largely on the predominant organisational characteristics of each enterprise.

Activity:

Obtain two annual reports from businesses in the same food service sector.

■ Compare and contrast the mission and the strategic direction of the business.

■ Draw conclusions about the financial performance of the business.

■ State which of the organisations you would invest in and why.

■ The reality of strategic decision-making

In this latter part of Chapter 10 we have considered some essential elements of the process of strategic decision-making. The intention has been to encourage the consideration of strategic issues in a systematic way through the application of a range of approaches, only some of which have been identified here. However, although it may appear from this presentation of the material that strategic management is a linear process starting at the establishment of a mission and ending with implementation, these elements in fact often run in parallel. Any operation will fail if it attempts to sets out its mission without knowing what its resources are or without considering the practicalities of implementation.

In reality strategic management is largely organic in nature and affected by a range of factors, such as organisational culture, which will mitigate against viewing the process as being simply scientific. The process of strategy that enables successful strategic management to be achieved certainly includes the need for some formal planning, but there is also a need for all managers to be involved in the continuous strategic management of the enterprise. In addition, no matter how well planned a strategy may seem to be, there will be many forces that will affect the extent to which the planned course of action will be achieved, and the possibility of this must always be taken into account in the strategy process. Strategic management therefore needs to be:

■ Recognised as being complex and judgemental

■ Continuous, rather than a once a year process

■ Developed using a combination of a variety of different approaches and techniques

■ Carried out by managers not planners

■ Based on a continuum of formulation and implementation, and

■ Flexible enough to cope with an uncertain future.

10

10.10 References and additional reading

Adams, D. (2019) *Management Accounting for the Hospitality, Tourism and Leisure Industries, A Strategic Approach*, 3rd edn, Oxford, Goodfellow Publishers.

Ansoff, H.I. (1988) *Corporate Strategy*, London: Penguin.

Balanced Scorecard Institute at: www.balancedscorecard.org (accessed January 2019).

BCG Classics Revisited: The Growth Share Matrix at www.bcg.com/en-gb/publications/2014/growth-share-matrix-bcg-classics-revisited.aspx (accessed January 2019).

Best Practice Forum at www.bestpracticeforum.org (accessed January 2019).

Bowie, D. and Buttle, F. (2011) *Hospitality Marketing, Principles and Practice*, 2nd edn, Oxford: Butterworth-Heinemann.

Bowie, D. Buttle, F., Brookes, M. and Mariussen, A. (2016) *Hospitality Marketing*, 3rd edn, Oxford: Routledge.

Harris, P. (2013) *Profit Planning for Hospitality and Tourism*, extended 3rd edition, Oxford: Goodfellow Publishers.

Hospitality Assured at www.hospitalityassured.com (accessed January 2019).

Johnson, G., Scholes, K. and Whittington, R. (2008) *Exploring Corporate Strategy*, Harlow: Prentice Hall.

Johnson, G., Whittington R., Scholes, K., Angwin, D. and Regnér, P. (2017) *Exploring Strategy: Text and Cases*, 11th edition, Harlow: Pearson Education.

Johnston, R., Clark, G. and Shulver, M. (2012) *Service Operations Management: Improving Service Delivery*, 4th edition, Harlow: Pearson.

Kaplan R., S. and Norton D., P. (1996) Using the Balanced Scorecard as a strategic management system, *Harvard Business Review*, January-February: 76.

Kotler, P., Keller, K., Brady, M. Goodman, M. and Hansen, T. (2016) *Marketing Management*, 3rd edition, Harlow: Pearson Education.

Parker, D. (2018) *Service Operations Management: The Total Experience*, 8th edition, Cheltenham: Edward Elgar Publishing Ltd.

Porter, M. (2004a) *Competitive Advantage*, New York: Free Press.

Porter, M. (2004b) *Competitive Strategy: Techniques for Analyzing Industries and Competitors*, New York: Free Press.

Rumelt, R. (2012) Good Strategy Bad Strategy: The Difference and Why it Matters, London: Profile Books Ltd.

Tribe, J. (2016) *Strategy for Tourism* 2nd edn, Oxford: Goodfellow Publishers.

A Appendices

A: Performance measures and Key Performance Indicators

The most of the common quantitative performance measures for a food service operation (as identified in Chapter 9) are the operational ratios and (as identified in Chapter 10) the financial ratios. The performance measures are also often referred to as Key Performance Indicators (KPIs). They can be grouped under seven main categories:

- Operational ratios
- Activity ratios
- Profitability ratios
- Liquidity ratio
- Gearing ratios
- Stock market ratios
- Social media and marketing.

The most common operational and financial ratios, their formulas and explanations of what the individual ratio can indicate, are grouped together under these six headings below:

Ratio	Formula	Meaning
Operational ratios		
Gross profit %	$\dfrac{\text{Sales revenue} - \text{cost of sales} \times 100}{\text{Sales}}$	A measure of operational efficiency (not profitability). Shows the gross profit, i.e. the sales less the costs of materials (food or beverage) as a percentage of sales. Conversely can be used to indicate the percentage of material costs. Can be used over time for budgeting and comparison purposes and for comparison with industry norms.
Net profit %	$\dfrac{\text{Sales revenue} - \text{total costs} \times 100}{\text{Sales}}$	Shows overall net profit percentage i.e. the sales less the total costs as a percentage of sales. Conversely can be used to indicate the percentage of costs. Can also be used over time for budgeting and comparison purposes and for comparison with industry norms.
Average check	$\dfrac{\text{Sales}}{\text{Number of bill transactions}}$	Measures the average amount spent per bill transaction. Usually calculated for a specific service period in order to compare spending power of customers and average customer group sizes over time. Useful when interpreting and comparing sales figures.
Average spend per head (ASPH)	$\dfrac{\text{Sales}}{\text{Number of customers}}$	Measures the average amount spent per person served. Usually calculated for a specific service periods in order to compare spending power of individual customers. Can be broken down further to indicate spend on food or beverages. Useful when interpreting and comparing sales figures over time.
Material costs %	$\dfrac{\text{Cost of materials} \times 100}{\text{Sales}}$	Identifies the cost of materials (either food or beverage) as a percentage of the sales revenue. Usually calculated separately for food and beverages and also then down to individual or groups of menu or beverage items. Useful for comparison over different service periods and for comparison against industry norms.
Labour costs %	$\dfrac{\text{Cost of labour} \times 100}{\text{Sales}}$	Identifies the cost of labour as a percentage of the sales revenue. Useful for comparison over different periods and for comparison against industry norms.
Productivity index	$\dfrac{\text{Sales}}{\text{Cost of labour}}$	Alternative method for showing labour costs in relation to sales. Low index would be where there is a high labour cost in relation to sales. Can be used as budget measure and also for comparison with industry norms.

Employee turnover %	$\dfrac{\text{No of employees who have left} \times 100}{\text{Average no of employees}}$	Indicates how frequently employees leave over a specific period of time. Less than 30% a year is considered good.
Prime cost %	$\dfrac{\text{Total cost of goods sold} + \text{labour} \times 100}{\text{Sales}}$	Checks on prime cost figures can give warnings if costs being likely to exceed revenue. Percentages below 60% are considered good but can be as high as 75%. Figures that are too low indicate that prices are too high for services provided.
Overhead cost %	$\dfrac{\text{Cost of sales} + \text{fixed costs} \times 100}{\text{Sales}}$	
Variance %	$\dfrac{\text{Actual} - \text{budget} \times 100}{\text{Budget}}$	Measures, in percentage terms, how far away the actual outcomes are from the budgeted figures. Valuable as a true monitor of actual performance against budget and comparison over time.
Revenue per employee	$\dfrac{\text{Sales}}{\text{No. of staff employed}}$	Gives sales revenue per member of staff. Can also be calculated for full time equivalent. Used as a measure of efficiency. Usually calculated for specific service periods and comparison made over time.
Sales per seat available	$\dfrac{\text{Sales}}{\text{No. of seats available}}$	Indicates the amount of sales that are generated per seat available. Can be referred to as revenue per available seat hour (RevPASH). Usually calculated for given service periods and compared over time. Can also be calculated on the sales per seat actually used. Comparison between these two figures can indicate efficiency of operation.
Seat turnover	$\dfrac{\text{No. of seats used}}{\text{No. of seats available}}$	Indicates the occupancy efficiency of the seating in a food service area. Usually calculated for specific service periods and compared over time.
Sales per square metre	$\dfrac{\text{Sales}}{\text{Total area of operation in m}^2}$	Can also be calculated per square foot. Commonly used in retail operations. Can be useful in bar areas or for takeaway operations where earnings per seat cannot be calculated.
Cost of premises %	$\dfrac{\text{Cost of premises} \times 100}{\text{Sales}}$	Cost of premises includes rent, council tax, property insurance etc. By dividing cost of premises by your sales will indicates if rent is too high. Above 7% is considered high.

A

Activity ratios

Net asset turnover	$\dfrac{\text{Sales}}{\text{Net assets}}$	Measures how effectively the net assets are used to generate sales; measures how many sales are generated by each pound of net assets.
Fixed asset turnover	$\dfrac{\text{Sales}}{\text{Fixed assets}}$	Measures the utilisation of the company's fixed assets (i.e. plant and equipment); measures how many sales are generated by each pound of fixed assets.
Stock turnover (rate)	$\dfrac{\text{Cost of sales}}{\text{Average value of stock}}$	Measures the number of times the stocks of food or beverage items were turned over during the year. Indicates management's ability to control investment in stocks.
Stock turnover (period)	$\dfrac{\text{Average value of stocks} \times 365}{\text{Cost of sales}}$	Indicates the stock level being held as shown by the number of days it takes to use and replace it.
Debt turnover	$\dfrac{\text{Sales}}{\text{Average level of debtors}}$	Indicates the number of times that debtors are cycled during the year.
Average collection period	$\dfrac{\text{Average level of debtors} \times 365}{\text{Sales}}$	The number of day's credit the firm gives to customers. The longer the period the more cost to the firm in outstanding debts.

Profitability ratios

Return on capital employed	$\dfrac{\text{Profit before interest and tax} \times 100}{\text{Capital employed}}$	Measures the performance of the firm regardless of the method of financing.
Return on equity	$\dfrac{\text{Profit after tax} \times 100}{\text{Shareholder' funds}}$	Measures the rate of return or profitability of the shareholders' investment in the company. . Also referred to as return on investment ROI
EBITDAR - Earnings Before Interest, Taxes, Depreciation, Amortisation and Rent	EBIT + Interest + Taxes + Depreciation + Amortisation + Rent	An indication of cash flow. Gives the amount of cash available after fixed expenses, such as rent and debt. It is different from operating profit EBIT (earnings before interest and tax), because it includes depreciation and amortisation (debt payments). Can be calculated as a percentage of sales which can indicate the efficiency of the business – typical figures are about 12%.
Gross profit margin	Sales – Gross profit before interest and tax	Shows the total margin available to cover operating expenses and still yield a profit. Useful for comparison over time and with industry norms.
Net profit margin	$\dfrac{\text{Net profit after tax}}{\text{Sales}}$	Shows how much after-tax profits are generated by each pound of sales. Also useful for comparison over time and with industry norms.

Liquidity ratios

Current ratio	$\dfrac{\text{Current assets}}{\text{Current liabilities}}$	Indicates the extent to which a firm can meet its short-term liabilities from short-term assets. This should be in the region of 2:1 or 1:1 to reflect a health proportion of current assets (stock, debtors and cash) to current liabilities (overdraft, creditors).
Acid test or quick ratio	$\dfrac{\text{Current assets} - \text{stocks}}{\text{Current liabilities}}$	Measures the firm's ability to pay off short-term liabilities from current assets without relying upon the sale of its stock. A stricter test of liquidity because it compares only money assets (cash and debtors) to current liabilities.

Gearing ratios

Debt ratio	$\dfrac{\text{Long-term debt}}{\text{Capital employed (net assets)}}$	Measures the extent to which borrowed funds have been used to finance the company's net assets. The more long-term debt the higher is the gearing and the greater the risk incurred. Gearing is generally considered to be high above 1:1.
Debt-to-equity ratio	$\dfrac{\text{Long-term debt}}{\text{Share capital}}$	Measures the funds provided by long-term creditors against the funds provided by shareholders.
Interest cover	$\dfrac{\text{Profit before interest and tax}}{\text{Interest payable}}$	Indicates the ability of the company to meet its annual interest costs. The higher the ratio the less risk is involved, as the interest being paid becomes a smaller proportion of the profit generated.

Stock market ratios

Earnings per share	$\dfrac{\text{Profit after tax}}{\text{No. of ordinary shares in issue}}$	Shows the after-tax earnings generated for each ordinary share. High earning per share can encourage new investors and promote investor loyalty.
Price/earnings	$\dfrac{\text{Market price per share}}{\text{Earnings per share}}$	Shows the esteem in which the market holds the company, the higher the ratio the more popular the share.
Net dividend yield	$\dfrac{\text{Dividend per share}}{\text{Market price per share}}$	Indicates the dividend rate of return to ordinary shareholders.
Dividend cover	$\dfrac{\text{Earnings per share}}{\text{Dividend per share}}$ or $\dfrac{\text{Profit to pay ordinary dividends}}{\text{Ordinary dividends}}$	Measures the extent to which the company pays dividends from earnings. High dividend cover is healthy provided that investors judge the gross dividend on ordinary shares to be adequate. Low dividend cover may indicate that gross dividends to ordinary shares have been set too high.

B

Social media and marketing – part of customer relationship management (CRM)

Email open rate	$\dfrac{\text{No. recipients who open email}}{\text{No. that did not}}$	These four sets of email metrics help to identify email open, click-through, and conversion rates and can monitor which type of emails are more successful e.g. information, event announcements or offers.
Email click through rate	$\dfrac{\text{No. who click the link in email}}{\text{No. that did not}}$	
Email conversion rate	$\dfrac{\text{No. who take the desired action}}{\text{No. that did not}}$	Email metrics also help to track the progress and effectiveness of email campaigns and make improvements. They can also be used as a basis for separating customers into groups, based on location or recent visitors, to create hyper-targeted email campaigns for each group.
Cost per lead / or conversion	$\dfrac{\text{Total spend for email campaign}}{\text{No. of leads / or conversion}}$	
Engagement rate	$\dfrac{\text{Total amount of interactions}}{\text{No. of followers}}$ (likes, *shares, comments etc.*)	Helps to monitor the number of followers against whether these are engaged with what is being posted. Low scores such as 0.05% means that content needs to be refreshed more regularly.
Customer reviews	Comments and scores	Most trusted scores are 4.00 and above. Positive reviews and be used as part of PR. Negative reviews provide opportunities for improvement. On public forums, reply to dissatisfied customers in a sympathetic and respectful way.
Website metrics	Metrics include: Average position in organic search results Volume of traffic Page views Bounce Rate Time on page	Helps to identify improvements necessary in website design. Most website hosting offers results for these. They are also available and calculated automatically, for example, in Google Analytics, for free.

B: Example calculations exercise

Being able to interpret operational data is an essential skill for the food and beverage manager. In order to be able to do that well it is necessary to have a sound understanding of the basis for operational calculations.

Chapter 9 details the appraisal of revenue, costs and profits. This appendix provides examples of operational figures and calculations.

Example figures

Below are examples of the figures that can be generated in a food service operation.

Type of operation

120-seat café restaurant

Operational hours

The restaurant is open six days a week all year

Opening hours

Lunch Service 12 noon to 2pm

Dinner Service 7pm to 10pm

Average customer numbers

Lunch – 40

Dinner – 75

Average customer spending

	Food	Beverage
Lunch	£12 per head	£6 per head
Dinner	£20 per head	£10 per head

Staffing establishment

Lunch – a daily average of one member of staff per 10 customers

Dinner – a daily average of one member of staff per 15 customers

All members of staff are employed for the entire service period plus one hour prior to the service and one hour after the service

Costs

The **food** costs are 40% of the annual food revenue

The **beverage** costs are 50% of the annual beverage revenue

The **staff** (labour) costs are averaged at £15.50 per hour per member of staff

The total **overhead cost** for one year is estimated at 20% of the total annual revenue (food and beverage)

B

Activity

Using the operational figures detailed above, calculate all of the following:

a. **Annual revenues**

The annual food revenue

The annual beverage revenue

The annual lunch revenue

The annual dinner revenue

The total annual revenue

b. **The total number of staff needed each day for the service of:**

lunch

dinner

c. **The total annual labour costs**

d. **The percentage of labour costs in relation to the total annual revenue**

e. **The average daily percentage seat occupancy during the year for:**

lunch

dinner

f. **The average daily overhead costs for each day of operation**

g. **The gross profit cash and percentage for the year for:**

food

beverage

total (food and beverage)

h. **The total amount of money left over at the end of the year (net profit) after all costs have been deducted and its percentage of the total revenue.**

The calculations

a. Annual revenues

The annual food revenue

Lunch food revenue	=	spend per head x No. of covers x No. of days x No. of weeks
	=	£12 × 40 covers x 6 days x 52 weeks
	=	£149,760
Dinner food revenue	=	spend per head x No. of covers x No. of days x No. of weeks
	=	£20 x 75 covers x 6 days x 52 weeks
	=	£468,000
Total annual food revenue	=	lunch food revenue + dinner food revenue
	=	£149,760 + £468,000
	=	£617,760

The annual beverage revenue

Lunch beverage revenue	= spend per head x No. of covers x No. of days x No. of weeks
	= £6 x 40 covers x 6 days x 52 weeks
	= £74,880
Dinner beverage revenue	= spend per head x No. of covers x No. of days x No. of weeks
	= £10 x 75 covers x 6 days x 52 weeks
	= £234,000
Total beverage revenue	= lunch beverage revenue + dinner beverage revenue
	= £74,880 + £234,000
	= £308,880
Total annual lunch revenue	= annual lunch food revenue + annual lunch beverage revenue
	= £149,760 + £74,880
	= £224,640
Total annual dinner revenue	= annual dinner food revenue + annual dinner beverage revenue
	= £468,000 + £234,000
	= £702,000
The total annual revenue	= annual lunch revenue + annual dinner revenue
	= £224.640 + £702,000
	= £926,640
OR	
	= annual food revenue + annual beverage revenue
	= £617,760 + £308,880
	= £926,640

b. **The total average number of staff needed for each day for the service of:**

Lunch

one member of staff is required for ten customers

the average number of customers per day = 40

therefore the average number of staff for lunch = 40/10 = 4

Dinner

one member of staff is required for 15 customers

the average number of customers per day = 75

therefore the average number of staff for dinner = 75/15 = 5

c. **Total annual labour costs**

Lunch labour costs per day	= No. of staff x working hours x rate per hour
	= 4 staff x 4 hours x £15.50
	= £248.00
Dinner labour costs per day	= No. of staff x working hours x rate per hour
	= 5 staff x 5 hours x £15.50
	= £387.50
Total labour costs per day	= lunch labour costs + dinner labour costs
	= £248.00 + £387.50
	= £635.50
Total annual labour costs	= total labour costs per day x No. of days x No. of weeks
	= £635.50 x 6 x 52
	= £198,276

d. **Percentage of labour cost in relation to total revenue**

Labour cost percentage

$$= \frac{\text{Labour costs} \times 100}{\text{Revenue}}$$

$$= \frac{£198,276 \times 100}{£926,640}$$

$$= 21.4\%$$

e. **The average daily percentage seat occupancy during the year for:**

Lunch

Percentage seat occupancy

$$= \frac{\text{covers actual} \times 100}{\text{covers available}}$$

$$= \frac{40 \times 100}{120}$$

$$= 33.33\%$$

Dinner

Percentage seat occupancy

$$= \frac{\text{covers actual} \times 100}{\text{covers available}}$$

$$= \frac{75 \times 100}{120}$$

$$= 62.50\%$$

f. **The average daily overhead cost**

Overheads = 20% of revenue

Total annual overheads

$$= \frac{20 \times £926,640}{100}$$

$$= £185,328$$

average daily overheads   =   annual cost
                                 ―――――――――――
                                 6 days x 52 weeks

                            = £185,328
                              ―――――――――
                                 312

                            = £594 per day

g. The gross profit cash and percentage for the year for:

Food cash gross profit and percentage

Food cost   = 40% of total food revenue

Therefore gross profit   = 60% of total food revenue

Gross profit on food   = 60 x £617,760
                              ―――――――――――――――
                                  100

                            = £370,656 cash, 60%

Beverage cash gross profit and percentage

Beverage cost   = 50% of total beverage revenue

Therefore gross profit   = 50% of total beverage revenue

Gross profit on beverage   = 50 x £308,880
                              ―――――――――――――――
                                  100

                            = £154,440 cash, 50%

Total cash gross profit and percentage

Total cash gross profit = food gross profit + beverage gross profit

                            = £370,656 + £154,440

                            = £525,096

Percentage gross profit   = cash gross profit x 100
                              ―――――――――――――――――――――――――
                                      revenue

                            = £525,096 x 100
                               ――――――――――――――
                                 £926,640

                            = 56.67%

h. Net profit – the total amount of money left over at the end of the year after all costs have been deducted and its percentage of total revenue

Net profit   = gross profit – (labour costs + overhead costs)

                            = £525,096 – (£198,276 + £185,328)

                            = £141,492

As a percentage of revenue = net profit x 100
                              ――――――――――――――――――
                                  revenue

                            = £141,492 x 100
                               ――――――――――――――
                                 £926,640

                            = 15.27%

B

Check matrix

In food service operations there is an established relationship between revenue, costs and profits. In order to check that all the cash and percentages figures are correct, a matrix can be constructed. This matrix is based on Figure 9.1, page 279, which summarises the relationship between revenue, costs and profits. The check matrix, for the figures used in the example above, is given in Table B.1.

Table B.1 Calculations check matrix

Check matrix	£	%		£	%
Material costs	401,544	43.33	Material costs	401,544	43.33
Labour cost	198,276	21.40			
Overheads	185,328	20.00	Gross profit	525,096	56.67
Net profit	141,492	15.27			
Revenue/sales	926,640	100.00	Revenue/sales	926,640	100.00

(Material costs = costs of food and beverages)

C: Example trading results: comparison and evaluation

Being able to interpret trading results is an essential skill for the food and beverage manager. In order to be able to do that well a manager needs to have a sound understanding of the basis of performance measures. The various performance measure ratios are detailed in Appendix A. In addition, Chapter 9 identifies that in order to interpret fully the meaning of operational ratios, it is necessary to have some basis of comparison. For operational ratios, there will usually be internal budgets and objectives against which to measure them.

Below is an example of the budget and trading results for a food service operation. This exercise is to carry out an analysis of the data provided and to present an evaluation of the current position of the operation.

The analysis should include:

- Trading figures together with percentages
- Stock turnover ratios
- Percentage variance against budget
- Percentage for food and drink sales of the total sales
- Average spend per head on food and beverage, and
- Average seat turnover.

The evaluation should identify:

- Strengths of the operation
- Areas for concern
- A general overview of the current potion, and,
- An identification of information that would help to make the evaluation more compete.

C

The budget and trading figures

The figures presented in Table C.1 are for a 62-seat, plated table service, café style restaurant. The restaurant holds a restaurant licence and is open from 8.30 a.m. to 9.30 p.m., Monday to Saturday.

Table C.1: Budget and trading results for 3 months

	Budget		1st month		2nd month		3rd month	
	(£)	(£)	(£)	(£)	(£)	(£)	(£)	(£)
Food								
Sales	40,575		40,109		41,003		39,624	
Food costs	14,201		14,711		15,200		13,824	
Gross profit		26,374		25,398		25,803		25,800
Beverage								
Sales	10,279		10,019		10,990		10,410	
Liquor costs	4,008		4,020		4,230		4,040	
Gross profit		6,271		5,999		6,760		6,370
Total sales	50,854		50,128		51,993		50,034	
Total cost of sales	18,209		18,731		19,430		17,864	
Total gross profit		32,645		31,397		32,563		32,170
Unallocated costs								
Labour costs	12,500		12,906		12,992		13,111	
Overheads	8,200		8,410		8,717		8,315	
Total costs		20,700		21,316		21,709		21,426
Net profit		11,945		10,081		10,854		10,744
Stockholding								
Food	7,710		8,010		7,924		7,999	
Beverage	1,520		1,670		1,910		1,710	
No. of customers	5,410		5,340		5,420		5,430	

Analysis

From the data provided in Table C.1:

- Table C.2 presents the trading figures together with a variety of performance measures.
- Table C.3 presents the percentage variance against budget.
- Table C.4 gives the percentage for food and drink sales of the total sales.
- Table C.5 shows the average spend per head on food and beverage.
- Table C.6 shows the average seat turnover.

Table C.2: Analysis of the budget and trading results for 3 months

	Budget			1st month			2nd month			3rd month		
	(£)	(£)	(%)	(£)	(£)	(%)	(£)	(£)	(%)	(£)	(£)	(%)
Food												
Sales	40,575			40,109			41,003			39,624		
Food costs	14,201		35	14,711		37	15,200		37	13,824		35
Gross profit		26,374	65		25,398	63		25,803	63		25,800	65
Beverage												
Sales	10,279			10,019			10,990			10,410		
Liquor costs	4,008		39	4,020		40	4,230		38	4,040		39
Gross profit		6,271	61		5,999	60		6,760	61		6,370	61
Total sales	50,854			50,128			51,993			50,034		
Total cost of sales	18,209			18 731			19,430			17,864		
Total gross profit		32,645	64		31,397	63		32,563	63		32,170	64
Unallocated costs												
Labour costs	12,500		24	12,906		26	12,992		25	13,111		26
Overheads	8,200		16	8,410		17	8,717		17	8,315		17
Total costs		20,700	41		21,316	42		21,709	42		21,426	43
Net profit		11,945	23		10,081	20		10,854	21		10,744	21
Stockholding		STO*			STO			STO			STO	
Food	7,710	1.84		8,010	1.83		7,924	1.91		7,999	1.72	
Beverage	1,520	2.63		1,670	2.40		1,910	2.21		1,710	2.36	

*STO: Stock turnover.

C

Table C.3: Variance percentage against budget

	1st month	2nd month	3rd month	To date
Food sales	−1.14	1.05	−2.34	−0.81
Food costs	3.59	7.03	−2.65	+2.65
Gross profit	−3.70	−2.16	−2.17	−2.68
Liquor sales	−2.52	6.91	1.27	+1.88
Liquor costs	0.29	5.53	0.79	+2.21
Gross profit	−4.33	7.79	1.57	+1.67
Total sales	−1.42	2.24	−1.61	−0.26
Total cost of sales	2.86	6.70	−1.89	+2.55
Total gross profit	−3.82	−0.25	−1.45	−1.84
Wage and staff	3.24	3.93	4.88	+4.02
Overheads	2.56	6.30	1.40	+3.42
Total costs	2.97	4.87	3.50	3.78
Net profit	−15.60	−9.13	−10.05	11.59
Net profit under budget	−£1 864	−£1 091	−£1201	−£4 156

Notes: Variance percentage = [(actual − budget) / budget] x 100
Variance percentage to date = [(actual to date − budget to date)/budget to date] x 100

Table C.4: Percentages of food and beverage sales of total sales

	Budget		1st month		2nd month		3rd month	
	(£)	(%)	(£)	(%)	(£)	(%)	(£)	(%)
Food	40,575	80.0	40,109	80.0	41,003	78.8	39,624	79.1
Beverage	10,279	20.0	10,019	20.0	10,990	21.1	10,410	20.8
Total	50,854	100	50,128	100	51 993	100	50,034	100

Table C.5: Average spend per head

	Budget	1st month	2nd month	3rd month
Food	7.50	7.51	7.56	7.29
Beverage	1.90	1.87	2.02	1.91
Total	9.40	9.38	9.58	9.20

Note: average spend per head = sales (food or/and beverages) ÷ number of customers

Table C.6: Average seat turnover

Budget	1st month	2nd month	3rd month
3.64	3.58	3.64	3.64

Note: seat turnover = No. of customers served ÷ No. of seats available
(Figures assume that establishment is open for 24 trading days per month (4 x 6 days)

Example evaluation

Evaluation of the operational data which has been generated might be as follows:

Apparent strengths:

- Conservative budget (given the number of seats) and targets for sales are being met.
- Reasonable match between spend and number of customers and budget.

Areas for concern:

- Food costs are higher in variance than sales, resulting in the gross profit running under budget at £2,121 to date (–2.68%).
- Although beverage sales were slightly above budget the costs were higher than forecasted.
- Stock turnover in food is slightly lower than budgeted possibly suggesting a problem with purchasing not matching rate of usage.
- Wage costs are between 3.24 and 4.88% over budget (+4.02% or £1509 to date) with upward trend indicating possible overstaffing.
- Overheads are increasing from 1.40 to 6.30% over budget (£842, or +3.42% to date).
- Overall performance of restaurant is poor against budget. Net profit is between –9.13 and –15.60% under budget and –11.59% under budget to date (£4156). The reduction in the net profit is mainly as a result of increasing labour costs but there are also increases in the food cost and overhead costs, which are contributing to this reduction in the net profit.

General overview:

- Sales on food are more or less static on budget while drink sales are slightly over budget.
- The main problems are seen to be costs: staff costs along with food costs are over budget and overhead costs are increasing.
- Overall there is a need to reduce costs to budget or increase sales to achieve targeted net profit.
- Assuming the budget to be accurate, and that costs can be brought under control, there may be little need for change. However without information on the nature of the customer demand being met, and the business environment in which this restaurant is operating, no further judgment can be made.

Additional information

Additional information required to make evaluation more complete will include:

- Basis of budget formulation including investigation of budgeting procedures to identify their appropriateness and accuracy.
- Previous trading information for comparison and to consider trends over the longer term.

C

- Analysis service period breakdown to show types of customer demand being met and analysis of sales mix date to determine popularity of menu and beverage items.

- Examination of food costs, purchasing and control system including pricing of food items. As well as possible problems with the relationship between demand and purchasing, which may lead to waste, there may also be difficulties with increases in prices of food.

- Identification of reason for drink sales increase and higher gross profit in order to determine cause (overages can indicate problems as much as shortages).

- Staffing information and breakdown of wage costs including investigation of staffing costs with a view to reducing them in line with budget.

- Examination of reasons for the high variance in actual overhead costs against budget.

- Assessment of the business environment.

Index

I

I

I